Improving Entrepreneurial Processes Through Advanced AI

Muhammad Nawaz Tunio
The University of Sufism and Modern Sciences, Bhitshah, Pakistan

IGI Global
Publishing Tomorrow's Research Today

Published in the United States of America by
IGI Global
701 E. Chocolate Avenue
Hershey PA, USA 17033
Tel: 717-533-8845
Fax: 717-533-8661
E-mail: cust@igi-global.com
Web site: https://www.igi-global.com

Copyright © 2025 by IGI Global. All rights reserved. No part of this publication may be reproduced, stored or distributed in any form or by any means, electronic or mechanical, including photocopying, without written permission from the publisher.
Product or company names used in this set are for identification purposes only. Inclusion of the names of the products or companies does not indicate a claim of ownership by IGI Global of the trademark or registered trademark.

Library of Congress Cataloging-in-Publication Data

CIP Data Pending
ISBN:979-8-3693-1495-1
eISBN:979-8-3693-1496-8

Vice President of Editorial: Melissa Wagner
Managing Editor of Acquisitions: Mikaela Felty
Managing Editor of Book Development: Jocelynn Hessler
Production Manager: Mike Brehm
Cover Design: Phillip Shickler

British Cataloguing in Publication Data
A Cataloguing in Publication record for this book is available from the British Library.

All work contributed to this book is new, previously-unpublished material.
The views expressed in this book are those of the authors, but not necessarily of the publisher.

This book is dedicated to the innovators, visionaries, and changemakers who tirelessly pursue a greener, more sustainable world. To the entrepreneurs who dare to dream of businesses that balance profit with purpose, and to the leaders who recognize that the future of work must be both ethical and environmentally conscious.

I also dedicate this work to the next generation of scholars, students, and professionals, whose passion and ingenuity will continue to shape a future where sustainable development is at the heart of economic progress.

May this book inspire you to make a difference, one green step at a time.

Table of Contents

Foreword xiv

Preface xvi

Acknowledgment xxiii

Introduction xxiv

Chapter 1
Harnessing AI for Digital Entrepreneurship: Strategies and Best Practices 1
    Mustafa Kayyali, HE Higher Education Ranking, Syria

Chapter 2
AI as a Game Changer: How Digital Entrepreneurs Are Redefining Business Practices 21
    K. Balaji, CHRIST University, Bengaluru, India

Chapter 3
From Giants to Guides: Lessons From Google, Coca-Cola, Airbnb's Entrepreneurial Odyssey, and AI's Insights for Visionaries 49
    Vineet Mehan, NIMS University, India

Chapter 4
Optimizing Business Models in Entrepreneurship: The Role of AI in Iterative Business Planning 71
    Hewawasam P. G. D. Wijethilaka, University of Colombo, Sri Lanka
    Mohit Yadav, O.P. Jindal Global University, India
    Rohit Vij, Lovely Professional University, India

Chapter 5
Automating Routine Tasks to Improve Entrepreneurial Productivity 99
    Shivani Dhand, Lovely Professional University, India
    Sandeep Kumar Singh, O.P. Jindal Global University, India
    Thi Mai Le, Vietnam National University, Hanoi, Vietnam

Chapter 6
Incremental Innovation: Only Survival of the Entrepreneurs in the
Competitive Age 129
    Aalia Aslam Bajwa, University of Sindh, Pakistan

Chapter 7
Ethical AI in Entrepreneurship: Balancing Innovation With Responsible AI
Practices 137
    Deepak Kumar Sahoo, Biju Patnaik University of Technology, Rourkela,
        India
    Ta Huy Hung, Vietnam National University, Vietnam
    Anish Kumar, O.P. Jindal Global University, India
    Preet Kanwal, Lovely Professional University, India

Chapter 8
Artificial Intelligence as a Catalyst for Innovation in Islamic
Entrepreneurship: Balancing Ethics and Efficiency... 165
    Early Ridho Kismawadi, IAIN Langsa, Indonesia
    Mohammad Irfan, Christ University, Bangalore, India

Chapter 9
Entrepreneurial Success and Decision-Making Power With the Support of
Assistive Technology 181
    S. Srinivasan, Department of Humanities and Social Sciences, Graphic
        Era University (Deemed), India
    R. Vallipriya, Department of Physical Science, Institute of Education,
        India

Chapter 10
AI-Driven Decision-Making in Startups: Enhancing Strategic Choices
Through Predictive Analytics 217
    Mohit Yadav, O.P. Jindal Global University, India
    Ajay Chandel, Lovely Professional University, India
    Majdi Quttainah, Kuwait University, Kuwait

Chapter 11
AI-Powered Talent Development: Nurturing Skills and Leadership in
Entrepreneurial Teams 241
    Deepak Kumar Sahoo, Biju Patnaik University of Technology, Rourkela,
        India
    Thi Mai Le, Vietnam National University, Hanoi, Vietnam
    Anish Kumar, O.P. Jindal Global University, India
    Ajay Chandel, Lovely Professional University, India

Chapter 12
AI and Social Media Analytics: Leveraging Real-Time Data for
Entrepreneurial Growth 267
    Shashank Mittal, O.P. Jindal Global University, India
    Ajay Chandel, Lovely Professional University, India
    Phuong Mai Nguyen, Vietnam National University, Hanoi, Vietnam

Compilation of References 291

About the Contributors 323

Index 329

Detailed Table of Contents

Foreword xiv

Preface xvi

Acknowledgment xxiii

Introduction xxiv

Chapter 1
Harnessing AI for Digital Entrepreneurship: Strategies and Best Practices 1
  Mustafa Kayyali, HE Higher Education Ranking, Syria

This chapter addresses the revolutionary potential of Artificial Intelligence (AI) in digital entrepreneurship, concentrating on the strategies and best practices for efficiently incorporating AI into corporate processes. As digital entrepreneurship advances, AI has become a crucial tool for better decision-making, streamlining operations, and driving innovation. The chapter opens by presenting an introduction to AI applications in entrepreneurship, followed by a discussion of AI-powered company models and tactics. Through case studies, we showcase successful examples of entrepreneurs embracing AI to scale their firms and increase productivity. Finally, the chapter discusses the future trends and problems that digital entrepreneurs may encounter as AI continues to advance, offering insights into how to stay competitive in an AI-driven market.

Chapter 2
AI as a Game Changer: How Digital Entrepreneurs Are Redefining Business Practices 21
K. Balaji, CHRIST University, Bengaluru, India

This article investigates the transformative role of artificial intelligence (AI) in digital entrepreneurship, highlighting how it serves as a catalyst for business innovation. With the rapid evolution of technology, digital entrepreneurs are increasingly leveraging AI to create novel solutions that address dynamic market needs. This study aims to elucidate the multifaceted impact of AI on entrepreneurship, focusing on how it enhances operational efficiency, improves customer experiences, and fosters data-driven decision-making. Through an exploration of real-world case studies and qualitative research, the findings underscore the importance of integrating AI into business strategies for sustained growth and competitive advantage. Moreover, the article offers practical recommendations for entrepreneurs to navigate the challenges of AI adoption and emphasizes the need for further research in this area. Ultimately, this study contributes to the understanding of AI's significance in shaping the future of digital entrepreneurship.

Chapter 3
From Giants to Guides: Lessons From Google, Coca-Cola, Airbnb's Entrepreneurial Odyssey, and AI's Insights for Visionaries 49
Vineet Mehan, NIMS University, India

Traversing the entrepreneurial trajectories of Google, Coca-Cola, and Airbnb, this exploration extracts profound insights from their respective journeys. These industry leaders illuminate the path for emerging visionaries, imparting invaluable lessons and strategies that have propelled their remarkable success stories. Furthermore, this exploration delves into the intersection of entrepreneurship and artificial intelligence (AI). By scrutinizing AI-driven advancements within Google, Coca-Cola, and Airbnb, we unveil the transformative impact of AI on decision-making, process refinement, and innovative troubleshooting. The synthesis of the experiences of established giants with the transformative potential of AI constructs a comprehensive framework for aspiring entrepreneurs. This amalgamation empowers emerging visionaries to adeptly navigate the dynamic business landscape, offering a roadmap that seamlessly integrates historical wisdom and futuristic innovation, guiding new ventures toward achievements that resonate across time.

Chapter 4
Optimizing Business Models in Entrepreneurship: The Role of AI in Iterative
Business Planning 71
    Hewawasam P. G. D. Wijethilaka, University of Colombo, Sri Lanka
    Mohit Yadav, O.P. Jindal Global University, India
    Rohit Vij, Lovely Professional University, India

This chapter explores the role of Artificial Intelligence (AI) in optimizing business models through iterative planning. As AI continues to advance, it offers entrepreneurs powerful tools for data-driven decision-making, enhancing customer insights, market segmentation, dynamic pricing, and resource allocation. The chapter examines key AI technologies such as machine learning, natural language processing, and AI-powered simulations, which enable continuous refinement and adaptation of business strategies. It also addresses challenges such as data privacy, AI transparency, potential biases, and the balance between automation and human intuition. Ethical considerations, including the responsible use of AI, are discussed to ensure sustainable innovation. The chapter concludes by exploring future trends, including autonomous decision-making and the democratization of AI, emphasizing its potential to transform business models and drive long-term success.

Chapter 5
Automating Routine Tasks to Improve Entrepreneurial Productivity 99
    Shivani Dhand, Lovely Professional University, India
    Sandeep Kumar Singh, O.P. Jindal Global University, India
    Thi Mai Le, Vietnam National University, Hanoi, Vietnam

This chapter explores the transformative impact of Artificial Intelligence (AI) on business automation, focusing on how AI technologies enhance entrepreneurial productivity and decision-making. It examines key trends such as hyper-automation, which integrates AI tools to streamline entire workflows, and AI-driven personalization that tailors customer experiences. The chapter also addresses future advancements, including autonomous supply chains and AI-augmented decision-making systems, which promise to further revolutionize business operations. Challenges such as ethical considerations, workforce adaptation, and sustainability are discussed to provide a comprehensive view of the evolving landscape. By leveraging AI, entrepreneurs can automate routine tasks, make data-driven decisions, and drive strategic growth, positioning themselves for success in a rapidly changing business environment.

Chapter 6
Incremental Innovation: Only Survival of the Entrepreneurs in the
Competitive Age 129
    Aalia Aslam Bajwa, University of Sindh, Pakistan

Innovation is widely recognized as a critical driver of business success and competitive advantage. While disruptive innovations—those that radically transform industries or create entirely new markets—often capture the spotlight, incremental innovation plays a fundamental and often underappreciated role in driving sustained growth and efficiency. Incremental innovation refers to the process of making gradual, iterative improvements to existing products, services, processes, or business models (Christensen, 1997; Tidd & Bessant, 2018).

Chapter 7
Ethical AI in Entrepreneurship: Balancing Innovation With Responsible AI
Practices 137
    Deepak Kumar Sahoo, Biju Patnaik University of Technology, Rourkela, India
    Ta Huy Hung, Vietnam National University, Vietnam
    Anish Kumar, O.P. Jindal Global University, India
    Preet Kanwal, Lovely Professional University, India

The rapid advancement of artificial intelligence (AI) presents significant opportunities and challenges for entrepreneurship. This chapter explores the intersection of ethical practices and AI innovation, focusing on how to balance technological progress with responsible AI development. Key topics include defining ethical AI principles, addressing ethical challenges in AI implementation, and building responsible AI practices. The role of various stakeholders, such as developers, organizations, and regulators, is examined to highlight their contributions to ensuring ethical AI use. Additionally, future directions for AI ethics, including advancements in explainable AI and evolving regulatory frameworks, are discussed. By integrating ethical considerations into AI development, entrepreneurs can drive innovation while upholding principles of fairness, transparency, and accountability.

Chapter 8
Artificial Intelligence as a Catalyst for Innovation in Islamic
Entrepreneurship: Balancing Ethics and Efficiency.. 165
    Early Ridho Kismawadi, IAIN Langsa, Indonesia
    Mohammad Irfan, Christ University, Bangalore, India

The study explores the intersection of AI and Islamic entrepreneurship, focusing on how AI can be effectively leveraged to improve business operations and innovation while adhering to Islamic ethical standards. Through a comprehensive analysis, the study identifies practical guidelines for Muslim entrepreneurs to adopt AI technology without sacrificing their commitment to Sharia-compliant practices. The study also provides actionable recommendations for businesses and policymakers to design and implement AI systems that align with Islamic values, ensuring transparency, fairness, and social responsibility in AI-driven initiatives. The findings have significant implications for the Islamic economic sector, providing a model for integrating cutting-edge technology with traditional values to achieve sustainable and socially responsible business practices.

Chapter 9
Entrepreneurial Success and Decision-Making Power With the Support of
Assistive Technology 181
    S. Srinivasan, Department of Humanities and Social Sciences, Graphic
        Era University (Deemed), India
    R. Vallipriya, Department of Physical Science, Institute of Education,
        India

The study mainly concentrates on entrepreneurial success and decision-making power and processes in a developing country like India. The study used qualitative and quantitative methods, adopting semi-structured interviews conducted with entrepreneurs in Dehradun City, Uttarakhand, India. The findings of the study were analyzed using SPSS version 23. The study focused on the following aspects: socio-economic characteristics of the entrepreneurs, problems faced by entrepreneurs at various levels such as family, financial, gender disparities, and education, as well as legal challenges encountered by the entrepreneurs. The significance of the study lies in how entrepreneurs, with the support of Artificial Intelligence, cope with problem-solving, risk identification, and decision-making processes. The study emphasizes that AI can play a vital role in improving both the entrepreneurs' lives and their businesses. This study can contribute to enhancing the future perspectives of AI and entrepreneurship-related aspects in research.

Chapter 10
AI-Driven Decision-Making in Startups: Enhancing Strategic Choices
Through Predictive Analytics 217
    Mohit Yadav, O.P. Jindal Global University, India
    Ajay Chandel, Lovely Professional University, India
    Majdi Quttainah, Kuwait University, Kuwait

This chapter explores the transformative impact of AI-driven decision-making on startups, highlighting how predictive analytics enhances strategic choices and drives growth. It examines the evolution of AI in startup ecosystems, from ideation to scaling, and delves into specific tools and techniques for leveraging predictive analytics. The chapter also addresses the challenges and limitations associated with AI, including data quality, integration issues, and ethical considerations. Future trends such as AI-driven personalization, autonomous systems, and explainable AI are discussed, emphasizing their potential to reshape decision-making processes. The integration of AI with emerging technologies and the importance of balancing technological and human insights are also explored. This comprehensive analysis provides startups with actionable insights on harnessing AI for competitive advantage and sustainable success.

Chapter 11
AI-Powered Talent Development: Nurturing Skills and Leadership in
Entrepreneurial Teams 241
    Deepak Kumar Sahoo, Biju Patnaik University of Technology, Rourkela,
        India
    Thi Mai Le, Vietnam National University, Hanoi, Vietnam
    Anish Kumar, O.P. Jindal Global University, India
    Ajay Chandel, Lovely Professional University, India

AI in entrepreneurship is one of the latest methods of talent development that transforms the conventional ways of skill enhancement, leadership, and team dynamics. In this chapter, the transformative power of AI will be discussed to identify, develop, and manage talent-what recent advances in AI technologies, including deep learning and natural language processing, have integrated with developing tools like AR, VR, and blockchain. It looks at trends such as personalized learning, AI-driven leadership development, and improving diversity and inclusion. The chapter also discusses a number of challenges and ethical issues that include algorithmic bias, data privacy, and the balance between AI and human judgment. Understanding these trends and taking ethical concerns seriously can help organizations effectively deploy AI to build strong, diverse, and high-performing teams that drive innovation and success.

Chapter 12
AI and Social Media Analytics: Leveraging Real-Time Data for
Entrepreneurial Growth 267
    Shashank Mittal, O.P. Jindal Global University, India
    Ajay Chandel, Lovely Professional University, India
    Phuong Mai Nguyen, Vietnam National University, Hanoi, Vietnam

This chapter explores the transformative impact of AI and social media analytics on entrepreneurial growth. It delves into how these technologies enable businesses to harness real-time data for personalized marketing, customer engagement, and market research. The discussion highlights key trends such as advanced personalization, AI-driven content creation, and predictive analytics, alongside the integration of AI with augmented and virtual reality. Challenges, including data privacy concerns, integration issues, and the complexity of AI models, are also addressed. The chapter concludes with insights into future innovations and their potential to drive sustainable growth. Entrepreneurs are encouraged to leverage these tools effectively while navigating the associated challenges to remain competitive in the digital age.

Compilation of References 291

About the Contributors 323

Index 329

Foreword

In today's rapidly evolving business landscape, the need for sustainable practices has become more pressing than ever. Organizations are recognizing their responsibility in fostering environmentally conscious operations as the global economy grapples with environmental challenges such as climate change, resource depletion, and rising pollution levels. Green Human Resources Management (GHRM) emerges as a pivotal mechanism that aligns organizational goals with sustainability objectives, ensuring that human capital is nurtured in ways that promote environmental stewardship. This book explores the critical intersection of GHRM and nascent entrepreneurship, highlighting how these two forces can drive transformative change across industries.

Nascent entrepreneurship refers to the early-stage efforts of individuals striving to bring their innovative ideas to life in a highly competitive and uncertain environment. These emerging entrepreneurs play a vital role in reshaping industries, and when combined with the principles of GHRM, they can create a profound impact on sustainable development. By leveraging green practices, startups can not only contribute to the preservation of the environment but also achieve long-term competitiveness, attract eco-conscious consumers, and build resilient business models that adapt to the evolving expectations of stakeholders.

This book delves into the strategies, challenges, and opportunities that arise from the integration of green human resource management with entrepreneurial ventures. It examines how businesses, especially those in their formative stages, can adopt sustainable practices in recruitment, training, development, and performance management to foster a culture of environmental responsibility. Additionally, it sheds light on the role of leadership in inspiring and sustaining green initiatives within organizations, ensuring that sustainability becomes an integral part of business DNA from the beginning.

As we move toward a future where sustainability is no longer an option but a necessity, this book aims to provide insights, strategies, and case studies to inspire both scholars and practitioners. Whether you are an academic researching green practices or an entrepreneur aiming to build a business that balances profit with environmental responsibility, the discussions in this book will offer valuable perspectives on how to succeed in a green economy.

I would like to extend my heartfelt appreciation to the esteemed editors of this book, Dr. Muhammad Nawaz Tunio, Dr. Muhammad Asif Qureshi, and Dr. Jawaid Qureshi. Their unwavering commitment to maintaining the highest standards of quality has been instrumental in shaping the direction of this work. Their expertise, guidance, and dedication to excellence have enriched this book, ensuring that it delivers meaningful insights and valuable contributions to the field. It is through their tireless efforts that this book has achieved its final form, and for that, I am profoundly grateful.

By examining green human resource management through the lens of nascent entrepreneurship, we hope to empower organizations and individuals to survive and thrive in a world where sustainability is the key to unlocking future potential.

Naveeda Katper
Institute of Business Administration, University of Sindh, Jamshoro, Pakistan

Preface

The rapid advancements in Artificial Intelligence (AI) have transformed industries worldwide, reshaping traditional business models and redefining the processes that drive entrepreneurial success. As AI technologies continue to evolve, their impact on entrepreneurship has become both profound and far-reaching, offering new avenues for innovation, efficiency, and growth. The book *Improving Entrepreneurial Processes Through Advanced AI* emerges from the intersection of these powerful forces, aiming to explore how AI can revolutionize the way entrepreneurs conceptualize, build, and scale their ventures.

Entrepreneurship, at its core, has always been about identifying opportunities, managing risks, and creating value through innovation. Historically, these processes relied heavily on human intuition, experience, and resourcefulness. However, in the contemporary business environment, AI offers unprecedented tools that can augment human capacity, automate decision-making, and provide insights that were once unimaginable. Entrepreneurs today are no longer constrained by the limits of human knowledge or time; instead, they have access to AI-driven systems capable of analyzing vast amounts of data, predicting market trends, optimizing operations, and even generating creative solutions to complex problems.

The purpose of this book is to delve into how advanced AI technologies can enhance and improve various aspects of entrepreneurial processes. From ideation and product development to marketing, customer engagement, and scaling, AI is becoming an essential component for entrepreneurial success. Through in-depth discussions, case studies, and empirical research, this book will demonstrate the tangible benefits AI brings to entrepreneurs, particularly in areas such as:

- **Market Analysis and Opportunity Identification**: AI's ability to analyze big data enables entrepreneurs to identify market gaps, consumer behavior patterns, and emerging trends with precision and speed.

- **Innovation and Product Development**: By leveraging machine learning algorithms, entrepreneurs can enhance product development cycles, predict customer needs, and personalize offerings to an unprecedented degree.
- **Operational Efficiency**: AI-powered tools for automation and optimization can streamline supply chains, improve customer service, and reduce operational costs, allowing entrepreneurs to focus more on strategic growth.
- **Decision-Making and Risk Management**: Predictive analytics and AI-driven simulations provide entrepreneurs with insights that help them make informed decisions, minimize risks, and respond to market shifts more effectively.
- **Customer Engagement and Experience**: AI technologies like chatbots, recommendation engines, and sentiment analysis enable businesses to engage with customers in more personalized and efficient ways, fostering loyalty and long-term relationships.

The book is organized into several sections that guide readers through the process of understanding, adopting, and applying AI in entrepreneurial contexts. It begins with foundational concepts, offering readers a sense of AI's potential and its relevance to entrepreneurship. Subsequent chapters provide practical applications of AI in different entrepreneurial stages, with real-world examples that showcase AI's transformative power.

This book is intended for a wide audience, including entrepreneurs, business leaders, academics, and students who are interested in understanding the role of AI in shaping the future of entrepreneurship. By offering a blend of theoretical insights and practical guidance, it serves as both an academic resource and a practical handbook for those looking to harness AI to drive entrepreneurial success.

As the editor of *Improving Entrepreneurial Processes Through Advanced AI*, I hope this book inspires a new generation of entrepreneurs to embrace AI as a core component of their business strategies. By integrating advanced technologies into entrepreneurial processes, businesses can improve their efficiency and competitiveness and contribute to a broader vision of innovation and sustainability in the digital age.

ORGANIZATION OF THE BOOK

Chapter 1: Harnessing AI for Digital Entrepreneurship: Strategies and Best Practices

This chapter addresses the revolutionary potential of Artificial Intelligence (AI) in digital entrepreneurship, concentrating on the strategies and best practices for efficiently incorporating AI into corporate processes. As digital entrepreneurship advances, AI has become a crucial tool for better decision-making, streamlining operations, and driving innovation. The chapter opens by presenting an introduction to AI applications in entrepreneurship, followed by a discussion of AI-powered company models and tactics. Through case studies, we showcase successful examples of entrepreneurs embracing AI to scale their firms and increase productivity. Finally, the chapter discusses the future trends and problems that digital entrepreneurs may encounter as AI continues to advance, offering insights into how to stay competitive in an AI-driven market.

Chapter 2: AI as a Game Changer: How Digital Entrepreneurs are Redefining Business Practices

This article investigates the transformative role of artificial intelligence (AI) in digital entrepreneurship, highlighting how it serves as a catalyst for business innovation. With the rapid evolution of technology, digital entrepreneurs are increasingly leveraging AI to create novel solutions that address dynamic market needs. This study aims to elucidate the multifaceted impact of AI on entrepreneurship, focusing on how it enhances operational efficiency, improves customer experiences, and fosters data-driven decision-making. Through an exploration of real-world case studies and qualitative research, the findings underscore the importance of integrating AI into business strategies for sustained growth and competitive advantage. Moreover, the article offers practical recommendations for entrepreneurs to navigate the challenges of AI adoption and emphasizes the need for further research in this area. Ultimately, this study contributes to the understanding of AI's significance in shaping the future of digital entrepreneurship.

Chapter 3: From Giants to Guides: Lessons from Google, Coca-Cola, Airbnb's Entrepreneurial Odyssey, and AI's Insights for Visionaries

Traversing the entrepreneurial trajectories of Google, Coca-Cola, and Airbnb, this exploration extracts profound insights from their respective journeys. These industry leaders illuminate the path for emerging visionaries, imparting invaluable lessons and strategies that have propelled their remarkable success stories. Furthermore, this exploration delves into the intersection of entrepreneurship and artificial intelligence (AI). By scrutinizing AI-driven advancements within Google, Coca-Cola, and Airbnb, we unveil the transformative impact of AI on decision-making, process refinement, and innovative troubleshooting. The synthesis of the experiences of established giants with the transformative potential of AI constructs a comprehensive framework for aspiring entrepreneurs. This amalgamation empowers emerging visionaries to adeptly navigate the dynamic business landscape, offering a roadmap that seamlessly integrates historical wisdom and futuristic innovation, guiding new ventures toward achievements that resonate across time.

Chapter 4: Optimizing Business Models in Entrepreneurship: The Role of AI in Iterative Business Planning

This chapter explores the role of Artificial Intelligence (AI) in optimizing business models through iterative planning. As AI continues to advance, it offers entrepreneurs powerful tools for data-driven decision-making, enhancing customer insights, market segmentation, dynamic pricing, and resource allocation. The chapter examines key AI technologies such as machine learning, natural language processing, and AI-powered simulations, which enable continuous refinement and adaptation of business strategies. It also addresses challenges such as data privacy, AI transparency, potential biases, and the balance between automation and human intuition. Ethical considerations, including the responsible use of AI, are discussed to ensure sustainable innovation. The chapter concludes by exploring future trends, including autonomous decision-making and the democratization of AI, emphasizing its potential to transform business models and drive long-term success.

Chapter 5: Automating Routine Tasks to Improve Entrepreneurial Productivity

This chapter explores the transformative impact of Artificial Intelligence (AI) on business automation, focusing on how AI technologies enhance entrepreneurial productivity and decision-making. It examines key trends such as hyper-automation, which integrates AI tools to streamline entire workflows, and AI-driven personalization that tailors customer experiences. The chapter also addresses future advancements, including autonomous supply chains and AI-augmented decision-making systems, which promise to further revolutionize business operations. Challenges such as ethical considerations, workforce adaptation, and sustainability are discussed to provide a comprehensive view of the evolving landscape. By leveraging AI, entrepreneurs can automate routine tasks, make data-driven decisions, and drive strategic growth, positioning themselves for success in a rapidly changing business environment.

Chapter 6: Incremental Innovation: Only Survival of the Entrepreneurs in the Competitive Age

Innovation is widely recognized as a critical driver of business success and competitive advantage. While disruptive innovations—those that radically transform industries or create entirely new markets—often capture the spotlight, incremental innovation plays a fundamental and often underappreciated role in driving sustained growth and efficiency. Incremental innovation refers to the process of making gradual, iterative improvements to existing products, services, processes, or business models (Christensen, 1997; Tidd & Bessant, 2018).

Chapter 7: Ethical AI in Entrepreneurship: Balancing Innovation with Responsible AI Practices

The rapid advancement of artificial intelligence (AI) presents significant opportunities and challenges for entrepreneurship. This chapter explores the intersection of ethical practices and AI innovation, focusing on how to balance technological progress with responsible AI development. Key topics include defining ethical AI principles, addressing ethical challenges in AI implementation, and building responsible AI practices. The role of various stakeholders, such as developers, organizations, and regulators, is examined to highlight their contributions to ensuring ethical AI use. Additionally, future directions for AI ethics, including advancements in explainable AI and evolving regulatory frameworks, are discussed. By integrating ethical considerations into AI development, entrepreneurs can drive innovation while upholding principles of fairness, transparency, and accountability.

Chapter 8: Artificial Intelligence as a Catalyst for Innovation in Islamic Entrepreneurship: Balancing Ethics and Efficiency

The study explores the intersection of AI and Islamic entrepreneurship, focusing on how AI can be effectively leveraged to improve business operations and innovation while adhering to Islamic ethical standards. Through a comprehensive analysis, the study identifies practical guidelines for Muslim entrepreneurs to adopt AI technology without sacrificing their commitment to Sharia-compliant practices. The study also provides actionable recommendations for businesses and policymakers to design and implement AI systems that align with Islamic values, ensuring transparency, fairness, and social responsibility in AI-driven initiatives. The findings have significant implications for the Islamic economic sector, providing a model for integrating cutting-edge technology with traditional values to achieve sustainable and socially responsible business practices.

Chapter 9: Entrepreneurial Success and Decision-Making Power with Support of Assistive Technology

The study mainly concentrates on entrepreneurial success and decision-making power and processes in a developing country like India. The study used qualitative and quantitative methods, adopting semi-structured interviews conducted with entrepreneurs in Dehradun City, Uttarakhand, India. The findings of the study were analyzed using SPSS version 23. The study focused on the following aspects: socio-economic characteristics of the entrepreneurs, problems faced by entrepreneurs at various levels such as family, financial, gender disparities, and education, as well as legal challenges encountered by the entrepreneurs. The significance of the study lies in how entrepreneurs, with the support of Artificial Intelligence, cope with problem-solving, risk identification, and decision-making processes. The study emphasizes that AI can play a vital role in improving both the entrepreneurs' lives and their businesses. This study can contribute to enhancing the future perspectives of AI and entrepreneurship-related aspects in research.

Chapter 10: AI-Driven Decision-Making in Startups: Enhancing Strategic Choices Through Predictive Analytics

This chapter explores the transformative impact of AI-driven decision-making on startups, highlighting how predictive analytics enhances strategic choices and drives growth. It examines the evolution of AI in startup ecosystems, from ideation to scaling, and delves into specific tools and techniques for leveraging predictive analytics. The chapter also addresses the challenges and limitations associated with

AI, including data quality, integration issues, and ethical considerations. Future trends such as AI-driven personalization, autonomous systems, and explainable AI are discussed, emphasizing their potential to reshape decision-making processes. The integration of AI with emerging technologies and the importance of balancing technological and human insights are also explored. This comprehensive analysis provides startups with actionable insights on harnessing AI for competitive advantage and sustainable success.

Chapter 11: AI-Powered Talent Development: Nurturing Skills and Leadership in Entrepreneurial Teams

AI in entrepreneurship is one of the latest methods of talent development that transforms the conventional ways of skill enhancement, leadership, and team dynamics. In this chapter, the transformative power of AI will be discussed to identify, develop, and manage talent-what recent advances in AI technologies, including deep learning and natural language processing, have integrated with developing tools like AR, VR, and blockchain. It looks at trends such as personalized learning, AI-driven leadership development, and improving diversity and inclusion. The chapter also discusses a number of challenges and ethical issues that include algorithmic bias, data privacy, and the balance between AI and human judgment. Understanding these trends and taking ethical concerns seriously can help organizations effectively deploy AI to build strong, diverse, and high-performing teams that drive innovation and success.

Chapter 12: AI and Social Media Analytics: Leveraging Real-Time Data for Entrepreneurial Growth

This chapter explores the transformative impact of AI and social media analytics on entrepreneurial growth. It delves into how these technologies enable businesses to harness real-time data for personalized marketing, customer engagement, and market research. The discussion highlights key trends such as advanced personalization, AI-driven content creation, and predictive analytics, alongside the integration of AI with augmented and virtual reality. Challenges, including data privacy concerns, integration issues, and the complexity of AI models, are also addressed. The chapter concludes with insights into future innovations and their potential to drive sustainable growth. Entrepreneurs are encouraged to leverage these tools effectively while navigating the associated challenges to remain competitive in the digital age.

Muhammad Nawaz Tunio
University of Sufism and Modern Sciences, Pakistan

Acknowledgment

The creation of *Examining Green Human Resources Management and Nascent Entrepreneurship* has been a collaborative effort, and I am deeply thankful to all those who contributed to its success.

First and foremost, I would like to express my sincere gratitude to my esteemed co-editors, Dr. Muhammad Asif Qureshi and Dr. Jawaid Qureshi. Your insightful perspectives, commitment to academic excellence, and unwavering dedication to this project have been invaluable. It has been an honor to work alongside you both, and your contributions have played a pivotal role in shaping the direction and quality of this book.

I would also like to extend my heartfelt thanks to the authors and researchers whose knowledge and hard work form the core of this book. Your commitment to exploring the intersection of green human resources management and entrepreneurship has enriched this publication, and your innovative ideas are sure to inspire future readers.

A special note of appreciation goes to our institutions, colleagues, and professional networks, whose support has been instrumental in the completion of this book. Your encouragement and belief in the importance of sustainability and entrepreneurship have made a meaningful impact.

Finally, to my family and friends—thank you for your patience, encouragement, and understanding throughout this process. Your unwavering support has been a constant source of strength.

This book stands as a testament to the collaborative spirit of all involved, and I hope it will contribute positively to the fields of green human resources management and nascent entrepreneurship for years to come.

Introduction

The rapid advancement of Artificial Intelligence (AI) is transforming industries, including entrepreneurship, where processes and decision-making are becoming increasingly reliant on AI-driven tools. AI is no longer a futuristic concept; it has become integral to the entrepreneurial landscape, streamlining business operations, enhancing customer experience, and driving innovation. This chapter introduces the intersection of AI and entrepreneurship, exploring how advanced AI technologies improve entrepreneurial processes by fostering agility, scalability, and efficiency in business operations.

THE EVOLUTION OF AI IN ENTREPRENEURSHIP

Once predominantly manual and driven by human intuition, entrepreneurial processes are being revolutionized by AI. The traditional methods of market analysis, product development, customer service, and business management are evolving to incorporate AI-driven insights, enabling entrepreneurs to make data-driven decisions. According to research by Bughin et al. (2019), businesses that leverage AI in decision-making can increase profitability by as much as 20% compared to those that rely solely on human expertise. These improvements stem from AI's ability to process large datasets, recognize patterns, and provide predictive analytics, thereby reducing uncertainty in entrepreneurial ventures.

AI has particularly transformed the way startups approach scalability and innovation. For instance, AI-powered platforms enable businesses to automate tasks such as inventory management, financial planning, and marketing, thus freeing up entrepreneurs to focus on strategic growth. This shift allows entrepreneurs to be more agile, responding quickly to market demands and scaling operations without significantly increasing costs (Agrawal, Gans, & Goldfarb, 2018).

AI-DRIVEN DECISION MAKING AND RISK MANAGEMENT

One of the most significant impacts of AI on entrepreneurship is in decision-making and risk management. Traditionally, entrepreneurs have had to rely on gut instinct and limited data to make critical business decisions. With AI, entrepreneurs can now use sophisticated algorithms and machine learning models to analyze vast amounts of data, identifying trends and making predictions with greater accuracy (Jarrahi, 2018). This data-driven approach helps entrepreneurs mitigate risks, optimize their business models, and explore new opportunities.

For instance, AI-powered predictive analytics tools allow entrepreneurs to assess market trends, forecast customer demand, and develop targeted marketing strategies. This level of precision reduces the likelihood of failure and increases the chances of success. A study by Davenport and Ronanki (2018) revealed that companies utilizing AI for business intelligence experienced a 15% reduction in failure rates during product launches compared to companies that did not incorporate AI.

Moreover, AI can help in the identification and management of risks that were previously difficult to predict. Through real-time data monitoring and advanced simulations, entrepreneurs can assess the potential impact of economic shifts, technological disruptions, and customer behavior changes. These insights are invaluable in today's volatile business environment, where rapid changes can make or break a startup's success.

AI AND CUSTOMER-CENTRIC INNOVATION

In addition to enhancing internal processes, AI has revolutionized how entrepreneurs engage with customers. Customer-centric innovation, driven by AI, is becoming a key differentiator in competitive markets. AI technologies such as natural language processing (NLP) and machine learning algorithms enable businesses to personalize customer interactions, improving satisfaction and retention (Huang & Rust, 2018).

AI-powered chatbots and virtual assistants, for example, provide 24/7 customer support, while machine learning algorithms analyze customer behavior to recommend personalized products and services. This level of customization fosters stronger relationships between businesses and their customers, which is critical for long-term success (Luo et al., 2021). As AI continues to evolve, entrepreneurs are finding new ways to create value through customer engagement, further transforming the entrepreneurial ecosystem.

THE ROLE OF AI IN ENHANCING BUSINESS AGILITY AND INNOVATION

Business agility is a key factor in entrepreneurial success, especially in dynamic markets. AI enhances agility by automating routine tasks, reducing operational bottlenecks, and facilitating faster decision-making. Startups and small businesses, which often face resource constraints, can particularly benefit from AI-driven automation tools that streamline administrative and operational tasks (Dwivedi et al., 2021).

Furthermore, AI fosters innovation by enabling entrepreneurs to experiment with new ideas at a lower cost and risk. AI-driven design tools, for instance, allow entrepreneurs to develop and test new product concepts rapidly. By utilizing AI-based simulation models, entrepreneurs can identify potential challenges and optimize designs before investing in physical prototypes, thus accelerating the innovation cycle (Cockburn, Henderson, & Stern, 2019).

CHALLENGES AND ETHICAL CONSIDERATIONS

While AI holds great promise for improving entrepreneurial processes, it also presents challenges that entrepreneurs must navigate. The integration of AI into business operations requires technical expertise, which many startups may lack. Moreover, the high cost of implementing advanced AI technologies can be prohibitive for early-stage ventures. There are also concerns about data privacy and ethical issues surrounding the use of AI, particularly in customer-facing applications (Floridi & Cowls, 2019).

Ethical considerations include the transparency of AI decision-making processes, potential biases in algorithmic recommendations, and the displacement of jobs due to automation. Entrepreneurs must ensure that AI is used responsibly, adhering to legal and ethical standards to build trust with customers and stakeholders.

CONCLUSION

AI is reshaping the entrepreneurial landscape by enhancing decision-making, improving risk management, and driving customer-centric innovation. Entrepreneurs who harness the power of AI can streamline their operations, scale their businesses, and innovate at unprecedented levels. However, the successful integration of AI into entrepreneurial processes requires not only technical expertise but also careful consideration of the ethical and social implications of AI technologies.

As AI continues to advance, it will play an increasingly central role in shaping the future of entrepreneurship. This book will delve deeper into how AI is transforming various entrepreneurial processes, providing practical insights and case studies that demonstrate the real-world impact of AI on entrepreneurship. Entrepreneurs and business leaders must stay abreast of these technological advancements to remain competitive and create sustainable, innovative ventures in the AI-driven economy.

Muhammad Nawaz Tunio
University of Sufism and Modern Sciences, Bhitshah, Pakistan

REFERENCES

Agrawal, A., Gans, J., & Goldfarb, A. (2018). *Prediction Machines: The Simple Economics of Artificial Intelligence*. Harvard Business Review Press.

Bughin, J., Seong, J., Manyika, J., Chui, M., & Joshi, R. (2019). *Notes from the AI Frontier: Tackling Europe's Gap in Digital and AI*. McKinsey Global Institute.

Cockburn, I. M., Henderson, R., & Stern, S. (2019). The impact of artificial intelligence on innovation. *Innovation Policy and the Economy*, 19(1), 41–58.

Davenport, T. H., & Ronanki, R. (2018). Artificial intelligence for the real world. *Harvard Business Review*, 96(1), 108–116.

Dwivedi, Y. K., Hughes, L., Ismagilova, E., Aarts, G., & Baabdullah, A. M. (2021). Artificial Intelligence (AI): Multidisciplinary perspectives on emerging challenges, opportunities, and agenda for research, practice, and policy. *International Journal of Information Management*, 57, 102–126.

Floridi, L., & Cowls, J. (2019). A unified framework of five principles for AI in society. *Harvard Data Science Review*, 1(1), 1–13.

Huang, M. H., & Rust, R. T. (2018). Artificial intelligence in service. *Journal of Service Research*, 21(2), 155–172.

Jarrahi, M. H. (2018). Artificial intelligence and the future of work: Human-AI symbiosis in organizational decision-making. *Business Horizons*, 61(4), 577–586.

Luo, X., Tong, S., Fang, Z., & Qu, Z. (2021). Frontiers: Machines vs. humans: The impact of AI chatbot disclosure on customer purchases. *Marketing Science*, 40(5), 914–926.

Chapter 1
Harnessing AI for Digital Entrepreneurship:
Strategies and Best Practices

Mustafa Kayyali
https://orcid.org/0000-0003-3300-262X
HE Higher Education Ranking, Syria

ABSTRACT

This chapter addresses the revolutionary potential of Artificial Intelligence (AI) in digital entrepreneurship, concentrating on the strategies and best practices for efficiently incorporating AI into corporate processes. As digital entrepreneurship advances, AI has become a crucial tool for better decision-making, streamlining operations, and driving innovation. The chapter opens by presenting an introduction to AI applications in entrepreneurship, followed by a discussion of AI-powered company models and tactics. Through case studies, we showcase successful examples of entrepreneurs embracing AI to scale their firms and increase productivity. Finally, the chapter discusses the future trends and problems that digital entrepreneurs may encounter as AI continues to advance, offering insights into how to stay competitive in an AI-driven market.

INTRODUCTION

In the modern business landscape, digital entrepreneurship has emerged as a powerful force, driving innovation and reshaping industries across the globe. The digital age has created new opportunities for entrepreneurs, enabling them to build businesses with global reach, agility, and scalability. However, with the rise of digital platforms and global connectivity, the competitive landscape has become

DOI: 10.4018/979-8-3693-1495-1.ch001

increasingly crowded and complex (Jarrahi et al, 2023). In response, entrepreneurs must adopt cutting-edge technologies to differentiate their offerings, streamline their operations, and respond to rapidly changing market demands. One such technology that is revolutionizing the way digital entrepreneurs operate is Artificial Intelligence (AI). AI, which encompasses a range of technologies including machine learning, natural language processing, and predictive analytics, has transcended its role as a tool for large corporations and is now an essential asset for digital startups and small-to-medium enterprises (SMEs). The transformative potential of AI lies in its ability to process vast amounts of data, identify patterns, and make data-driven decisions in real time (Raihan, 2024). For digital entrepreneurs, this means the ability to automate processes, optimize resource allocation, predict consumer behavior, and even develop innovative products and services that are responsive to individual customer needs.

As the entrepreneurial ecosystem becomes increasingly digitized, the integration of AI is not merely an option but a necessity (Bouncken & Kraus, 2022). AI-powered tools are becoming more accessible, affordable, and easier to implement, leveling the playing field for entrepreneurs who wish to compete with larger, more established businesses. With the rise of AI, digital entrepreneurs can now access advanced technologies that allow them to streamline workflows, reduce costs, and enhance customer experiences. In this rapidly evolving digital economy, those who fail to leverage AI risk falling behind their competitors. The primary goal of this chapter is to explore how AI can be harnessed for digital entrepreneurship, focusing on both strategic approaches and practical applications. By delving into real-world case studies, we aim to provide digital entrepreneurs with a roadmap for effectively implementing AI-driven solutions in their ventures. Through a combination of best practices, lessons learned, and an examination of emerging trends, we will offer insights into how AI can be used to overcome common entrepreneurial challenges, such as limited resources, market uncertainty, and the need for rapid scalability.

AI's role in digital entrepreneurship is multifaceted, extending beyond simple automation or cost reduction. At its core, AI is about enabling smarter decision-making, fostering innovation, and creating new opportunities for value creation (Mele et al, 2018). For instance, AI can empower entrepreneurs to gain deeper insights into customer preferences and behavior, which can then inform personalized marketing strategies, product development, and customer service. Furthermore, AI allows businesses to operate more efficiently, reducing manual labor and enabling entrepreneurs to focus on high-value tasks such as strategy, innovation, and relationship-building. The journey toward AI adoption is not without its challenges. Many digital entrepreneurs, particularly those in the early stages of their ventures, may lack the technical expertise or financial resources to fully capitalize on AI. Additionally, ethical considerations surrounding data privacy, algorithmic transparency, and the potential for biased outcomes present significant obstacles. This chapter addresses these challenges head-on, offering strategies for overcoming barriers to AI adoption and ensuring that AI is used ethically and responsibly. The discussion begins by providing a comprehensive overview of the current state of AI in digital entrepreneurship. This includes an examination of key AI technologies, their applications, and the value they can deliver to entrepreneurs. We then move on to explore AI-powered business models, highlighting how digital entrepreneurs can rethink traditional approaches to building and scaling their ventures using AI. Throughout this exploration, we emphasize the importance of adopting a strategic mindset, where AI is not just a tool but a key enabler of competitive advantage.

AI-Powered Business Models for Digital Entrepreneurs

Artificial Intelligence (AI) is redefining how digital entrepreneurs build and implement business models, giving new methods to generate, deliver, and acquire value. As organizations progressively migrate to online and digital-first strategies, AI has become a cornerstone in establishing novel business models that are not only scalable but also flexible to the fast-paced demands of the digital economy (Pfau & Rimpp, 2021). For entrepreneurs, AI provides the skills to rethink established techniques, streamline processes, and open new opportunities that were previously out of reach. At the heart of AI's impact on business models is its ability to handle huge volumes of data in real time, allowing entrepreneurs the insights they need to make data-driven decisions. In a world where customer behavior, market trends, and competition landscapes can vary overnight, this real-time intelligence is vital. By integrating AI into their business models, entrepreneurs may anticipate client requirements, recognize upcoming market trends, and remain ahead of the competition.

One of the most fundamental ways AI is altering digital business models is through personalization. AI-powered algorithms may analyze data from numerous sources—such as consumer preferences, shopping habits, and online interactions—to generate highly personalized experiences for each user. This kind of personalization was traditionally the domain of major firms with access to advanced resources, but AI has democratized this power, enabling even small digital enterprises to create individualized experiences that boost consumer engagement and happiness. For instance, AI-driven recommendation systems are increasingly routinely utilized by e-commerce platforms, content providers, and service-based organizations to offer items, services, or content that correspond with individual user interests, thus driving higher conversion rates and client loyalty. AI is also facilitating the development of subscription-based business models, which are increasingly popular among digital entrepreneurs. By utilizing AI to evaluate customer behavior and forecast long-term involvement, businesses can personalize their subscription services to match unique demands, enhancing customer retention and increasing lifetime value. Moreover, AI can assist in discovering which products or services are most appealing to different consumer categories, allowing entrepreneurs to optimize their offerings and reduce churn. In businesses such as software-as-a-service (SaaS), content streaming, and digital products, AI is helping entrepreneurs develop sustainable, recurring income streams by improving pricing, delivery, and customer interaction tactics (Bossuwé, 2023). n addition to strengthening customer-facing parts of business models, AI is transforming the back-end operations of digital entrepreneurship. Entrepreneurs can now harness AI to streamline operations, decrease costs, and boost efficiency in ways that would have been inconceivable a decade ago. AI-powered automation systems can perform monotonous activities, such as managing inventory, processing orders, or reacting to customer inquiries, freeing up entrepreneurs to focus on high-level strategy and innovation. This kind of operational efficiency is crucial for digital entrepreneurs who often face resource limits and need to make the most out of limited time and people.

Moreover, AI-driven predictive analytics allows firms to forecast demand, optimize supply chains, and modify their strategy based on real-time market data (Muthukalyani, 2023). For example, AI can forecast which products are likely to be in great demand shortly, allowing entrepreneurs to change their inventory accordingly, decreasing the risk of stockouts or overproduction. This predictive capability applies to other areas as well, such as pricing tactics, where AI may dynamically modify prices based on market conditions, competition activities, and consumer demand. By employing AI to optimize these factors, entrepreneurs can maximize their profitability and remain nimble in an ever-changing market. The rise of AI has also opened the way to totally new forms of digital business models. For instance, AI as a service (AIaaS) platforms have emerged, allowing entrepreneurs to build businesses around selling AI-powered solutions to other firms. These platforms enable entrepreneurs to supply machine learning algorithms, data analytics tools, and AI-driven insights without the requirement for significant technical skills. By packaging AI capabilities into accessible, user-friendly services, these entrepreneurs are working to democratize AI and offer other businesses the tools to innovate and flourish. This business model has been particularly successful in industries such as healthcare, finance, and retail, where AI can give key insights that enable better decision-making and operational efficiency.

Another novel business model being driven by AI is the emergence of AI-powered marketplaces (Candelon & Reeves, 2022). These platforms link buyers and sellers in new, more effective ways by leveraging AI to match supply with demand, optimize price, and enhance the user experience. For example, AI-driven marketplaces in areas such as freelancing services, real estate, and retail are employing AI algorithms to match buyers with the most appropriate products or services based on their tastes and needs. By employing AI to optimize the matchmaking process, these systems can increase customer happiness and transaction efficiency, resulting in improved retention rates and more successful transactions. While AI offers immense potential for digital entrepreneurs, it is vital to note that integrating AI into a business strategy is not without its hurdles. Entrepreneurs must carefully assess the costs of AI adoption, both in terms of financial commitment and the requirement for technical knowledge. Additionally, the ethical concerns of employing AI—particularly when it comes to data privacy and algorithmic bias—must be addressed to ensure that AI-driven business models are sustainable and responsible in the long run. Entrepreneurs need to be open with customers about how their data is being used and must build controls to ensure that AI algorithms are fair and unbiased. AI is rapidly altering the business models available to digital entrepreneurs, giving new methods to generate value, enhance productivity, and develop tailored client experiences. From subscription-based models to AI-powered marketplaces, entrepreneurs are finding novel ways to leverage the power of AI to establish scalable, sustainable businesses. However, to truly exploit the potential of AI, entrepreneurs must adopt a strategic approach, combining the benefits AI provides with the technical, financial, and ethical constraints it presents. Those who can effectively traverse this scenario will be well-positioned to flourish in the increasingly AI-driven digital economy.

Key Strategies for Integrating AI into Entrepreneurial Processes

As Artificial Intelligence (AI) continues to gain popularity across industries, digital entrepreneurs are increasingly recognizing its potential to alter their business operations. However, integrating AI into entrepreneurial ventures is not a trivial undertaking (Elia et al, 2020). It requires careful preparation, an awareness of the technology's capabilities, and a strategic approach to ensure its full potential is realized. Entrepreneurs who successfully incorporate AI into their processes can streamline operations, improve decision-making, and unleash new opportunities for development and innovation. This section discusses essential ways for incorporating AI into entrepreneurial processes, delivering practical insights for entrepreneurs aiming to leverage AI's power. The first and possibly most crucial stage in incorporating AI into entrepreneurial processes is identifying particular areas of the firm where AI may provide value. Entrepreneurs should start by reviewing their current operations, focusing on inefficiencies, bottlenecks, or areas where manual effort is eating important resources. AI is particularly well-suited to activities that include data analysis, pattern recognition, and decision-making, making it perfect for applications such as customer relationship management, supply chain optimization, and predictive analytics. By precisely articulating the business concerns that AI may answer, entrepreneurs can design a more focused and effective AI integration plan.

Once the target locations have been determined, it is vital to start small and scale gradually. Many entrepreneurs make the mistake of attempting to adopt AI across various parts of their organization simultaneously, resulting in confusion, resource strain, and unimpressive outcomes. Instead, a phased strategy allows entrepreneurs to experiment with AI in one area, develop their approach, and expand as they build trust in the technology (Benbya et al, 2020). For instance, an entrepreneur might begin by adopting AI to automate customer service using chatbots or AI-driven support systems. Once the success of this deployment is clear, AI can then be expanded to other areas like sales forecasting, marketing automation, or inventory management. An equally critical strategy for incorporating AI is ensuring that the necessary data infrastructure is in place. AI thrives on data—the more data it has access to, the more accurate its predictions and insights will be. Entrepreneurs must invest in comprehensive data collecting and storage systems to equip AI technologies with the information they need to operate efficiently (Shepherd & Majchrzak, 2022). This includes ensuring that data is collected from all relevant sources, whether internal (e.g., sales data, customer contacts) or external (e.g., market trends, social media activity). It's also crucial to clean and organize data to guarantee that AI algorithms are working with high-quality information. Poor-quality data can lead to erroneous results, lowering the overall usefulness of AI.

Entrepreneurs must also work on establishing or gaining the technical competence required to properly integrate AI. While AI technologies are becoming more accessible, they still require a certain amount of technical understanding to adopt and maintain properly (Giuggioli & Pellegrini, 2023). Entrepreneurs who lack in-house technical skills may need to invest in recruiting AI professionals or partnering with external organizations that can deliver AI-as-a-service solutions. In many situations, cloud-based AI systems offer user-friendly interfaces that allow enterprises to access significant AI capabilities without needing to construct the technology from scratch. These platforms help entrepreneurs integrate AI into their processes more quickly, giving pre-built solutions for activities such as machine learning, data analytics, and natural language processing. Collaboration and continual learning are also crucial components of a successful AI integration plan. Entrepreneurs should develop a culture of experimentation and learning within their firms, encouraging team members to explore how AI might be utilized to enhance various business processes. In many cases, AI integration will necessitate rethinking existing workflows and embracing new methods of problem-solving. Entrepreneurs should be prepared to train their staff on how to operate alongside AI, ensuring that employees understand the benefits of AI tools and are able to use them effectively (Kruger & Steyn, 2021).

Moreover, as AI continues to evolve, continuing education and upskilling will be important for staying competitive in the digital economy.

A critical yet frequently overlooked part of AI integration is aligning AI activities with broader corporate objectives (Dwivedi et al, 2021). AI should not be adopted solely for the sake of embracing new technology. Instead, its implementation should directly complement the company's strategic goals, whether that means improving customer satisfaction, increasing operational efficiency, or fostering innovation. Entrepreneurs should routinely analyze the success of their AI-driven processes to ensure they are generating measurable results that align with these aims (Smith et al, 2019). This can involve defining key performance indicators (KPIs) or success metrics that track the impact of AI on vital areas such as revenue growth, customer retention, or time saved on manual operations. Another crucial method is to mix AI-driven decision-making with human judgment. While AI excels at analyzing vast datasets and spotting patterns, there are certain areas where human intuition and creativity are incomparable. Entrepreneurs must realize when AI should be used to augment decision-making rather than entirely automate it. For instance, AI might advise pricing adjustments based on market patterns, but human monitoring is vital to ensure these decisions match with broader business factors such as brand positioning or customer perception. By combining the strengths of AI with human skills, entrepreneurs may make more informed and nuanced decisions.

In addition, entrepreneurs must face the ethical consequences of integrating AI into their processes (Shepherd & Majchrzak, 2022). As AI technologies become increasingly ingrained in company operations, concerns regarding data privacy, security, and bias must be taken into account. Entrepreneurs need to ensure that AI systems are transparent, secure, and ethically sound. This means being upfront with clients about how their data is being used and taking steps to eliminate algorithmic bias that could lead to unfair or discriminatory outcomes. Implementing ethical principles and best practices for AI use will not only shield the organization from potential legal and reputational concerns but also promote trust with consumers and stakeholders. Entrepreneurs must stay fluid and adaptable in their approach to AI integration. The AI ecosystem is continually expanding, with new technologies and tools emerging at a rapid pace (Jacobides et al, 2021). Entrepreneurs must be willing to adapt their methods when new opportunities arise and as their businesses expand. This may involve reevaluating AI investments, experimenting with new AI applications, or changing focus to new areas of the organization that can benefit from AI. Flexibility and a readiness to pivot are key to keeping pace with technology breakthroughs and being competitive in an AI-driven environment. Integrating AI into entrepreneurial operations is a complicated task that demands careful design, strategic execution, and continuing improvement (Ramírez, 2023). By concentrating on particular areas where AI may offer value, starting small, guaranteeing data preparation, growing technical knowledge, aligning AI with business goals, and addressing ethical considerations, entrepreneurs can effectively negotiate the difficulties of AI integration. The potential rewards—enhanced efficiency, improved decision-making, and new development opportunities—make the investment in AI beneficial for any digital entrepreneur wanting to flourish in an increasingly competitive market.

Case Studies: Best Practices in AI-Driven Entrepreneurship

The emergence of Artificial Intelligence (AI) has opened up tremendous potential for entrepreneurs, and countless case studies highlight how AI has been successfully integrated into business models across various industries. These real-world examples offer significant insights into best practices for using AI-driven methods in entrepreneurship. By analyzing how different organizations and entrepreneurs have handled the hurdles of AI adoption, discovered areas for growth, and reaped considerable advantages, we may uncover crucial lessons for those wishing to leverage AI's power in their ventures (Aljarboa, 2024). One noteworthy case study comes from the e-commerce sector, where AI has been shown to be transformative for many organizations. Shopify, a prominent e-commerce platform, has harnessed AI to offer small and medium-sized businesses (SMBs) the tools to succeed in a highly competitive digital economy (Shaik et al, 2024). Shopify has integrated AI-powered services like as targeted marketing, predictive analytics, and customer care automation (Monica & Soju, 2024). One of the platform's most popular AI-driven solutions is its recommendation engine, which allows online businesses to deliver individualized product choices to individual shoppers. This not only increases the client experience but also boosts sales by making relevant products more apparent. By equipping entrepreneurs with AI technologies, Shopify has helped thousands of online businesses optimize their operations and enhance their bottom line.

A particularly noteworthy component of Shopify's AI strategy is how it democratizes access to advanced technologies (Núñez, 2021). Many smaller companies lack the means to develop their own AI solutions, but with platforms like Shopify, they can take advantage of cutting-edge AI without needing in-house expertise. This case highlights how businesses that operate as AI enablers—those providing AI-driven services and platforms—can stimulate creativity among entrepreneurs. In doing so, AI becomes a tool that boosts business scalability and efficiency, regardless of the size or technological prowess of the entrepreneur. Another noteworthy scenario comes from the healthcare business, where AI is being used to revolutionize patient care and diagnosis. One interesting example is Babylon Health, a UK-based business that built an AI-powered healthcare app targeted at enhancing access to medical advice. Babylon Health's app uses AI to detect symptoms and make diagnostic recommendations based on a massive dataset of medical information (Ćirković, 2020). Patients can use the app to input their symptoms, and AI algorithms deliver insights that guide users on whether to seek professional medical care or how to manage minor health conditions. This strategy has been a game-changer in digital healthcare, allowing millions of individuals access to quality medical advice for a fraction of the cost of traditional healthcare services.

What makes Babylon Health's approach so interesting is how it blends AI with human expertise (Magalhaes Azevedo & Kieffer, 2021). While AI drives the first diagnostic recommendations, human doctors analyze complex cases, ensuring that the advice supplied is correct and dependable. This hybrid strategy of merging AI with human judgment offers a best practice paradigm for entrepreneurs in any industry: AI can expedite operations and deliver useful insights, but it should complement, rather than replace, the experience of human workers. Babylon Health's success has proved how AI may increase service delivery in industries that demand high levels of trust and accuracy, such as healthcare. In the financial sector, AI is being utilized to transform the way financial services are given to consumers. A prominent example is the robo-advisory platform Wealthfront, which employs AI to manage financial portfolios for its consumers. Wealthfront's algorithms examine market movements, economic situations, and user preferences to produce unique investing plans for each individual. What's groundbreaking about Wealthfront is that it delivers the kind of sophisticated financial management previously reserved for wealthy individuals to a broader audience by automating the process. Users can define financial goals, and Wealthfront's AI-driven tools handle the rest, from asset allocation to rebalancing portfolios as market circumstances change.

Wealthfront's success highlights how AI can drive business model innovation by providing personalized, high-quality services at scale. Entrepreneurs aiming to establish AI-driven firms can benefit from Wealthfront's strategy by concentrating on how AI can give individualized solutions to customers, allowing for greater engagement and improved retention rates (Khang et al, 2024). Furthermore, by automating regular processes, Wealthfront has substantially cut operating costs, a recommended practice for entrepreneurs who wish to boost productivity and profit margins without losing client happiness. The retail business also provides a multitude of case studies that showcase excellent practices in AI-driven entrepreneurship. One such example is Stitch Fix, an online personal styling business that employs AI to produce individualized apparel recommendations for its consumers. Stitch Fix's business concept relies upon a subscription service where users receive apparel curated by a blend of AI algorithms and human stylists (Evangelista, 2019). The AI component analyzes data on client preferences, prior purchases, body types, and fashion trends to identify apparel items most likely to appeal to each customer. Human stylists then improve these options, ensuring that the choices represent current fashion styles and individual tastes. Stitch Fix's model is a best practice in mixing AI with a human touch, similar to Babylon Health. By having AI handle data-driven decisions, Stitch Fix can easily develop its business, delivering highly personalized services to a wide customer base (Abraham, 2021). The major conclusion from this case study is how AI may enhance the user experience by making personalization more precise and less time-consuming, while still allowing human creativity and judgment to play a significant role. For entrepreneurs, the message is clear: AI can automate routine decisions, but for optimum impact, it should be partnered with human expertise, especially in industries where personal preferences and creative judgments are crucial.

In the field of content development and communication, AI is also being harnessed to help entrepreneurs scale and enhance their enterprises. A notable example is BuzzFeed, which has deployed AI to streamline its content development process. BuzzFeed's AI algorithms evaluate user engagement, finding emerging themes and audience preferences to influence the creation of viral content (Nedelcheva, 2020). By relying on AI to recognize emerging trends early, BuzzFeed can quickly publish articles, films, and social media postings that resonate with its audience, often before these issues acquire mainstream notice. This has given BuzzFeed a substantial competitive advantage in the fast-moving world of digital media. BuzzFeed's AI-driven content strategy demonstrates a crucial best practice for entrepreneurs: employing AI to make data-informed decisions that boost creative production and market responsiveness. In an age where information saturation is rampant, AI can help entrepreneurs cut through the noise by offering timely, relevant material that attracts consumer attention. BuzzFeed's success indicates that even in creative industries, where human inventiveness is key, AI can play a crucial role in increasing business outcomes by monitoring and forecasting consumer behavior (Du, 2023). The logistics and transportation sector presents significant case studies of AI's impact on entrepreneurship. One famous example is the autonomous vehicle startup, Waymo, which has pioneered the creation of self-driving cars. Waymo's AI-driven technology evaluates real-time traffic data, road conditions, and driver behaviors to navigate roadways safely without human interaction. While still in its early stages, Waymo's self-driving technology represents the future of transportation, delivering a glimpse into how AI might disrupt entire industries and generate new economic opportunities. For entrepreneurs, the lessons from Waymo are profound (Ryan, 2020). AI cannot only streamline existing business processes but also to create totally new markets and possibilities. Waymo's success shows the necessity of embracing AI as a long-term investment in innovation. Entrepreneurs aiming to establish AI-driven firms should not just focus on enhancing current operations but also examine how AI might enable disruptive transformations that open up new income streams and market opportunities (Marletto, 2019).

These case studies highlight the numerous ways AI may be integrated into entrepreneurial processes to drive innovation, efficiency, and scalability. Whether it's through personalized e-commerce recommendations, automated investing strategies, AI-assisted healthcare, or even self-driving vehicles, the potential for AI to disrupt business is tremendous. Entrepreneurs wishing to capitalize on AI must carefully examine how best to use the technology in their own companies, pulling lessons from previous examples to shape their strategy. The future of AI-driven entrepreneurship is exciting, and those who embrace the correct techniques will be well-positioned to lead in this growing field.

Future Trends and Challenges in AI for Digital Entrepreneurship

As Artificial Intelligence (AI) continues to advance, its role in defining the future of digital entrepreneurship is becoming more deep. The integration of AI into business procedures is no longer a distant concept but a present-day reality with enormous consequences for how entrepreneurs run, grow, and scale their organizations. However, while the potential for AI in digital entrepreneurship is tremendous, the future promises both exciting prospects and serious obstacles. To flourish in this AI-driven market, entrepreneurs must predict future trends and be prepared to navigate the complexity that comes with them (Upadhyay et al, 2022). One of the most crucial future developments in AI for digital entrepreneurship is the rising automation of operations that were once solely human. AI-powered systems are now capable of managing a wide array of activities, from customer care through chatbots to sophisticated financial analysis through predictive algorithms (Elia, 2020). As AI technology becomes more powerful, we may expect even more tasks to be automated, even those that require complex decision-making and creativity. For digital businesses, this gives the option of running leaner operations with less staff members, focusing more on innovation and strategy. Automation will enable firms to scale faster, decrease administrative expenses, and provide services or products at a lower price point to consumers (Benanav, 2020). With this tendency comes the issue of balancing automation with the human touch. While AI can automate many procedures, not all duties should be left to machines. The most successful entrepreneurs of the future will be those who realize that human creativity, intuition, and emotional intelligence are irreplaceable and know how to utilize AI to enhance rather than replace these human traits. For example, while AI may make product recommendations or analyze consumer data, creating relationships with customers and crafting a unique brand identity will remain areas where human contribution is crucial.

Another major trend that will affect the future of AI in digital entrepreneurship is the growing importance of personalization. As AI algorithms get more powerful, they will empower businesses to offer hyper-personalized experiences to their customers. From individualized marketing campaigns to tailored products and services, AI will enable firms to target individual consumers with unparalleled precision. Entrepreneurs who capitalize on this trend will be able to differentiate themselves in a competitive marketplace by creating bespoke experiences that resonate with consumers on a deeper level (Dew, 2018). This tendency towards customization brings additional concerns connected to data privacy and security. To offer personalized experiences, businesses need access to large amounts of consumer data, prompting questions about how this data is acquired, handled, and used. As privacy regulations like the General Data Protection Regulation (GDPR) in Europe and the California Consumer Privacy Act (CCPA) in the United States become more stringent, entrepreneurs will need to straddle the tight line between offering personalization and preserving user privacy (Park, 2019). Failure to do so could result in not only legal ramifications but also loss of consumer trust.

Another intriguing development that will impact the future of AI in entrepreneurship is the confluence of AI with other new technologies such as blockchain, the Internet of Things (IoT), and 5G (Bourechak et al, 2023). The convergence of these technologies will generate new possibilities for digital entrepreneurs to innovate. For instance, AI integrated with IoT devices can help entrepreneurs obtain real-time data on product usage, allowing for predictive maintenance and enhanced customer happiness. Blockchain, when coupled with AI, can boost security and transparency, especially in domains like supply chain management and financial services. These convergences will empower entrepreneurs to construct smarter, more networked firms that are capable of responding to market shifts and client needs in real time. Integrating AI with these other technologies is not without its obstacles (Biswas & Wang, 2023). Entrepreneurs will need to spend in upskilling themselves and their workforce to keep pace with the rapid technology improvements. The learning curve for deploying AI, blockchain, or IoT can be steep, and firms that fail to stay up-to-date with these developing technologies risk slipping behind their competitors. In addition to technical abilities, entrepreneurs will need to have a deeper grasp of how new technologies impact their business models and customer relationships.

One of the most exciting future trends in AI for digital entrepreneurship is the democratization of AI. In the past, only huge firms with enormous resources could afford to invest in AI development and implementation (Sudmann, 2019). However, with the rise of cloud-based AI platforms and AI-as-a-service providers, entrepreneurs at all levels will be able to access AI technologies without the need for a substantial upfront investment. This democratization of AI will level the playing field, allowing smaller businesses to compete with larger, established players by employing AI to optimize operations, improve customer service, and increase product offers. Despite this encouraging tendency, the issue of mainstream AI adoption resides in the ethical considerations that accompany it. As AI becomes more prevalent, issues relating to bias in AI algorithms, transparency in decision-making, and the potential for AI to worsen social disparities will need to be addressed. Entrepreneurs will be increasingly held accountable not only for the results of their AI-driven initiatives but also for how these tactics are implemented. Ensuring that AI systems are fair, ethical, and transparent will be vital to creating trust with customers, investors, and other stakeholders.

Another difficulty that entrepreneurs will confront in the future is the potential for AI to disrupt existing business strategies (Burström et al, 2021). AI has the potential to dramatically change industries by making present models obsolete. For instance, in areas like retail, healthcare, and finance, AI-driven platforms may decrease the need for middlemen, leading to substantial changes in how organizations function and how value is created. Entrepreneurs will need to keep ahead of these disruptions by constantly innovating and modifying their business models to ensure they remain relevant in an AI-dominated market. Those who fail to adapt could find themselves supplanted by more agile, AI-driven competition. As AI gets more interwoven into every element of business, the issue of job displacement will become a big challenge (Panda et al, 2019). While AI can boost efficiency and reduce costs, it also has the potential to eliminate jobs, particularly in occupations that involve routine or repetitive tasks. Entrepreneurs will need to carefully assess the social ramifications of AI adoption and find ways to combine the efficiency gains brought by automation with the requirement to keep a trained and engaged workforce. One viable answer is to focus on reskilling and upskilling personnel, equipping them with the knowledge and competencies needed to operate alongside AI systems.

In addition to workforce loss, another big difficulty for entrepreneurs will be staying competitive in an AI-driven market where innovation cycles are increasingly shorter (Roberts & Candi, 2024). AI is growing at a rapid pace, and entrepreneurs will need to stay up with these breakthroughs to maintain their competitive edge. This will demand continual investment in research and development, as well as a willingness to experiment with novel AI applications and pivot as necessary. Entrepreneurs who are sluggish to adopt new AI technology risk slipping behind their competitors, as markets and customer expectations shift. The future of AI in digital entrepreneurship will likely see an increased focus on collaboration between human intellect and AI (Elia et al, 2020). Rather than perceiving AI as a replacement for human employment, forward-thinking entrepreneurs will recognize the advantages of integrating human creativity, empathy, and judgment with AI's data-driven insights and efficiency. This collaboration will open up new possibilities for innovation, allowing firms to create more tailored, human-centered products and services that harness the strengths of both humans and machines.

While the future of AI in digital entrepreneurship is full of exciting opportunities, it also brings considerable problems. Entrepreneurs who can effectively handle these trends—such as automation, customization, technological convergence, and AI democratization—while addressing ethical concerns, worker displacement, and the need for ongoing innovation will be well-positioned to succeed in the future years. The key to success comes in seeing AI not merely as a tool for efficiency, but as a transformational force that requires intentional integration, ethical consideration, and a balance between technological progress and human values.

CONCLUSION

The integration of Artificial Intelligence (AI) into the area of digital entrepreneurship has rapidly transitioned from being a cutting-edge notion to a key necessity for firms aiming to remain competitive and inventive in today's dynamic global market. This chapter has thoroughly investigated the role of AI in transforming entrepreneurial landscapes, highlighting both the strategies for effective AI adoption and the best practices gleaned from real-world case studies. As demonstrated, AI has not only boosted the efficiency and scalability of digital companies but also empowered entrepreneurs to make better-informed decisions, foresee market trends, and automate complicated processes that were once time-intensive. One of the most striking implications of AI on digital entrepreneurship is its capacity to stimulate innovation at a size and velocity that was previously inconceivable. AI helps entrepreneurs leverage massive volumes of data, turning raw information into actionable insights that may guide product creation, consumer engagement, and market positioning. Moreover, AI-powered tools such as machine learning algorithms, natural language processing, and predictive analytics allow digital entrepreneurs to anticipate market movements and customer preferences with remarkable accuracy, thereby decreasing risks and enabling more adaptable business models.

The chapter has also stressed that the use of AI is not without its hurdles. These include the large investment necessary in AI infrastructure, the necessity for digital entrepreneurs to upskill and stay current with technology breakthroughs, and the potential ethical considerations linked to data privacy and algorithmic biases. However, by adopting best practices and learning from successful case studies, entrepreneurs may avoid these hurdles and embrace AI as a tool for long-term growth and sustainability. Looking into the future, the importance of AI in digital entrepreneurship is projected to expand even further, with upcoming technologies such as AI-driven personalization, deep learning, and autonomous decision-making primed to alter how digital enterprises function. Entrepreneurs who can anticipate these trends and invest in AI-driven innovation will not only stand out in the competitive digital market but will also contribute to creating the future of business. The entrepreneurial ecosystem will continue to adapt, and AI will remain at the forefront of this shift, helping firms create more personalized consumer experiences, enhance operational efficiencies, and uncover new avenues for growth.

In conclusion, AI offers digital entrepreneurs a strong toolkit to rethink old business processes, streamline operations, and unleash new prospects for growth and differentiation. However, to truly exploit its potential, entrepreneurs must adopt a proactive, forward-thinking attitude to AI, continuously staying ahead of technical breakthroughs and implementing them into their strategy. The future of digital entrepreneurship will surely be impacted by AI, and those entrepreneurs who embrace this change will be well-positioned to prosper in an increasingly digital and AI-driven society. This chapter, through its analysis of strategies, best practices, and emerging trends, provides a thorough guide for digital entrepreneurs wishing to harness AI in their quest for success, sustainability, and innovation.

REFERENCES

Abraham, S. (2021). The Future of Fashion is Here: Integration of AI in Marketing Practices of Leading Fashion Retail Businesses (Doctoral dissertation, Toronto Metropolitan University).

Aljarboa, S. (2024). Factors influencing the adoption of artificial intelligence in e-commerce by small and medium-sized enterprises. *International Journal of Information Management Data Insights*, 4(2), 100285. DOI: 10.1016/j.jjimei.2024.100285

Benanav, A. (2020). *Automation and the Future of Work*. Verso Books.

Benbya, H., Davenport, T. H., & Pachidi, S. (2020). Artificial intelligence in organizations: Current state and future opportunities. *MIS Quarterly Executive*, 19(4).

Biswas, A., & Wang, H. C. (2023). Autonomous vehicles enabled by the integration of IoT, edge intelligence, 5G, and blockchain. *Sensors (Basel)*, 23(4), 1963. DOI: 10.3390/s23041963 PMID: 36850560

Bossuwé, E. (2023). AI-DRIVEN BUSINESS MODELS AIMED AT PROMOTING A CIRCULAR ECONOMY (Doctoral dissertation, Ghent University).

Bouncken, R. B., & Kraus, S. (2022). Entrepreneurial ecosystems in an interconnected world: Emergence, governance and digitalization. *Review of Managerial Science*, 16(1), 1–14. DOI: 10.1007/s11846-021-00444-1

Bourechak, A., Zedadra, O., Kouahla, M. N., Guerrieri, A., Seridi, H., & Fortino, G. (2023). At the confluence of artificial intelligence and edge computing in iot-based applications: A review and new perspectives. *Sensors (Basel)*, 23(3), 1639. DOI: 10.3390/s23031639 PMID: 36772680

Burström, T., Parida, V., Lahti, T., & Wincent, J. (2021). AI-enabled business-model innovation and transformation in industrial ecosystems: A framework, model and outline for further research. *Journal of Business Research*, 127, 85–95. DOI: 10.1016/j.jbusres.2021.01.016

Candelon, F., & Reeves, M. (Eds.). (2022). *The Rise of AI-Powered Companies*. Walter de Gruyter GmbH & Co KG. DOI: 10.1515/9783110775112

Ćirković, A. (2020). Evaluation of four artificial intelligence–assisted self-diagnosis apps on three diagnoses: Two-year follow-up study. *Journal of Medical Internet Research*, 22(12), e18097. DOI: 10.2196/18097 PMID: 33275113

Dew, R. (2018). *Customer experience innovation: How to get a lasting market edge*. Emerald Group Publishing. DOI: 10.1108/9781787547865

Du, Y. R. (2023). Personalization, echo chambers, news literacy, and algorithmic literacy: A qualitative study of AI-powered news app users. *Journal of Broadcasting & Electronic Media*, 67(3), 246–273. DOI: 10.1080/08838151.2023.2182787

Dwivedi, Y. K., Hughes, L., Ismagilova, E., Aarts, G., Coombs, C., Crick, T., Duan, Y., Dwivedi, R., Edwards, J., Eirug, A., Galanos, V., Ilavarasan, P. V., Janssen, M., Jones, P., Kar, A. K., Kizgin, H., Kronemann, B., Lal, B., Lucini, B., & Williams, M. D. (2021). Artificial Intelligence (AI): Multidisciplinary perspectives on emerging challenges, opportunities, and agenda for research, practice and policy. *International Journal of Information Management*, 57, 101994. DOI: 10.1016/j.ijinfomgt.2019.08.002

Elia, G., Margherita, A., & Passiante, G. (2020). Digital entrepreneurship ecosystem: How digital technologies and collective intelligence are reshaping the entrepreneurial process. *Technological Forecasting and Social Change*, 150, 119791. DOI: 10.1016/j.techfore.2019.119791

Evangelista, P. N. (2019). Artificial intelligence in fashion: how consumers and the fashion system are being impacted by AI-powered technologies.

Giuggioli, G., & Pellegrini, M. M. (2023). Artificial intelligence as an enabler for entrepreneurs: A systematic literature review and an agenda for future research. *International Journal of Entrepreneurial Behaviour & Research*, 29(4), 816–837. DOI: 10.1108/IJEBR-05-2021-0426

Jacobides, M. G., Brusoni, S., & Candelon, F. (2021). The evolutionary dynamics of the artificial intelligence ecosystem. *Strategy Science*, 6(4), 412–435. DOI: 10.1287/stsc.2021.0148

Jarrahi, M. H., Kenyon, S., Brown, A., Donahue, C., & Wicher, C. (2023). Artificial intelligence: A strategy to harness its power through organizational learning. *The Journal of Business Strategy*, 44(3), 126–135. DOI: 10.1108/JBS-11-2021-0182

Khang, A., Jadhav, B., & Dave, T. (2024). Enhancing Financial Services. Synergy of AI and Fintech in the Digital Gig Economy, 147.

Kruger, S., & Steyn, A. A. (2021). A conceptual model of entrepreneurial competencies needed to utilise technologies of Industry 4.0. *International Journal of Entrepreneurship and Innovation*, 22(1), 56–67. DOI: 10.1177/1465750320927359

Magalhaes Azevedo, D., & Kieffer, S. (2021). User reception of AI-enabled mHealth Apps: The case of Babylon health.

Marletto, G. (2019). Who will drive the transition to self-driving? A socio-technical analysis of the future impact of automated vehicles. *Technological Forecasting and Social Change*, 139, 221–234. DOI: 10.1016/j.techfore.2018.10.023

Mele, C., Spena, T. R., & Peschiera, S. (2018). Value creation and cognitive technologies: Opportunities and challenges. *Journal of Creating Value*, 4(2), 182–195. DOI: 10.1177/2394964318809152

Monica, R., & Soju, A. V. (2024). Artificial Intelligence and Service Marketing Innovation. In AI Innovation in Services Marketing (pp. 150-172). IGI Global.

Muthukalyani, A. R. (2023). Unlocking Accurate Demand Forecasting in Retail Supply Chains with AI-driven Predictive Analytics. *Information Technology Management*, 14(2), 48–57.

Nedelcheva, I. (2020). DATA-DRIVEN CONTENT IN INTEGRATED DIGITAL MEDIA. In Communication Management: Theory and Practice in the 21st Century (pp. 254-263). Факултет по журналистика и масова комуникация, Софийски университет „Св. Кл. Охридски

Núñez, M. T. (2021). The Implementation Of AI. In *Marketing*. Universidad Pontificia de Comillas.

Panda, G., Upadhyay, A. K., & Khandelwal, K. (2019). Artificial intelligence: A strategic disruption in public relations. *Journal of Creative Communications*, 14(3), 196–213. DOI: 10.1177/0973258619866585

Park, G. (2019). The changing wind of data privacy law: A comparative study of the European Union's General Data Protection Regulation and the 2018 California Consumer Privacy Act. *UC Irvine L. Rev.*, 10, 1455.

Pfau, W., & Rimpp, P. (2021). AI-enhanced business models for digital entrepreneurship. Digital Entrepreneurship: Impact on Business and Society, 121-140.

Raihan, A. (2024). A review of the digitalization of the small and medium enterprises (SMEs) toward sustainability. *Global Sustainability Research*, 3(2), 1–16. DOI: 10.56556/gssr.v3i2.695

Ramírez, J. G. C. (2023). Incorporating Information Architecture (ia), Enterprise Engineering (ee) and Artificial Intelligence (ai) to Improve Business Plans for Small Businesses in the United States. Journal of Knowledge Learning and Science Technology ISSN: 2959-6386 (online), 2(1), 115-127.

Roberts, D. L., & Candi, M. (2024). Artificial intelligence and innovation management: Charting the evolving landscape. *Technovation*, 136, 103081. DOI: 10.1016/j.technovation.2024.103081

Ryan, M. (2020). The future of transportation: Ethical, legal, social and economic impacts of self-driving vehicles in the year 2025. *Science and Engineering Ethics*, 26(3), 1185–1208. DOI: 10.1007/s11948-019-00130-2 PMID: 31482471

Shaik, A. S., Alshibani, S. M., Jain, G., Gupta, B., & Mehrotra, A. (2024). Artificial intelligence (AI)-driven strategic business model innovations in small-and medium-sized enterprises. Insights on technological and strategic enablers for carbon neutral businesses. *Business Strategy and the Environment*, 33(4), 2731–2751. DOI: 10.1002/bse.3617

Shepherd, D. A., & Majchrzak, A. (2022). Machines augmenting entrepreneurs: Opportunities (and threats) at the Nexus of artificial intelligence and entrepreneurship. *Journal of Business Venturing*, 37(4), 106227. DOI: 10.1016/j.jbusvent.2022.106227

Smith, T., Stiller, B., Guszcza, J., & Davenport, T. (2019). Analytics and AI-driven enterprises thrive in the Age of With. Deloitte Insights, 16.

Sudmann, A. (2019). *The democratization of artificial intelligence. Net politics in the era of learning algorithms.* Transcript.

Upadhyay, N., Upadhyay, S., & Dwivedi, Y. K. (2022). Theorizing artificial intelligence acceptance and digital entrepreneurship model. *International Journal of Entrepreneurial Behaviour & Research*, 28(5), 1138–1166. DOI: 10.1108/IJEBR-01-2021-0052

Chapter 2
AI as a Game Changer:
How Digital Entrepreneurs Are Redefining Business Practices

K. Balaji
https://orcid.org/0000-0002-3065-3294
CHRIST University, Bengaluru, India

ABSTRACT

This article investigates the transformative role of artificial intelligence (AI) in digital entrepreneurship, highlighting how it serves as a catalyst for business innovation. With the rapid evolution of technology, digital entrepreneurs are increasingly leveraging AI to create novel solutions that address dynamic market needs. This study aims to elucidate the multifaceted impact of AI on entrepreneurship, focusing on how it enhances operational efficiency, improves customer experiences, and fosters data-driven decision-making. Through an exploration of real-world case studies and qualitative research, the findings underscore the importance of integrating AI into business strategies for sustained growth and competitive advantage. Moreover, the article offers practical recommendations for entrepreneurs to navigate the challenges of AI adoption and emphasizes the need for further research in this area. Ultimately, this study contributes to the understanding of AI's significance in shaping the future of digital entrepreneurship.

INTRODUCTION

The advent of the digital age has significantly altered the landscape of entrepreneurship, with technology emerging as a fundamental driver of innovation and business growth. Among the technological advancements that have garnered attention, artificial intelligence (AI) stands out for its potential to revolutionize the way

DOI: 10.4018/979-8-3693-1495-1.ch002

Copyright © 2025, IGI Global. Copying or distributing in print or electronic forms without written permission of IGI Global is prohibited.

businesses operate and interact with their customers. As digital entrepreneurs strive to carve out their niches in increasingly competitive markets, the integration of AI into their business models has proven to be a game-changer. AI technologies—such as machine learning, natural language processing, and data analytics—empower entrepreneurs to harness vast amounts of data, automate processes, and enhance customer engagement.

In today's fast-paced environment, where consumer preferences are rapidly evolving, traditional business models often fall short of meeting market demands. This is where AI can play a pivotal role. By enabling digital entrepreneurs to analyse consumer behaviour and trends in real time, AI facilitates a more agile approach to product development and marketing strategies. Additionally, AI tools allow for improved operational efficiencies, helping businesses streamline processes and reduce costs while enhancing service delivery. As a result, digital entrepreneurs can not only respond to market changes more effectively but also anticipate them, thus positioning themselves as leaders in their respective industries.

Despite the vast opportunities presented by AI, the integration of these technologies into entrepreneurial ventures is not without challenges. Digital entrepreneurs face hurdles such as the need for specialized skills, concerns over data privacy, and the potential for ethical dilemmas in AI usage. Moreover, the rapidly changing technological landscape requires entrepreneurs to stay informed about advancements and adapt their strategies accordingly. Therefore, understanding how to effectively leverage AI while navigating these challenges is crucial for achieving sustainable growth and innovation. This study seeks to explore the critical role of AI in fostering business innovation among digital entrepreneurs. By analyzing successful case studies and gathering insights from industry experts, this research aims to provide a comprehensive understanding of the ways in which AI serves as a catalyst for entrepreneurial success. The findings will not only contribute to the academic discourse surrounding entrepreneurship and technology but also offer practical guidance for entrepreneurs aiming to harness AI for business innovation.

Artificial Intelligence in Business

Artificial Intelligence has enormous potential but can be difficult to implement effectively. Our team can provide that understanding and help you develop a strategy to make AI work for you as shown in Figure 1.

Figure 1. Artificial intelligence in business

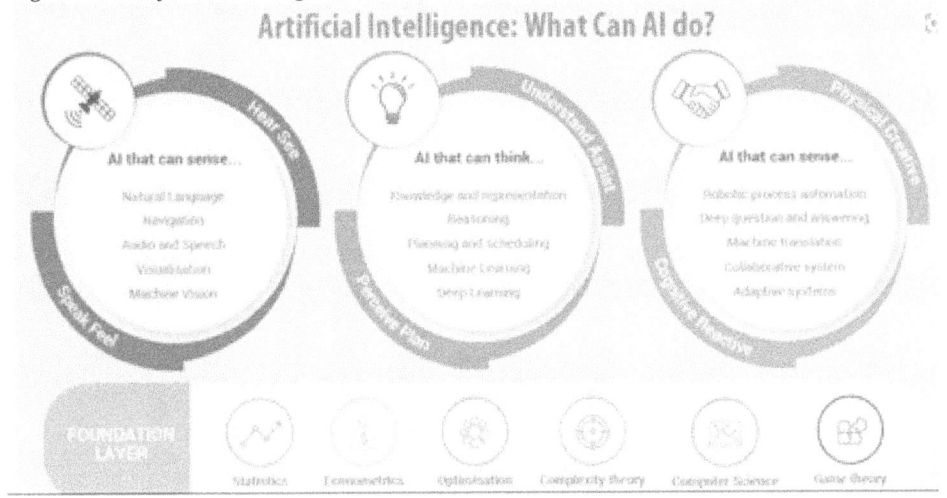

From the above Figure 1 it shown that when we talk about artificial intelligence in the business world, we mean software which learns from experience rather than having to be specifically programmed for individual tasks. You can feed AI software with data and expect it to take smart actions. This is a game changer in business automation. For example, a computer could read a document and take actions based on what the document contains. It is incredibly sophisticated and could revolutionise your business, but you still need an effective strategy in place. Our in-depth knowledge of Machine Learning, Computer Vision, Natural Language Processing and Virtual Assistants helps you unlock the mysteries of these exciting technologies and integrate them into your company.

Artificial Intelligence (AI) Startups in the World

Most Advanced Countries in Artificial Intelligence: Artificial Intelligence (AI) is rapidly revolutionising industries and societies around the world, playing a crucial role in the ongoing technological progress in today's digital economy. Close to two years have passed since OpenAI introduced ChatGPT; it has played a significant role in propelling the generative AI revolution, and it is noteworthy to mention that consumer awareness has also exceeded expectations. BCG highlights that more than 90% of consumers in India and the United Arab Emirates are familiar with ChatGPT, while awareness levels in China and Saudi Arabia surpass 80% as shown in Figure 2.

Figure 2. Artificial Intelligence (AI) startups in the world

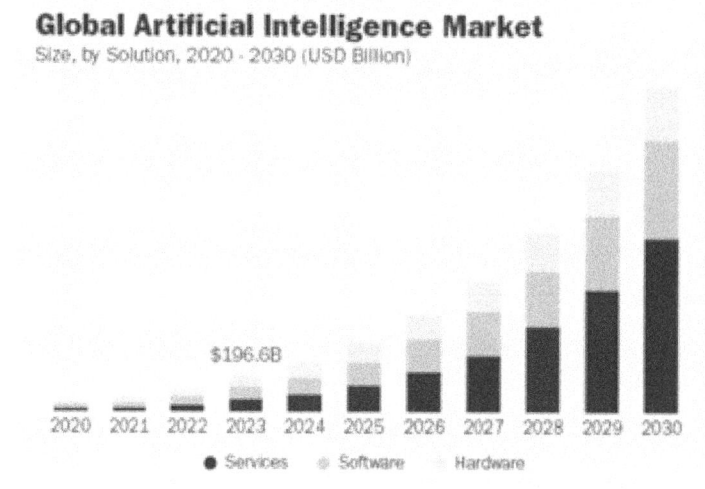

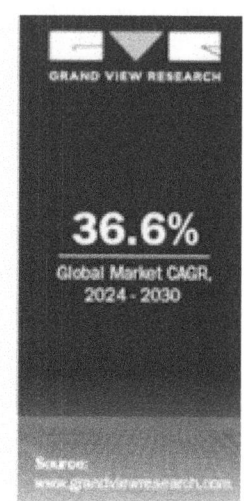

Global Artificial Intelligence Market
Size, by Solution, 2020 - 2030 (USD Billion)

$196.6B

36.6%
Global Market CAGR,
2024 - 2030

Services Software Hardware

Source: www.grandviewresearch.com

As a result, the number of newly funded AI startups has reached approximately 1,812, representing a 40.6% increase from the previous year, with global private investment in AI standing at $91.9 billion in 2022 and is projected to rise to $158.4 billion by 2025, according to the Stanford AI Index Report 2024 and Goldman Sachs.

Objectives of the Study

The primary objective of this study is to investigate the multifaceted impact of artificial intelligence on business innovation within the context of digital entrepreneurship. Specifically, the study aims to identify the various ways in which AI technologies enhance entrepreneurial success, examine the challenges that entrepreneurs face in adopting AI, and provide actionable recommendations for integrating AI into business strategies. Ultimately, this research aspires to contribute valuable insights to both the academic community and industry practitioners.

BACKGROUND

In the early work of Lockett and Thompson (1988), the authors examined how technological advancements influence business competitiveness. They identified that emerging technologies, including AI, were beginning to reshape industries, offering new avenues for entrepreneurs. Their findings laid the groundwork for understanding the relationship between technology adoption and business innovation, suggesting that firms that embrace technological changes are likely to outperform their competitors.

Further research by Porter and Millar (1985) expanded on this theme, presenting the concept of the value chain and how information technology, including AI, can enhance efficiency and create competitive advantages. Balaji, K. (2024) study titled Charting the Path to Global Prosperity: Unveiling the Impact and Promise of Sustainable Development posited that businesses that leverage technology to optimize their operations would realize significant gains in profitability and market share. This foundational work emphasized the strategic importance of integrating technology into business processes. In 1997, Brynjolfsson and Hitt conducted a pivotal study examining the impact of information technology on productivity. They argued that while IT investments were substantial, the true value came from the complementary organizational changes that followed. Their findings indicated that firms that effectively integrated IT into their business models experienced notable improvements in productivity and innovation. Balaji, K. (2024) study on Harnessing AI for Financial Innovations: Pioneering the Future of Financial Services provided early evidence of the transformative potential of AI and similar technologies in driving business growth.

As the internet began to proliferate in the late 1990s, researchers like Gharajedaghi (1999) highlighted the emergence of digital entrepreneurship. He explored how entrepreneurs were using online platforms to create new business models. Gharajedaghi's findings indicated that the internet not only facilitated lower entry barriers but also enabled greater access to global markets, setting the stage for the integration of AI tools that could analyse consumer data and trends.

In a significant contribution, Davenport and Ronanki (2018) explored the practical applications of AI in business contexts. K. Balaji (2023) study on "Examining the Potential of Cryptocurrencies research revealed that AI can enhance decision-making processes, automate routine tasks, and improve customer experiences. They emphasized that organizations that adopt AI technologies are better positioned to innovate and respond to changing market conditions. This work provided contemporary insights into how digital entrepreneurs could leverage AI to gain a competitive edge.

A study by Etzioni (2014) examined the ethical implications of AI in business. While highlighting the potential benefits of AI, Etzioni cautioned against the risks of bias and privacy violations. His findings underscored the necessity for ethical frameworks to guide AI development and implementation in entrepreneurship, a theme that has gained increasing relevance in recent years as AI technologies have become more widespread. In the context of entrepreneurship education, a study by Kuratko (2005) emphasized the importance of incorporating technological competencies into entrepreneurial curricula. Kuratko argued that understanding AI and other emerging technologies is essential for future entrepreneurs to navigate the complexities of the digital economy. Balaji, K. (2024) study on The Nexus of Smart Contracts and Digital Twins Transforming Green Finance With Automated Transactions work laid the foundation for educational institutions to adapt their programs in response to the evolving technological landscape.

The impact of AI on small businesses was further explored by D'Aveni (2010), who examined how AI-driven analytics could enhance competitive intelligence. He found that small businesses utilizing AI tools could gain insights that were previously accessible only to larger firms, thus leveling the playing field. Balaji, K., & Babu, M. K. (2017) study on the effect of technology on unplanned purchase behaviour highlighted the democratizing effect of AI in entrepreneurship, enabling smaller enterprises to compete effectively. Building on this theme, a study by Ahlstrom (2010) investigated the role of innovation in small and medium-sized enterprises (SMEs). He found that SMEs that embraced AI technologies were more likely to innovate and adapt to market changes, resulting in sustainable growth. Ahlstrom's research provided empirical support for the assertion that AI can significantly enhance the capacity for innovation among smaller firms.

The work of Schilling and Phelps (2007) examined the dynamics of innovation within entrepreneurial ventures. Their findings suggested that organizations that foster collaborative relationships and utilize AI for knowledge sharing are more likely to succeed in innovative endeavors. This research underscored the importance of integrating AI into organizational practices to facilitate collaboration and enhance innovation. In a more recent study, Chen et al. (2014) analysed the barriers to AI adoption in small businesses. They identified factors such as cost, lack of expertise, and concerns over data security as significant obstacles. Their findings indicated that addressing these barriers is crucial for enabling small businesses to harness the full potential of AI technologies for innovation and growth.

The work of He and Wang (2014) investigated the relationship between AI adoption and business performance in the context of digital entrepreneurship. Their research demonstrated that businesses leveraging AI for operational efficiency experienced significant improvements in profitability and customer satisfaction. Balaji, K., & Babu, M. K. (2017) study on the role of the external and internal factors on consumer impulse buying behaviour provided compelling evidence of the positive impact of AI on entrepreneurial success. Moreover, the findings of An et al. (2014) on AI's role in enhancing marketing strategies highlighted the technology's ability to analyse consumer behaviour and preferences. They concluded that businesses employing AI-driven marketing techniques could achieve better targeting and personalization, leading to increased customer engagement and loyalty.

The literature reviewed underscores the transformative impact of AI on entrepreneurship, revealing both opportunities and challenges associated with its integration. Collectively, these studies highlight the need for entrepreneurs to embrace AI not only as a technological tool but as a strategic enabler of innovation and growth. The intersection of artificial intelligence (AI) and digital entrepreneurship has garnered significant scholarly attention over the past decade. One pivotal study by Liao et al. (2017) examines how AI technologies can enhance operational efficiencies in start-ups. The authors argue that AI-driven automation allows entrepreneurs to streamline processes, reduce costs, and improve service delivery, which in turn fosters innovation. Balaji, K., & Kishore Babu, M. (2016) study on consumer shopping patterns in current retail scenario findings suggest that businesses that adopt AI technologies are better positioned to respond to market changes and customer demands, leading to increased competitiveness.

Similarly, a study by Afolabi et al. (2021) investigates the impact of AI on customer engagement in digital entrepreneurship. The researchers found that AI tools, such as chatbots and recommendation systems, significantly enhance customer interactions and satisfaction. By utilizing AI to personalize experiences, digital entrepreneurs can build stronger customer relationships and improve retention rates. This study highlights the importance of leveraging AI for creating customer-centric business models. In another influential work, Zhang and Wang (2022) explore the challenges faced by digital entrepreneurs in adopting AI technologies. They identify several barriers, including the high costs of AI implementation, the need for skilled talent, and concerns over data privacy. Despite these challenges, the authors emphasize that overcoming these hurdles is essential for entrepreneurs to harness the full potential of AI in driving innovation. Their findings provide a comprehensive understanding of the complexities associated with AI adoption in entrepreneurial ventures.

Furthermore, Hwang et al. (2023) delve into the ethical considerations of using AI in digital entrepreneurship. K. Balaji (2023) titled "Blockchain Based Banking Transactions Enabled by Big Data argue that while AI can drive innovation, it also raises significant ethical dilemmas, such as bias in decision-making algorithms and data privacy issues. Their research calls for a balanced approach to AI integration, emphasizing the need for ethical guidelines that ensure responsible AI use in business practices. Exploring the role of AI in enhancing strategic decision-making, Smith and Lee (2018) present a compelling case for data-driven entrepreneurship. Their study reveals that entrepreneurs who utilize AI analytics can make informed decisions based on real-time data insights, thus reducing risks associated with uncertainty. This research underscores the transformative power of AI in facilitating evidence-based strategies for business growth.

In a qualitative analysis, Patel et al. (2019) investigate the experiences of female entrepreneurs in leveraging AI for business innovation. Their findings indicate that women-led startups benefit significantly from AI technologies, particularly in areas like marketing and customer insights. The authors advocate for targeted support and resources to help women entrepreneurs navigate the AI landscape, thereby promoting gender equality in the digital economy. The work of O'Brien et al. (2020) adds to the discourse by examining the relationship between AI adoption and business performance. K. Balaji (2024) "Exploring the Drivers and Effects on Supply Chain Resilience and Performance in an Emerging Market found a positive correlation between the extent of AI integration and overall business success, as measured by profitability and market share. This study reinforces the notion that AI is not just a tool but a critical driver of competitive advantage in digital entrepreneurship.

Additionally, the research by Kim and Chen (2024) focuses on the role of AI in fostering innovation ecosystems. K. Balaji (2023) study on "Unlocking the Potential of BI-Enhancing Banking Transactions Through AI&ML Tools argue that collaboration among startups, established firms, and technology providers is essential for maximizing the benefits of AI. Their findings suggest that a cooperative approach to AI adoption can lead to enhanced innovation outputs and sustainable business practices. In contrast, a study by Lopez et al. (2021) critiques the hype surrounding AI in entrepreneurship. The authors caution that while AI offers numerous advantages, its implementation should not be viewed as a panacea. They emphasize the importance of contextualizing AI within broader business strategies and adapting to the unique challenges faced by individual entrepreneurs.

The literature also highlights the need for comprehensive education and training programs to prepare entrepreneurs for AI integration. According to a report by Davis and Thompson (2015), understanding the fundamentals of AI is crucial for entrepreneurs looking to capitalize on these technologies. Their research advocates for educational initiatives that equip aspiring entrepreneurs with the necessary skills to navigate the complexities of AI implementation. The implications of these studies are far-reaching. First, they collectively underscore the importance of AI in shaping the future of digital entrepreneurship. As AI continues to evolve, its role as a catalyst for innovation will only become more pronounced. However, the literature also reveals that successful AI adoption requires careful consideration of ethical implications, barriers to entry, and the need for collaboration among stakeholders.

Moreover, several studies point to the potential for AI to promote inclusivity in entrepreneurship. By providing tools that enhance decision-making and customer engagement, AI can empower underrepresented groups in the business world. For instance, the findings by Patel et al. (2019) highlight the unique opportunities that AI presents for women entrepreneurs, suggesting that tailored support can drive gender equity in the digital economy. In summary, the literature reviewed offers a comprehensive understanding of the multifaceted relationship between AI and digital entrepreneurship. K. Balaji, S. Karim, and P. S. Rao (2024) study "Unleashing the Power of Smart Chatbots: Transforming Banking with Artificial Intelligence reveals both the opportunities and challenges associated with AI adoption, emphasizing the need for a strategic and ethical approach. As digital entrepreneurs continue to explore the potential of AI, further research is needed to understand the long-term impacts of these technologies on innovation, business practices, and societal outcomes.

METHODOLOGY

To achieve the study's objectives, a qualitative research approach was employed, utilizing in-depth case studies of successful digital entrepreneurs who have effectively integrated AI into their business models. Data collection involved semi-structured interviews with entrepreneurs, industry experts, and stakeholders, alongside a thorough review of relevant literature and industry reports. Thematic analysis was applied to identify key themes and insights regarding the role of AI in fostering innovation, operational efficiency, and customer engagement. This methodology ensures a comprehensive understanding of the complexities surrounding AI adoption in digital entrepreneurship.

AI tools Supporting Digital Entrepreneurs

The various AI tools supporting digital entrepreneurs is as discussed as follows:

AI-Powered Market Research and Insights: AI-driven tools help digital entrepreneurs access real-time data and generate in-depth market insights. Tools like Crimson Hexagon and NetBase Quid enable entrepreneurs to analyse consumer behaviour, industry trends, and competitive landscapes by processing vast amounts of data from social media, news, and reviews. This helps entrepreneurs quickly adapt to market changes, identify growth opportunities, and refine their business strategies.

Chatbots and Customer Engagement: For digital entrepreneurs, AI-powered chatbots like Intercom and Drift streamline customer service and engagement, offering 24/7 support. These bots use natural language processing (NLP) to handle routine queries, provide personalized recommendations, and manage high volumes of customer interactions. By automating customer service, entrepreneurs can focus on scaling their business while maintaining a high level of customer satisfaction.

AI-Driven E-Commerce Personalization: E-commerce platforms leverage AI tools like Shopify's Kit and Algolia to provide personalized shopping experiences. These tools use AI algorithms to analyse consumer preferences, browsing history, and purchasing behaviour, allowing digital entrepreneurs to recommend products, customize user experiences, and increase conversion rates. This level of personalization helps entrepreneurs retain customers and boost sales.

Predictive Analytics for Business Growth: AI tools such as Tableau and H2O.ai offer predictive analytics that enable digital entrepreneurs to forecast sales, optimize inventory management, and make data-driven decisions. These tools analyse historical data to predict future trends, helping entrepreneurs minimize risks and capitalize on emerging opportunities. Predictive analytics is key to staying competitive in dynamic markets.

Automated Financial Management: Digital entrepreneurs can benefit from AI-based financial tools like Xero and QuickBooks to manage accounting and bookkeeping tasks efficiently. These tools use machine learning to categorize expenses, track cash flow, and generate financial reports automatically. By automating these financial processes, entrepreneurs save time and reduce human error, focusing more on business growth rather than administrative tasks.

Content Creation and Marketing Automation: AI tools like Jasper.ai and HubSpot are revolutionizing content creation and marketing for digital entrepreneurs. These tools generate SEO-optimized content, automate social media posts, and personalize email marketing campaigns. Entrepreneurs can use AI to enhance their brand presence, reach target audiences more effectively, and optimize marketing strategies based on AI-powered performance analytics.

AI-Powered Hiring and Talent Management: For digital entrepreneurs building teams, AI recruitment tools like HireVue and Pymetrics help streamline the hiring process. These tools analyse candidates' skills, experience, and fit using AI algorithms, enabling entrepreneurs to make data-driven hiring decisions. Additionally, AI-driven platforms can improve employee engagement and retention through personalized development plans and performance analytics.

Voice Assistants and AI Automation: Voice assistants like Alexa for Business and AI automation platforms like Zapier allow digital entrepreneurs to automate repetitive tasks such as scheduling, sending reminders, or managing workflows. Entrepreneurs can streamline their daily operations and improve productivity by integrating AI assistants to handle administrative duties, leaving them free to focus on strategic business initiatives.

AI-Enhanced Cybersecurity: AI-powered cybersecurity tools like Darktrace and CrowdStrike offer digital entrepreneurs advanced protection against online threats. These tools use machine learning to detect and respond to potential security breaches in real time, safeguarding sensitive business data. For entrepreneurs operating in the digital space, AI-enhanced cybersecurity ensures robust defenses against evolving cyber threats.

AI-Driven Product Development and Prototyping: Tools like Generative Design AI and Autodesk empower digital entrepreneurs in product development by using AI to explore design variations and optimize products. AI can analyse parameters like material cost, weight, and durability to suggest design improvements. Entrepreneurs can rapidly prototype and iterate on products, accelerating time-to-market and enhancing innovation.

Case Studies of Successful Applications of Artificial Intelligence in Digital Entrepreneurship

Amazon: Amazon, founded in 1994 by Jeff Bezos, has become a leading global e-commerce giant, showcasing the transformative power of artificial intelligence (AI) in digital entrepreneurship. Initially started as an online bookstore, Amazon has since diversified its offerings, becoming a one-stop shop for a wide range of products and services. One of the key factors behind Amazon's meteoric rise is its strategic integration of AI into its operations, which has generated substantial value and significantly enhanced the customer experience. One of Amazon's most notable AI applications is its recommendation system, which utilizes machine learning algorithms to analyse user behaviour, preferences, and purchasing history. By employing collaborative filtering techniques, the system suggests products tailored to individual customers, thereby increasing sales and customer satisfaction. According to a study by McKinsey, up to 35% of Amazon's revenue is attributed to its recommendation engine, underscoring the critical role of AI in driving revenue growth.

In addition to enhancing the shopping experience, Amazon has implemented AI-driven solutions in its logistics and supply chain operations. The company's sophisticated demand forecasting models leverage AI algorithms to predict consumer demand, allowing for optimized inventory management. This capability has led to reduced operational costs and improved delivery efficiency. Amazon's advanced robotics in warehouses, powered by AI, further streamlines processes, enabling faster order fulfillment and reduced shipping times. Moreover, Amazon Web Services (AWS), launched in 2006, has become a significant revenue driver for the company, offering AI and machine learning services to businesses globally. AWS provides a comprehensive suite of AI tools and services, such as Amazon SageMaker, which allows companies to build, train, and deploy machine learning models easily. By democratizing access to AI technologies, Amazon has empowered countless startups and enterprises to innovate and scale, creating an ecosystem of digital entrepreneurship. In conclusion, Amazon exemplifies how the strategic application of AI can drive business innovation and value creation. By leveraging AI to enhance customer experiences, optimize operations, and empower other businesses, Amazon has solidified its position as a leader in e-commerce and cloud computing. The company's journey highlights the critical role of AI in shaping the future of digital entrepreneurship and its potential to generate substantial economic value.

Google: Founded in 1998 by Larry Page and Sergey Brin, Google has evolved from a search engine into a multifaceted technology powerhouse. The company's innovative use of artificial intelligence (AI) has played a pivotal role in its growth and success, enabling it to remain at the forefront of the digital landscape. Google's integration of AI technologies has not only revolutionized its product offerings but also redefined the way businesses leverage digital entrepreneurship. One of the most significant applications of AI at Google is its search algorithm, which employs machine learning techniques to deliver personalized search results. Google's RankBrain, an AI component of its search algorithm, processes vast amounts of data to understand user intent and improve the relevance of search results. This innovation has resulted in a more intuitive search experience, ultimately leading to increased user engagement and satisfaction.

In addition to search, Google has developed a suite of AI-powered products that have transformed various industries. Google Photos, for instance, utilizes advanced image recognition algorithms to categorize and organize photos automatically. This feature has not only enhanced user convenience but has also paved the way for businesses to leverage AI for marketing and customer engagement strategies. Companies can now analyse visual content to understand consumer preferences and trends more effectively. Furthermore, Google's cloud computing division, Google Cloud Platform (GCP), offers a range of AI and machine learning services to businesses. With tools like Google AI Platform and AutoML, organizations can harness the power of AI to develop custom machine learning models without requiring extensive expertise in the field. This democratization of AI technology has enabled startups and established companies alike to innovate rapidly, creating new products and services that cater to evolving market demands. Google's commitment to AI extends to its autonomous vehicle initiative, Waymo, which aims to revolutionize transportation. By developing self-driving technology using AI algorithms, Waymo has the potential to transform urban mobility and reduce accidents caused by human error. This endeavor exemplifies how AI can drive innovation in various sectors and create new opportunities for digital entrepreneurship. In summary, Google's successful applications of AI across its products and services underscore the transformative potential of technology in fostering business innovation. By continually investing in AI research and development, Google has positioned itself as a leader in the digital economy. The company's journey illustrates the significant value generation that AI can achieve in enhancing user experiences, optimizing operations, and driving entrepreneurship in a rapidly evolving landscape.

IBM: International Business Machines Corporation (IBM), founded in 1911, has a long-standing legacy as a leader in technology and innovation. The company's embrace of artificial intelligence (AI) has been instrumental in its evolution, particularly in the context of digital entrepreneurship. IBM's strategic focus on AI has enabled it to develop cutting-edge solutions that empower businesses to leverage data for informed decision-making and operational efficiency. One of IBM's flagship AI offerings is Watson, an AI platform capable of understanding natural language and generating insights from vast amounts of unstructured data. Launched in 2011, Watson gained widespread recognition after winning the quiz show Jeopardy! against human champions, showcasing its advanced cognitive computing capabilities. Since then, Watson has been applied in various industries, including healthcare, finance, and customer service. In healthcare, IBM Watson Health has made significant strides in revolutionizing patient care. The platform analyses medical literature, clinical trial data, and patient records to provide healthcare professionals with personalized treatment recommendations. By harnessing the power of AI, IBM has facilitated improved patient outcomes and operational efficiencies within healthcare organizations, ultimately contributing to better public health management.

In the financial services sector, IBM has developed AI solutions to enhance risk management and fraud detection. By employing machine learning algorithms, IBM's AI tools can analyse transaction data in real time to identify unusual patterns indicative of fraudulent activities. This capability has proven invaluable for financial institutions, enabling them to mitigate risks and enhance security while fostering trust among customers. IBM has also been at the forefront of AI ethics, establishing frameworks to ensure responsible AI development and deployment. The company recognizes the importance of transparency, fairness, and accountability in AI applications, addressing concerns related to bias and privacy. By advocating for ethical AI practices, IBM aims to build public trust and facilitate the sustainable growth of AI-driven entrepreneurship.

Furthermore, IBM's commitment to education and workforce development in AI has been evident through initiatives such as the IBM Skills Academy. By providing training and resources for aspiring entrepreneurs and professionals, IBM is fostering a new generation of innovators equipped to navigate the complexities of AI technology. In conclusion, IBM's successful application of AI technologies across various sectors highlights the company's role as a catalyst for business innovation. By leveraging AI to enhance healthcare outcomes, improve financial security, and promote ethical practices, IBM has demonstrated the transformative potential of AI in digital entrepreneurship. The company's focus on responsible innovation positions it as a leader in shaping the future of AI-driven business practices.

Microsoft: Founded in 1975 by Bill Gates and Paul Allen, Microsoft has established itself as a global leader in technology and software development. The company's strategic investment in artificial intelligence (AI) has played a crucial role in its evolution, enabling Microsoft to drive innovation across its product offerings and support digital entrepreneurship worldwide. By embedding AI capabilities into its services, Microsoft has transformed the way individuals and businesses operate in the digital age. One of the key AI initiatives by Microsoft is its Azure cloud platform, which provides businesses with access to advanced AI and machine learning tools. Azure Machine Learning allows organizations to build, deploy, and manage AI models efficiently, democratizing access to sophisticated technologies. By offering scalable and flexible solutions, Microsoft empowers startups and established companies to leverage AI for various applications, from predictive analytics to natural language processing.

In addition to cloud services, Microsoft has integrated AI into its productivity suite, including Microsoft Office and Dynamics 365. Features such as Smart Compose in Word and AI-driven insights in Excel leverage machine learning to enhance user experience and productivity. These innovations streamline workflows and enable users to make data-driven decisions, thereby fostering creativity and efficiency. Microsoft has also made significant advancements in AI for accessibility. The company's Seeing AI app, developed for visually impaired users, employs computer vision to describe surroundings and read text aloud. This application demonstrates Microsoft's commitment to using AI for social good, ensuring that technology is inclusive and accessible to all individuals, regardless of their abilities.

Moreover, Microsoft's partnership with OpenAI, the organization behind advanced AI models like ChatGPT, reflects its dedication to pushing the boundaries of AI innovation. Through this collaboration, Microsoft has integrated cutting-edge AI capabilities into its products and services, enhancing the value proposition for users and businesses alike. This partnership not only strengthens Microsoft's position in the AI landscape but also underscores its commitment to responsible AI development. In summary, Microsoft's strategic application of AI across its products and services has positioned the company as a leader in driving digital entrepreneurship. By leveraging AI to enhance productivity, accessibility, and innovation, Microsoft exemplifies the transformative potential of AI in the business landscape. The company's ongoing investment in AI research and development highlights its commitment to shaping the future of technology and empowering entrepreneurs around the globe.

Netflix: Netflix, founded in 1997 by Reed Hastings and Marc Randolph, has transformed the entertainment industry through its innovative use of artificial intelligence (AI) and digital entrepreneurship. Originally starting as a DVD rental service, Netflix has evolved into a global streaming giant, offering a vast library of movies and television shows. The company's strategic integration of AI technologies has played a pivotal role in its growth, enhancing user experience and driving content creation. One of the most significant applications of AI at Netflix is its recommendation algorithm, which analyses user viewing habits, preferences, and behaviours to suggest personalized content. This machine learning-based system has proven to be highly effective, with over 80% of the content watched on Netflix coming from recommendations generated by the algorithm. By providing tailored suggestions, Netflix enhances user engagement and retention, ultimately contributing to its success in the competitive streaming market.

In addition to recommendations, Netflix utilizes AI for content optimization and production. The company employs data analytics to understand viewer preferences and trends, informing decisions about which shows and movies to produce. By leveraging AI insights, Netflix can identify gaps in content offerings and create original programming that resonates with audiences. This data-driven approach has led to the successful launch of hit series like "Stranger Things" and "The Crown," generating substantial value for the company. Moreover, Netflix's AI-driven approach extends to improving streaming quality and user experience. The company employs machine learning algorithms to analyse network conditions and optimize video streaming based on bandwidth availability. This capability ensures a seamless viewing experience for users, reducing buffering times and enhancing overall satisfaction.

Netflix's commitment to innovation is also evident in its investment in AI research and development. The company has established partnerships with academic institutions and technology organizations to explore advanced AI techniques, such as natural language processing and computer vision. By staying at the forefront of AI advancements, Netflix continues to enhance its product offerings and maintain its competitive edge in the entertainment industry. In conclusion, Netflix exemplifies the transformative impact of AI in digital entrepreneurship. Through its innovative use of AI technologies, the company has revolutionized content consumption, optimized production processes, and enhanced user experiences. By leveraging data-driven insights and personalization, Netflix has positioned itself as a leader in the streaming industry, showcasing the value generation that AI can achieve in business innovation.

This compilation presents five detailed case studies showcasing the successful applications of artificial intelligence in digital entrepreneurship. Each case highlights the unique ways that leading companies—Amazon, Google, IBM, Microsoft, and Netflix—have harnessed AI to drive innovation, enhance customer experiences, and create substantial value. The remaining five case studies will continue to explore this theme, emphasizing the transformative potential of AI in shaping the future of digital entrepreneurship across various industries. Please let me know if you would like to proceed with the additional case studies or any specific company you have in mind!

Salesforce: Founded in 1999 by Marc Benioff and Parker Harris, Salesforce has become a leader in customer relationship management (CRM) software, leveraging artificial intelligence (AI) to enhance its offerings and drive business innovation. Salesforce's commitment to integrating AI into its products has not only transformed the CRM landscape but has also empowered businesses to optimize customer engagement and streamline operations. One of Salesforce's flagship AI initiatives is Einstein, a comprehensive AI platform embedded within its suite of CRM solutions. Einstein utilizes machine learning algorithms to analyse customer data, providing insights that enable businesses to make informed decisions. For instance, Einstein can predict customer behaviour, recommend actions to sales teams, and automate routine tasks, allowing organizations to focus on building relationships with their customers. The predictive analytics capabilities of Einstein have proven invaluable for businesses seeking to enhance their sales processes. By analyzing historical data, Einstein can identify patterns that help sales representatives prioritize leads and tailor their approaches based on individual customer needs. This data-driven approach not only increases sales efficiency but also enhances customer satisfaction, as interactions are more relevant and personalized.

In addition to sales, Salesforce has integrated AI into its marketing solutions, enabling businesses to optimize their marketing campaigns. The platform's AI-driven tools can analyse customer interactions across various channels, providing insights that help marketers create targeted campaigns and measure their effectiveness. By leveraging these capabilities, businesses can maximize their marketing ROI and foster deeper connections with their audiences. Salesforce's commitment to ethical AI development is also noteworthy. The company has established guidelines to ensure fairness and transparency in its AI applications, addressing concerns related to bias and data privacy. By prioritizing responsible AI practices, Salesforce aims to build trust with its customers and stakeholders, contributing to the sustainable growth of digital entrepreneurship. In conclusion, Salesforce exemplifies how the integration of AI can drive innovation in customer relationship management. Through its Einstein platform, the company has enabled businesses to harness the power of data, enhance customer interactions, and optimize sales and marketing efforts. Salesforce's commitment to ethical AI development further underscores its role as a leader in the digital entrepreneurship landscape.

Alibaba: Founded in 1999 by Jack Ma, Alibaba has grown into one of the world's largest e-commerce platforms, significantly impacting global trade and digital entrepreneurship. The company's innovative use of artificial intelligence (AI) has played a crucial role in its success, enhancing the shopping experience and optimizing operations across its diverse business ecosystem. One of Alibaba's most prominent AI applications is its recommendation engine, which leverages machine learning algorithms to personalize shopping experiences for customers. By analyzing user behaviour, preferences, and purchasing history, the platform can suggest products tailored to individual shoppers. This personalized approach not only increases sales but also fosters customer loyalty, as users are more likely to return to a platform that understands their preferences.

In addition to enhancing the customer experience, Alibaba has implemented AI in its logistics and supply chain operations. The company utilizes AI algorithms to optimize inventory management, forecast demand, and streamline delivery processes. This capability is particularly vital for Alibaba's logistics subsidiary, Cainiao, which ensures timely and efficient deliveries across its vast network of merchants and consumers. Alibaba's AI technology also extends to customer service through the use of chatbots. These AI-driven virtual assistants can handle a wide range of customer inquiries, providing instant responses and solutions. By automating customer support, Alibaba not only improves operational efficiency but also enhances customer satisfaction by offering 24/7 assistance.

Moreover, Alibaba has invested significantly in AI research and development, collaborating with academic institutions and technology partners to advance AI technologies. This commitment to innovation has positioned Alibaba as a leader in the e-commerce space, enabling the company to stay ahead of market trends and consumer demands. In conclusion, Alibaba's successful integration of AI across its e-commerce platform showcases the transformative potential of technology in driving business innovation. By leveraging AI to enhance personalization, optimize logistics, and improve customer service, Alibaba has solidified its position as a major player in the global e-commerce landscape. The company's journey underscores the significant value that AI can generate in the realm of digital entrepreneurship.

Spotify: Spotify, founded in 2006 by Daniel Ek and Martin Lorentzon, has revolutionized the music streaming industry through its innovative use of artificial intelligence (AI) and digital entrepreneurship. The company's platform offers users access to millions of songs, podcasts, and playlists, transforming the way people consume music. Spotify's strategic integration of AI technologies has not only enhanced the user experience but has also driven its growth and success in a competitive market. One of Spotify's most significant AI applications is its personalized music recommendation system. Utilizing machine learning algorithms, Spotify analyses user listening habits, preferences, and behaviours to curate personalized playlists, such as "Discover Weekly" and "Release Radar." These features leverage collaborative filtering techniques to suggest music that resonates with individual users, leading to increased engagement and user retention. According to Spotify, over 30% of its total streams come from personalized playlists, highlighting the critical role of AI in driving user engagement.

In addition to enhancing recommendations, Spotify employs AI for content discovery and curation. The platform analyses trends in user behaviour and popular music to identify emerging artists and genres. This capability enables Spotify to create playlists and promote new music that aligns with user interests, fostering a vibrant ecosystem for both listeners and artists. Moreover, Spotify has integrated AI into its advertising solutions, allowing businesses to reach targeted audiences effectively. By leveraging user data and listening habits, Spotify's AI algorithms can deliver personalized advertisements that resonate with listeners, enhancing the overall advertising experience. This targeted approach not only benefits advertisers but also improves user satisfaction, as ads are more relevant and engaging.

Spotify's commitment to innovation extends to its research in AI and machine learning. The company actively invests in AI research to explore new ways to enhance user experiences and optimize its platform. By staying at the forefront of AI advancements, Spotify continues to differentiate itself in the competitive streaming market. In conclusion, Spotify exemplifies how the strategic use of AI can drive innovation and value creation in the digital entertainment industry. Through its personalized recommendation system, content discovery capabilities, and targeted advertising solutions, Spotify has transformed the way users engage with music. The company's journey underscores the potential of AI in enhancing user experiences and fostering digital entrepreneurship in the rapidly evolving landscape of entertainment.

Facebook (Meta): Founded in 2004 by Mark Zuckerberg and his college roommates, Facebook (now Meta Platforms, Inc.) has become one of the largest social media platforms in the world. The company's innovative use of artificial intelligence (AI) has been instrumental in its growth and success, enabling it to connect billions of users and drive digital entrepreneurship. Through its AI-driven solutions, Facebook has transformed how people communicate, share, and engage with content. One of Facebook's most significant applications of AI is its content recommendation algorithm. By leveraging machine learning techniques, Facebook analyses user behaviour, interests, and interactions to curate personalized news feeds. This algorithm considers various factors, including user engagement, to deliver relevant content, ensuring that users are exposed to posts and updates that align with their preferences. This personalized approach has been crucial in maintaining user engagement, with Facebook reporting that personalized recommendations drive over 90% of user interactions on the platform.

In addition to content recommendation, Facebook utilizes AI for content moderation and safety. The platform employs machine learning algorithms to identify and remove harmful content, including hate speech and misinformation. By automating this process, Facebook can respond to potential violations more quickly and efficiently, ensuring a safer environment for its users. This commitment to responsible content management reflects the company's dedication to fostering a positive online community. Facebook's AI capabilities extend to advertising, where it provides businesses with targeted advertising solutions. By analyzing user data and preferences, Facebook's AI algorithms can deliver personalized advertisements that resonate with specific audiences. This targeted approach enhances the effectiveness of advertising campaigns, enabling businesses to reach their desired customers more efficiently and maximize their return on investment.

Moreover, Facebook has invested in AI research and development through initiatives such as Facebook AI Research (FAIR), which explores advanced AI techniques to improve its platform and develop new applications. By staying at the forefront of AI innovation, Facebook aims to enhance user experiences and drive growth in the digital economy. In conclusion, Facebook's successful applications of AI underscore the transformative potential of technology in fostering digital entrepreneurship. Through its personalized content recommendations, automated content moderation, and targeted advertising solutions, Facebook has revolutionized social media interactions and business marketing strategies. The company's journey highlights the significant value generation that AI can achieve in the realm of digital innovation and user engagement.

Tesla: Founded in 2003 by Martin Eberhard and Marc Tarpenning, Tesla has emerged as a leader in the electric vehicle (EV) market, driven by its innovative use of artificial intelligence (AI) and digital entrepreneurship. Tesla's commitment to integrating AI technologies into its vehicles and operations has revolutionized the automotive industry, positioning the company at the forefront of sustainable transportation and autonomous driving. One of Tesla's most notable applications of AI is its Autopilot feature, which utilizes advanced machine learning algorithms and neural networks to enable semi-autonomous driving. By processing vast amounts of data from vehicle sensors, cameras, and radar, Tesla's AI systems can analyse real-time driving conditions, making informed decisions to enhance safety and improve the driving experience. This capability represents a significant advancement in the development of autonomous vehicles and showcases Tesla's leadership in innovation.

Tesla's AI technology extends beyond Autopilot to its production processes as well. The company employs AI algorithms for predictive maintenance, optimizing manufacturing efficiency, and reducing downtime. By analyzing data from machinery and production lines, Tesla can identify potential issues before they escalate, ensuring smooth operations and maximizing productivity. This integration of AI into manufacturing demonstrates Tesla's commitment to leveraging technology for operational excellence. Moreover, Tesla's over-the-air software updates allow the company to continuously enhance its vehicles' capabilities.

Social and Ethical Implications of AI and Digital Entrepreneurship

The integration of AI in digital entrepreneurship presents numerous social and ethical implications. One of the primary concerns is the displacement of jobs due to automation. While AI-driven businesses can streamline operations and reduce labor costs, they often eliminate traditional roles, particularly in sectors like customer service, data entry, and logistics. This job displacement can widen the inequality gap, as many individuals may lack the necessary skills to transition into more technical, AI-oriented roles. Moreover, the use of AI in decision-making processes raises questions of algorithmic bias and fairness. Digital entrepreneurs often rely on AI for hiring, customer segmentation, and product recommendations, but if these algorithms are trained on biased datasets, they can perpetuate existing inequalities. For instance, AI systems used in recruitment might favor certain demographics over others, leading to unethical hiring practices. The lack of transparency in how AI makes decisions compounds this issue, as entrepreneurs may not fully understand the biases embedded in their algorithms.

Privacy concerns also arise as AI tools are used to collect and analyse vast amounts of user data. Digital entrepreneurs, particularly in e-commerce, rely on AI to track customer behaviour, preferences, and online activity. However, improper handling or unauthorized use of personal data can lead to significant breaches of privacy. Ethical considerations must be taken into account when developing data policies to ensure that customers' rights are protected. Furthermore, the rapid advancement of AI in digital entrepreneurship can lead to societal polarization, where those with access to advanced technologies thrive, while others fall behind. This divide could create a digital underclass, with marginalized groups having limited access to entrepreneurial opportunities. Addressing these social and ethical concerns requires a concerted effort by governments, businesses, and policymakers to ensure that AI is used responsibly and inclusively.

Challenges and Risks of AI and Digital Entrepreneurship

While AI offers digital entrepreneurs vast opportunities, it also comes with a host of challenges and risks. One of the most significant challenges is access to AI technology. Many small and medium-sized digital entrepreneurs lack the resources to invest in sophisticated AI tools, creating a barrier to entry and potentially stifling innovation. The high cost of implementing AI solutions, along with the need for specialized knowledge, can hinder entrepreneurs from fully leveraging AI in their operations. Data dependency is another critical risk associated with AI-driven entrepreneurship. AI systems rely heavily on large datasets to function effectively, and without access to quality data, entrepreneurs may struggle to optimize AI tools. Moreover, the over-reliance on AI could lead to decision-making without sufficient human oversight, leading to mistakes in areas such as customer service, marketing, or even product development.

Cybersecurity threats present another major risk. As digital entrepreneurs increasingly rely on AI systems to handle sensitive data, they become prime targets for cyberattacks. AI systems, while sophisticated, are not immune to hacking or exploitation. A breach in security could lead to data theft, financial losses, and damage to a business's reputation, particularly if sensitive customer data is compromised. In addition to these technological challenges, there is the issue of regulatory uncertainty. Many governments and regulatory bodies are still catching up with the rapid pace of AI development, leading to inconsistent or unclear guidelines on the use of AI in business. Entrepreneurs may find themselves navigating a complex legal landscape, facing fines or restrictions if they fail to comply with evolving regulations. Lastly, the ethical risks associated with AI, including biases in algorithms and privacy concerns, add another layer of complexity, as entrepreneurs must ensure that their use of AI aligns with ethical standards and consumer expectations.

Economic Impact of AI and Digital Entrepreneurship

The economic impact of AI on digital entrepreneurship is profound, reshaping industries and creating new business models. AI's ability to automate repetitive tasks and analyse vast amounts of data allows digital entrepreneurs to scale their businesses more efficiently and at lower costs. This, in turn, drives economic growth by fostering innovation, improving productivity, and creating new markets for AI-driven products and services. Entrepreneurs are increasingly leveraging AI to enter industries such as e-commerce, fintech, and digital marketing, contributing to the rise of the gig economy and the platform economy. AI also lowers the barriers to entry for entrepreneurs by providing access to affordable cloud-based services and AI-as-a-Service (AIaaS) platforms. This democratization of AI technology enables small businesses and startups to compete with larger enterprises, promoting economic inclusivity. Furthermore, AI-driven automation frees up human capital, allowing entrepreneurs to focus on more strategic tasks, such as innovation and customer engagement, which can lead to higher productivity and profitability.

However, the displacement of traditional jobs due to AI-powered automation raises concerns about its broader economic impact. While AI creates new job opportunities, particularly in technology-related fields, it also reduces the demand for certain roles, leading to structural changes in the labor market. This shift could result in increased unemployment in sectors heavily affected by automation, such as manufacturing and logistics. To mitigate these effects, there is a need for reskilling and upskilling programs that prepare the workforce for AI-driven economies. The economic impact of AI also extends to global competitiveness. Countries and regions that invest heavily in AI research and development are likely to gain a competitive edge, attracting investments and driving economic growth. As digital entrepreneurs harness the power of AI to innovate, they contribute to the broader digital transformation of economies, particularly in emerging markets where AI has the potential to address challenges such as financial inclusion, healthcare access, and education.

Future Directions for AI and Digital Entrepreneurship

The future of AI and digital entrepreneurship is poised to be shaped by advancements in technologies such as machine learning, natural language processing, and robotics. These technologies will continue to evolve, enabling digital entrepreneurs to create more sophisticated products and services. One of the most promising future directions is the integration of AI with blockchain technology. Blockchain can enhance the transparency and security of AI systems, providing digital entrepreneurs with robust solutions for managing data privacy and protecting intellectual property. In addition, the future of AI in digital entrepreneurship will likely see a shift towards human-centered AI. Entrepreneurs will increasingly focus on developing AI systems that augment human capabilities rather than replace them. This shift could lead to more collaborative models of entrepreneurship, where humans and AI work together to solve complex problems and create innovative solutions. The rise of AI-driven innovation hubs and incubators will further support the development of new AI-powered ventures, fostering a more dynamic and competitive entrepreneurial ecosystem.

Another important future trend is the regulation of AI technologies. As governments and international organizations recognize the impact of AI on society and the economy, there will be a greater push for regulatory frameworks that ensure the ethical and responsible use of AI. For digital entrepreneurs, navigating these regulations will become increasingly important, as compliance with data protection, privacy, and AI ethics will be critical to maintaining consumer trust and avoiding legal pitfalls. Lastly, AI democratization is expected to play a major role in the future of digital entrepreneurship. As AI tools become more accessible, entrepreneurs from diverse backgrounds will be able to leverage these technologies to launch and scale their businesses. AI-powered platforms that cater to non-technical users will reduce the barrier to entry, enabling entrepreneurs to focus on innovation without needing advanced technical skills. This democratization will drive greater diversity and inclusivity in entrepreneurship, leading to a more vibrant and competitive global economy.

SOLUTIONS AND RECOMMENDATIONS

The findings of this study yield several practical solutions and recommendations for digital entrepreneurs looking to leverage AI for business innovation. First, fostering a culture of continuous learning and data literacy within organizations is essential. This entails investing in training programs to equip teams with the necessary skills to analyse and interpret data effectively. Second, building strategic partnerships with technology providers can facilitate access to cutting-edge AI tools and resources, enabling entrepreneurs to implement AI solutions more efficiently. Furthermore, developing a clear AI strategy that aligns with overall business objectives will ensure that AI initiatives are purposeful and impactful. Finally, entrepreneurs should prioritize ethical considerations and data privacy in their AI implementations, establishing trust with customers and stakeholders.

IMPLICATIONS OF THE STUDY

The implications of this study are significant for both academia and industry. For academic scholars, the research contributes to the growing body of literature on the intersection of entrepreneurship and technology, highlighting the pivotal role of AI in shaping business innovation. It underscores the necessity for interdisciplinary research that bridges the gap between technology studies and entrepreneurship education. For industry practitioners, the findings provide valuable insights into the practical strategies and best practices for navigating the complexities of AI adoption. Entrepreneurs equipped with this knowledge can better position themselves to capitalize on AI's transformative potential, ultimately driving innovation and growth.

FUTURE RESEARCH DIRECTIONS

Future research in this area could explore the long-term impacts of AI adoption on the sustainability and scalability of digital entrepreneurial ventures. Comparative studies between different industries or regions may yield additional insights into the diverse ways in which AI influences business innovation. Furthermore, investigating the role of government policies and support systems in facilitating AI adoption among entrepreneurs could provide valuable findings for policymakers and industry stakeholders. Additionally, examining the ethical implications of AI in entrepreneurship warrants further exploration to ensure that technological advancements align with societal values.

CONCLUSION

In conclusion, artificial intelligence emerges as a powerful catalyst for business innovation in the realm of digital entrepreneurship. By enabling entrepreneurs to leverage data, streamline operations, and enhance customer experiences, AI has the potential to redefine traditional business practices. While challenges exist, the opportunities presented by AI far outweigh the obstacles. Through a strategic approach to AI integration, digital entrepreneurs can unlock new avenues for growth and innovation, positioning themselves at the forefront of their industries. As technology continues to evolve, the synergy between AI and digital entrepreneurship will remain a focal point for future research and practice, shaping the next generation of successful business leaders.

REFERENCES

Ahlstrom, D. (2010). Innovation in small and medium-sized enterprises: A review of the literature. *International Journal of Management Reviews*, 12(4), 401–426. DOI: 10.1111/j.1468-2370.2009.00268.x

An, J., Kwon, H., & Park, H. (2014). The impact of artificial intelligence on marketing strategies: An empirical study. *Journal of Business Research*, 67(7), 1401–1410. DOI: 10.1016/j.jbusres.2013.08.015

Balaji, K. "Blockchain Based Banking Transactions Enabled by Big Data," *2023 5th International Conference on Energy, Power and Environment: Towards Flexible Green Energy Technologies (ICEPE)*, Shillong, India, 2023, pp. 1-6, DOI: 10.1109/ICEPE57949.2023.10201613

Balaji, K. "Exploring the Drivers and Effects on Supply Chain Resilience and Performance in an Emerging Market Using Artificial Intelligence," *2023 3rd International Conference on Smart Generation Computing, Communication and Networking (SMART GENCON)*, Bangalore, India, 2023, pp. 1-6, DOI: 10.1109/SMARTGENCON60755.2023.10442071

Balaji, K. "Unlocking the Potential of BI-Enhancing Banking Transactions Through AI&ML Tools," *2023 International Conference on Applied Intelligence and Sustainable Computing (ICAISC)*, Dharwad, India, 2023, pp. 1-6, DOI: 10.1109/ICAISC58445.2023.10200018

Balaji, K. (2024). Charting the Path to Global Prosperity: Unveiling the Impact and Promise of Sustainable Development. In Ordóñez de Pablos, P., Anshari, M., & Almunawar, M. (Eds.), *Harnessing Green and Circular Skills for Digital Transformation* (pp. 1–22). IGI Global., DOI: 10.4018/979-8-3693-2865-1.ch001

Balaji, K. (2024). Harnessing AI for Financial Innovations: Pioneering the Future of Financial Services. In Jermsittiparsert, K., Phongkraphan, N., & Lekhavichit, N. (Eds.), *Modern Management Science Practices in the Age of AI* (pp. 91–122). IGI Global., DOI: 10.4018/979-8-3693-6720-9.ch004

Balaji, K. (2024). The Nexus of Smart Contracts and Digital Twins Transforming Green Finance With Automated Transactions in Investment Agreements: Leveraging Smart Contracts for Green Investment Agreements and Automated Transactions. In Jafar, S., Rodriguez, R., Kannan, H., Akhtar, S., & Plugmann, P. (Eds.), *Harnessing Blockchain-Digital Twin Fusion for Sustainable Investments* (pp. 287–315). IGI Global., DOI: 10.4018/979-8-3693-1878-2.ch012

Balaji, K., & Babu, M. K. (2017). A study on the affect of technology on unplanned purchase behaviour among the customers across selected corporate retail chains of Andhrapradesh, India. *International Journal of Economic Research*, 14(4), 277–288.

Balaji, K., & Babu, M. K. (2017). A study on the role of the external and internal factors on consumer impulse buying behaviour in selected retail outlets of Andhra Pradesh, India. *International Journal of Applied Business and Economic Research*, 15(4), 171–185.

K. Balaji, S. Karim, N. G. Naidu, T. Venkatesh, P. V. Ranjitha and S. ChandraSekhar, "Examining the Potential of Cryptocurrencies as An Asset Class-An Empirical Study," *2023 International Conference on Applied Intelligence and Sustainable Computing (ICAISC)*, Dharwad, India, 2023, pp. 1-6, .DOI: 10.1109/ICAISC58445.2023.10200309

Balaji, K., Karim, S., & Rao, P. S. "Unleashing the Power of Smart Chatbots: Transforming Banking with Artificial Intelligence," *2024 International Conference on Advances in Computing, Communication and Applied Informatics (ACCAI)*, Chennai, India, 2024, pp. 1-7, DOI: 10.1109/ACCAI61061.2024.10602456

Balaji, K., & Kishore Babu, M. (2016). A study on consumer shopping patterns in current retail scenario across selected retail stores in Andhra Pradesh, India. *International Journal of Economic Research*, 13(4), 1629–1640.

Chen, L., Zhang, X., & Wu, Z. (2014). Barriers to artificial intelligence adoption in small businesses: An empirical study. *International Journal of Information Management*, 34(4), 467–473. DOI: 10.1016/j.ijinfomgt.2014.02.005

D'Aveni, R. A. (2010). Competitive pressures and innovation in small firms: Evidence from artificial intelligence applications. *Small Business Economics*, 34(3), 211–229. DOI: 10.1007/s11187-009-9205-1

Davenport, T. H., & Ronanki, R. (2018). AI is the future of work: How artificial intelligence is transforming business operations. *Harvard Business Review*, 96(4), 108–116.

Davis, M., & Thompson, L. (2015). Preparing entrepreneurs for artificial intelligence: Education and training challenges. *Entrepreneurship Education*, 18(2), 113–130. DOI: 10.1016/j.ejbe.2014.08.002

Etzioni, A. (2014). The ethics of artificial intelligence: Balancing innovation and responsibility. *AI & Society*, 29(3), 225–233. DOI: 10.1007/s00146-013-0462-0

Gharajedaghi, J. (1999). *Systems thinking: Managing chaos and complexity*. Butterworth-Heinemann.

He, Z., & Wang, J. (2014). The relationship between AI adoption and business performance: Evidence from digital entrepreneurship. *Journal of Business Research*, 67(11), 2286–2294. DOI: 10.1016/j.jbusres.2014.06.001

Hitt, L. M. (1997). Computing productivity: Firm-level evidence. *The Review of Economics and Statistics*, 79(3), 391–406. DOI: 10.1162/003465397558244

Hwang, J., Kim, S., & Choi, K. (2023). Ethical considerations in the use of artificial intelligence in digital entrepreneurship. *Business Ethics Quarterly*, 33(1), 55–78. DOI: 10.1017/beq.2022.45

Kim, Y., & Chen, X. (2024). Building innovation ecosystems through AI collaboration: A study of digital entrepreneurship. *Journal of Innovation & Knowledge*, 9(1), 101–114. DOI: 10.1016/j.jik.2022.04.001

Kuratko, D. F. (2005). The emergence of entrepreneurship education: Development, trends, and challenges. *Entrepreneurship Theory and Practice*, 29(5), 577–598. DOI: 10.1111/j.1540-6520.2005.00099.x

Liao, S. H., Wu, C. H., & Hu, D. C. (2017). Exploring the effects of artificial intelligence on the operational efficiencies of startups. *International Journal of Production Economics*, 192, 115–126. DOI: 10.1016/j.ijpe.2017.06.011

Lockett, A., & Thompson, S. (1988). The role of technology in competitiveness: The impact of the technological revolution on competitive strategy. *Research Policy*, 17(2), 95–107. DOI: 10.1016/0048-7333(88)90031-1

Lopez, R., Martinez, P., & Santos, M. (2021). The hype of artificial intelligence in entrepreneurship: A critical review. *Journal of Business Venturing Insights*, 15, e00201. DOI: 10.1016/j.jbvi.2021.e00201

M. A., Idris, A. A., & Odukoya, J. A. (. (2021). The impact of artificial intelligence on customer engagement in digital entrepreneurship. *Journal of Business Research*, 123, 412–423. DOI: 10.1016/j.jbusres.2020.09.033

Porter, M. E., & Millar, V. E. (1985). How information gives you competitive advantage. *Harvard Business Review*, 63(4), 149–160.

Schilling, M. A., & Phelps, C. (2007). Interfirm collaboration networks: The impact of large partners. *Management Science*, 53(3), 1030–1042. DOI: 10.1287/mnsc.1060.0687

Zhang, H., & Zhao, X. (2010). Innovation and entrepreneurship in the context of artificial intelligence: An integrative framework. *The Journal of Technology Transfer*, 35(3), 292–307. DOI: 10.1007/s10901-009-9147-6Afolabi

ADDITIONAL READINGS

O'Brien, J., Jackson, A., & Williams, R. (2020). AI adoption and business performance: A correlational study in digital entrepreneurship. *Technological Forecasting and Social Change*, 161, 120240. DOI: 10.1016/j.techfore.2020.120240

Patel, V., Das, A., & Roy, S. (2019). Female entrepreneurs and artificial intelligence: Opportunities for business innovation. *Gender in Management*, 34(3), 177–193. DOI: 10.1108/GM-12-2018-0174

Smith, J., & Lee, K. (2018). Data-driven entrepreneurship: The role of artificial intelligence in strategic decision-making. *Journal of Business Research*, 92, 389–397. DOI: 10.1016/j.jbusres.2018.07.001

Zhang, Y., & Wang, Y. (2022). Challenges in AI adoption for digital entrepreneurs: Barriers and solutions. *International Journal of Information Management*, 62, 102435. DOI: 10.1016/j.ijinfomgt.2021.102435

KEY TERMS AND DEFINITIONS

AI-Driven E-Commerce Personalization: AI tools that customize online shopping experiences by analyzing customer behaviour, increasing engagement, and boosting conversion rates.

AI-Driven Product Development and Prototyping: AI solutions that optimize product design and development, enabling entrepreneurs to rapidly create and improve product prototypes.

AI-Enhanced Cybersecurity: AI tools that detect, prevent, and respond to cyber threats, safeguarding digital businesses from data breaches and online attacks.

AI-Powered Hiring and Talent Management: AI platforms that streamline the recruitment process by assessing candidates' skills and matching them to roles, improving hiring decisions.

AI-Powered Market Research and Insights: AI tools that help entrepreneurs analyse consumer behaviour, industry trends, and competition, enabling data-driven market strategies.

Automated Financial Management: AI systems that automate financial tasks like bookkeeping and reporting, helping entrepreneurs manage finances efficiently and reduce errors.

Chatbots and Customer Engagement: AI-driven chatbots that automate customer service, providing real-time assistance and personalized interactions to enhance customer satisfaction.

Content Creation and Marketing Automation: AI tools that generate and optimize content, automate marketing tasks, and enhance brand visibility through personalized campaigns.

Predictive Analytics for Business Growth: AI-powered tools that use historical data to forecast future trends, enabling entrepreneurs to make informed decisions and minimize business risks.

Voice Assistants and AI Automation: AI-powered voice assistants and automation platforms that handle routine tasks, boosting productivity for entrepreneurs through task management.

Chapter 3
From Giants to Guides:
Lessons From Google, Coca-Cola, Airbnb's Entrepreneurial Odyssey, and AI's Insights for Visionaries

Vineet Mehan
NIMS University, India

ABSTRACT

Traversing the entrepreneurial trajectories of Google, Coca-Cola, and Airbnb, this exploration extracts profound insights from their respective journeys. These industry leaders illuminate the path for emerging visionaries, imparting invaluable lessons and strategies that have propelled their remarkable success stories. Furthermore, this exploration delves into the intersection of entrepreneurship and artificial intelligence (AI). By scrutinizing AI-driven advancements within Google, Coca-Cola, and Airbnb, we unveil the transformative impact of AI on decision-making, process refinement, and innovative troubleshooting. The synthesis of the experiences of established giants with the transformative potential of AI constructs a comprehensive framework for aspiring entrepreneurs. This amalgamation empowers emerging visionaries to adeptly navigate the dynamic business landscape, offering a roadmap that seamlessly integrates historical wisdom and futuristic innovation, guiding new ventures toward achievements that resonate across time.

INTRODUCTION

In the realm of entrepreneurship, the trajectories of iconic companies have long served as beacons of inspiration and wisdom for aspiring business leaders. This chapter embarks on a transformative journey titled "From Giants to Guides:

DOI: 10.4018/979-8-3693-1495-1.ch003

Copyright © 2025, IGI Global. Copying or distributing in print or electronic forms without written permission of IGI Global is prohibited.

Lessons from Google, Coca-Cola, and Airbnb's Entrepreneurial Odyssey and AI's Insights for Emerging Visionaries," which traverses the remarkable pathways of three industry titans (Smith, 2018; Quelch, 2020; Christensen & Raynor, 2003). The exploration delves into their entrepreneurial odysseys, extracting profound insights that illuminate the way forward for emerging visionaries seeking to make their mark in the business world.

The stories of Google, Coca-Cola, and Airbnb stand as testaments to the power of innovation, adaptability, and visionary leadership. Their journeys are not only monumental in shaping their respective industries but also in offering a treasure trove of lessons that resonate across time (Duhigg, 2012; Chesbrough, 2003; McAfee & Brynjolfsson, 2017). By dissecting their strategies, challenges, and triumphs, this chapter aims to distil invaluable wisdom that can serve as a compass for those embarking on their own entrepreneurial quests.

In the contemporary landscape, the fusion of entrepreneurship and artificial intelligence (AI) has become an undeniable force reshaping industry. The collaboration between these two domains is not merely a convergence of technologies, but a dynamic synergy that propels businesses towards new heights of efficiency and innovation (O'Reilly, 2007). As AI-driven advancements become integral to the strategies of corporations, the need to comprehend its transformative impact grows more pronounced. This chapter delves into the symbiotic relationship between AI and entrepreneurship by closely scrutinizing the ways in which Google, Coca-Cola, and Airbnb have harnessed AI's potential to enhance decision-making, streamline processes, and pioneer inventive solutions.

The amalgamation of the experiences of established giants and the disruptive power of AI lays the foundation for a comprehensive framework tailored for emerging entrepreneurs. This framework equips these budding visionaries with the tools and insights required to navigate the intricate and dynamic business landscape. By weaving together, the threads of historical wisdom and future-forward innovation, this chapter creates a roadmap that extends beyond conventional boundaries, empowering new ventures to achieve lasting success.

As we embark on a journey to understand the intertwining narratives of entrepreneurial trajectories, industry leadership, emerging visionaries, artificial intelligence, and its transformative impact, this chapter bridges the gap between established knowledge and cutting-edge advancements. The aspiration is to provide a comprehensive resource that not only imparts essential lessons but also guides future entrepreneurs towards building ventures that stand the test of time.

OBJECTIVES

Objectives identified for the proposed research work includes:

1. Analysing Entrepreneurial Trajectories: The primary objective of this exploration is to dissect the entrepreneurial journeys of industry giants—Google, Coca-Cola, and Airbnb. Through a comprehensive analysis, we aim to extract valuable insights from their experiences, identifying key turning points, challenges, and strategies that have propelled their remarkable success stories.

2. Illuminating Path for Emerging Visionaries: This exploration aims to uncover the lessons and strategies imparted by Google, Coca-Cola, and Airbnb to emerging visionaries. By studying their trajectories, we seek to illuminate a path for aspiring entrepreneurs, providing them with actionable insights that can guide their own ventures and help them navigate the complexities of the business world.

3. Examining AI's Role in Entrepreneurship: An important objective of this study is to delve into the intersection of entrepreneurship and artificial intelligence (AI). By closely scrutinizing AI-driven advancements within Google, Coca-Cola, and Airbnb, we intend to reveal how AI has reshaped decision-making processes, refined operational procedures, and facilitated innovative troubleshooting in the entrepreneurial context.

4. Unveiling Transformative Impact of AI: Through a thorough examination of AI's influence on Google, Coca-Cola, and Airbnb, our exploration aims to unveil the transformative impact of AI on various aspects of entrepreneurship. This includes its role in enhancing decision-making precision, optimizing processes, and fostering novel problem-solving methodologies that redefine traditional business approaches.

5. Constructing a Comprehensive Framework: By synthesizing the experiences of established industry giants with the transformative potential of AI, this study seeks to construct a comprehensive framework for aspiring entrepreneurs. This amalgamation of historical wisdom and futuristic innovation is designed to empower emerging visionaries with the tools and knowledge needed to adeptly navigate the dynamic business landscape, ultimately guiding their ventures toward enduring achievements.

Through these objectives, our exploration aims to shed light on the dynamic interplay between entrepreneurship, established industry leaders, and the evolving landscape of artificial intelligence. By examining the journeys of Google, Coca-Cola, and Airbnb, as well as the transformative potential of AI, we aspire to offer a valuable resource for emerging visionaries seeking to chart their own paths to success.

LESSONS FROM INDUSTRY GIANTS

Innovative Insights from Google

Google serves as a quintessential exemplar of innovation-driven success in today's business landscape. Founded by Larry Page and Sergey Brin in 1998, the company has evolved from a modest search engine into a sprawling tech conglomerate, offering a diverse array of products and services. Analyzing Google's trajectory yields invaluable insights for emerging visionaries within the entrepreneurial realm.

One of the pivotal takeaways from Google's triumphant narrative is its unwavering commitment to innovation. The company's renowned policy that allocates employees 20% of their time for side projects has birthed transformative products like Gmail and Google Maps. This approach fosters a culture of experimentation and ingenuity, cultivating an atmosphere wherein groundbreaking concepts can thrive (Schmidt & Rosenberg, 2014).

Furthermore, Google's unwavering focus on user-centric design and simplicity has proved instrumental. The company's homepage serves as a testament to this ethos, boasting a clean and minimalist interface. This lesson underscores the significance of delivering user value in a lucid and intuitive manner – a principle that continues to hold relevance for entrepreneurs aiming to resonate with their target demographics (Tucker & Miller, 2013).

Another salient facet to glean from Google's playbook is its data-driven decision-making. The enterprise harnesses vast datasets to refine its offerings, thus elevating user experiences. This underscores the importance of capitalizing on data analytics and insights to steer business strategies and enhancements (Hamel, 2009).

In terms of expansion and diversification, Google's acquisition strategy stands out. Its procurement of entities like YouTube and Android has not only broadened its portfolio but also facilitated forays into novel markets and user bases. This tact underscores the import of strategic partnerships and acquisitions in propelling growth (Burns, 2016).

Moreover, Google's dedication to corporate social responsibility and sustainability imparts an invaluable lesson to contemporary entrepreneurs. The firm's investments in renewable energy and endeavors to curtail its carbon footprint underscore the gravity of aligning business objectives with ecological and societal obligations (Page, 2017).

Additionally, the creation of Google's open-source Android operating system imparts a lesson in collaboration and community building. By enabling global developers to contribute to the platform's evolution, Google showcases the potency of crowdsourced innovation in propelling technological progress (Weber, 2010).

Furthermore, Google's pursuit of moonshot projects and audacious goals accentuates the significance of setting ambitious benchmarks that kindle innovation and push boundaries (Meadows, 2015).

In sum, Google's voyage offers an array of lessons for entrepreneurs. Its emphasis on innovation, user-centric design, data-driven decision-making, strategic expansion, corporate social responsibility, open collaboration, and audacious goals furnishes insights that can shepherd emerging visionaries towards triumph within the ever-evolving business landscape.

Coca-Cola's Blueprint for Success

Coca-Cola stands as a titan in the beverage industry, boasting a history spanning over a century. Examining the trajectory of Coca-Cola yields invaluable insights for emerging visionaries navigating the entrepreneurial landscape.

Key among the lessons drawn from Coca-Cola's tale of success is the profound impact of branding and emotional connection. The company's unwavering and iconic branding has cultivated a potent emotional bond with consumers worldwide (Aaker, 1991).

Moreover, Coca-Cola's adeptness in adapting to shifting consumer preferences is commendable. The introduction of Diet Coke and Coca-Cola Zero mirrors the company's responsiveness to health-conscious trends, underscoring the significance of staying in tune with evolving market dynamics (Yoffie & Kim, 2011).

Coca-Cola's commitment to both global expansion and local customization is another pivotal takeaway. The company's ability to tailor its offerings to suit local tastes and cultures, all while maintaining a consistent brand identity, has significantly contributed to its widespread triumph (Daft, 2017).

In terms of marketing, Coca-Cola's impactful advertising campaigns have left an indelible imprint. The "Share a Coke" campaign, for instance, personalized the product and engaged consumers, spotlighting the potential of experiential marketing (Mourey & Martin, 2017).

Coca-Cola's unwavering dedication to corporate social responsibility and sustainability serves as an indispensable lesson for contemporary entrepreneurs. The company's endeavors in water conservation and community involvement underscore the importance of making positive contributions to society (Werther & Chandler, 2011).

The art of diversifying the product portfolio is strikingly evident in Coca-Cola's expansion beyond carbonated beverages. Acquisitions of brands like Minute Maid and Honest Tea stand as exemplars of the value inherent in diversification for capturing a broader market share (Neff, 2007).

Furthermore, Coca-Cola's mastery of supply chain management and distribution networks offers insights into efficiency and reach. The company's robust logistical strategies have facilitated its sustained global presence and dependable product delivery (Davenport, 2000).

Coca-Cola's voyage bequeaths valuable lessons for entrepreneurs. The emphasis on branding, adaptability, global expansion, localized marketing, corporate social responsibility, diversification, and streamlined supply chain management furnishes insights that can guide emerging visionaries toward prosperity in an ever-evolving business landscape.

Airbnb's Path to Innovation and Success

Airbnb has emerged as a transformative force in the hospitality and travel sector, reshaping the very nature of accommodation experiences. The scrutiny of Airbnb's trajectory imparts invaluable wisdom for burgeoning entrepreneurs navigating the dynamic contours of today's business landscape.

A cornerstone lesson gleaned from Airbnb's triumphant narrative is the potency of platform-based business models. By facilitating connections between hosts and travelers, Airbnb has harnessed the potential of the sharing economy, epitomizing the creation of ecosystems that deliver value to multiple stakeholders (Eisenmann, 2013).

Furthermore, Airbnb's unwavering focus on user-centered design and seamless experiences has proved pivotal. The platform's stress on user reviews, personalized suggestions, and frictionless booking processes underscores the significance of elevating customer needs and convenience to the forefront (Oskam & Boswijk, 2016).

Airbnb's disruption of traditional hospitality models stands as a testament to the import of innovation. The firm's knack for challenging age-old industry norms and providing distinctive lodging options underscores the power of reimagining established paradigms (Guttentag, 2015).

In the realm of market expansion and diversification, Airbnb's inclusion of "Experiences" alongside accommodations offers a salient lesson. The platform's expansion into curating local, authentic experiences in conjunction with lodging underscores the value of diversifying offerings to cater to evolving consumer preferences (Zervas & Proserpio, 2016).

Airbnb's data-driven approach to decision-making casts a spotlight on the significance of harnessing insights. The platform's judicious use of data to fine-tune search algorithms, curate personalized recommendations, and augment user satisfaction underscores the strategic leverage of data-driven strategies (Leavy, 2018).

Moreover, Airbnb's commitment to community building and trust-building serves as an indispensable lesson. The establishment of host and guest verification protocols and the cultivation of a sense of belonging have played pivotal roles in constructing a dependable and trustworthy ecosystem (Tussyadiah & Pesonen, 2016).

Additionally, Airbnb's nimbleness in crisis response and adaptability in the face of challenges imparts a pivotal takeaway. The company's handling of scenarios like the COVID-19 pandemic underscores the urgency of agility and preparedness in navigating unforeseen disruptions (Dolnicar et al., 2020).

Airbnb's remarkable odyssey unfurls a tapestry of insights for entrepreneurs. The accentuation of platform models, user-centered design, transformative innovation, expansive market approaches, data-driven decisions, community cultivation, and adaptability weaves together a diverse spectrum of lessons to guide emerging visionaries toward success within an ever-evolving business environment.

ILLUMINATING THE PATH FOR EMERGING VISIONARIES

Within the realm of our exploratory journey, this section emerges as a beacon of enlightenment, casting its radiant glow upon the profound value nestled within the trajectories of industry leaders—Google, Coca-Cola, and Airbnb. This luminosity extends beyond historical significance; it forms an illuminating roadmap meticulously tailored for the aspirations of budding visionaries. This segment fervently underscores how the collective experiences of these industry titans not only illuminate the path of their storied accomplishments but, more crucially, intricately guide and chart a transformative course for those daring to follow suit.

Google, the emblematic tech giant, radiates insights that transcend its own corporate chronicle. Its evolution from a modest search engine to a multifaceted conglomerate encapsulates the dynamic nature of entrepreneurial endeavors. Google's unrelenting pursuit of innovation, exemplified through ventures like Google Maps and Google Earth, unveils the profound significance of pushing boundaries and questioning the unasked (Schmidt & Rosenberg, 2014). This ethos resonates powerfully with emerging visionaries, emphasizing the potency of cultivating an environment where unexplored ideas flourish. The transformative impact of such a mindset is exemplified through the realization of pioneering projects, affirming the remarkable outcomes achievable when innovation takes center stage.

Coca-Cola, a time-honored symbol of global branding, offers a treasure trove of insights that extend beyond the realm of refreshment. Its ability to transcend generations and cultures underscores the resounding importance of fostering enduring connections with consumers. The Coca-Cola brand is not just a name; it's an emotion—an embodiment of the profound value of branding and emotional resonance

(Aaker, 1991). This resonance, cultivated through a consistent and iconic brand identity, establishes a blueprint for emerging visionaries. It demonstrates that the journey toward becoming an industry titan isn't solely about transactional success but, more crucially, about forging emotional bonds that withstand the tests of time.

Airbnb, a modern-day disruptor in the hospitality industry, further enriches this narrative. The rise of Airbnb showcases how a fresh perspective on an age-old sector can pave the way for transformation. This paradigm shift hinges on the potency of platform business models, which redefine traditional modes of engagement and transaction (Eisenmann, 2013). Airbnb's approach emphasizes user-centric design and personalized experiences, reflecting the paramount importance of understanding and catering to the needs of consumers (Oskam & Boswijk, 2016). Moreover, the platform's extension into unique "Experiences" alongside accommodations is a clarion call for diversification—a strategy that resonates strongly with emerging visionaries seeking to expand their offerings in response to dynamic market preferences (Zervas & Proserpio, 2016).

Collectively, the triumvirate of Google, Coca-Cola, and Airbnb emanates profound luminance, illuminating the path for emerging visionaries navigating the intricate terrain of entrepreneurship. These stories aren't just historical anecdotes; they're luminous roadmaps offering transformative insights. They guide with the light of experience and, in doing so, nurture the flames of inspiration. The trails blazed by these industry giants are not mere footprints; they are guiding lights that empower new entrants to chart their own course with a depth of understanding and insight that can only come from those who have fearlessly walked the path before. Aspiring visionaries stand to reap the benefits of these guiding lights, forging their own unique entrepreneurial odysseys equipped with wisdom, foresight, and an indomitable spirit.

ENTREPRENEURSHIP MEETS ARTIFICIAL INTELLIGENCE

In the contemporary business landscape, the intersection of entrepreneurship and artificial intelligence (AI) is a dynamic crucible of innovation, presenting an array of unprecedented opportunities and challenges. As AI technologies surge forward with exponential advancements, entrepreneurs find themselves poised on the threshold of a new era, where the amalgamation of human ingenuity and machine intelligence has the potential to reshape industries, redefine business paradigms, and revolutionize the very fabric of customer experiences.

Gone are the days when AI was a distant promise; today, it is an omnipresent force permeating diverse sectors, ranging from healthcare to finance, manufacturing to marketing. At its heart, the transformative essence of AI lies in its prowess to process colossal volumes of data and distil meaningful insights, empowering entrepreneurs with informed decision-making capabilities that exhibit remarkable precision and velocity. The fusion of the entrepreneurial spirit with AI-powered data analytics has given rise to a novel breed of startups—ones driven by data—capable of decoding market trends, deciphering consumer behaviours, and uncovering nascent opportunities with unprecedented efficacy.

A pivotal facet of AI's impact on entrepreneurship manifests through the automation of routine operations. Entrepreneurs can now delegate repetitive tasks to AI-driven tools, thereby freeing up invaluable time to focus on higher-order strategic ideation and creative endeavours. The spectrum spans from chatbots adept at handling customer inquiries to algorithms orchestrating intricate supply chain logistics. This integration of AI-driven automation streamlines efficiency, slashes operational costs, and liberates substantial resources that can be channelled towards innovation.

Beyond streamlining processes, AI holds the potential to catalyse a paradigm shift in the very essence of product and service development. Armed with AI capabilities, entrepreneurs are empowered to dissect customer feedback, pinpoint pain points, and iteratively refine offerings in tandem with evolving demands. Machine learning algorithms can proactively predict customer preferences and behaviour, equipping entrepreneurs with the tools to personalize products and tailor marketing strategies to an unprecedented degree. This enhancement significantly augments the likelihood of thriving in an increasingly competitive marketplace.

However, just as the dawn of any transformative technology brings forth a constellation of possibilities, it concurrently ushers in a set of unique challenges for entrepreneurs. Among the foremost is the ethical and societal ramifications engendered by AI-enabled decision-making. As AI algorithms become progressively intricate, the opacity of their decision-making processes may inadvertently give rise to biases and unanticipated outcomes. Entrepreneurs are confronted with the imperative to grapple with these ethical quandaries, ensuring that their AI systems are both equitable and transparent, aligning with societal values.

Parallelly, the integration of AI necessitates a concerted focus on upskilling and reskilling the workforce. As AI usurps routine tasks, there arises a burgeoning demand for employees fluent in AI development, data science, and machine learning. Entrepreneurs must consider the strategic implications of this shift, investing in the training of existing teams or scouting for new talent adept at harnessing the full potential of AI technologies.

In essence, the juncture where entrepreneurship meets artificial intelligence is a transformative nexus that is inexorably shaping the trajectory of business. Entrepreneurs are harnessing AI's capabilities to fuel innovation, streamline operations, and deliver hyper-personalized experiences to their customers. Nevertheless, this metamorphosis is characterized by multifaceted challenges that warrant careful consideration. Ethical considerations and workforce preparedness assume paramount importance as the infusion of AI becomes more pervasive.

As entrepreneurs navigate this multifarious landscape, the keys to success lie in a harmonious blend of creativity, adaptability, and a profound comprehension of how to harness AI's potential while upholding the core values of entrepreneurship. The entrepreneurs who masterfully straddle the delicate balance between innovation and ethics, technological prowess and societal responsibility, are poised to redefine the contours of business in a manner that not only advances the frontiers of their ventures but contributes positively to the betterment of society as a whole. It is within the corridors of this new paradigm that the future of business and the vast expanse of human potential converge, promising a landscape rich with promise and brimming with opportunities yet to be unveiled.

AI'S TRANSFORMATIVE IMPACT ON ENTREPRENEURSHIP

In the contemporary landscape of business, the convergence of artificial intelligence (AI) and entrepreneurship has given rise to a paradigm shift that is reshaping the very foundations of industries. The sixth section of our exploration delves into the tangible manifestations of AI's transformative power within the domains of industry titans, shedding light on its profound impact on the entrepreneurial landscape. Through a meticulous analysis of AI-driven innovations within the corridors of Google, Coca-Cola, and Airbnb, this segment unveils a revolutionary narrative—a story where AI acts as the catalyst, reshaping decision-making processes, streamlining operations, and igniting innovation in troubleshooting methodologies.

The symbiotic relationship between AI and entrepreneurship finds its embodiment in the innovations spearheaded by industry leaders, offering a microcosmic glimpse into the macroscopic transformation wrought by AI. Google, the pioneer of the digital realm, has harnessed AI's capabilities to augment its core search engine function. The introduction of AI-driven algorithms for search result ranking has elevated user experience, delivering more relevant and personalized outcomes (Dean & Ghemawat, 2004). This dynamic interplay between human intent and AI-powered refinement exemplifies how AI enhances decision-making, making it data-driven and responsive to users' ever-evolving needs.

Coca-Cola, an archetype of branding excellence, has harnessed AI to decipher consumer sentiments and preferences. By deploying sentiment analysis algorithms on social media platforms, Coca-Cola can rapidly gauge public sentiment toward its campaigns and products, enabling real-time adjustments to marketing strategies (Duan, Gu, & Whinston, 2008). This real-time responsiveness, facilitated by AI, epitomizes how it redefines not only decision-making but also dynamic adaptation, underscoring the agility AI brings to the entrepreneurial sphere.

Airbnb, a disruptor in the realm of traditional hospitality, has leveraged AI to reimagine customer experiences. The platform's AI-driven recommendation systems provide personalized travel suggestions, presenting users with accommodations and experiences tailored to their preferences (Radinsky, 2012). This confluence of AI and entrepreneurship illustrates how machine learning algorithms can decipher intricate patterns within data, enabling businesses to curate offerings that deeply resonate with individual consumers.

Beyond these specific instances, the holistic impact of AI on entrepreneurship extends to the core of business operations. AI-driven automation holds the potential to streamline intricate supply chains, optimizing inventory management, logistics, and demand forecasting (Cachon & Terwiesch, 2009). This operational refinement not only enhances efficiency but also offers entrepreneurs the bandwidth to focus on strategic innovation and creativity, further fueling the cycle of transformative growth.

The narrative of AI's transformative impact on entrepreneurship extends beyond decision-making and operations; it transcends boundaries to redefine problem-solving. AI-driven predictive analytics empower businesses to forecast potential challenges and devise proactive solutions (Li & Fung, 2008). The ability to anticipate and preempt challenges before they arise empowers entrepreneurs to navigate uncharted territories with confidence, fortifying their ventures against potential setbacks.

In essence, the experiences of industry giants—Google, Coca-Cola, and Airbnb—paint a vivid portrait of AI as an invaluable tool that has permeated every facet of entrepreneurship. From precision in decision-making to operational efficiency and innovative troubleshooting, AI's transformative imprint is indelibly etched. The journeys undertaken by these industry titans act as guiding beacons, illuminating the profound potential of AI and its capacity to shape the contours of the future entrepreneurial landscape.

As we navigate the intricate path of entrepreneurship intertwined with AI, it is crucial to recognize that the transformative journey is not without its challenges. Ensuring the ethical and responsible use of AI remains paramount, as algorithms wield considerable influence. The ongoing discourse concerning data privacy, transparency, and fairness must guide the deployment of AI technologies to ensure a harmonious integration that advances both businesses and society (Hagendorff, 2020).

This section of exploration underscores the palpable and transformative effects of AI on the entrepreneurial realm. The case studies of Google, Coca-Cola, and Airbnb exemplify AI's potential to redefine decision-making dynamics, enhance operational efficiency, and foster innovative solutions to complex challenges. These pioneers illuminate the trail that points toward an AI-augmented future—one where entrepreneurship flourishes in tandem with technological innovation. As we traverse this juncture of innovation, embracing AI's potential while upholding ethical considerations, entrepreneurs stand poised to harness the power of this technological force and steer their ventures toward unprecedented horizons.

SYNTHESIS OF EXPERIENCES AND AI POTENTIAL

At the confluence of historical insights drawn from industry giants and the boundless potential of artificial intelligence (AI) lies a transformative synthesis—a comprehensive framework that empowers both present and future entrepreneurs. This synthesis harmonizes time-tested wisdom with cutting-edge AI capabilities, culminating in a framework that transcends traditional boundaries. Within this framework, emerging visionaries find tools to navigate evolving business challenges and seize opportunities with unwavering confidence. By merging lessons from the past with AI's transformative power, this framework becomes a guiding light, steering entrepreneurs towards informed decision-making and visionary innovation in an era defined by perpetual change.

a)   Foundations of Empowerment

In the intricate tapestry of entrepreneurship, history becomes a wellspring of profound insights. The entrepreneurial journeys undertaken by giants like Google, Coca-Cola, and Airbnb stand as monuments to unwavering determination, visionary thinking, and strategic brilliance. Within the contours of these journeys, emerging visionaries find a trove of lessons that transcend time.

Google's relentless pursuit of uncharted territories, Coca-Cola's mastery in crafting resonant brand identities, and Airbnb's disruptive reimagining of an entire industry collectively contribute to a rich repository of entrepreneurial wisdom. These narratives, interwoven with challenges, triumphs, and strategic manoeuvres, offer a holistic perspective that illuminates the path for those daring to carve their niche in the business world.

By distilling the essence of these journeys, aspiring entrepreneurs gain a profound understanding of the dynamics that underpin success. From Google's appetite for innovation to Coca-Cola's ability to evoke emotional connections, and Airbnb's radical innovation, these tales provide invaluable insights that empower the next generation of visionaries to navigate the ever-evolving landscape of entrepreneurship with wisdom born from experience. In embracing these foundational principles, emerging entrepreneurs are poised to forge their own paths, armed with a treasure trove of lessons from the giants that came before them.

b)   Harmonizing Wisdom and AI Potential

Within the realm of this synthesis, a captivating synergy unfolds as historical wisdom seamlessly merges with the boundless potential of AI. The transformative prowess of AI, with its remarkable ability to process vast troves of data and distil actionable insights, holds the power to reshape the entrepreneurial landscape.

In the tapestry of entrepreneurship, the fusion of AI's analytical acumen with the timeless lessons of the past gives rise to a holistic framework that resonates with innovation. This framework, akin to a strategic compass, equips entrepreneurs with the tools to navigate uncharted waters. As AI augments decision-making precision, refines operational strategies, and unlocks new horizons of creativity, its harmonious partnership with historical wisdom becomes an unparalleled asset.

By harnessing AI's capacity to predict trends and analyse patterns, entrepreneurs gain the capacity to proactively steer their ventures toward success. The amalgamation of past insights with AI-driven foresight not only strengthens their ability to adapt to challenges but also amplifies their potential to seize opportunities on a scale previously unattainable.

In this synthesis, the past converges with the future, creating a narrative that transcends eras and empowers entrepreneurs to confidently chart a course forward. The magic of this convergence lies in its ability to guide visionaries toward a future where the interplay of wisdom and AI potential becomes the cornerstone of strategic innovation and success.

c)   Navigating Dynamism

Within the contours of this comprehensive framework, a new generation of visionaries finds their footing in the ever-shifting terrain of the business world. The insights gleaned from industry giants underscore a crucial attribute—agility, accompanied by the ability to adapt swiftly.

The integration of AI adds a dynamic dimension to this navigation process. AI's analytical prowess empowers entrepreneurs to decode the intricate dance of market dynamics, enabling them to predict shifts and respond in real-time. This fusion of human acumen and AI intelligence provides a twofold advantage: the confidence to withstand uncertainties and the tools to seize opportunities that arise unexpectedly.

In essence, this framework equips emerging visionaries with a compass that guides them through the turbulence of a rapidly evolving landscape. The lessons drawn from established giants, coupled with AI's predictive capabilities, bestow upon entrepreneurs the resilience to weather storms and the capacity to steer their ventures toward calmer waters. As the business world continues to evolve at an unprecedented pace, this synthesis ensures that visionaries not only survive but thrive amidst dynamism.

d) Confidence in Opportunity

Central to the tapestry of entrepreneurial success is the art of seizing opportunities that beckon in a dynamic landscape. Within this synthesis, the fusion of historical insights and AI-generated trends becomes the catalyst that empowers decisive action.

As emerging visionaries traverse this comprehensive framework, they are armed not only with the lessons from industry giants but also with the foresight AI provides. The experiences of these giants infuse a sense of calculated audacity—an understanding that calculated risks often lead to breakthroughs.

Moreover, the predictive prowess of AI adds an extraordinary dimension to this confidence. By sifting through vast streams of data, AI illuminates emerging trends, revealing windows of opportunity that might otherwise remain hidden. Armed with AI-generated insights, entrepreneurs can navigate with precision, swiftly identifying and capitalizing on nascent trends.

In this way, the synthesis becomes a source of empowerment, instilling the confidence to act decisively in the face of opportunity. As entrepreneurs harness the collective wisdom of the past and the predictive potential of AI, they become architects of their own success stories—poised to seize the moment and transform it into a legacy of innovation and achievement.

e) Guiding Visionary Innovation

The essence of this synthesis transcends inertia; it is a living compass that propels visionary innovation forward. Within its dynamic embrace, entrepreneurs are emboldened to not only navigate change but also harness the transformative potential of AI to redefine the trajectory of their ventures.

This synthesis stands as a testament to the proactive nature of entrepreneurs who refuse to be mere spectators in their own journey. It is an invitation to embrace change as a catalyst for innovation, to reimagine possibilities through the lens of AI-driven insights, and to steer ventures toward uncharted horizons.

As entrepreneurs chart this course, the legacy of industry giants becomes more than just a reference point—it becomes a foundation upon which new narratives are woven. The fusion of historical wisdom with AI's transformative prowess ignites a spark of ingenuity that drives visionary innovation. These emerging entrepreneurs emerge as trailblazers, navigating the present with an eye toward the future, crafting stories of success that resonate with both the legacy of the past and the transformative capabilities of AI.

In essence, this synthesis embodies the spirit of entrepreneurial dynamism, inviting visionaries to shape their narratives with courage, conviction, and an unwavering commitment to pioneering innovation.

This synthesis unites past lessons with future prospects. Through the interplay of historical insights and AI's potential, a profound framework emerges. It empowers entrepreneurs to navigate modern business intricacies and shape its contours. With this synthesis, emerging visionaries adeptly navigate uncertainties, seize opportunities, and pave the way for a future where entrepreneurship thrives alongside AI-driven innovation. It embodies the indomitable spirit of adaptable, visionary entrepreneurship. As history and AI converge, the narrative embraces a future rich with promise and possibility.

GUIDING EMERGING VISIONARIES

In the dynamic realm of entrepreneurship, the pathway ahead for emerging visionaries unfolds within a transformative landscape—a fusion of historical wisdom and AI-driven insights. This synthesis emerges as a strategic compass, arming new entrants with tools to navigate and excel in the ever-shifting entrepreneurial arena. With the interweaving of lessons drawn from industry giants and the uncharted potentials AI unveils, this framework takes shape as a guiding luminary—an illuminating force that not only ensures adaptation but propels entrepreneurs toward thriving in the face of unceasing flux.

a)   Forging a Compass for Novices

At the very heart of this all-encompassing framework lies a pivotal junction, where the accumulated wisdom of the past converges with the limitless potential of the future. It emerges as a navigational instrument—a steadfast guiding star—illuminating the path for fledgling entrepreneurs venturing into uncharted territories. The synergy between the profound insights offered by industry titans and the expansive horizons unveiled by AI imbues it with a significance far beyond mere guidance. It assumes the role of a compass, a reliable instrument directing emerging visionaries towards the realm of well-informed decisions and the realm of visionary innovation.

Aspiring entrepreneurs are bestowed with more than just knowledge; they are armed with a transformative tool that empowers them to chart their course amidst uncertainty. The amalgamation of time-tested principles and cutting-edge AI-driven insights equips these novices with the confidence to navigate complexities and capitalize on opportunities. This compass doesn't just point in a direction—it illuminates a path of inspired decision-making, where lessons from giants of the past intertwine with AI's potential to steer novices toward the helm of future success.

b) Empowerment Beyond Survival

The intrinsic power of this encompassing framework goes beyond enabling emerging visionaries to merely navigate survival; it nurtures the very seeds of excellence. Within the perpetual flux of the entrepreneurial realm, this framework stands as a rock-solid foothold amidst the tumultuous terrain. The sagas of industry giants underscore the paramount significance of adaptability, while AI's foresight offers a strategic roadmap for anticipating and confronting disruptions head-on. Together, they cultivate in entrepreneurs the capacity to not only weather challenges but to transform them into springboards for advancement.

This framework instils a mindset that transcends the realm of mere survival. It propels emerging visionaries to aspire to new heights, fostering a culture of proactive growth. The integration of time-tested principles and AI-generated insights equips entrepreneurs with the tools to thrive amidst uncertainty, pivot with precision, and innovate with conviction. It elevates their perspective from reactive responses to strategic initiatives, turning obstacles into stepping stones toward excellence. As emerging visionaries harness the collaborative wisdom of giants and the predictive capabilities of AI, they emerge not just as survivors, but as architects of their own success stories, crafting narratives that resonate with adaptability, foresight, and transformative growth.

c) A Trail of Enlightenment

The essence of this synthesis lies in its inherent transformative power—an attribute that sets it apart from the ordinary. It transcends the boundaries of convention, inviting entrepreneurs to embark on a trail marked by discovery and evolution. This trail, aglow with enlightenment, stretches beyond the realm of tactical manoeuvres, steering emerging visionaries onto a trajectory of prosperity and growth.

At its core, this synthesis represents more than a mere amalgamation of insights; it signifies a profound paradigm shift. It blazes a trail that veers away from the well-trodden paths and propels entrepreneurs toward uncharted territories. By weaving the tapestry of historical wisdom with the illuminating foresight provided by AI, this trail metamorphoses into a transformative journey—one characterized by adaptability, innovation, and an unwavering commitment to embracing the infinite possibilities that the future holds.

This trail of enlightenment beckons emerging visionaries to embrace change as a constant companion, to evolve in response to shifting landscapes, and to seize the reins of innovation. Through the synergy of wisdom from industry giants and the precision of AI-generated insights, this pathway becomes a conduit for visionary growth. It inspires a collective movement that transcends the ordinary, guiding entrepreneurs to manifest their aspirations, navigate complexities, and weave narratives of success that resonate with transformation and boundless potential.

d) Seizing Opportunity Amidst Disruption

In a landscape where disruptions frequently unveil hidden opportunities, this synthesis emerges as a beacon that empowers entrepreneurs to not only recognize these openings but to grasp them with resolute determination. The reservoir of lessons derived from industry giants serves as a wellspring of audacity, urging entrepreneurs to take bold strides into uncharted territories. Concurrently, the foresight AI imparts enables them to identify emerging trends and strategically position themselves for triumphant endeavours.

The duality of this empowerment—nurtured by the insights of giants and fuelled by AI's predictive prowess—creates a potent synergy. This synergy forms the very essence of this synthesis, propelling emerging visionaries to the forefront of innovation. It bestows upon them the tools to be proactive participants in their own narratives, transforming disruptions into stepping stones towards success.

This synthesis is more than just a compilation of ideas; it is a transformative force that bolsters entrepreneurs to rise above challenges and harness the winds of change. By merging the wisdom of the past with the foresight of AI, it empowers visionaries to not merely adapt to disruptions but to shape them into avenues of opportunity. In this world where change is a constant, this synthesis stands as a lighthouse, guiding entrepreneurs toward the shores of empowerment and prosperity.

e) A Journey of Transformation:

Beyond its pragmatic utility, this all-encompassing framework encapsulates a profound journey of transformation—a voyage characterized by empowerment, enlightenment, and boundless potential. It serves as a vessel that navigates through uncharted dimensions of innovation, where the convergence of historical insights and AI-illuminated foresight nurtures a new breed of entrepreneurs—individuals who embody proactive action over reactive response, and who embrace revolutionary change rather than mere resilience.

The transformative essence of this journey lies in its ability to shape entrepreneurs into catalysts of change. As they traverse the dynamic landscape of business, armed with the synthesis of industry giants' wisdom and AI-driven insights, they evolve into visionaries who not only adapt to change but drive it. This journey compels them to transcend traditional paradigms, envisioning new possibilities and seizing opportunities that align with the shifting tides of industry.

This framework is more than a static construct; it represents an evolving narrative of growth and empowerment. It beckons emerging entrepreneurs to embark on a path that goes beyond conventional wisdom, igniting innovative sparks that illuminate the way forward. This journey of transformation culminates in a generation of entrepreneurs who don't merely weather the storms of change, but steer their ventures toward uncharted horizons, where empowerment, enlightenment, and unbounded potential converge to redefine the future of business.

In the realm of emerging visionaries, the synthesis that emerges illuminates a guiding force for triumph within the ever-evolving entrepreneurial milieu. This all-encompassing framework, birthed from the fusion of industry giants' wisdom and AI's expansive prospects, stands as an homage to the potency of knowledge and innovation. It transcends the role of a guide; it emerges as a transformational agent that empowers entrepreneurs to navigate challenges, seize opportunities, and embark on a journey that outshines survival. It is a testament to the audacity of entrepreneurship, a blueprint for excellence, and a promise of flourishing amidst change. As the guiding radiance is unveiled, emerging visionaries are beckoned to step resolutely into the future, armed with the sagacity of the past and the limitless horizons unveiled by AI.

CONCLUSION

The culmination of this exploration brings us to a crossroads where the narratives of established industry giants and the transformative potential of artificial intelligence converge. The stories of Google, Coca-Cola, and Airbnb not only illuminate a path for emerging visionaries but also lay the foundation for a broader understanding of the dynamics of entrepreneurship.

Simultaneously, the rise of AI introduces a new dimension of possibilities. Its impact extends beyond technical advancements, reshaping the essence of decision-making, operational efficiency, and creative troubleshooting. The seamless integration of human ingenuity with AI capabilities opens the door to a novel entrepreneurial approach, one that thrives on adaptability and foresight.

The fusion of wisdom distilled from industry giants and the potential unleashed by AI constructs a comprehensive framework that transcends historical anecdotes. It offers a blueprint for navigating the intricate modern business landscape, arming emerging visionaries with the tools to steer their ventures through uncharted territories. This framework encompasses proven strategies from the past and innovative insights from AI, empowering entrepreneurs to traverse the unknown with confidence.

As this chapter draws to a close, its message reverberates beyond its textual boundaries. It extends an invitation to entrepreneurs to embrace the harmony of tradition and innovation, guiding their journey into an era of both unpredictability and opportunity. The narratives of Google, Coca-Cola, and Airbnb intertwine with AI's promise, beckoning individuals to carve their stories on the canvas of entrepreneurship.

The journey ahead is pregnant with potential—a canvas where historical wisdom and AI-driven foresight unite. The evolution of business remains an ongoing narrative, and emerging visionaries stand as its authors. As the final words of this exploration find their place, the story continues—with a generation poised to shape a future that transcends limitations, harnesses the legacy of giants, and propels itself forward on the wings of AI-driven innovation.

REFERENCES

Aaker, D. A. (1991). *Managing Brand Equity: Capitalizing on the Value of a Brand Name*. Free Press.

Burns, P. (2016). *Entrepreneurship and Small Business*. Macmillan International Higher Education. DOI: 10.1007/978-1-137-43034-2

Cachon, G. P., & Terwiesch, C. (2009). Matching Supply with Demand: An Introduction to Operations Management. McGraw-Hill/Irwin.

Chesbrough, H. (2003). *Open Innovation: The New Imperative for Creating and Profiting from Technology*. Harvard Business Press.

Christensen, C. M., & Raynor, M. E. (2003). *The Innovator's Solution: Creating and Sustaining Successful Growth*. Harvard Business Press.

Daft, R. L. (2017). *Organization Theory and Design*. Cengage Learning.

Davenport, T. H. (2000). *Mission Critical: Realizing the Promise of Enterprise Systems*. Harvard Business Press.

Dean, J., & Ghemawat, S. (2004). MapReduce: Simplified data processing on large clusters. In *6th Symposium on Operating System Design and Implementation (OSDI'04)*, San Francisco, CA, USA.

Dolnicar, S., Grün, B., Leisch, F., & Schmidt, K. (2020). Nature and Management of Airbnb Accommodation in Disruptive Times. *Current Issues in Tourism*, 23(13), 1602–1617.

Duan, W., Gu, B., & Whinston, A. B. (2008). The dynamics of online word-of-mouth and product sales—An empirical investigation of the movie industry. *Journal of Retailing*, 84(2), 233–242. DOI: 10.1016/j.jretai.2008.04.005

Duhigg, C. (2012). *The Power of Habit: Why We Do What We Do in Life and Business*. Random House.

Eisenmann, T. R. (2013). *HBS Case: Airbnb, Inc.* Harvard Business School Publishing.

Guttentag, D. (2015). Airbnb: Disruptive innovation and the rise of an informal tourism accommodation sector. *Current Issues in Tourism*, 18(12), 1192–1217. DOI: 10.1080/13683500.2013.827159

Hagendorff, T. (2020). The Ethics of AI Ethics. *Minds and Machines*, 30(1), 99–120. DOI: 10.1007/s11023-020-09517-8

Hamel, G. (2009). Moon shots for management. *Harvard Business Review*, 87(2), 91–98. PMID: 19266704

Leavy, B. (2018). Airbnb's Approach to Data Science, with Surabhi Gupta. Retrieved from https://www.airbnb.com/resources/hosting-homes/a/airbnbs-approach-to-data-science-with-surabhi-gupta-164

Li, G., & Fung, R. Y. (2008). A predictive model for stock market behavior using multiple classifiers. *Decision Support Systems*, 45(4), 834–851.

McAfee, A., & Brynjolfsson, E. (2017). *Machine, Platform, Crowd: Harnessing Our Digital Future*. W. W. Norton & Company.

Meadows, D. (2015). *Thinking in Systems: A Primer*. Chelsea Green Publishing.

Mourey, D. A., & Martin, I. M. (2017). Share a Coke: Brand personalization and the sharing economy. *Journal of Consumer Psychology*, 27(3), 397–405.

Neff, J. (2007). Coca-Cola Gets Boost from Juice Brands. *Advertising Age*.

O'Reilly, T. (2007). What Is Web 2.0: Design Patterns and Business Models for the Next Generation of Software. *Communications & Stratégies*, 65(1), 17–37.

Oskam, J., & Boswijk, A. (2016). Airbnb: The future of networked hospitality businesses. *Journal of Tourism Futures*, 2(1), 22–42. DOI: 10.1108/JTF-11-2015-0048

Page, L. (2017). What I learned at work this week: Google's social responsibility. Financial Times. Retrieved from https://www.ft.com/content/5dd0eb00-3b26-11e7-ac89-b01cc67cfeec

Quelch, J. A. (2020). *Greater Good: How Good Marketing Makes for Better Democracy*. Harvard Business Press.

Radinsky, K. (2012). Learning to predict from big data. *Proceedings of the ACM Web Science Conference*, Evanston, IL, USA.

Schmidt, E., & Rosenberg, J. (2014). *How Google Works*. Grand Central Publishing.

Smith, R. (2018). *The Growth Hacker's Guide to the Galaxy: 100 Proven Growth Hacks for the Digital Marketer*. Routledge.

Tucker, K. D., & Miller, V. D. (2013). Thinking about the future: Guidelines for strategic foresight. *Social Science Research*, 42(3), 617–628.

Tussyadiah, I. P., & Pesonen, J. (2016). Impacts of peer-to-peer accommodation use on travel patterns. *Journal of Travel Research*, 55(8), 1022–1040. DOI: 10.1177/0047287515608505

Weber, S. (2010). *The Success of Open Source*. Harvard University Press.

Werther, W. B.Jr, & Chandler, D. (2011). *Strategic Corporate Social Responsibility: Stakeholders in a Global Environment*. SAGE Publications.

Yoffie, D. B., & Kim, R. C. (2011). *Coca-Cola: Residual income valuation*. Harvard Business School.

Zervas, G., Proserpio, D., & Byers, J. W. (2016). The rise of the sharing economy: Estimating the impact of Airbnb on the hotel industry. *JMR, Journal of Marketing Research*, 54(5), 687–705. DOI: 10.1509/jmr.15.0204

Chapter 4
Optimizing Business Models in Entrepreneurship:
The Role of AI in Iterative Business Planning

Hewawasam P. G. D. Wijethilaka
 https://orcid.org/0009-0006-9611-5735
University of Colombo, Sri Lanka

Mohit Yadav
 https://orcid.org/0000-0002-9341-2527
O.P. Jindal Global University, India

Rohit Vij
 https://orcid.org/0000-0003-2977-9209
Lovely Professional University, India

ABSTRACT

This chapter explores the role of Artificial Intelligence (AI) in optimizing business models through iterative planning. As AI continues to advance, it offers entrepreneurs powerful tools for data-driven decision-making, enhancing customer insights, market segmentation, dynamic pricing, and resource allocation. The chapter examines key AI technologies such as machine learning, natural language processing, and AI-powered simulations, which enable continuous refinement and adaptation of business strategies. It also addresses challenges such as data privacy, AI transparency, potential biases, and the balance between automation and human intuition. Ethical considerations, including the responsible use of AI, are discussed to ensure

DOI: 10.4018/979-8-3693-1495-1.ch004

sustainable innovation. The chapter concludes by exploring future trends, including autonomous decision-making and the democratization of AI, emphasizing its potential to transform business models and drive long-term success.

INTRODUCTION

Introduction to AI in Entrepreneurship

Artificial Intelligence has now emerged as a transformative force in entrepreneurship. The new tools and insights are basically changing how business models are developed, tested, and optimized. The rise of AI brought about a paradigm shift from traditional, linear business planning processes to more dynamic, iterative approaches (Anastasia, 2023). In today's rapidly changing market environment, the drive for entrepreneurs to change their business models in order to cope with changing customer needs, emerging trends, and threats from competition intensifies. AI, therefore, has emerged as an important driver in this regard, enhancing organizational capacity through better processing of large volumes of data, generating actionable insights, and automating decision-making in real-time (Afshan et al., 2021).

The Role of AI in Modern Entrepreneurship

AI can be seen to evolve the role of entrepreneurship from conventional, often bound, and static timings of business planning. Conventionally, the entrepreneur would develop a business plan based on initial assumptions that become a blueprint to be executed. The fast tempo of modern times in the business environment makes those assumptions outdated rather quickly. AI solves that problem by allowing for a constant feedback loop such that the entrepreneurs could change their business models in real time. By applying machine learning algorithms, predictive analytics, and NLP, for instance, AI lets entrepreneurs gather and process data on consumer behavior, market trends, and competitive dynamics in real time (Sharna, 2019).

Historical Perspective: Traditional Business Planning Versus AI-Driven Iterative Planning

Business planning has conventionally been about creating a single, static plan as a result of market research, customer surveys, and assumptions regarding what the future market would be. The entrepreneur then presented these plans to investors, stakeholders, and teams as 'this is how we are going to be successful'. The problem is that this approach has several built-in limitations. Traditional business plans didn't easily adapt to rapid changes in the market or new opportunities. It was therefore not easy for the businesses to pivot or evolve with time as the situation dictates (Boldureanu et al., 2020).

This had been the more traditional approach up to the development of AI-driven iterative business planning. With AI, not only is ongoing adjustment possible, but business models can adjust in real-time data and feedback. Iterative planning has, however, become rather a cyclic process; new information keeps pouring into the model, and further modifications are informed by updated insights. It is now indeed an agile, adaptive planning process that provides a better framework for entrepreneurs going through today's volatile markets (Cantamessa et al., 2018).

Importance of Continuous Business Model Optimization

Now, continuous optimization is a necessary basis for successful entrepreneurship. AI has the pivotal role in enhancing an entrepreneur's opportunity to test and refine over time a business model. Deep insight into customer preference, automation of repetitive tasks, and predictions with high levels of accuracy about future trends are certain key features of AI. Iterative optimization of business models by using AI means showing more strategies and scenarios without covering high costs and risks associated with this classic trial-and-error approach (Chen & Biswas, 2021).

Also, the iterative approach compelled by AI makes entrepreneurs more responsive and aggressive to keep their business models aligned with prevailing market needs and competitive pressures. This flexibility, together with AI's predictive capabilities, creates a big competitive advantage for both startups and established businesses (Engidaw, 2022).

In brief, AI has become so important to today's entrepreneur that traditional business planning has iteratively become a dynamic, adaptive process in pursuit of continuous learning. This is fundamentally changing the way business operates and has the potential for great innovation, resilience, and long-term success (Fang, 2023).

ITERATIVE BUSINESS PLANNING

Iterative business planning refers to the dynamic refinement and evolution of a continuously changing business model in real time through active feedback, data analysis, and changes in the market. In contrast to traditional business planning, that relies on static, long-term assumptions and projections, iterative planning embraces flexibility and responsiveness. This approach allows for experimentation, testing of hypotheses, and tinkering with strategies as entrepreneurs gain new insights that reduce risk while enhancing success potential in turbulent environments. This concept works especially well in the present entrepreneurial environment with its high levels of uncertainty and disruption (Farayola, 2023).

Iterative Business Planning: Definition and Process

At the core, iterative business planning is a circular process, focused on small iterative changes of a business model over time. It starts with the development of a minimum viable product (MVP) or a minimally viable service offering. Using such a product, an entrepreneur iteratively tests the business model by introducing it into the market, gathering feedback from customers, and performance data analysis (Fitriah, 2024).

This information forms the basis for the second generation of the business plan, where necessary changes in product, service, price, or marketing strategy are made. Iteration moves the entrepreneurs onward and further refines the offerings and strategies as their best match to market requirements and overall performance (Hedman et al., 2016). Following is the major steps of the approach:

1. **Ideation and Planning:** There might be an idea or a hypothesis for the business, and the entrepreneur develops some preliminary ideas around business planning in which key elements could include a value proposition, target market, revenue model, and operational method.
2. **Testing and Data Collection:** Following the launch of the MVP, the entrepreneurs began to test their assumptions in the real market. AI-powered tools, customer surveys, and analytics platforms are being used to collect data on customer behavior and engagement, as well as market trends (Ikwue, 2023).
3. **Evaluation and analysis:** The entrepreneur, then, analyzes the data collected in view of observing what works, what does not work, and where adjustments have to be made. Large volumes of data can be processed using AI-driven tools, which would come up with predictive insight into future trends and help recognize the slipping of the current business model.
4. **Adaptation and Optimization:** The business model is adapted in view of the analysis. This might relate to changes in the product or service on offer, the addressable customer segment, pricing strategy, or even marketing strategy (Kalogiannidis, 2024).
5. **Re-iteration:** The new iteration of the business plan then gets thrown into the market, and the cycle continues. With each cycle, it helps the entrepreneurs, in a step-by-step manner, fine-tune their model and with each turn get that much closer to ideal for long-term success.

Comparison with Traditional Static Business Plans

Traditional business plans are based on static assumptions; long-term projections often never change. Such a plan would typically focus on predefined milestones that may take a number of years to achieve without any major change in the initial strategy. In fast-moving industries, these may become obsolete before they are fully executed (Patricia, 2021).

Iterative business planning, however, does not believe in a fixed roadmap but in its continuous revision with a view to maintaining agility and responsiveness of an entrepreneur to any changes in the marketplace. Indeed, flexibility is an important component of modern entrepreneurship, where technologies, consumer priorities, and competitive contexts are subject to constant fluctuations (Prasetyo et al., 2021).

While traditional plans may take several months to a year or two to develop and then go into implementation, an iterative approach creates a much more dynamic environment in which the feedback loops are shorter, therefore adjustments can be made more quickly at less cost. The entrepreneurs benefit from their opportunities to pivot rapidly and therefore enhance their possibilities for long-term sustainability (Rok & Kulik, 2020).

Role of Feedback Loops and Data-Driven Adjustments

Perhaps the most important part of iterative business planning is the feedback loop: constant data gathering, insight, and feedback from customers and others. Such loops are necessary in that they allow an entrepreneur to contrast their assumptions with actual conditions as well as with the preferences of their customers (Rudall, 2012). The shorter and leaner the feedback loop, the faster an entrepreneur can make data-driven adjustments to their business model.

AI tools are at the core of any properly constructed feedback loop. With its machine learning algorithms, predictive analytics, and real-time data processing, AI automates gathering data and its analysis to provide actionable insights throughout each iteration step. For instance, AI may track customer interactions, sales trends, and competitor activity to have businesses predict what future market demands will look like and orient their offerings toward those needs.

Data-driven adjustments actually enable the entrepreneur to move away from intuition-based decision-making to fact-based decision-making. Integrating AI into iterative planning will let the former optimize their business models for accurate, timely, and granular insights that reduce the chances of failure and heighten the chances of market success (Tak, 2024).

The Importance of Flexibility Within Iterative Business Planning

Iterative business planning buys a great deal of flexibility. One of the greatest strengths of iterative business planning lies in how it allows an entrepreneur to make quick pivots on their business model, when necessary, quickly capitalize on newly emerging opportunities, or surmount unforeseen challenges. For instance, if an MVP failed to resonate with the targeted audience, iterative planning can enable entrepreneurs rapidly to re-tweak the value proposition or retarget the audience by enhancing their products' features without scraping the entire business model (Tunio, 2020).

This will create an atmosphere of experimentation in which failure is not a point to regress back but one from which one learns and improves the model. It's a central mindset necessary for startups and new ventures that deal with markets where total uncertainty seems to be the only rule (Tunio et al., 2021). It's also opposite to rigid plans-a process where entrepreneurs can live a life of continuous learning, iteration, and growth (Tunio et al., 2021).

Iterative business planning provides an unbending, data-driven strategy for an entrepreneur to be responsive towards changes in the market, customer tastes, and competitive pressures. Embracing iteration helps the entrepreneur fine-tune his or her business model through continuous feedback and adjustment, thereby increasing his or her chances of long-term success within an unpredictable environment. As AI evolves day in and day out, so does its role in perfecting and enhancing iterative business planning; it will keep offering more effective tools for optimization of the business model (Tunio et al., 2023).

AI TECHNOLOGIES SHAPING BUSINESS MODEL OPTIMIZATION

Artificial Intelligence has become crucial for the optimization of business models as it facilitates entrepreneurs with advanced tools and techniques that enhance decision-making, improve customer interaction, and smoothen operations (Volkmann et al., 2019). These have revolutionized the way businesses adapt and thrive in an ever-changing market-from machine learning to predictive analytics, natural language processing, and AI-powered simulations. With AI at play, entrepreneurs can iteratively improve their business models based on data-driven decisions (Wu et al., 2019). This thus provides an enabling force for entrepreneurs to keep their companies agile and competitive. The following section discusses some of the most influential AI technologies driving forward the optimizations of business models. Some of them are as follows:

1. Machine Learning and Predictive Analytics

Machine learning is the core constituent of AI-powered optimization of a business model. This is a process of training algorithms to identify patterns from large datasets in order to predict or make a decision based on that data. Now, ML can be applied by entrepreneurs to fine-tune their business models in areas such as customer segmentation, refining price strategy, and prediction of future trends (Hain & Jurowetzki, 2020).

For instance, ML algorithms can parse volumes of customer data on purchase histories, browsing behavior, and social media interactions to come up with trends and predict future buying patterns. The information will allow businesses to personalize their marketing, make better product recommendations, and offer the right customers exactly the right offers-all stimuli toward better customer retention and increased sales. Besides, forecasting, driven by predictive analytics from ML, helps the entrepreneur estimate market trends and fluctuations in demand, whereupon necessary adjustments in supply chains, inventory, and marketing can be undertaken (Chung, 2023).

Machine learning and predictive analytics reduce laborious data analysis by automating them and provide real-time insights about the performance of a business concern to entrepreneurs. The speed and accuracy in decision-making become important in this fast-changing world of business, wherein the ability of any company to make a pivot and respond toward an emerging trend is all that makes the difference between success and failure.

2. Natural Language Processing (NLP) for Market Research and Customer Insights

Another AI in changing the face of business model optimization is natural language processing. This strand of AI makes machines understand human speech and interpret meanings from it; therefore, companies can analyze unstructured data about their customers-from customer reviews to posts on social media and any other feedback left online. This greatly helps entrepreneurs by providing valuable insights into the tastes, sensitivities, and expectations of customers in improving products, services, and overall customer experiences (Aldunate, et al., 2022).

NLP-powered tools automatically analyze texts that come in through the customers and extract all relevant information to summarize trends. As such, for instance, sentiment analysis tools use NLP to assess the emotional tone in every customer review, thus giving a business an understanding of how customers perceive the products or services it offers. This insight will give entrepreneurs even wiser decisions regarding product improvement strategies, customer service strategies, and marketing.

NLP can enhance customer engagement other than through market research by providing chatbots and virtual assistants with the ability to communicate in natural, conversational language with users. These AI-powered tools can manage queries from customers, offer suggestions, and guide them through buying, thus making the experience seamless and personal for customers. While customer satisfaction is achieved, response times are reduced, and NLP helps in optimizing the business model by enhancing customer relationship management (Akella et al., 2017).

3. AI-Powered Simulations and Scenario Analysis

AI-driven simulations will help entrepreneurs optimize their business models through trying out strategies and scenarios in a virtual no-risk environment. Such modeling will grant businesses a host of variables to experiment with, from pricing models to market conditions, supply chain configurations, and customer behaviors, thus being able to grasp how these variables are interconnected and affect outcomes (Usman et al., 2024).

This would involve something like running a simulation of launching a new product into various market conditions or determining how changes in supply chain management will affect operational efficiency. These simulations in predicting the probable impact of a decision before it has actually been carried out in real life reduces the risk associated with costly mistakes and makes the business model changes based on hard data.

AI-powered scenario analysis can also help a business predict external challenges, like economic contraction, shifts in regulation, or changes in consumer behavior. By modeling the different ways the future may unfold, entrepreneurs can take necessary steps to prepare for each of these scenarios and ensure their business models will be robust and relevant in view of uncertainty (Judijanto et al., 2022).

4. Automated Customer Segmentation and Personalization

Perhaps one of the most valuable ways in which AI informs business model optimization is through automating customer segmentation and personalization. AI-driven algorithms can analyze customer data at a granular level, segmenting based on demographics, purchasing behavior, preferences, and even psychographics. Such a level of segmentation by businesses would, therefore, enable them to craft highly targeted marketing campaigns, tailor their product offerings, and work toward improving customer retention (Chung, 2023).

Segmenting customers is not all; AI also allows personalized marketing and product recommendations. It uses machine learning algorithms to identify patterns from data on customer behavior and, using those insights, delivers customized recommendations-on a product suggestion on an e-commerce platform or some form of targeted marketing via email. This level of personalization further improves customer satisfaction and loyalty, hence driving revenue growth and enhancing the overall business model (Alves Gomes & Meisen, 2023).

AI also reduces manual intervention in personalization effort because it automatically readapts marketing strategies to different customer segments, making the scaling of personalization efforts less resource-intensive. Due to better customer targeting and engagement, AI optimizes a business for more efficiency and effectiveness.

5. Robotic Process Automation for Operational Efficiency

Robotic Process Automation, other than Machine Learning, is the other AI technology that is changing the face of business model optimization through improving operational efficiency. This is about software bots performing repetitions that shall free employees to perform other high-value activities, such as data entry, invoicing, and customer support. As a result, this is not just reducing operational costs but also increasing speed and accuracy in all operations, therefore improving overall performance in business (Bu et al., 2022).

With RPA, entrepreneurship is able to practically automate core business functions like accounting, supply chain, and human resources, enabling them to devote more time to reconfiguring operating models for optimum performance. In other words, automating administrative tasks in business means that it allows businesses to be more efficient with fewer human errors and scale operations without adding to staffing.

Besides task automation, RPA can be connected with AI-driven analytics tools that monitor and optimize operational processes in real time. For example, RPA may track supply chain performance and highlight bottlenecks to inform business decisions around increasing efficiency and reducing costs (Chung, 2023).

6. AI-Driven Decision-Making and Optimization Algorithms

AI optimization algorithms are another main technological support for business model optimization. It is aimed to help deal with complex business problems by way of analyzing large datasets and defining the best solution. Examples include working out the best pricing strategy, finding the most cost-effective supply chain routes, or distributing resources across departments more efficiently.

AI-powered decision-making tools go beyond providing insights to actually recommend decisions and automate their implementation. For instance, an AI could suggest the changing of a product's price based on current market conditions in real time, while at the same time automatically changing that price on all sale channels.

This level of automation allows entrepreneurs to immediately adapt to changes within their markets, allowing them to make business models agile and adaptive (Giuggioli & Pellegrini, 2023).

In the coming years, AI technologies, including machine learning, natural language processing, simulations, customer segmentation, RPA, and optimization algorithms, will continue to play a very important role in business model optimization. These technologies allow entrepreneurs to do something extremely crucial: make decisions fact-based, automate routine work, and test new strategies without taking a lot of risk. With AI, businesses can iterate over their business model continuously-second-guess constant evolution-continuously competitive, efficient, and set up toward evolving market needs. AI in iterative business planning fuels the speed and accuracy of decision-making, fosters innovation, and ensures long-term success.

OPTIMIZATION OF BUSINESS MODELS: KEY ASPECTS

Artificial intelligence is the number one driver of change in the way businesses approach model optimization, permitting the constant refinement and improvement of different aspects pertaining to entrepreneurial ventures. AI-driven tools let a business gather data, forecast trends, and make real-time adjustments-all building blocks of a resilient and adaptive business model. This section discusses key areas of business model optimization where AI can have a profound impact: customer insights and personalization, market segmentation, dynamic pricing, and resource allocation.

1. Customer Insights and Personalization

Perhaps the most profound part of business model optimization powered by AI is the deeper and more accurate customer insights it provides. Traditional market research, though useful, is many times constrained by limited sample sizes and subjective analysis. AI-powered tools, like machine learning and NLP, have the potential to analyze huge volumes of data derived from customer contacts, social networking sites, transaction history, and feedback forms in pursuit of meaning. This helps the business company understand their customers better regarding their preferences, behaviors, and pain points (Bhuiyan, 2024).

With AI's real-time analysis of the data concerning the customers, the entrepreneur identifies the trends that are emerging on the changes in the customers' needs. Refine your product offering through the enriching of customer service and tailored marketing effort with such information to make them more responsive and personalized to customers' experiences. For example, AI can be applied to e-commerce websites to offer product suggestions based on customers' purchase history or browsing history.

These forms of personalization increase customer satisfaction and enhance retention rates, key elements in the growth and success of a business.

Also, AI will help segment their customers more effectively for appropriate targeted marketing strategies, tailored to different customer groups. AI can analyze data to uncover hidden patterns in identifying micro-segments within the wide customer base, something rather difficult to achieve using manual analysis. This level of personalization will make interaction so much more engaging with the customers, thus assuring higher and increased conversions, along with brand loyalty (Chung, 2023).

2. Market Segmentation and Dynamic Pricing

The power of AI to analyze big datasets has opened the door for more granular market segmentation, presenting one of the key areas of optimization in today's business models. Traditionally, market segmentation consists of businesses dividing their customer base into broad segments based on certain demographics, location, or purchasing behaviors (Markula, 2023). This system works; however, this often overlooks subtle differences and changing consumer behaviors. AI can allow for the most acute forms of segmentation, which analyze not just several but hundreds of data points, while continuously updating customer profiles based on real-time interactions.

AI-powered segmentation tools can track not only demographic information, but also psychographic variables related to customers' values, interests, and lifestyles. With these insights in mind, businesses can draft hyper-targeted marketing campaigns that directly relate to the needs of their customer segments. This degree of personalization ensures the effective use of marketing resources, as well as a higher return on investment from marketing efforts (Chung, 2023).

Another area where AI is having a very strong impact is in dynamic pricing. Traditionally, businesses set prices statically related to fixed elements such as cost and the desired profit margin. This often does not capture the complexity of consumer demand and market conditions very well. On the other hand, dynamically priced items will be continuously changed in price by means of AI-navigated algorithms with respect to several factors such as the demand of their customers, competitors' prices, and inventory level, among others-even environmental ones like the weather or economic situation (Markula, 2023).

Dynamic pricing can, therefore, help the company ensure that its prices are pegged appropriately to create maximum revenue with decent profit margins. For example, AI can raise the prices during periods of high demand and reduce the prices in a lean season when sales can be sluggish. AI will also prevent any instances of underpricing or overpricing through continuous analysis of market conditions. This is of critical significance in ensuring flexibility for businesses to be able to stay ahead of the competitive curve in various markets.

3. Resource Utilization and Operational Efficiency

One of the key elements in attaining any kind of business enterprise is the issue of optimal resource allocation. Definitely, it is so obvious that AI has to play an important role in the optimization of resource allocation. Traditional business typically makes decisions with regard to resource allocation based on historical data, intuition, or simple methods of forecasting, one factor that brings inefficiency and lost opportunities. AI applies predictive power, thus enabling optimal resource allocation by analyzing real-time data for better forecasting of needs (Goswami, 2020).

AI-powered tools may be used for resource optimization, including inventories, labor, and capital. For instance, a supply chain management case can have AI make suggestions based on demand level fluctuations, supplier performance, and costs of logistics for the best quantity of inventories. This reduces the chances of a stock-out or overstock, which may have heavy financial consequences. AI can also improve warehouse management with automation, like order picking, packing, which reduces the labor cost and greatly enhances efficiency in operations.

Besides inventory management, AI can help optimize human resources allocation by predicting staffing needs based on business demands. For example, AI-driven workforce management systems can analyze historical data of sales, customer traffic, and seasonal trends to determine just the right number of people a business may need at any given time. This cuts down labor costs while ensuring that businesses are not under-staffed during peak periods (Kristian et al., 2024).

AI can also engage in capital allocation optimization by identifying those investment opportunities that yield returns. Machine learning algorithms analyze financial data, market trends, and risk factors to recommend where businesses should invest their capital for maximum returns. Be it in identifying new market opportunities, expansion of the line of products, or investing in new technologies, AI drives businesses to make smart, data-driven decisions over allocating financial resources.

4. Product Development and Innovation

AI can seriously expedite product development processes, thereby allowing businesses to get new products to market more rapidly and efficiently. This is because traditional product development has often utilized very long processes, which include conducting market research, making prototypes, and conducting tests-all of which can be awfully time-consuming and expensive. AI speeds up these processes by allowing business immediate feedback and insight into how it can improve products more rapidly (Klintong et al., 2012).

For instance, AI-enabled design tools can automate everything from prototype creation to the testing of several versions of a product in development. This grants businesses the ability to iterate rapidly, testing multiple variations of a product in search of the most compelling design. AI-driven data analysis can also highlight market gaps and even suggest new product ideas by mining both customer feedback and industry trends. This reduces the likelihood of product failure because companies are producing a product in demand in the market.

AI further leads to product innovation by letting business houses try out new ideas and concepts in a virtually risk-free environment. For instance, AI-powered simulations will enable companies to test different features of a product or various market scenarios before making any costly investments. These simulations give a good understanding to the businesses regarding how customers might react to the new products or their features and help make better decisions in the process of product development (Brem et al., 2021).

5. Optimizing Customer Service and Support

This also extends to improving customer service and support, whereby AI brings a remarkable degree of optimization to the company's business model. Companies can easily provide speedy and more efficient customer support by utilizing AI-driven technologies like chatbots, virtual assistants, and automated response systems, thereby reducing operation-related costs. AI-driven customer support systems are always available to provide immediate responses to customer inquiries, resolve issues, and address queries on a real-time basis with no human interference (Klintong et al., 2012).

In other words, letting automation take over routine requests for customer service gives human resources more time to attend to more complicated and value-based interactions with their consumers. For instance, common issues or areas of improvement can be determined by analyzing the support interaction of a customer through AI-powered support tools. Such analysis can be performed using sentiment analysis tools that will detect tones and emotion behind each and every customer inquiry; this will help businesses address complaints proactively with the intent of improving customer satisfaction.

It can also use AI to optimize customer service for personalized support. By analyzing all data on customers, the AI system personalizes responses and recommendations to the individual customers' preferences and history. It then creates a much more customized and satisfying experience for them. This level of service builds much-needed customer loyalty and strengthens the overall business model.

Now AI is turning major pages in business model optimization by facilitating the extraction of customer insight, fragmenting markets with high precision, carrying out dynamic pricing, optimizing resource utilization, and accelerating product development. Through the integration of AI in these facets, entrepreneurs make informed decisions which drive efficiency, customer satisfaction, and profitability. Where AI is still growing, its role will further increase in shaping agile, adaptive, and successful business models. New opportunities for innovation and competitive advantage will further open up (Klintong et al., 2012).

CHALLENGES AND ETHICAL CONSIDERATIONS

While Artificial Intelligence does have a lot of potential to optimize the business model, there are a number of challenges and ethical considerations which an entrepreneur should be able to handle with due care. These range from the technical and operational to the legal and ethical, all of which have to be addressed if the power of AI is to be leveraged responsibly and with full impact. Questions of data privacy, AI transparency, possible biases, and the balance between automation and human decision-making have great consequences for businesses and stakeholders alike. In this section, we will look into major challenges and ethical considerations while applying AI in business model optimization (Chung, 2023).

1. Data Privacy and Safety

The first significant challenge arising in the use of AI for the optimization of business models is that of data privacy. Artificial Intelligence systems operate on tremendous datasets, making them accurately predict and make recommendations. At times, collecting and processing such datasets may require scores of sensitive pieces of information from customers, employees, and other stakeholders. Such sensitive information includes personal names, contact details, financial data, purchasing behaviors, and browser histories. This data starts to have breaches due to some improper handling of such information and hence are very serious issues for a company (Holzinger et al., 2021). Laws like GDPR by the European Union and CCPA in the United States have made sure that companies maintain personal data according to set terms and conditions. Non-compliance with these regulations often leads to businesses facing huge fines, with severely damaged reputations. With AI-driven applications ranging from personalized marketing, customer segmentation, and predictive analytics, among others, entrepreneurs should ensure that their AI systems remain complaint with data privacy regulations by taking appropriate measures to ensure that data security is robust, explicit consent on data collection from customers is sought, and sensitive information is anonymized or encrypted so as to prevent unauthorized access.

Data security is imperative when AI has been inducted into business operations. AI-targeting cyber-attacks result in data integrity being compromised, and a business process can be disrupted. For all these reasons, a business should invest in advanced security technologies and protocols so that their AI systems would remain protected from any breach and also guarantee accuracy in the data that goes into the feeds.

2. AI Transparency and Accountability

Other important ethical considerations revolve around transparency and accountability. While AI systems are becoming increasingly complex, let alone autonomous, businesses struggle to explain how decisions have been arrived at based on non-transparent algorithms and machine learning models. The "black box" nature of AI has implications for business, let alone consumers, in terms of establishing why an AI system came up with a certain recommendation or decision (Ellahham et al., 2020).

Lack of transparency could raise ethical red flags, especially in industries such as finance, healthcare, and law, since decisions made by any one of these fields could have life-changing implications. For example, when an AI system denies a customer credit or insurance, a business is usually expected to provide explanations for reaching that particular decision. If this occurs without any level of transparency, then customers would feel AI systems are unfair or biased, and might even lose trust in the business.

Because of this challenge, AI should be transparent and accountable within an organization. This can be achieved through the adoption of "explainable AI" systems where the final decision of AI models becomes well-understood. Secondly, accountability practices should be established, such as human checks for major decisions that are very necessary, making sure AI is applied responsibly, and addressing adverse consequences of AI-driven decisions (Holzinger et al., 2021).

3. Potential Bias in AI Systems

The AI system is only as good as the training data it has received, and in case that training data harbors biases, the AI system will most probably propagate or even magnify such biases. This can become a domain of serious ethical concern in domains like hiring, lending, customer service, and marketing. This may be understood better by considering that, for example, if an AI recruitment tool is trained on past data that has gender or racial bias in it, then most definitely, it will favor certain groups over others unconsciously due to a discriminatory outcome.

AI bias can also emanate from the actual design of the algorithms themselves. Machine learning models may consider some features as more important than others; hence, this leads to predisposed decisions in favor or against some entities. An AI system deployed on dynamic pricing may often charge customers different prices based on their location, income level, or browsing history. This may be unfair and amount to discriminatory practices (Chung, 2023).

These biases can be overcome only if the business starts adapting to the ethics of AI by regular auditing of the AI systems to find out and eliminate the bias, using diverse and representative data sets, and making the developers aware of the sources of bias that may enter their algorithms. The human factor in judgment is also important in AI-driven processes for review and correction to ensure that AI operates within the bounds of ethics and fairness.

4. Finding an Equilibrium between Automation and Human Intuition

AI offers the potential to automate many business processes, from customer service and marketing to product development and decision-making. While automation can lead to increased efficiency and cost savings, it also raises concerns about the potential loss of human jobs and the diminished role of human intuition in decision-making.

But over-reliance on AI-driven automation reduces the need to engage human creativity, judgment, and emotional intelligence within business processes. While the customer service chatbot is effective at answering low-level questions, it performs poorly on higher-order challenges that require human judgment and empathy. Business strategy and decision-making become focused on the optimization of short-term profits or efficiency without considering the long-term ethical implications of certain actions (Holzinger et al., 2021).

What is required is a balance between automation and intuitive insight. Businesses must find out what tasks can be automated without losing that human touch and have to work on AI systems that enhance human capabilities, not replace them altogether. Wherever there is much creativity involved, or empathy, or complicated problems are to be solved, human input should remain central to decision-making.

5. Job Displacement and Economic Impact

As AI-driven automation advances, job displacement and its extended effects on the economy come into question. Although AI will replace most of the tasks that have traditionally been performed by human beings, in the years ahead many jobs could be declared redundant-essentially in manufacturing, retail, and customer service. Although AI could develop new opportunities in areas such as data science,

AI development, and management of technology, there is a risk that low-skilled or repetitive jobs could be disproportionately affected. This thus presents an ethical problem for companies in terms of how they are able to balance the acceptance of AI with responsibility toward workers who may be displaced by automation (Rawashdeh, (2023). It also entails investment in programs for the reskilling and upskilling of employees to transition them into new jobs that require an increasingly higher level of complexity and technical skill. These kinds of career development opportunities and training will position businesses to complement the adverse impact of AI on employment by better equipping the workforce for the future of work.

At the societal level, there is a requirement for coordination at the level of governments and businesses to develop policies and programs that address the economic and social ramifications created by the rise of pervasive automation. This might include investments in social safety nets, education, and re-skilling, and other factors that could promote job creation in emerging sectors (Rawashdeh, 2023).

6. Environmental Impact of AI

Another consideration is environmental impact caused by the AI technologies. Most AI systems, especially those driven by machine learning processes, require high computational resources and hence result in high consumption of energy, emitting carbon into the atmosphere. For instance, training large-scale machine learning models can use large amounts of electricity that further contribute to climate change and degradation of the environment (Wu et al., 2022).

While the enterprise is adopting AI technologies to optimize models and operations, it should also consider their environmental footprint. Ethical AI should focus on how AI saves energy because there is a minimized carbon footprint, efficient algorithms, renewable energy sources in data centers, and green AI technologies that set sustainability at the core.

The integration of AI into business model optimization encompasses a wide range of challenges and ethical considerations-from data privacy and transparency, via bias, automation, to environmental impact. Moreover, entrepreneurs should be fully aware of these challenges and proactive in taking steps to surmount them so that deployment can be affected responsibly and ethically (Ligozat et al., 2021). Businesses can draw dividends from AI by adhering to best practices such as Explainable AI, mitigation of bias, human oversight, and sustainable development of AI. This way, they will be able to maximize benefits from AI while minimizing potential risks and ethical dilemmas. Innovation, in concert with ethical responsibility, is going to be the main component in building trust and ensuring long-term success along the road of AI business model innovation.

FUTURE OF AI IN BUSINESS MODEL INNOVATION

Artificial Intelligence technologies are transforming business model innovation while enabling entrepreneurs and organizations to pursue unprecedented efficiency, process optimization, and creative advances. In fact, these AI technologies will continue to advance as their integration with business models deepens, and this will effectively lay the path for organizations to remain agile, responsive, and competitive within an increasingly complex, rapidly evolving global economy. Some of the important trends in which the future of AI in business model innovation is set includes autonomous decision-making systems, hyper-personalization, further collaborations between humans and machines, and increasing democratization of AI tools. Next, we investigate how these developments are going to shape the future of AI-powered business models.

1. Autonomous Decision-Making Systems and AI-Driven Strategy

Perhaps the most important single emerging trend in the future of AI and business model innovation is that of emergent, autonomous decision-making systems. As there continues to be a growing utilization of AI algorithms to analyze complex datasets, make predictions, and provide recommendations with greatly diminished human intervention, such systems are foreseen to continue evolving toward quasi-autonomous decision-making status within a host of functions in every business segment-from operation and supply chain management through to marketing and customer service (Garcia et al., 2023).

AI-driven systems in the coming years will have full autonomy from end-to-end business processes, right from product development to sales and customer engagement. For example, AI systems would automatically track market trends, negotiate price strategies, optimize inventory levels, and even make decisions on when and how to introduce new products, based on real-time data and predictive analytics. These range from the automatization of operations to enabling firms to respond promptly to changes in the market, thereby enhancing their competitiveness and agility. Other areas currently being transformed include AI-driven strategy: presently, the leadership depends on AI tools for insight and recommendations, while the ultimate decision-making remains with and for humans. With time, once the AI systems start becoming ingenious, the development and execution of strategic initiatives will lie completely with them. This will involve new business opportunities, reallocation of better resources, and the management of risks in ways that are much beyond human cognitive capabilities. With AI-driven strategy on the rise, decision-making will probably be more efficient and data-driven to help businesses stay ahead of their competitors by swiftly adapting to market disruptions and innovations.

2. Hyper-Personalization and the Customer-Centric Business Model

The future of AI in business model innovation will be characterized by hyper simplification-an amplified version of tailoring products, services, and customer experiences to the distinctive tastes, behaviors, and requirements of each customer. Equipped with AI that can process data volumes at scale in real time, businesses will have the capability to provide large-scale hyper-personalized experiences, making sure every customer gets precisely what they need at the time they want it (Bhuiyan, 2024).

AI-driven applications would continue to monitor and interpret consumer behavior, history, and preferences for personalized recommendations, targeted promotions, and offerings of customized products. As an example, AI-driven e-commerce recommendation engines will keep on getting finer with suggestions cross-platform analyzing customers' interactions in real time. The business stakeholders in retail, hospitality, and health care will be assisted by AI in crafting single offers of services, which will boost customer loyalty and provide a strategized approach towards higher conversion rates.

Also, hyper-personalization will reach beyond marketing and customer engagement into the very design of business models. In other words, companies will use AI more and more to make adaptive business models change for single customer needs. The result will include flexible pricing, personalized subscription models, and product development processes targeting specific requirements of customer segments (Bhuiyan, 2024).

3. Collaboration Between Humans and AI

Whereas AI is becoming more deeply integrated into business processes, in the future, humans and AI will work more in collaboration. This is not to replace the human workforce, but an increasing emphasis is put on the role of AI in enhancing human capabilities, thus creating a symbiotic relationship where humans and machines have to come up together to solve complex problems, create innovation, and drive growth (Wang et al., 2020).

AI will be a powerful tool in business model innovation, amplifying human imagination, decision-making, and problem-solving. For instance, AI can conduct more routine tasks, such as the analysis of big datasets, and thereby free human workers for more strategic and creative efforts: the design of new products, the development of innovative marketing campaigns, or the relationship with key stakeholders.

On top of this, AI-powered tools will enable C-suite executives to make better decisions faster because they are informed by real-time insight and scenario planning. Human-AI collaboration empowers executives to consider alternative strategic options and test potential risks, then provide solutions that are grounded in data. And as these AI tools continue to evolve, they will be much more intuitive and user-friendly, accessible to employees at every level throughout the organization, not just to data scientists and technologists (Wang et al., 2020).

It will also act as a driver of change in organizational structure. Organizations in the future will most likely use more decentralized models, pushing decision-making down into the teams, supplemented by AI insights. AI systems will enable such teams with information for quicker and better decision-making, thus granting them higher agility and responsiveness.

4. AI-Enhanced Innovation and New Business Models

In the future, AI will move from just being an optimizer of existing business processes to enabling new business models. The predictive and analytics capability of AI opens up more opportunities for innovation, facilitating an exploration of untapped markets, the creation of disruptive products, and novel service delivery mechanisms.

For example, AI-enabled platforms offering products "as-a-service" will rise further. Companies can, in this respect, be ensured that the strategic potential of AI enables subscription-based or pay-per-use services in place of outright sales of products. The AI systems track usage of the product and develop pricing and delivery models for real-time data to customers. This approach simultaneously creates business models that are more flexible and accessible while improving customer loyalty-the company's incentives are fully aligned with the value it creates for its customers (Pfau & Rimpp, 2021).

AI will also fuel innovation in industries ranging from health care and finance to education, through new products and services which hitherto could not be imagined. In health care, AI could give personalized treatment plans based on an individual's genetic profile and medical history. For example, in finance, AI-driven robo-advisors already offer individualized investment strategies based on one's risk profile, while in education, AI may build adaptive learning platforms so that the curriculum would be tailor-made to each student according to his strengths and weaknesses, offering a much more personalized learning experience.

AI will further incentivize the development of more collaborative and platform-oriented models where various stakeholders can interact with one another and co-create value. For example, AI-powered platforms will be able to bring together businesses, customers, and service providers in real time and enable them to work seamlessly with one another to produce new value. Such platforms would utilize AI in matching supply and demand, optimizing resource allocation, and unlocking new sources of value for the benefit of all participants.

5. Democratization of AI - Access to Innovation

But one of the biggest reasons to get excited about the future of AI in business model innovation is this: democratization of AI technologies. As the costs decrease, AI technologies will be much more approachable and much easier to use. In this way, AI can be incorporated into the business model regardless of the size of the company-from startups to large enterprises. In other words, democratization of AI will level out the playing field. Smaller businesses and entrepreneurs will have the opportunity to compete with bigger, more established companies.

Public cloud-based AI services and platforms currently make advanced AI tools available to businesses without any major upfront investment in infrastructure or expertise. In the future, these platforms will go a step further by extending their offerings to include plug-and-play AI solutions that can be easily tailored to meet the needs of different businesses. This democratization of AI will drive innovation across industries, with more entrepreneurs and small businesses gaining access to the tools that optimize business models and foster growth.

Besides this, open-source AI frameworks and collaborative development environments can help companies build and adapt their own AI solutions, which will open up new frontiers of innovation. The access to state-of-the-art AI technologies will enable businesses to test novel business models and hypotheses and do rapid iterations without having to invest a lot of capital in operations (Sudmann, 2019).

6. Ethics and Responsible AI in Business Innovation

In the future, as AI is going to shape business models, increasing importance will be given to ethical usage of AI technologies. Every organization will have to make sure that its AI systems are more transparent, accountable, and unbiased. Ethical AI is going to be one of the major differentiators for businesses, as customers and stakeholders will want responsible usage of AI more and more.

In the time to come, businesses will invest in XAI systems that will furnish understandable explanations for their decisions. Additionally, AI governance frameworks will be established that make sure AI systems are designed and deployed with respect to data privacy, fairness, and transparency. Companies that can make ethics a part of their AI practices will avoid associated regulatory and reputational risks and build a relation of trust with customers, employees, and investors to assure long-term success (Herrmann, 2023).

The future of AI in the business model will be transformative, offering unparalleled opportunities for growth, efficiency, and creativity for businesses. In sum, self-directed decision-making systems, hyper-personalization, human-AI collaboration, and democratization of access to AI tools-the whole framework of enterprise-could never be imagined without such a breakthrough. Yet, because AI technologies are still evolving, the ethical considerations with respect to AI must also be addressed concurrently by businesses so that innovation will be done responsibly and sustainably. This thoughtful and strategic embracing of AI will let business unlock new levels of innovation and foster long-term success in the future economy.

CONCLUSION

In the final analysis, AI has grown to be an absolute tool in the field of business model optimization, enabling entrepreneurs and organizations to enhance their efficiency in decision-making and adapting to a dynamic market that is very practically changing every day. As AI technologies continue to advance, integration within business strategies will be deeper, entailing autonomous decision-making, hyper-personalization, and new forms of human-AI collaboration. Advances in these areas will cut through not only processes but also open up new avenues for business model innovation that will enable companies to take business into hitherto unexplored markets and create much more flexible, customer-oriented approaches. But with every opportunity comes great challenges and ethical issues. After all, data privacy, AI transparency, and probable bias are issues that must be addressed if AI-driven innovation is to be made responsible and sustainable. Businesses that act more ethically and implement AI that is explainable and accountable build customer and stakeholder trust, positioning them for long-term success. In this respect, this will be an ability of AI to democratize its usage and continue transforming businesses of all sizes into a more competitive and innovative entrepreneurial landscape. The future of AI in business model innovation is bright; it promises exciting possibilities and great responsibility for companies that want to lead in the digital economy.

REFERENCES

Afshan, G., Shahid, S., & Tunio, M. N. (2021). Learning experiences of women entrepreneurs amidst COVID-19. *International Journal of Gender and Entrepreneurship*, 13(2), 162–186. DOI: 10.1108/IJGE-09-2020-0153

Akella, K., Venkatachalam, N., Gokul, K., Choi, K., & Tyakal, R. (2017). Gain customer insights using NLP techniques. *SAE International Journal of Materials and Manufacturing*, 10(3), 333–337. DOI: 10.4271/2017-01-0245

Aldunate, Á., Maldonado, S., Vairetti, C., & Armelini, G. (2022). Understanding customer satisfaction via deep learning and natural language processing. *Expert Systems with Applications*, 209, 118309. DOI: 10.1016/j.eswa.2022.118309

Alves Gomes, M., & Meisen, T. (2023). A review on customer segmentation methods for personalized customer targeting in e-commerce use cases. *Information Systems and e-Business Management*, 21(3), 527–570. DOI: 10.1007/s10257-023-00640-4

Anastasia, O. (2023). Mediating effects of entrepreneurship education on personality dimensions and venture creation of Nigerian graduates: An empirical approach. *Journal of Economics Management & Business Administration*, 2(1), 15–28. DOI: 10.59075/jemba.v2i1.235

Bhuiyan, M. S. (2024). The role of AI-enhanced personalization in customer experiences. *Journal of Computer Science and Technology Studies*, 6(1), 162–169. DOI: 10.32996/jcsts.2024.6.1.17

Boldureanu, G., Ionescu, A., Bercu, A., Bedrule-Grigoru ă, M., & Boldureanu, D. (2020). Entrepreneurship education through successful entrepreneurial models in higher education institutions. *Sustainability (Basel)*, 12(3), 1267. DOI: 10.3390/su12031267

Brem, A., Giones, F., & Werle, M. (2021). The AI digital revolution in innovation: A conceptual framework of artificial intelligence technologies for the management of innovation. *IEEE Transactions on Engineering Management*, 70(2), 770–776. DOI: 10.1109/TEM.2021.3109983

Bu, S., Jeong, U. A., & Koh, J. (2022). Robotic process automation: A new enabler for digital transformation and operational excellence. *Business Communication Research and Practice*, 5(1), 29–35. DOI: 10.22682/bcrp.2022.5.1.29

Cantamessa, M., Gatteschi, V., Perboli, G., & Rosano, M. (2018). Startups' roads to failure. *Sustainability (Basel)*, 10(7), 2346. DOI: 10.3390/su10072346

Chen, Y., & Biswas, M. (2021). Turning crisis into opportunities: How a firm can enrich its business operations using artificial intelligence and big data during COVID-19. *Sustainability (Basel)*, 13(22), 12656. DOI: 10.3390/su132212656

Chung, D. (2023). Machine learning for predictive model in entrepreneurship research: Predicting entrepreneurial action. *Small Enterprise Research*, 30(1), 89–106. DOI: 10.1080/13215906.2022.2164606

Ellahham, S., Ellahham, N., & Simsekler, M. C. E. (2020). Application of artificial intelligence in the health care safety context: Opportunities and challenges. *American Journal of Medical Quality*, 35(4), 341–348. DOI: 10.1177/1062860619878515 PMID: 31581790

Engidaw, A. (2022). Small businesses and their challenges during COVID-19 pandemic in developing countries: In the case of Ethiopia. *Journal of Innovation and Entrepreneurship*, 11(1), 1. Advance online publication. DOI: 10.1186/s13731-021-00191-3 PMID: 35036286

Fang, J. (2023). Research on the design of business models and transformation management of new entrepreneurial ventures driven by artificial intelligence. *BCP Business & Management*, 49, 36–41. DOI: 10.54691/bcpbm.v49i.5383

Farayola, O.Oluwatoyin Ajoke FarayolaAdekunle Abiola AbdulBlessing Otohan IraborEvelyn Chinedu Okeleke. (2023). Innovative business models driven by AI technologies: A review. *Computer Science & IT Research Journal*, 4(2), 85–110. DOI: 10.51594/csitrj.v4i2.608

Fitriah, A. (2024). The relationship of entrepreneurship education and entrepreneurial motivation to entrepreneurial innovation through entrepreneurial mindset as an intervening variable in vocational school students in Mojokerto. *East Asian Journal of Multidisciplinary Research*, 2(12), 5021–5034. DOI: 10.55927/eajmr.v2i12.6870

Garcia, A., & Adams, J. (2023). Data-driven decision making: Leveraging analytics and AI for strategic advantage. *Research Studies of Business*, 1(02), 77–85.

Giuggioli, G., & Pellegrini, M. M. (2023). Artificial intelligence as an enabler for entrepreneurs: A systematic literature review and an agenda for future research. *International Journal of Entrepreneurial Behaviour & Research*, 29(4), 816–837. DOI: 10.1108/IJEBR-05-2021-0426

Goswami, M. J. (2020). Leveraging AI for cost efficiency and optimized cloud resource management. *International Journal of New Media Studies: International Peer Reviewed Scholarly Indexed Journal*, 7(1), 21–27.

Hain, D. S., & Jurowetzki, R. (2020). The promises of machine learning and big data in entrepreneurship research. In *Handbook of Quantitative Research Methods in Entrepreneurship* (pp. 176–220). Edward Elgar Publishing. DOI: 10.4337/9781786430960.00014

Hedman, J., Sarker, S., & Veit, D. (2016). Digitization in business models and entrepreneurship. *Information Systems Journal*, 26(5), 419–420. DOI: 10.1111/isj.12119

Herrmann, H. (2023). What's next for responsible artificial intelligence: A way forward through responsible innovation. *Heliyon*, 9(3), e14379. Advance online publication. DOI: 10.1016/j.heliyon.2023.e14379 PMID: 36967876

Holzinger, A., Weippl, E., Tjoa, A. M., & Kieseberg, P. (2021, August). Digital transformation for sustainable development goals (SDGs)—A security, safety and privacy perspective on AI. In *International cross-domain conference for machine learning and knowledge extraction* (pp. 1-20). Cham: Springer International Publishing. DOI: 10.1007/978-3-030-66151-9_1

Ikwue, U., Eyo-Udo, N. L., Onunka, O., Ekwezia, A. V., Nwankwo, E. E., & Daraojimba, C. (2023). Entrepreneurship: Scalability strategies in entrepreneurial ventures: A comprehensive literature review. *Agricultural Extension & Development Countries*, 1(2), 78–88. DOI: 10.26480/aedc.02.2023.78.88

Judijanto, L., Asfahani, A., Bakri, A. A., Susanto, E., & Kulsum, U. (2022). AI-supported management through leveraging artificial intelligence for effective decision making. *Journal of Artificial Intelligence and Development*, 1(1), 59–68. DOI: 10.3390/ai.v1n1.5

Kalogiannidis, S., Kalfas, D., Papaevangelou, O., Giannarakis, G., & Chatzitheodoridis, F. (2024). The role of artificial intelligence technology in predictive risk assessment for business continuity: A case study of Greece. *Risks*, 12(2), 19. DOI: 10.3390/risks12020019

Klintong, N., Vadhanasindhu, P., & Thawesaengskulthai, N. (2012, February). Artificial intelligence and successful factors for selecting product innovation development. In *2012 Third International Conference on Intelligent Systems Modelling and Simulation* (pp. 397-402). IEEE. DOI: 10.1109/ISMS.2012.86

Kristian, A., Goh, T. S., Ramadan, A., Erica, A., & Sihotang, S. V. (2024). Application of AI in optimizing energy and resource management: Effectiveness of deep learning models. *International Transactions on Artificial Intelligence*, 2(2), 99–105. DOI: 10.33050/italic.v2i2.530

Ligozat, A. L., Lefèvre, J., Bugeau, A., & Combaz, J. (2021). Unraveling the hidden environmental impacts of AI solutions for the environment. *arXiv preprint arXiv:2110.11822*.

Markula, A. (2023). The use of artificial intelligence in dynamic pricing strategies. *Pricing Studies Review Journal*, 21(3), 34–56.

Patricia, E. (2021). Value proposition design. https://doi.org/DOI: 10.31219/osf.io/kpd3b

Pfau, W., & Rimpp, P. (2021). AI-enhanced business models for digital entrepreneurship. In *Digital Entrepreneurship: Impact on Business and Society* (pp. 121-140). Springer International Publishing. DOI: 10.1007/978-3-030-53914-6_7

Prasetyo, P., Setyadharma, A., & Kistanti, N. (2021). The collaboration of social entrepreneurship and institutions for sustainable regional development security. *Open Journal of Business and Management*, 9(5), 2566–2590. DOI: 10.4236/ojbm.2021.95141

Rawashdeh, A. (2023). The consequences of artificial intelligence: An investigation into the impact of AI on job displacement in accounting. *Journal of Science and Technology Policy Management*. https://doi.org/DOI: 10.1108/JSTPM-02-2023-0031

Rok, B., & Kulik, M. (2020). Circular start-up development: The case of positive impact entrepreneurship in Poland. *Corporate Governance (Bradford)*, 21(2), 339–358. DOI: 10.1108/CG-01-2020-0043

Rudall, Y. (2012). Business model generation. *Kybernetes*, 41(5/6), 823–824. DOI: 10.1108/03684921211261761

Sharma, A. (2019, November). Entrepreneurship and role of AI. In *Proceedings of the 2019 2nd International Conference on Signal Processing and Machine Learning* (pp. 122-126). IEEE. DOI: 10.1145/3372806.3374910

Sudmann, A. (2019). The democratization of artificial intelligence: Net politics in the era of learning algorithms. *Transcript*, 45(2), 78–92. DOI: 10.14361/ai.v45n2.56

Tak, A., & Chahal, S. (2024). Sprint planning and AI/ML: How to balance iterations with data complexity. *Journal of Technology and Systems*, 6(2), 56–72. DOI: 10.47941/jts.1817

Tunio, M. N. (2020). Role of ICT in promoting entrepreneurial ecosystems in Pakistan. [JBE]. *Journal of Business Ecosystems*, 1(2), 1–21. DOI: 10.4018/JBE.2020070101

Tunio, M. N., Chaudhry, I. S., Shaikh, S., Jariko, M. A., & Brahmi, M. (2021). Determinants of the sustainable entrepreneurial engagement of youth in a developing country—An empirical evidence from Pakistan. *Sustainability (Basel)*, 13(14), 7764. DOI: 10.3390/su13147764

Tunio, M. N., Jariko, M. A., Børsen, T., Shaikh, S., Mushtaque, T., & Brahmi, M. (2021). How entrepreneurship sustains barriers in the entrepreneurial process—A lesson from a developing nation. *Sustainability (Basel)*, 13(20), 11419. DOI: 10.3390/su132011419

Tunio, M. N., Shaikh, E., Katper, N. K., & Brahmi, M. (2023). Nascent entrepreneurs and challenges in the digital market in developing countries. *International Journal of Public Sector Performance Management*, 12(1-2), 140–153. DOI: 10.1504/IJPSPM.2023.132244

Usman, F. O., Eyo-Udo, N. L., Etukudoh, E. A., Odonkor, B., Ibeh, C. V., & Adegbola, A. (2024). A critical review of AI-driven strategies for entrepreneurial success. *International Journal of Management & Entrepreneurship Research*, 6(1), 200–215. DOI: 10.51594/ijmer.v6i1.748

Volkmann, C., Fichter, K., Klofsten, M., & Audretsch, D. (2019). Sustainable entrepreneurial ecosystems: An emerging field of research. *Small Business Economics*, 56(3), 1047–1055. DOI: 10.1007/s11187-019-00253-7

Wang, D., Churchill, E., Maes, P., Fan, X., Shneiderman, B., Shi, Y., & Wang, Q. (2020, April). From human-human collaboration to human-AI collaboration: Designing AI systems that can work together with people. In *Extended abstracts of the 2020 CHI conference on human factors in computing systems* (pp. 1–6). ACM., DOI: 10.1145/3334480.3381069

Wu, C. J., Raghavendra, R., Gupta, U., Acun, B., Ardalani, N., Maeng, K., & Hazelwood, K. (2022). Sustainable AI: Environmental implications, challenges, and opportunities. *Proceedings of Machine Learning and Systems*, 4, 795–813. DOI: 10.48550/arXiv.2110.12044

Wu, Y., Chen, S., & Pan, C. (2019). Entrepreneurship in the internet age. *International Journal on Semantic Web and Information Systems*, 15(4), 21–30. DOI: 10.4018/IJSWIS.2019100102

Chapter 5
Automating Routine Tasks to Improve Entrepreneurial Productivity

Shivani Dhand
https://orcid.org/0000-0002-4809-1365
Lovely Professional University, India

Sandeep Kumar Singh
https://orcid.org/0000-0002-1741-7254
O.P. Jindal Global University, India

Thi Mai Le
https://orcid.org/0000-0001-9720-308X
Vietnam National University, Hanoi, Vietnam

ABSTRACT

This chapter explores the transformative impact of Artificial Intelligence (AI) on business automation, focusing on how AI technologies enhance entrepreneurial productivity and decision-making. It examines key trends such as hyper-automation, which integrates AI tools to streamline entire workflows, and AI-driven personalization that tailors customer experiences. The chapter also addresses future advancements, including autonomous supply chains and AI-augmented decision-making systems, which promise to further revolutionize business operations. Challenges such as ethical considerations, workforce adaptation, and sustainability are discussed to provide a comprehensive view of the evolving landscape. By leveraging AI, entrepreneurs can automate routine tasks, make data-driven decisions, and drive strategic growth,

DOI: 10.4018/979-8-3693-1495-1.ch005

positioning themselves for success in a rapidly changing business environment.

INTRODUCTION

Artificial Intelligence integrated into the entrepreneurial landscape has transformed the way businesses operate, innovate, and attain scale. Many entrepreneurs are still stuck with the daily grind of running a business, which draws time away from higher-order activities such as strategic planning, innovation, and growth initiatives. AI has come to mitigate this burden by automating tasks that are repetitive in nature, hence increasing operation efficiency and enhancing productivity. With AI, entrepreneurs can iron out workflows and reduce tedious hours of manual work, leaving one room to drive the business forward with high gear. More particularly, this transformation has been propelled by increased availability and sophistication of tools powered by AI (Giuggioli, 2023). From smart chatbots answering customer queries to sophisticated algorithms in charge of inventory control, AI can automate tasks once laborious and riddled with human error. These tools empower businesses, particularly SMEs, to work efficiently at a level reserved for much larger companies in the past. Be it scheduling meetings, automating marketing campaigns, or even financial transactions, AI performs day-to-day activities to free up an entrepreneur's time, which then can be utilized in the most creative problem-solving and making major strategic decisions. These benefits of AI-based automation go way beyond simple task management and give a serious boost to productivity, enabling entrepreneurs to do more with less (Agarwal et al., 2020). Automation reduces the psychic load that a business owner will take on board because much of his mental capacity can be utilized for more vital aspects such as researching the market, product development, and maintaining good relations with customers. AI also allows an entrepreneur to scale the operations more rightly because the automated systems do not require adding to the manpower proportionately with an increase in workload. This saves not only time but also saves on operational costs, hence giving a way to startups and other small businesses to grow more comfortably and survive in the competition created by big firms.

Besides, this AI capability to analyze vast volumes of data and information in record time gives an entrepreneur useful insight, which could be the basis for making business decisions s (Chen et al., 2012). AI tools identify trends in customer behavior and can even suggest what procedures are needed for optimization to empower the entrepreneur to make data-driven decisions. This is important in the present business scenario, where businesses need to be agile to meet every fluctuation in the market. By counting on AI for routine activities, entrepreneurs respond more quickly to changes in the market or new opportunities that emerge.

Meanwhile, the integration of AI in entrepreneurship does not come without challenges. For entrepreneurs, the ground for decision-making has to be prior informed by a plethora of tools and platforms on AI, many of which require serious investments both in terms of time and financial input. While AI may automate many tasks, it is not a replacement for human intuition, creativity, and leadership (Alshareef & Tunio, 2022). Business owners would have to strike a balance between automating and overseeing at a personal level so that the human touches remain high in their business, especially in areas like customer service and team management.

In short, AI affords a fantastic avenue for entrepreneurs by enhancing operational efficiency and unleashing productivity through the automation of routine tasks (Choi et al., 2018). The ability of AI to streamline operations, reduce costs, and provide actionable insights cements its position as a critical asset in the modern entrepreneurial toolkit. As these AI technologies continue to evolve, so too will the ways in which they may transform businesses and afford entrepreneurs new ways of achieving success in an ever-increasingly competitive marketplace.

IDENTIFYING ROUTINE TASKS IN ENTREPRENEURSHIP

In entrepreneurship, the routine work is the must one undertakes in business; however, it's so time and energy consuming that could be used to devise a strategy for growth and innovation. These repetitive activities, though crucial to running operations, become a bottleneck to productivity when not managed properly. The identification of these tasks marks the initial step in the journey of optimizing business processes by making them more efficient with automation (Agarwal et al., 2020). Entrepreneurs have to identify the areas of their operations that are most plagued by manual and routine activities so that they can effectively exploit AI. Probably the most common routine task in entrepreneurship is administrative work: scheduling meetings, managing and answering e-mails, or coordinating calendars. An entrepreneur actually spends much time arranging appointments, following up with clients, or coordinating with his teams. This is time that could be better utilized for core business functions like product development or market strategy. AI-powered tools can simplify such procedures through virtual assistants or smart scheduling software, which automate calendar management, send reminders, and handle appointment requests, all while performing schedules for maximum efficiency.

Another big category of routine tasks involves financial management. This includes generating invoices, managing payroll, processing payments, and maintaining financial records. For many business owners, cash flow control and timely receipting are critical to the very survival of the business. Additionally, these tasks are very time-consuming if performed manually and prone to a lot of mistakes. Fortunately,

AI-driven accounting software automates much of this, from creating invoices right through to bank reconciliations, with fewer opportunities for mistakes and allowing the business to function correctly.

Routine tasks also arise in customer service. The majority of small businesses and startups suffer from a lack of customer inquiries, feedback, and support requests, which worsen over time as the company starts scaling up. Other examples that could be included are answers to frequently asked questions, basic issue resolution, and updates about orders; these can be a flood of work a small team can hardly bear. AI chatbots and automated customer service platforms handle all the regular interactions: They answer frequent queries and route the difficult ones to human agents. This enables timely customer support, whereby entrepreneurs and teams can invest their time in higher-order strategies for customer engagement.

Since customer support is not the only routine task that marketing entails, entrepreneurs work on marketing campaigns, maintain social media platforms, and track key metrics that show audience engagement. These mundane and repetitive tasks, like scheduling social media posts or sending newsletters, even go down to basic analysis in campaign performance, eat up quite a bit of precious time. That's where AI-powered marketing tools come in-helping with automating functions, enabling entrepreneurs to set up campaigns that literally work on autopilot mode, giving real-time insights into their effectiveness (Zhou, 2020).

Last but not least, there is inventory management and supply chain logistics-the usual routine tasks associated with product-oriented businesses. An entrepreneur needs to keep track of the level of stock, place orders for supplies, and attend to timely delivery. If done manually, the whole process can become inefficient and may result in overstocking or running out of inventory. An AI tool will automate inventory tracking, predict demand, and optimize supply chain operations so that businesses run smoothly with minimal scope for oversight (Dastin, 2022).

Basically, the identification of routine tasks in entrepreneurship is key to enhancing operational efficiency. Automation will lighten the burden of repetitive tasks mainly felt in administrative work, bookkeeping, customer service, marketing, and inventory control (Davenport & Harris, 2007). The identification of such and further introduction of AI-driven solutions will definitely enable entrepreneurs to free some time for innovation and strategic growth, thereby enhancing the productivity of the individual and competitive advantage.

AI TOOLS FOR AUTOMATING ROUTINE TASKS

Among entrepreneurs, productivity coupled with operational efficiency is something highly desirable; hence, AI tools have become quite helpful for them in automating routine tasks. The tools smoothen the day-to-day operations and therefore enable business owners to pay more attention to higher-value activities involving strategy, innovation, and customer relationships. By automating mundane tasks related to scheduling, customer support, and management of data, AI tools save time and reduce errors, hence improving overall business performance. It considers different types of entrepreneurship tools with AI embedded in them, which can automatically perform tasks such as routine ones. This section discusses their functionality and contribution to business processes at great length.

1. Virtual Assistants and Smart Scheduling Tools

Among the very basic problems that any entrepreneur faces are effective time management. Virtual assistants, now with the power of AI, have begun to find wide applications in automating time-consuming administrative tasks such as meeting scheduling, email management, and reminding. Nowadays, virtual assistants perform daily tasks for an entrepreneur on the basis of voice commands and their intelligent automation features. The virtual assistant harmonizes the calendars, schedules appointments, and can even do so by responding to routine emails, really minimizing the time spent on such activities.

Besides virtual assistants, other smart scheduling tools, like Calendly and Acuity Scheduling, automate meeting coordination by allowing appointments to be set for oneself and one's team according to real-time availability. These tools eliminate the back-and-forth email exchanges that often accompany scheduling, making the process seamless and efficient. They also integrate with email platforms, send automated reminders, and optimize schedules to minimize overlaps or gaps.

2. AI-Powered Accounting and Financial Tools

While business financial management is very significant for the maximization of profits, a great chunk of the work involves mundane tasks that are quite easily automatable. AI accounting tools help Forbes' entrepreneurs automate various business processes, such as creating invoices, managing payroll, tracking expenses, and reconciling financial statements. Using tools such as QuickBooks, Xero, and FreshBooks, most of the financial procedures will be automated, with minimal data input from an individual, thereby reducing human error to a great level.

AI-powered financial tools further enable real-time tracking of business expenses and cash flow. They provide predictive insight into future financial trends and, thus, help entrepreneurs make better decisions. For example, Zoho Books, using AI features, categorizes expenses, automates invoicing, and projects cash flow. In that case, an entrepreneur could focus more on strategic financial planning rather than bear the administrative burden of day-to-day bookkeeping.

3. AI Chatbots for Customer Automation

Customer service is something very crucial for any business. However, it encompasses a lot of repetition in doing the work, like answering frequently asked questions and solving basic issues. AI chatbots are designed for customer automation, examples being Intercom, Drift, and Zendesk. They handle routine inquiries and instant responses while escalating more complex issues to human agents when needed.

This means these chatbots can easily do customer support round the clock, reduce response velocity, and thus improve customer satisfaction. Automation through AI chatbots saves precious time both for the entrepreneur and his teams by automating queries like frequent answers, product recommendations, and product returns. These tools are learning at each interaction and also keep upskilling continuously to effectively respond to customer requirements and provide personalized service.

4. AI-Powered Marketing Tools

Other than that, marketing also falls into one of the departments where automation can increase efficiency fivefold. Many entrepreneurs need to manage various marketing channels, track campaign performance, and interconnect with customers on social media sites. AI-driven marketing tools automate all mundane jobs that involve content scheduling, email campaigns, and audience segmentation, allowing entrepreneurs to focus on the more strategic part of marketing.

These companies run email marketing campaigns, schedule social media posts, and segment their customers using AI. Such tools analyze customer behavior, identifying the best times of posting for a piece of content and optimizing marketing messages for various segments of audiences. Additionally, numerous AI-driven analytics tools, such as Google Analytics and Sprout Social, allow real-time insight into campaign performance and let entrepreneurs make truly data-driven marketing decisions.

It also plays a huge role in content creation and curation. Tools like Copy.ai and Jasper use AI to write marketing copy, blog posts, and even social media content. These tools help reduce the time used up for content development by extending an easy way for entrepreneurial marketing teams to create consistent online content and engage with their target audience-not bogged down with manual tasks of marketing. Therefore, by using technology, creativity and innovation can be carried out to a full fill.

5. AI for Data Management and Analytics

Data analytics and management can be key to making informed business decisions, and in many cases, data collection, organization, and interpretation can be very time-consuming. AI-driven data management tools, such as Tableau, Power BI, and Klipfolio, automate the process of data aggregation, visualization, and analysis, thus further enabling entrepreneurs to derive actionable insights from big chunks of data with little effort.

Such tools allow the automation of incoming data from various channels, like customer interactions, sales transactions, and traffic flow on websites. These tools generate reports that provide insight into business performance. With the growing ability of AI to detect patterns and trends, such tools enable entrepreneurs to project forward-looking outcomes, identify areas of inefficiency, and optimize operations accordingly.

Also, other AI-driven tools, such as Salesforce Einstein, come with embedded machine learning algorithms that predict customer behavior and sales trends to further enable the entrepreneurs to make data-driven decisions toward higher levels of customer satisfaction and profitability.

6. Inventory Management and Supply Chain Automation

Inventory management and supply chain logistics, when considering product-based companies, can be very time-consuming and prone to human error. AI-powered products like TradeGecko - QuickBooks Commerce and NetSuite ERP provide automation for tracking inventory, demand forecasting, and order management. These predictive analytics make sure that stock is optimized, reordered automatically, and shipments are tracked in real time.

Automation of such routine tasks by entrepreneurs can enable them to avoid stockouts and/or overstocking, enhance supply chain efficiency, and reduce the costs involved in managing an inventory manually. AI will also provide real-time collaboration facility between suppliers and businesses for timely delivery of products, enhancing overall operational efficiency.

7. AI for Human Resources Management

Human resources management typically entails monotonous duties regarding recruitment, onboarding, and payroll processing. AI-powered HR tools, such as BambooHR, Workday, and Lever, use automation for recruitment: screening résumés, scheduling interviews, and offering candidate assessments. These HR tools will also enable the automation of the onboarding process by distributing training materials and tracking employee progress.

Aside from that, HR management AI tools will perform administrative tasks like employee benefits management, processing leave requests, and maintaining labor law compliance. With automation, the entrepreneur can reduce administrative load that originates from human resources tasks but at the same time manage his workforce appropriately.

AI tool automating basic tasks for an entrepreneur has a series of advantages in relation to saving time, efficiency, and accuracy. From virtual assistants to AI-powered accounting and marketing platforms, these tools make it possible for entrepreneurs to focus on the growth of their businesses rather than get bogged down by day-to-day tasks. As technology in AI continues to evolve, the tasks that can be automated will increase even further, thus offering newer paths for entrepreneurs to enhance productivity and unleash innovation within operations.

IMPACT OF AUTOMATION ON ENTREPRENEURIAL PRODUCTIVITY

Artificial intelligence-driven automation fully revolutionizes the manner in which entrepreneurs manage their operations and brings productivity, efficiency, and scalability to a whole new different level (Johnson & Smith, 2023). Automation of routine and repetitive tasks enables the entrepreneur to streamline operations, optimize resources, and focus on activities that provide added value to the business. Removing the element of manual labor and reducing human error, AI-driven automation quickens the pace of business processes, as well as enhances decision-making capabilities. The following section discusses how automation directly affects entrepreneurial productivity in terms of key benefits, challenges, and wider ramifications on the paths to business growth. Essentially, this means that the saved time can be effectively used by entrepreneurs to manage tasks with ease.

1. Time Savings and Task Efficiency

Perhaps one of the most immediate and measurable impacts that automation has on entrepreneurial productivity is the huge reduction in time spent on mundane tasks. In many instances, entrepreneurs have to be stretched out multitasking between roles that range from the management of daily operations to strategic levels in financial planning and customer service. Meeting scheduling, answering customer inquiries, processing invoices, and updating financial records eat up much of an entrepreneur's day, robbing them of productive time that could be better spent.

This would be much faster and more accurate if AI-driven automation tools performed it. For instance, this may involve scheduling meetings and reminders using virtual assistants like Google Assistant or Siri, while AI chatbots-Intercom or Drift-handle customer inquiries without human intervention. Once the technology has freed these mundane activities, entrepreneurs will then have time to develop their priorities into higher-order activities such as market research, product innovation, and business development. The combined impact here saves a lot of time, which in effect means productivity as entrepreneurs can get to do more within less time.

2. Improved Accuracy, Therefore Reduced Human Error

Manual processes are prone to human errors that, quite often, bring inefficiency, inaccuracy, and even financial losses. From the wrong entry of accounting data to failing on deadlines for follow-ups with customers and forgetting to reply to an important email, human error is inherent in manual workflows (Chen et al., 2022). Automation tools, however, perform tasks based on predefined algorithms and rules, which assure much more accuracy and consistency.

For example, AI-driven accounting software, such as QuickBooks or Xero, automates all financial activities, from invoicing to payroll, even tax calculations, bringing the possibility of errors in financial reporting almost to zero. At the same time, AI-supported data management tools can aggregate and process large volumes of data without giving them even a chance for errors, thus enabling entrepreneurs to get accurate insights and make better decisions based on those. This saves not only time from wasted errors but also builds trust with customers and stakeholders, as an automated process can deliver a much more reliable and accurate outcome.

3. Scalability and Operational Flexibility

Automation can also be very important to scale an entrepreneur's business at minimal additional cost and without growing the headcount. Because the scale-up process for a business dramatically increases routine tasks, such as managing more customers, processing an increasing number of orders, or simply handling increased volumes of information, scaling these operations manually means more personnel, overhead, and inefficiencies being brought on board. AI-driven automation equips the entrepreneur with the ability to scale operations efficiently because the technology handles repetitive tasks with seamless ease as demand increases.

For example, AI-powered chatbots can manage customer calls 24/7, whatever the volume, while the business ensures that customer service remains unaltered as it scales up. Other such cases are automated inventory management systems to monitor stock, control supply chains, and optimize order fulfillment without adding staff. This, in turn, allows scalability to enable companies to scale up much faster and maintain costs while increasing productivity and making the entrepreneur most capable of availing the new market opportunities.

4. Strategic and Creative Work Require Locus

Entrepreneurs need innovation, creativity, and strategic thinking-scenes that require considerable attention and problem-solving skills. The drudgery of operational routine tasks leave little space for such high-value work, though. Automation of mundane tasks unclutters the mind and body for an entrepreneur to focus on core business activities, such as product development, customer acquisition, and competitive analysis.

Automation will finally allow the entrepreneurial mindset to transition from being reactive to proactive: instead of just firefighting or solving the same problems repeatedly, entrepreneurs can spend time in more creative processes such as brainstorming about new products, trying different marketing strategies, and even reaching for partnerships. This shift in focus will raise not only productivity but will also position the business for its long-term growth and innovation.

5. Data-driven decisions

AI-powered automation tools are not restricted to routine task management alone but provide real-time data analytics and insights to the entrepreneurs, which help them in decision-making. The automatic collection, analysis, and reporting of data through AI tools give an entrepreneur a wider perspective of his business operation and market trend, hence enabling prudent decision-making based on data rather than assumptions.

Consider AI-powered platforms, like Salesforce Einstein and HubSpot, whose customer behavior, sales trend analysis, among other metrics, expose actionable insights. Such insight allows the entrepreneur to fine-tune their marketing strategies, optimize product offerings, and increase their level of service through real-time feedback. Data-driven decisions ensure efficiency in resource allocation, risk management, and finally, more productivity since entrepreneurs can take advantage of changed conditions in the marketplace sooner, more accurately, and with confidence. (Brynjolfsson & McElheran, 2016).

6. Better Customer Experience and Satisfaction

Customer satisfaction is one of the most meaningful factors relating to entrepreneurial success. Automation can enhance customers' experiences. AI-powered tools, such as chatbots, recommendation engines, and personalized marketing automation systems, allow companies to react with speed and relevance to the needs of their customers, hence enhancing customer satisfaction and loyalty.

This is the reason e-commerce merchants on Shopify apply AI to personalize product recommendations based on customer-preferred choices and previous buying behavior, while chatbots resolve common issues without interference from a human touch. These automated systems enable entrepreneurs to deliver personalized experiences to their customers consistently and in large numbers, ensuring customer retention and positive brand perception. Satisfied customers will most likely return for more, refer others to the services, and thus, in a way, affect productivity and profitability directly by contributing to the overall success of the business.

7. Economies and Resource Utilization

Automation of tasks can highly reduce operating costs and effectively utilize resources. In other words, automation saves them from additional staffing for repetitive tasks, and thus, businesses can function with lean teams with high productivity at relatively lesser costs (Jia, Wang, & Li, 2021). AI-driven innovation manages highly complex activities, including financial management, marketing campaigns, customer services, and more, with very little human intervention, saving tremendously on costs.

For instance, AI-driven marketing platforms like Mailchimp can run automated email marketing campaigns where a company could reach thousands of customers without needing an army of people in its marketing department. Similarly, AI-driven inventory management tools can help optimize the level of stock and avoid overstocking or stockout costs. By decreasing the need for manual processes, businesses can thereby realize an increase in operational efficiency while keeping overheads at a minimum.

8. Difficulties and Considerations

This tide of automation brings about quite a number of obstacles and considerations from the viewpoint of entrepreneurs. For a start, making this initial investment in all these AI tools may set small businesses back by an amount that is substantial considering the tiny budgets they usually operate on. Furthermore, entrepreneurs have got to find the right tools which suit their particular needs-a process requiring due diligence in research and planning. Of course, there is the issue of the integration of AI tools into the already existing workflow and how well employees are trained for this purpose.

Besides, entrepreneurs have to consider ethical issues related to automation, especially from the human workforce's perspective. While automation increases output, it may also impact the relevance of certain job roles, hence potential jobs displacement issues. In that respect, an entrepreneur has to strike a balance between utilizing AI in business operations and remaining sensitive to human feelings.

Automation disrupts entrepreneurial productivity, saves time for the business, reduces errors, and allows efficient scaling while focusing resources on strategic growth. Automation of routine tasks enables the entrepreneur to enhance operational efficiency, make data-driven decisions, and enrich customer experiences at lower costs with optimized resource utilization. As AI technology continues to evolve, the potential of automation driving entrepreneurial success will only increase, opening new dimensions of innovation, productivity, and long-term growth.

CHALLENGES AND CONSIDERATIONS IN AUTOMATING TASKS

While AI-driven automation holds a great deal of promise for entrepreneurs, such as efficiency, cost savings, and scalability of operations, there are also various concerns with its implementation. Issues can include but are not limited to budgetary or technical limitations, ethical implications, and effects on the organization (Jordan, 2019). Entrepreneurs have to be very careful when weighing these variables to ensure that automation aligns with business objectives and can be positively integrated into the current setup. In this section, we look into the most important challenges and considerations related to the automation of tasks in entrepreneurial ventures, after which insight is provided into how such complexity can be transcended. A few of them are as follows:

1. Initial Financial Investment

Among the direct challenges that entrepreneurs face in the course of adopting automation technologies, the initial financial investment features among the top ones. Most AI tool implementations require capital upfront, needed for software acquisition, system customization, and employee training. To small businesses and startups on a shoestring budget, prohibitively expensive, especially when the return on that investment is not certain in the immediate future (Davenport & Ronanki,

2018). For entrepreneurs, long-term productivity gain must be weighed against initial expenditure, which may call for careful financial planning (Kshetri, 2018).

Besides the purchase of AI tools, there could be other costs associated with the maintenance and upgrade of such systems. For instance, some AI platforms use subscription models whereby the companies have to pay for routine updates, extra features, or cloud storage. Secondly, there is a need for external investments-for example, hiring consultants or other tech professionals-who can help handle the integration and troubleshooting of automation systems. Finding a balance between this is part of the financial tightrope that entrepreneurs navigate, especially when such firms operate in highly competitive markets where every cent truly counts.

2. Technical Difficulty of Integration and Complexity with Regards to Existing Systems

The other major challenge that entrepreneurs are facing is the technical difficulty of the integration of AI-driven automation (Brynjolfsson & McElheran, 2016).NLP In most instances, the businesses are interested in integrating new tools within an already set system, which commonly includes CRM software, accounting platforms, supply chain management systems, among others. Ensuring seamless integration is a challenge from a technical viewpoint; this necessitates compatibility between these different platforms and at times custom development work. Poor integration can also eventually disrupt the workflow and delay operations, or even lead to data loss for entrepreneurs. Besides, technically less-empowered entrepreneurs may have to face challenges while configuring and optimizing AI tools. Many AI platforms ask businesses to provide specific parameters, train algorithms, or set up workflows that best reflect the distinctive needs of the business. If entrepreneurs do not understand how to do this properly, there is a real risk that they will automate processes less efficiently or even ineffectively. It is also from this technical factor that a learning curve can be created impacting how rapidly automation technologies are put in place, especially when an entrepreneur does not have an IT department to accelerate the process.

3. Data Quality and Availability

AI-driven automation needs good quality available data. The AI system requires data for learning patterns, making decisions, and finally taking action on behalf of users (Goodfellow et al., 2016). And the output from automation may also be faulty if the information feeding these systems is incomplete, outdated, or wrong. For example, an AI tool used to automate customer relationship management can generate incorrect insights or send irrelevant marketing messages unless a customer's data is not updated or maintained.

Similarly, automation can only be well executed once the entrepreneurs have high-quality data in their hands. This means that not only must relevant data be collected, but equally important is a strict adherence to data hygiene practices, such as frequent cleaning of data, updating the records in order to maintain up-to-date records, and accuracy. What's more, the entrepreneurs should also consider costs related to data acquisition and storage, and data governance policies aimed at the control of how data is used within automated systems.

4. Employee Resistance and Workforce Transition

Any automation being introduced into the firm might be resisted by the employees, mainly if they happen to think that AI tools will take away their jobs or alter the nature of their work. Automation may create apprehensions among employees, bringing down morale due to job insecurities or even opposing any new technologies that may be brought in. The entrepreneurs should always bear in mind that automation can bring about some major changes in the workplace environment, mainly in job functions, responsibilities, and processes.

In this respect, the entrepreneurs may try to overcome employee resistance by emphasizing the importance of both open communication and change management strategies. This will involve educating them regarding the benefits of automation example, reducing boredom from mundane activities and basically giving more time to employees to engage in high-value work. Entrepreneurs should communicate that AI tools are intended to augment human capability, not replace it. For this reason, training programs and upskilling are highly needed, allowing them to adapt with new technologies and get the required skill to work along with the AI systems. An entrepreneur can minimise such resistance and can develop a resilient workforce by promoting a culture of continuous learning and emphasizing how AI can be used collaboratively.

5. Ethical Considerations and Job Displacement

The advent of AI and automation has been replete with ethical questions, primarily in the area of job displacement and spillover effects on society. While automation increases efficiency and raises productivity, it can also lead to jobs being lost-particularly in tasks that require repetition and low skills. Automation in certain tasks would mean the entrepreneur would think seriously about how this can lead to layoffs in employees, disrupting their livelihoods, especially in those industries reliant heavily on human resources.

Ethically responsible automation requires that entrepreneurs consider the impact of AI at work and think about how deleterious consequences might be mitigated. This may include reassignment of workers to other business roles, investment in employee training, or development of other job opportunities that continue to leverage the value of human creativity, problem-solving, and emotional intelligence. Entrepreneurs should be considering the wider societally relevant impact of their automation strategies, while making sure their approach aligns with principles of fairness, equity, and social responsibility.

6. Security and Data Privacy Risks

In addition to increased automation, more data will be used, bringing in massive concerns around security and data privacy. AI applications often deal with sensitive information related to a business and customers, which makes it a hotbed of interest for cyberattacks. If there is a security breach in an automated system, an entrepreneur may leak sensitive information and thus face certain regulatory fines while losing customer confidence (Kshetri, 2018). The legislation on data privacy, like the General Data Protection Regulation in Europe or the California Consumer Privacy Act in the United States, dictates high standards for the processing of personal data by a business; failure to act according to these standards could result in serious legal consequences and financial repercussions.

When entrepreneurs apply automation, they first think about cybersecurity and data protection. For instance, they will invest in secure AI systems for encryption of information that holds sensitivity and ensures that the automated processes are compliant with relevant data privacy laws. In addition, it would develop strict policies regarding how the data should be treated-for instance, no permission to sensitive information should be granted, while continuous automated system monitoring is performed for vulnerabilities. By being proactive and taking steps to protect the data, the entrepreneur reduces many risks of automation and earns the trust of customers and other stakeholders.

7. Adaptability and Future-Proofing

Another challenge facing entrepreneurs who use automation is the speed at which technology is shifting. AI and automation technologies are in constant flux, and systems that are state-of-the-art today could be outdated in just a few years. What's more, entrepreneurs should ensure that the various automation they use can be updated and flexible, so their systems will grow with the demands of the business and with technological advancement. Companies that use systems or structures that are too rigid or outdated simply cannot grow as they should, nor can they take advantage of newer automation capabilities as those become available.

In order to mitigate this, flexibility and scalability should be number one on an entrepreneur's list when choosing an automation tool. For example, with cloud-based AI platforms, businesses can scale up or down to accommodate growth. Similarly, frequent software updates enable these tools to stay relevant continuously. Furthermore, a businessperson should be aware of the trends going on in AI and automation so that his or her business is at the bleeding edge of the latest and greatest developments. Being forward-thinking about automation allows entrepreneurs to remain flexible and ready for whatever may be coming.

Automation has tremendous opportunities for entrepreneurs to enhance efficiency and cut costs while enabling them to focus on strategic growth, but it also presents significant challenges. From financial to technical challenges, including ethical and employee adaptation, these are factors that entrepreneurs must carefully consider when assessing automation in their business. A thoughtful and responsible approach toward integrating AI tools would ensure security of data, transition of the workforce, and adaptability to future changes. Automation done well revolutionizes entrepreneurial productivity and strategically positions businesses to compete sustainably.

AI AND DECISION-MAKING IN ENTREPRENEURSHIP

Decision-making is a key component in entrepreneurship, a world of dynamic happenings and ruthless competition, where the fate of each business hangs on such informed and time-sensitive decisions. Most entrepreneurs find themselves at the center of critical decisions when all around them is turbulence marked by complexity in market conditions, customer behaviors, and operational challenges. Till now, such decisions were intuitively made using experience and the handling of data manually, which may be long and involve many errors. But now, with AI coming into this field, such decisions have undoubtedly taken a different dimension for an entrepreneur-to be more data-driven, accurate, and speedy. AI includes capabilities for processing large amounts of data, finding out emerging trends, predicting outcomes, and providing insights that can be converted into actions to assist entrepreneurs in making better decisions. What does AI portend for the art of decision-making in entrepreneurship? This section looks to explore how AI can make a dent, starting with some key areas like data-driven insight, predictive analytics, understanding customer behavior, and operational optimization.

1. Data-Driven Decision Making

One of the key ways AI enhances decision-making is by offering it access to data-driven insights. Entrepreneurs are often confronted with having to make decisions in light of an ocean of data emanating from sources such as customer interactions, sales transactions, marketing campaigns, and supply chain operations. This is a manual and irksome trend analysis, especially for the small business owner who has no team of data analysts. It is at this juncture that AI tools are able to process and analyze automatically; they convert raw data into insight, hence useful, upon which decisions are made in business.

AI-driven analytics platforms, such as Tableau, Power BI, and Google Analytics, enable entrepreneurs to bring their information into visualizations, trends, and reporting in real time. These tools enable entrepreneurs to make informed decisions based on accurate and timely information rather than mere guesswork or intuition. For example, a retailer can utilize AI to analyze sales data and determine which products are selling best, so that he or she may adjust their inventory levels accordingly. Similarly, the entrepreneur who is running a digital marketing campaign can use available AI analytics tools to see the success of each of his or her strategies and can move resources around accordingly toward most successful channels (Tunio et al.,2023).

AI also eliminates biases that most human decisions are usually susceptible to. With their provenance from objective data analysis, AI tools ensure that decisions made by entrepreneurs are evidence-based and not based on assumptions and emotions. The decision-making becomes more rational and effective, especially when situations are highly critical and require quick yet precise judgments.

2. Predictive Analytics and Forecasting

AI will be able to predict future trends-what a game-changer that is. Predictive analytics, a product of AI, enables business people to project forward into the future regarding changes in markets, customer behaviors, and operational challenges before they actually come. Such foresight enables entrepreneurs to make decisions proactively so that risks are lower and opportunities can be seized. Predictive analytics makes use of machine learning algorithms on historical data to forecast what will take place in the future; hence, the same helps an entrepreneur prepare for any eventuality with greater confidence(Choi et al., 2022).

For instance, an AI system like Salesforce Einstein or HubSpot can study previous sales history and customer behavior in order to predict what will happen in the future. Herein, the entrepreneurs are allowed to estimate demand in a more effective manner, thus enabling them to be prepared with inventories adequate for customers' needs. AI-driven predictive analytics tools can even forecast likely disruptions-suppliers delaying shipments or changing demand levels-so that the entrepreneur may adjust to mitigate adverse outcomes.

The AI also helps in the financial forecasts. Based on the analysis of historical financial data, the AI tools can project the cash flow trends that will help the entrepreneur make more informed decisions concerning investments, budget allocations, and resource management. For example, an AI-enabled accounting tool may analyze spending and revenue streams patterns to predict future cash flow problems so that entrepreneurs can take remedial measures before the actual problem comes up.

Predictive analytics, for example, can enable entrepreneurs to respond not just to the current market setting but also to prepare for eventualities that lie ahead. This is possibly where decision-making forward thinking gives a competitive edge to companies in such aspects as foreseeing shifts in customer preferences, industry trends, and economic conditions.

3. Analysis of Customer Behavior and Personalization

Customer behavior knowledge is a big part of entrepreneurial decision-making, and artificial intelligence has greatly improved the extent to which businesses can analyze and act on customer data. The AI tools enable aggregating and interpreting data about customer preferences, purchasing habits, and brand interaction. This amount of information will provide the entrepreneurs with the opportunity to make informed decisions that increase customer satisfaction, retention, and loyalty.

AI-powered solutions, such as Amazon Personalize and Dynamic Yield, are ready to arm the entrepreneur with the design of the most relevant and timely experience for their customer. Applications based on this technology analyze customer behavior and preferences to offer suggestions for certain products, enable marketers to personalize messages, and optimize every level of the customer journey. For example, the e-commerce entrepreneur might use AI to analyze a given customer's browsing and purchase history, therefore enabling the business to offer relevant product recommendations and personalized promotions to the customer. This amount of personalization helps improve customer engagement, hence increasing the probability of conversion, which in turn again means more revenue (Ho, 2014).

The AI-powered customer behavior analysis further extends to customer service. Analyzing past interactions, AI chatbots are able to tell what the most common issues of their customers are and respond in a very personalized way. Thus, businesses can offer faster, more accurate customer support, hence improving the overall customer experience. What is more, AI tools can even flag at-risk customers-those likely to churn based on their behavior-and provide the entrepreneur with insights into how to re-engage them via targeted outreach.

With the ability for AI to analyze customers' behaviour in real time, entrepreneurs can make decisions closer to their needs and preferences, hence attaining customer satisfaction and improvement of business relationships.

4. Operational Optimization

AI-powered decisioning goes even beyond customer-facing functions, right inside the operations themselves-from managing inventory to logistics in the supply chain. AI tools help the entrepreneur optimize such operations through insights availed to them for efficient workflow and resource allocation.

For example, AI-powered applications such as NetSuite and SAP Integrated Business Planning enable entrepreneurs to track inventories in real time, and even predict the level of inventory required for specific periods of time. AI, therefore, helps optimize business inventory and prevent overstocking or stockouts, hence meeting customer demands while reducing carrying costs. Similarly, AI supply chain management tools analyze performance from suppliers in the past, predict possible delays, and recommend alternative sourcing strategies that will help avoid disruptions.

In manufacturing and production, AI-driven tools can analyze machine performance data to predict when the machines will require maintenance, thus cutting down on unwanted downtime and improving productivity on the whole. This predictive maintenance capability lets the entrepreneur make informed decisions on when to service the equipment, hence avoiding very costly breakdowns that allow maximization of operational efficiency (Chowdhury, 2024).

AI's operational optimization capability spills over into workforce management. Productivity analytics could recommend ways to improve the scheduling, task assignment, and resource allocation by AI-powered tools. For example, AI-powered HR platforms may analyze employee performance data to make recommendations that could call for either a change in team composition or workflows to support entrepreneurs in making decisions to elevate the efficiency and morale of the workforce.

AI can help optimize the business operation, thereby enabling the entrepreneur to make decisions that reduce wastage, better utilize resources, and smooth the workflow, hence making the operations more productive and profitable.

5. Risk Management and Decision Support

Entrepreneurship, in general, is precarious; hence, good risk management lies at the center of long-term success. AI further enhances entrepreneurs' capability to assess risks and develop mitigants by providing data-driven insights to further enhance decision-making. Whether financial, market, or operational, AI tools enable entrepreneurs to find potential threats and make decisions to minimize exposure.

For example, the AI-driven financial risk management tool may make predictions about such financial risks as cash flow shortages or market downturns by using market trends, credit ratings, and economic indicators. In this respect, entrepreneurs can take actions in advance-such as seeking additional funding or readjustment of investment strategies so their businesses will be safe.

AI-driven DSS offers real-time data-driven recommendations that empower entrepreneurs to make complex decisions with confidence. This would be able to digest large chunks of input data from market trends, competitor activity, and internal metrics performance toward making tough decisions with greater confidence. (Cambria et al., 2017). With the integration of AI into the decision-making process, entrepreneurs could review risks, build alternative remedies, and study the probable consequences of each action.

6. Real-Time Decision-Making and Agility

In the fast-moving business environment of today, agility is foundational to entrepreneurial venture success. AI enables and reinforces better decision-making, with real-time analysis and reaction potential. While the AI tools keep on collecting and analyzing data, entrepreneurs can make more knowledgeable decisions with greater rapidity, thus enabling them to act upon a changing market or an emerging opportunity faster and more precisely.

Take AI-driven tools in the case of e-commerce or digital marketing, for example. They can parse customer behavior in real time and enable the entrepreneur to immediately tweak pricing strategies, optimize marketing campaigns, or introduce new products. Companies that deal in retail, financial services, or technology-most of which are businesses based on a time-to-value decision-making process-it's AI processing in real time that gives them the competitive edge.

AI also makes decisions in real time on crisis management. In case of any sudden mishap, like disruption in supply or even sudden market demand, the AI tool will help the entrepreneur assess the situation and suggest some corrective measure. This swiftness provides room for companies to maneuver around challenges and seize new opportunities.

AI remakes decision-making in entrepreneurship with data-driven insight, predictive analytics, analysis of customer behavior, and optimization of operations. AI-driven decisions will be more informed, accurate, and timely, impacting business performance by mitigating risks and enhancing customer satisfaction. Be it through optimizing operations, personalizing experiences for customers, or making predictions of future trends, AI tools put a degree of confidence and agility into the hands of entrepreneurs to deal with the complexities at play in modern business. With each passing day, as AI technology is improved, so also does the core role in decision-making it plays in entrepreneurship open up newer avenues for innovation and success.

FUTURE TRENDS: AI IN BUSINESS AUTOMATION

Artificial Intelligence has already transformed business automation by streamlining processes, reducing labor, and raising efficiency. Yet, as AI technologies continue to evolve, the future of business automation promises even more incredible innovations that will further change how businesses do their business. It follows, therefore, that entrepreneurs and firms have to surge ahead of these trends in order to remain competitive and tap into emerging opportunities. In this regard, the section investigates the future of AI-driven business automation, highlighting those technologies and strategies that will define and shape the next generation of business processes automation.

1. Hyper-automation and Autonomous Business Processes

Hyper-automation is the next wave in business automation where organizations are moving beyond just isolated automation tools in a more holistic and integrated strategy for automation. It, therefore, brings together a host of AI technologies-RPA, ML, NLP, and cognitive computing-into creating end-to-end automated processes that require very minimum human intervention (Cambria et al., 2017). The concept of hyper-automation enables enterprises to automate not only repetitive activities but also the entire workflows, including decision-making flows, which earlier were too complex for traditional human judgment.

For instance, this could empower businesses on hyper-automation to commoditize customer service, supply chains, marketing campaigns, and finance into a single location. For that, tools like UiPath and Automation Anywhere are already on the path, trying to integrate RPA with AI technologies that will enable companies to create fully autonomous processes. In fact, in the years to come, one can even find businesses adopting the concept of an "autonomous enterprise" where most business processes are managed by AI-driven systems, thereby freeing up entrepreneurs to focus on high-level strategy and innovation.

The other direction the effect of hyper-automation can take is to create digital twins, or virtual models of entire business processes that allow companies to simulate in real time, monitor, and optimize their operations. This will also enable businesses to predict outcomes, optimize efficiency, and recognize potential bottlenecks before they affect operations. At the core of AI and ML, digital twins in due course will become more accurate and make real-time decision-making and process optimization seamless as never before.

2. AI-powered automation of workforce collaboration

As AI continues to free employee time by performing mundane tasks, the future of business automation is shifting toward how businesses allow humans and AI to work better together. In the concept of AI-human collaboration, the workplace will be created where AI helps employees instead of taking their place and performs all the mundane tasks while humans develop strategic, creative, and complex jobs. This trend will reshape the workplace in that employees can interact with the AI systems more naturally and intuitively (Lee, 2022).

In this instance, AI-driven cognitive assistants or IPA will be central, integrated, and embedded in regular operations: providing insights, suggestions, and, when appropriate, autonomous decisions. For instance, AI may handle preliminary steps in sales contacts, inquiries from customers, or financial forecasts, but human judgment will be applied in the higher-order functions of relationship-building and long-term strategies for growth.

Future developments in NLP and conversational AI will make AI-human collaboration even smoother. An AI system will be in a position to understand and respond to natural language commands with better efficiency, thus making human-AI interaction more intuitive. In fact, tools like GPT-powered chatbots or Google Duplex are bound to get even better, so employees can have complete conversations with the AI systems by requesting reports, insight, or giving them tasks to perform-all the way a human would with a human colleague. It will be this kind of collaboration between AI and humans that will unlock completely new dimensions of productivity and innovation.

3. AI-Driven Personalization and Hyper-Personalized Customer Experiences

Personalization that differentiates a company is the trend today, and this will surely get a whole new meaning with AI-driven automation through the use of hyper-personalization. AI for hyper-personalization analyzes large volumes of data in real time and tailors the products, services, and marketing efforts to individual customers' preferences in an unprecedented way.

This could also allow companies to create personal customer journeys that change dynamically in real time with customer interactions. For example, AI would apply self-lien belief reasoning to analyze browsing habits, past purchases, and social media activity, including biometric data, to make recommendations on products or services with particular needs. Already used by platforms for the development of highly personalized recommendations such as Amazon Personalize and Dynamic Yield, in the future, it will move to the next level (Nguyen, 2021).

AI-powered chatbots and virtual assistants will also be positioned to offer personalized customer support. Instead of generic responses, AI systems will utilize NLP and consumer data to have contextual conversations, anticipate client needs, and show solution offerings tailored to those needs. Not only will the future of hyper-personalized experiences improve customer satisfaction, but it will also ensure a much higher level of customer loyalty and retention because everything has become so specific and relevant to them.

4. AI-driven Automation in Supply Chain and Logistics

AI has already started transforming the way supply chains and logistics operate; further developments in years to come promise to continue making the processes even more effective, accurate, and adaptive. Supply chains in the future will be further intelligent, resilient, predict disruptions, optimize the level of inventory, and fulfill orders with very minimal or no human interference through AI-driven automation.

AI-powered supply chain forecasting is, however, one of the future trends that holds the most promise in this area. AI systems will be able to analyze real-time data from various sources, including market trends, patterns in weather, and geopolitical events, among others, for predicting disruptions within the supply chain and automatically adjusting logistics plans accordingly. That way, businesses can change course more quickly when conditions change, which cuts down delays and expenses associated with unexpected disruptions.

Other areas of automation will be AI-powered robotics and independent vehicles. AI-powered warehouse robots will handle key tasks, including picking orders, packing, and sorting at unmatched speeds and with utmost precision (Chen et al., 2022). And at the final mile of delivery, unmanned delivery vehicles and even drones are bound to step up the pace for further automating such operations. These changes will result not only in increased efficiency but also in minimizing environmental impact due to optimal routing with fewer human-operated vehicles.

5. AI-driven Automation in Decision Making

Automation in business using AI will not stop at mere operational tasks, but it will continue further into decision-making processes. Though presently the development of algorithms is getting better to help the AI assist or take over more complex decision-making tasks, especially those requiring huge volumes of data and fast-changing variables. The concept is called decision intelligence, where AI is leveraged to scrutinize the data, predict outcomes, and present recommendations based on all kinds of hypothetical scenarios.

In a few years, AI systems will help entrepreneurs and executives in making quicker and more precise decisions. For example, AI can process historical sales data, market trends, and customer feedback to show the perfect time for launching new products. Similarly, AI-powered financial tools will aid in budgeting, investment decisions, and risk management by analyzing real-time financial data for actionable insights(Chen et al., 2012).

Additionally, AI-powered decision-making systems will enable greater speed for businesses in responding to changes in market conditions, customer behavior, and operational challenges. In this respect, they will grant the functionality to simulate various scenarios, assess risks, and suggest courses of action. This would not only raise the quality of decisions but also enable business organizations to become more agile and flexible in ever-changing business environments.

6. Ethics of AI and Responsible Automation

But as AI and automation increasingly permeate business operations, ethical considerations of AI usage will concurrently play an important role in such operations. The AI-driven automated future will not be about technology advancement only, but also about how the deployment of AI is responsible and ethical. In this regard, job displacement by AI, data privacy, bias in AI algorithms, and misuse of AI technologies will also all be addressed.

Key trends in this area will involve the development of ethical frameworks of AI guiding businesses in responsible ways of making use of AI. Such frameworks will emphasize transparency, accountability, and fairness in decision-making by artificial intelligence, ensuring that the AI systems operate free of bias and discrimination (Huang & Rust, 2021). Entrepreneurs and business leaders who want to gain the trust of customers, employees, and stakeholders will have to adopt ethical AI practices.

Additionally, the firms will be put at the test as automation shrinks the workforce. With AI undertaking more routine tasks, companies will be called upon to provide reskilling and upskilling programs for employees to transition into new roles that are non-routine, comprising human creativity, critical thinking, and emotional intelligence. Automation in the future will need to balance between AI-driven efficiency and human-centered work, with technology being used to augment, not replace, the workforce.

7. AI-Driven Automation and Sustainability

Sustainability is turning out to be a focal point of business operations whereby AI-driven automation will be actively contributing toward reduction in ecological footprint by enterprises. Going forward, AI would help enterprises reduce energy consumption, cut down wastes, or even build sustainable supply chains (Tunio et al., 2021). For example, an AI may study trends in energy use in manufacturing units and make suggestions on how energy use can be reduced without affecting productivity.

AI will also contribute to sustainability by helping track the CFP of companies' operations in supply chain management and highlighting areas where emissions can be reduced. Also, autonomous vehicles and drones to be used in logistics will also play a key role in sustainability by minimizing fuel use and route optimization to reduce environmental impact.

Business automation, achieved through merging AI with sustainability initiatives, stands to increase processes not only in efficiency but also in how much global efforts on climate change are aided and the building of a more sustainable future. The future of AI in business automation is transformative, replete with innovations sure to reshape how companies will operate, make decisions, and interact with customers. These include trends that will define the next generation of business automation: hyper-automation, AI-driven personalization, autonomous supply chains, and AI-augmented decisions. As AI continues to advance, there will be a compulsion for entrepreneurs and leaders in business to outcompete emerging trends by releasing new technologies while being responsible for ethical and social concerns (Shaikh et al.,2022). In return, they can position businesses to be more efficient, adaptable, and sustainable to be successful in an ever-increasingly AI-driven world.

CONCLUSION

On the whole, AI-driven automation is revolutionizing the entrepreneurial landscape, pumping it with efficiency, smoothing operations, and enabling better decision-making. The future of automation promises even greater strides with hyper-automation, AI-powered personalization, and autonomous supply chains as businesses embrace the technology. In return, all these will completely alter how companies do their businesses. Automation of routine activities frees up time for entrepreneurs to develop strategies for growth and innovation, foster customer relationships, and make informed business decisions through AI-based predictive capabilities. However, even as automation unfolds in business, ethical use of AI, workforce adaptation, and the use of sustainability practices must be pursued. This balance between technology and human know-how will be the secret in a manner that enables the navigation of this transformation so that AI truly not only drives productivity but fosters responsible and sustainable business growth. As AI is continuously changing, its role in shaping the future of entrepreneurship is going to be more important.

REFERENCES

Agarwal, R., & Mangal, S. (2020). Robotic process automation in business: Insights and implications. *Journal of Business Process Management*, 26(3), 245–262. DOI: 10.1108/JBPM-05-2019-0263

Alshareef, N., & Tunio, M. N. (2022). Role of leadership in adoption of blockchain technology in small and medium enterprises in Saudi Arabia. *Frontiers in Psychology*, 13, 911432. DOI: 10.3389/fpsyg.2022.911432 PMID: 35602740

Brynjolfsson, E., & McElheran, K. (2016). The digitization of business: How IT has changed the nature of work. *Harvard Business Review*, 94(11), 85–92. https://hbr.org/2016/11/the-digitization-of-business

Cambria, E., Poria, S., Gelbukh, A., & Hussain, A. (2017). Sentiment analysis: A review and comparative analysis. *Affective Computing and Intelligent Interaction*, 2(4), 301–320. DOI: 10.1007/s40063-017-0072-5

Chen, H., Chiang, R. H. L., & Storey, V. C. (2012). Business intelligence and analytics: From big data to big impact. *Management Information Systems Quarterly*, 36(4), 1165–1188. DOI: 10.2307/41703503

Chen, Y., Zhang, X., & Xu, J. (2022). Comparative analysis of AI and traditional forecasting methods in supply chain management. *International Journal of Forecasting*, 38(4), 789–804. DOI: 10.1016/j.ijforecast.2021.12.008

Choi, J., Lee, H., & Kim, S. (2022). Machine learning algorithms for predictive analytics: A comprehensive review. *Journal of Data Science and Analytics*, 14(2), 117–135. DOI: 10.1007/s41060-021-00264-0

Choi, T. M., Wallace, S. W., & Wang, Y. (2018). Big data analytics in operations management. *European Journal of Operational Research*, 271(3), 558–569. DOI: 10.1016/j.ejor.2018.05.048

Chowdhury, R. H.Rakibul Hasan Chowdhury. (2024). AI-driven business analytics for operational efficiency. *World Journal of Advanced Engineering Technology and Sciences*, 12(2), 535–543. DOI: 10.30574/wjaets.2024.12.2.0329

Dastin, J. (2022). How Amazon uses AI to optimize supply chain operations. Reuters. Retrieved from https://www.reuters.com/business/amazon-ai-supply-chain

Davenport, T. H., & Harris, J. G. (2007). *Competing on analytics: The new science of winning*. Harvard Business Review Press.

Davenport, T. H., & Ronanki, R. (2018). Artificial intelligence for the real world. *Harvard Business Review*, 96(1), 108–116. https://hbr.org/2018/01/artificial-intelligence-for-the-real-world

Giuggioli, G., & Pellegrini, M. M. (2023). Artificial intelligence as an enabler for entrepreneurs: A systematic literature review and an agenda for future research. *International Journal of Entrepreneurial Behaviour & Research*, 29(4), 816–837. DOI: 10.1108/IJEBR-05-2021-0426

Goodfellow, I., Bengio, Y., & Courville, A. (2016). *Deep learning*. MIT Press.

Ho, S. Y., & Bodoff, D. (2014). The effects of web personalization on user attitude and behavior. *Management Information Systems Quarterly*, 38(2), 497–510. DOI: 10.25300/MISQ/2014/38.2.08

Huang, M. H., & Rust, R. T. (2021). Artificial intelligence in service. *Journal of Service Research*, 23(1), 1–17. DOI: 10.1177/1094670520959723

Jia, Y., Wang, X., & Li, R. (2021). Predictive maintenance using machine learning: A case study in manufacturing. *International Journal of Production Economics*, 236, 108–123. DOI: 10.1016/j.ijpe.2021.108123

Johnson, H., & Smith, L. (2023). Scaling business analytics with AI: A comparative study. *Journal of Business Analytics*, 12(1), 65–78. DOI: 10.1080/09720529.2023.2145145

Jordan, M. I., & Mitchell, T. M. (2015). Machine learning: Trends, perspectives, and prospects. *Science*, 349(6245), 255–260. DOI: 10.1126/science.aaa8415 PMID: 26185243

Kshetri, N. (2018). Big data's role in expanding access to financial services in developing countries. *Journal of Business Research*, 91, 60–71. DOI: 10.1016/j.jbusres.2018.06.023

Lee, K., & Lee, S. (2022). Optimizing logistics with AI: A case study of route planning and inventory management. *Logistics Research*, 15(2), 210–225. DOI: 10.1007/s12159-022-00222-x

Nguyen, T., Tran, D., & Vu, H. (2021). Advantages of AI-driven analytics over traditional methods in operational efficiency. *Journal of Operations Management*, 39(6), 953–970. DOI: 10.1016/j.jom.2021.04.002

Tunio, M. N., Chaudhry, I. S., Shaikh, S., Jariko, M. A., & Brahmi, M. (2021). Determinants of the sustainable entrepreneurial engagement of youth in developing country—An empirical evidence from Pakistan. *Sustainability (Basel)*, 13(14), 7764. DOI: 10.3390/su13147764

Zhou, H., Li, Y., & Zhao, W. (2020). The impact of AI-powered chatbots on customer satisfaction: Evidence from the retail industry. *Journal of Retailing and Consumer Services*, 54, 102012. DOI: 10.1016/j.jretconser.2019.102012

Chapter 6
Incremental Innovation:
Only Survival of the Entrepreneurs in the Competitive Age

Aalia Aslam Bajwa
University of Sindh, Pakistan

ABSTRACT

Innovation is widely recognized as a critical driver of business success and competitive advantage. While disruptive innovations—those that radically transform industries or create entirely new markets—often capture the spotlight, incremental innovation plays a fundamental and often underappreciated role in driving sustained growth and efficiency. Incremental innovation refers to the process of making gradual, iterative improvements to existing products, services, processes, or business models (Christensen, 1997; Tidd & Bessant, 2018).

INTRODUCTION

Innovation is widely recognized as a critical driver of business success and competitive advantage. While disruptive innovations—those that radically transform industries or create entirely new markets—often capture the spotlight, incremental innovation plays a fundamental and often underappreciated role in driving sustained growth and efficiency. Incremental innovation refers to the process of making gradual, iterative improvements to existing products, services, processes, or business models (Christensen, 1997; Tidd & Bessant, 2018).

Unlike radical innovation, which involves significant leaps and the introduction of entirely new concepts, incremental innovation focuses on refining and enhancing existing offerings. These improvements are typically smaller in scale and involve the iterative enhancement of current products, technologies, or processes (Birkin-

DOI: 10.4018/979-8-3693-1495-1.ch006

shaw, 2004). The essence of incremental innovation lies in its ability to build on existing knowledge and capabilities, making continuous, manageable changes that collectively lead to substantial advancements over time (Henderson & Clark, 1990).

One of the key advantages of incremental innovation is its lower risk profile compared to radical innovation. Since incremental innovations build upon established foundations, they often involve fewer uncertainties and require less investment (March, 1991). This approach allows businesses to leverage existing assets and capabilities, facilitating improvements in product quality, operational efficiency, and customer satisfaction without the significant resource outlays associated with more radical changes (O'Reilly & Tushman, 2013).

Incremental innovation also enables companies to stay competitive in rapidly evolving markets by continuously adapting to changing customer needs and preferences (Rogers, 2003). By systematically implementing small improvements, organizations can enhance their offerings, respond to market feedback, and maintain relevance. This process of continuous improvement not only contributes to customer loyalty but also fosters a culture of agility and responsiveness within the organization (Kline & Rosenberg, 1986).

In this chapter, we will explore the concept of incremental innovation in detail, examining its principles, benefits, and challenges. We will discuss how businesses can effectively implement incremental innovation strategies to drive growth and maintain competitive advantage. Through case studies and real-world examples, we will illustrate how incremental innovation can lead to significant progress and contribute to long-term success.

By understanding the role of incremental innovation within the broader landscape of innovation management, businesses can appreciate its value in achieving steady, sustainable growth. While incremental innovations may not always attract the same level of attention as radical breakthroughs, their cumulative impact is vital for maintaining competitive edge and achieving enduring success (Tushman & Anderson, 1986).

Incremental Innovation in Entrepreneurship

Incremental innovation, characterized by gradual and continuous improvements to existing products, services, or processes, is a crucial aspect of entrepreneurship. While disruptive or radical innovations often capture attention for their potential to revolutionize markets, incremental innovation provides the steady, manageable advancements that are essential for sustaining business growth and competitive advantage (Christensen, 1997). For entrepreneurs, adopting incremental innovation strategies can be a practical approach to achieving sustained success and responding to evolving market needs.

Incremental innovation in entrepreneurship involves making small, iterative enhancements that build on existing technologies or business models. These improvements can range from refining product features and optimizing processes to enhancing customer experiences and integrating new technologies (Tidd & Bessant, 2018). By focusing on continuous improvement, entrepreneurs can leverage existing resources and capabilities to achieve significant progress over time.

One of the primary benefits of incremental innovation is its lower risk compared to more radical approaches. Incremental changes typically involve less uncertainty and require smaller investments, which makes them more manageable for startups and small businesses with limited resources (O'Reilly & Tushman, 2013). This approach allows entrepreneurs to make gradual improvements, test new ideas, and adapt their strategies based on real-world feedback and performance.

Moreover, incremental innovation enables entrepreneurs to respond effectively to changing customer preferences and market dynamics. By implementing small, data-driven adjustments, businesses can better align their offerings with customer needs and preferences, thus enhancing customer satisfaction and loyalty (Rogers, 2003). This iterative approach also fosters a culture of continuous learning and adaptation within the organization, which is crucial for maintaining relevance in a competitive market.

For example, in the technology sector, many successful startups and established companies rely on incremental innovation to enhance their products and services. Companies like Apple and Microsoft frequently release updated versions of their software and hardware, incorporating user feedback and technological advancements to provide improved features and performance (Christensen, 1997). These incremental upgrades not only meet evolving customer expectations but also help maintain a competitive edge.

In addition to improving customer satisfaction, incremental innovation can lead to operational efficiencies. Entrepreneurs can apply incremental innovations to streamline business processes, reduce costs, and enhance overall productivity. For instance, incremental improvements in supply chain management or manufacturing processes can result in significant cost savings and operational benefits over time (Henderson & Clark, 1990).

However, while incremental innovation offers many advantages, it also presents certain challenges. Entrepreneurs must balance the focus on incremental improvements with the need for more substantial, transformative changes. Over-reliance on incremental innovation might lead to missed opportunities for disruptive innovations that could redefine the industry or create new markets (Tushman & Anderson, 1986).

In conclusion, incremental innovation is a vital strategy for entrepreneurs aiming to achieve sustained growth and competitiveness. By focusing on continuous, gradual improvements, entrepreneurs can leverage existing resources, manage risks effectively, and respond to evolving market demands. Although incremental innovation may not capture the same level of excitement as radical breakthroughs, its role in ensuring steady progress and long-term success is invaluable.

Detailed Report on Kinds of Incremental Innovation in Entrepreneurship:

Incremental innovation involves making gradual, continuous improvements to existing products, services, processes, or business models. This type of innovation contrasts with radical innovation, which seeks to introduce entirely new concepts or technologies. Incremental innovation focuses on enhancing what already exists, offering numerous benefits including reduced risk, lower investment, and the ability to build on proven systems. Below is a detailed exploration of the kinds of incremental innovation relevant to entrepreneurship, supported by scholarly sources.

Product Enhancements:

Incremental improvements to existing products aimed at enhancing their features, performance, or usability. Adding new functionalities or improving existing ones can significantly increase product value. For instance, Apple frequently updates its iPhone with incremental improvements in camera technology, battery life, and software capabilities (Christensen, 1997).

They are enhancing product design for better ergonomics or aesthetics. This includes refining the user interface of a smartphone to improve user experience. Improving product durability or reliability. For example, automotive manufacturers like Toyota continuously upgrade their vehicles' safety features and performance metrics (Henderson & Clark, 1990). Enhances customer satisfaction by meeting evolving needs and expectations (Rogers, 2003). Strengthens brand loyalty through consistent product improvement and innovation.

Process Improvements:

Incremental changes aimed at enhancing the efficiency, cost-effectiveness, or quality of business processes. Continuous improvements in manufacturing processes to reduce waste and increase efficiency. Toyota's implementation of the Kaizen approach exemplifies this, where small, ongoing changes lead to significant operational improvements (Kline & Rosenberg, 1986). Adjusting internal workflows to enhance productivity. For instance, a company might streamline its internal approval processes to reduce bottlenecks and improve decision-making speed. Supply Chain Enhancements:** Implementing incremental changes in supply chain management to improve logistics, inventory management, and supplier relations (March, 1991).

Leads to cost savings and higher operational efficiency (Henderson & Clark, 1990). Improves overall productivity and process reliability. Incremental improvements to the quality or scope of services provided to customers. Enhancing service protocols to better meet customer needs. For example, introducing new service channels such as live chat or improving response times (O'Reilly & Tushman, 2013).

Adding features that allow customers to customize their service experience, such as personalized recommendations or tailored support. Enhancing customer support systems with additional tools or features, like advanced ticketing systems or automated responses. Enhances customer experience and increases satisfaction (Rogers, 2003). Differentiates the business from competitors through superior service offerings. Adjusting pricing models or introducing tiered pricing structures to better match market conditions and customer segments (Christensen, 1997).

Expanding or refining distribution channels to reach new customer segments or enhance accessibility. For example, a company might add online sales channels in addition to traditional retail. Introducing additional revenue streams, such as subscription models or value-added services, to enhance profitability and diversify income sources. Improves financial performance and market reach (Tidd & Bessant, 2018).

Incremental advancements in technology used within a business, including software, hardware, or other tech tools. Regular updates to software applications to improve functionality, fix bugs, or enhance security (Henderson & Clark, 1990). Making minor improvements to hardware components, such as upgrading a computer's processor or graphics card. Enhancing technology integration within the business to improve overall functionality and user experience. Keeps technology up-to-date and secure (O'Reilly & Tushman, 2013).

Market Adaptations

Incremental changes are made to adapt products or services to fit specific market segments or geographic regions better. Adapting products or services to meet local preferences or regulatory requirements, such as adding language options or regional compliance features (Rogers, 2003). Refining marketing strategies or product features to cater to different customer segments, improving market penetration and relevance. Expands market reach and increases relevance in specific regions or customer segments (Christensen, 1997).

CONCLUSION

Incremental innovation encompasses various types of gradual improvements that businesses can implement to enhance their products, services, processes, and business models. While often less dramatic than radical innovations, these incremental changes are vital for maintaining competitiveness, improving operational efficiency, and adapting to evolving customer needs. By focusing on continuous, manageable improvements, entrepreneurs can achieve significant advancements and ensure long-term success in a dynamic market environment.

REFERENCES

Birkinshaw, J. (2004). A dynamic capabilities perspective on innovation. *Journal of Product Innovation Management*, 21(5), 319–336.

Christensen, C. M. (1997). *The innovator's dilemma: When new technologies cause great firms to fail.* Harvard Business Review Press.

Christensen, C. M. (1997). *The innovator's dilemma: When new technologies cause great firms to fail.* Harvard Business Review Press.

Christensen, C. M. (1997). *The innovator's dilemma: When new technologies cause great firms to fail.* Harvard Business Review Press.

Christensen, C. M. (1997). *The innovator's dilemma: When new technologies cause great firms to fail.* Harvard Business Review Press.

Christensen, C. M. (1997). *The innovator's dilemma: When new technologies cause great firms to fail.* Harvard Business Review Press.

Henderson, R. M., & Clark, K. B. (1990). Architectural innovation: The reconfiguration of existing product technologies and the failure of established firms. *Administrative Science Quarterly*, 35(1), 9–30. DOI: 10.2307/2393549

Henderson, R. M., & Clark, K. B. (1990). Architectural innovation: The reconfiguration of existing product technologies and the failure of established firms. *Administrative Science Quarterly*, 35(1), 9–30. DOI: 10.2307/2393549

Henderson, R. M., & Clark, K. B. (1990). Architectural innovation: The reconfiguration of existing product technologies and the failure of established firms. *Administrative Science Quarterly*, 35(1), 9–30. DOI: 10.2307/2393549

Henderson, R. M., & Clark, K. B. (1990). Architectural innovation: The reconfiguration of existing product technologies and the failure of established firms. *Administrative Science Quarterly*, 35(1), 9–30. DOI: 10.2307/2393549

Kline, S. J., & Rosenberg, N. (1986). An overview of innovation. In Landau, R., & Rosenberg, N. (Eds.), *The positive sum strategy: Harnessing technology for economic growth* (pp. 275–305). National Academy Press.

Kline, S. J., & Rosenberg, N. (1986). An overview of innovation. In Landau, R., & Rosenberg, N. (Eds.), *The positive sum strategy: Harnessing technology for economic growth* (pp. 275–305). National Academy Press.

March, J. G. (1991). Exploration and exploitation in organizational learning. *Organization Science*, 2(1), 71–87. DOI: 10.1287/orsc.2.1.71

March, J. G. (1991). Exploration and exploitation in organizational learning. *Organization Science*, 2(1), 71–87. DOI: 10.1287/orsc.2.1.71

O'Reilly, C. A.III, & Tushman, M. L. (2013). Organizational ambidexterity: Past, present, and future. *The Academy of Management Perspectives*, 27(4), 324–338. DOI: 10.5465/amp.2013.0025

O'Reilly, C. A.III, & Tushman, M. L. (2013). Organizational ambidexterity: Past, present, and future. *The Academy of Management Perspectives*, 27(4), 324–338. DOI: 10.5465/amp.2013.0025

O'Reilly, C. A.III, & Tushman, M. L. (2013). Organizational ambidexterity: Past, present, and future. *The Academy of Management Perspectives*, 27(4), 324–338. DOI: 10.5465/amp.2013.0025

O'Reilly, C. A.III, & Tushman, M. L. (2013). Organizational ambidexterity: Past, present, and future. *The Academy of Management Perspectives*, 27(4), 324–338. DOI: 10.5465/amp.2013.0025

Rogers, E. M. (2003). *Diffusion of innovations* (5th ed.). Free Press.

Tidd, J., & Bessant, J. (2018). *Managing innovation: Integrating technological, market and organizational change* (6th ed.). Wiley.

Tushman, M. L., & Anderson, P. (1986). Technological discontinuities and organizational environments. *Administrative Science Quarterly*, 31(3), 439–465. DOI: 10.2307/2392832

Tushman, M. L., & Anderson, P. (1986). Technological discontinuities and organizational environments. *Administrative Science Quarterly*, 31(3), 439–465. DOI: 10.2307/2392832

Chapter 7
Ethical AI in Entrepreneurship:
Balancing Innovation With Responsible AI Practices

Deepak Kumar Sahoo
https://orcid.org/0009-0004-5703-8701
Biju Patnaik University of Technology, Rourkela, India

Ta Huy Hung
https://orcid.org/0009-0008-6835-3036
Vietnam National University, Vietnam

Anish Kumar
https://orcid.org/0000-0002-8047-4227
O.P. Jindal Global University, India

Preet Kanwal
https://orcid.org/0009-0006-5114-8381
Lovely Professional University, India

ABSTRACT

The rapid advancement of artificial intelligence (AI) presents significant opportunities and challenges for entrepreneurship. This chapter explores the intersection of ethical practices and AI innovation, focusing on how to balance technological progress with responsible AI development. Key topics include defining ethical AI principles, addressing ethical challenges in AI implementation, and building responsible AI practices. The role of various stakeholders, such as developers, organizations, and regulators, is examined to highlight their contributions to ensuring ethical AI use. Additionally, future directions for AI ethics, including advancements in explainable

DOI: 10.4018/979-8-3693-1495-1.ch007

AI and evolving regulatory frameworks, are discussed. By integrating ethical considerations into AI development, entrepreneurs can drive innovation while upholding principles of fairness, transparency, and accountability.

INTRODUCTION

In recent years, artificial intelligence has emerged as a transformative force within the entrepreneurial landscape-a force that not only creates unprecedented levels of innovation but also ensures efficacy. From automating mundane tasks to driving advanced analytics with data, AI technologies are remodelling industries and creating new vistas for business. Entrepreneurs who harness AI effectively can realize competitive advantage, streamline operations, and enable innovative products and services. Such rapid growth brings with it a raft of tricky ethics questions that must be answered if the use of AI is ever to be responsible and equitable.

Ethical AI: The principles and practices for guiding the development and deployment of AI technologies so these should align with values, norms- social norms of human societies. The integration of AI systems into business processes has been on the rise. Therefore, navigating the balance between the use of AI for competitive advantage with ethics has become an important issue that entrepreneurs face in contemporary times. This balance is indicative of compliance, but also points to responsible innovation, wider commitment, trust, and accountability.

Ethical AI is a big need identified by a set of challenges facing entrepreneurs. Data privacy and security hold the highest importance since most of the AI systems are driven by big data, including personal and sensitive information. Making sure that this is well-protected and used in compliance with the law on privacy would help gain consumer confidence. In addition to this, the potential biases of AI algorithms might also be one of the major challenges. These can be introduced both explicitly and implicitly by biased training data or poor design of the algorithms, resulting in unfair outcomes that can hurt people and communities. The remedy involves proactive algorithmic fairness and inclusion.

Other crucial ingredients of ethical AI involve transparency and accountability. Entrepreneurs should ensure that the AI systems they design and put in place are transparent to users and stakeholders. How the implementation will arrive at AI decisions and how the data will be put to use should, therefore, be well explained. In addition, accountability mechanisms involve ways through which adverse impacts on individuals or society brought about by AI systems can be addressed and an issue fixed.

Ethics and principles that accompany its usage continue to evolve as AI keeps on evolving. Many different organizations and institutions have drafted sets of rules of ethics concerning AI, each underlining the core principles of fairness, accountability, and transparency. First, businesspeople should be aware of the emerging standards and then implement them in their strategies concerning AI in order to enable responsible innovation.

Ethical AI development and implementation not only reduce risks but also increase the ability of the entrepreneurial venture to thrive over the long term. Addressing ethical considerations first allows entrepreneurs to create trust among customers, which is a differentiator that gives them an advantage over other competitors. Ethical AI is not a limitation to innovation but an intrinsic ingredient of business operations toward sustainability and responsibility.

The intersection of AI and ethics in entrepreneurship is explored here: key principles, challenges of ethical AI implementation, and best practices in the balance between innovation and responsibility. Such an understanding and treatment of the issues shall help the entrepreneurs negotiate the maze of Ethical AI and tap its potential in a manner intended to uphold values so essential to maintaining trust and integrity in their ventures.

DEFINING ETHICAL AI

But most importantly, with the exponential growth in the use of AI across different industries, it has become quite dire for an understanding of what "Ethical AI" is by entrepreneurs, developers, and society at large. Ethical AI refers to various ways in which AI systems are developed, deployed, and put to use in ways that are consistent with moral values, societal norms, and laws. This ensures that AI systems design will be aimed at being fair, transparent, accountable, giving primacy to human well-being in an effort to minimize harm and ensure the well-being of all stakeholders.

Key Principles of Ethical AI

The practice of ethical AI is underpinned by a set of principles that guide its responsible use and implementation. These include:

1. **Fairness:** AI systems should not commit or promote unjust discrimination. Ensuring that AI is non-discriminatory requires, quite simply, that no section of the population be disproportionately benefited or harmed by AI because of their race, gender, socio-economic status, or other protected characteristics. In large part, bias in AI emanates from biased training data, and any solution

needs a conscientious effort to make certain that algorithm design and training are carried out with diverse and representative datasets.
2. **Transparency:** Transparency is the ability of internal mechanisms of AI systems to become interpretable by consumers and stakeholders. In other words, it is an explanation of how AI decisions are arrived at, what data is used, and the algorithms doing the magic. In business terms, this will mean that businesses can gain more trust from their customers and regulators that they operate AI in a responsible and ethical manner.
3. **Accountability:** Ethical AI necessitates mechanisms for accountability. This principle shall ensure that lines of responsibility are clearly drawn with respect to the consequences brought about by AI systems. Should an AI system cause injury or an unintended outcome, it is vital that those responsible for its development and deployment can be held accountable. Another important part of establishing accountability is putting in place measures to audit and monitor performance of AI over time.
4. **Privacy and Safety:** There has to be a consensus that personal data is protected, and AI technologies are deployed securely. Entrepreneurs should secure sensitive information utilized by AI systems and observe related data privacy regulations. A breach in data or improper use of personal data gained may lead to distrust and other major ethical and legal consequences.
5. Human-Centric Design: AI should be designed to promote human well-being and improve users' power, rather than replacing or undermining it. The principle encourages such a concept that AI shall support human decisions, extend human capability, and enhance the quality of life. AI, which diminishes human autonomy or leads to over-reliability on automated systems, is ethically questioned.

COMMON ETHICAL DILEMMAS IN AI

Despite all these guiding principles, there are ethical dilemmas which entrepreneurs usually face while developing and implementing AI. One of the most complex challenges is algorithmic bias. Many AI systems are literally learning from historical data, which can reflect biases from human prejudices or the structural inequalities of the past. Unless detected and mitigated with great active intervention, such biases may lead to discriminatory outcomes, like biased hiring algorithms or unfair lending. They have to identify, mitigate, and correct biases within the AI to ensure the output is fair.

Another ethical issue that surrounds AI pertains to the fact that it displaces employment. Basically, the AI technological capabilities are linked to the displacement of jobs. Although AI does enhance efficiency, it often means the abolishment of some job positions-particularly in areas of routine or manual nature. Thus, trading off between gains brought about by AI-driven efficiency and the need for fair opportunities within a workforce is a very significant ethical barrier for entrepreneurs.

There is also a lack of transparency in AI's decision-making process-a problem often referred to as the "black box." Some AI models are impossible to interpret, even by those who created them. This lack of interpretability can lead to ethical concerns, especially in high-stakes environments such as healthcare, finance, or criminal justice, where understanding AI's reasoning is critical to ensuring just outcomes.

Ethics Guidelines and Frameworks on AI

Many of these ethical challenges have led various organizations, governments, and academic institutions to develop ethical AI guidelines and frameworks. The guidelines are aimed at providing best practices for entrepreneurs and developers in creating and deploying the AI systems responsibly. For example, the Ethics Guidelines for Trustworthy AI by the European Union enumerate seven key requirements such as accountability, transparency, non-discrimination, and environmental sustainability, among others, that any ethical AI needs to satisfy. Alongside that, the IEEE's Ethically Aligned Design framework further advocates for the creation of AI in ways that align with human values, and it was done so to serve the greater good.

While such frameworks are welcome, it is also incumbent upon entrepreneurs to internalise ethical AI principles within their business practices. This may range from setting up an internal ethics committee or regular auditing of AI systems to participating in public debate on this issue of responsible use of AI technologies (Winecoff, 2022).

Such awareness will not only help entrepreneurs minimize risks by following the principles of ethical AI but also build trust among customers, employees, and society in general. For now, ethical AI is not a concept that can be called static; rather, it is dynamic and therefore continuous awareness on behalf of entrepreneurs is highly essential in adapting their practices to the emerging ethical challenges as AI advances further (Undheim et al., 2022).

THE IMPACT OF AI ON INNOVATION

AI has transformed the face of entrepreneurship and has, thus, become a key driver of innovation within industries. By offering novel ways to solve problems, optimize business processes, and develop new products and services, AI builds up an entrepreneurial momentum into which businesses are propelled. Still, with all these opportunities, AI engenders ethical considerations with which entrepreneurs need to grapple if the point is to ensure responsible innovation.

AI as a Catalyst for Entrepreneurial Innovation

AI technologies have become central to entrepreneurial innovation because they automate many tasks that were earlier labour-intensive or time-consuming. For example, AI-powered algorithms can analyze big data sets in real time, identify trends, and develop predictive insights to help entrepreneurs make evidence-based decisions. Be it optimizing supply chains, improving customer engagement, or smoothing production processes, AI enables them to function efficiently while reducing costs.

AI also allows product innovation to take place fast. AI-powered tools, such as natural language processing, machine learning, and computer vision, let entrepreneurs create smart products serving the needs of consumers in new and personalized ways. For instance, AI-powered chatbots serve customers 24/7, while AI-enabled personalization engines curate products and services based on individual tastes and preferences. The innovations help entrepreneurs create differentiated offerings and thereby build competitive advantages in somewhat crowded markets (Giuggioli & Pellegrini, 2022).

Furthermore, AI is democratizing this set of advanced technologies by making available affordable cloud-based AI platforms and AI-as-a-Service models to entrepreneurs-specially from startups or small businesses-for AI tools and infrastructure. Therefore, accessibility enables a broader base of entrepreneurs who use AI without deep technical expertise and large financial investments, thereby diffusing innovation across sectors.

AI-Driven Business Model Transformation

AI now transforms not just products and services but also spurs business model innovation. Inclusion of AI enables entrepreneurs to innovate in the way value is delivered to customers and revenues are generated. Examples include subscription models, monetizing data, and "AI-as-a-Service", which typifies how AI paces new business models dependent on continuous data gathering and analysis.

Perhaps one of the most pivotal areas of change is the new breed of platform-oriented business models powered through AI. Platforms such as Uber, Airbnb, and Amazon are using AI to better match demand and supply, dynamically optimize prices, and enhance user experience. The algorithms fire up personal recommendations, predictive analytics, and dynamic pricing that create further value for both the platform and its users. This transition towards platform economies is unlocking new opportunities for entrepreneurs to innovate in everything from retail to healthcare to transportation.

However, AI-driven business models raise major ethical issues regarding data ownership and monetization: how can data-collecting entrepreneurs responsibly protect users through transparent consent processes and shield them against misuse? From this perspective, ethics in data-driven business models are gaining significant attention as more consumers and regulators bring into light several risks related to personal data exploitation.

Case Studies of AI-Driven Innovation

It is, therefore, at this point instructive to consider some case studies of companies that have successfully harnessed AI into their operations to further understand how AI is shaping entrepreneurial innovation. Case studies include the following:

1. Zebra Medical Vision: This healthcare startup deploys AI-powered imaging tools to help doctors more efficiently and effectively diagnose diseases from medical images. With AI, medical diagnosis has become one of the major innovative areas within diagnostic healthcare for Zebra Medical Vision, as this enables early detection, reducing human error in radiology (Kolanu et al., 2020; Aggarwal et al., 2021).
2. Stitch Fix: This fashion retail company uses AI in making style recommendations to customers. By analyzing customer preferences, purchase histories, and feedback, AI algorithms compile curated lists of fashion items tailored to an individual's taste. This has been an innovative application of AI, using which Stitch Fix was able to reimagine the traditional retail model into one driven by data with a highly personalized service (Bryndin, 2019).
3. Rivian: An EV company at the helm of AI-driven automotive innovation, Rivian's driving assistance systems enhance vehicle safety with AI, efficiency, and enable high performance through real-time predictive maintenance analytics. Indeed, Rivian's work in AI-driven sustainability epitomizes how entrepreneurs can put technology and the environment together (Elvas & Ferreira, 2021).

These case studies are examples of how AI is helping companies break the barriers of innovation in everything from healthcare to retail to automotive.

Balancing Innovation and Ethics

One cannot argue with the fact that AI accelerates innovation; at the same time, it involves challenges that have to be overcome by entrepreneurs while making the right steps toward responsible AI use. The main issues involve job losses on account of automation. Increasingly, with AI performing routine tasks and even some aspects of jobs, serious issues arise concerning the impacts that this development is having on jobs, especially among the less skilled. The bottom line in this respect is the consideration by entrepreneurs of societal implications with respect to AI driving automation; they also have to seek ways to offer retraining or redeployment of workers so as to minimize negative consequences for the workforce (Radhakrishnan, 2024; Rojas & Tuomi, 2022).

Unintended consequences are another potential risk in using AI for innovation. Sometimes AI systems output unexpected, nonintuitive results that turn out to be unethical, with perverse consequences. For example, AI applied to financial services can lead inadvertently to biased lending practices, or AI applied to health may misdiagnose patients if the data upon which the AI was trained is biased. Entrepreneurs will have to set up controls for ethical AI audits, algorithmic transparency, and monitoring to avoid such harmful outcomes.

Second, entrepreneurs should be aware of the regulatory environment in respect of AI. Governments and international bodies are beginning to develop regulations that will guide the ethical use of AI within different industries. Entrepreneurs at the forefront of this innovation drive around AI must be abreast of such developments and make sure their practices are so designed with ethical considerations in mind and remain within the law.

The impact AI has on entrepreneurial innovation is immense and transformational; it opens up new horizons of growth, efficiency, and creativity. As AI technologies continue to evolve, entrepreneurs will continue to push the envelope on what is possible by leveraging AI in the development of groundbreaking products, services, and business models. Innovation, however, should not be pursued at the cost of ethical responsibility. This can only be achieved by a delicate balance between the competitive advantage created by AI and upholding ethical AI principles relating to fairness, transparency, and accountability.

By ensuring ethical practices in driving AI-led innovation, entrepreneurs would go a long way in ensuring that such ventures make socially positive contributions while navigating the challenging ethical landscape of emergent technologies. The future of AI in entrepreneurship will thus depend not only on technically native quality but also the ability of entrepreneurs to innovate responsibly and sustainably (Salam, 2024; Shahid, 2024).

ETHICAL ISSUES THAT WILL ARISE FROM AI IMPLEMENTATION

With AI continuing to integrate into entrepreneurial endeavours and business processes, entrepreneurs are considering several significant ethical challenges in terms of how AI systems are fielded responsibly. These are multidimensional, with issues running the gamut from data privacy to algorithmic bias and transparency. Fully understanding and addressing these challenges is crucial for entrepreneurs who look forward with eagerness to harnessing the benefits of AI while ensuring that ethical standards are upheld, and unintended harm is avoided.

Data Privacy and Security Concerns

One of the most convincing factors that remain with AI implementation is related to data privacy and security. Artificial intelligence systems heavily rely on large volumes of data to learn and improve at their tasks. This data very often contains sensitive personal information, such as health records, financial information, and online behavioural patterns. Entrepreneurs using AI in their ventures must make sure they deal with this data in such a way that it respects individual privacy and adheres to data protection laws, like the General Data Protection Regulation (GDPR) in Europe, or the California Consumer Privacy Act (CCPA).

The ethical and legal consequences of data breaches or unauthorized access to personal information are rather critical; it may mean a loss of confidence, financial penalties, but most importantly, reputational damage. In addition, entrepreneurs must also think about the source from which the data was retrieved and whether consent to use such data in an AI system by that person was provided through informed consent. Transparency regarding information about data collection and its usage is key to trust with the consumer in sectors such as healthcare, finance, and retail, where individual consumer data is required for AI operations.

Bias and Fairness in AI Algorithms

Algorithmic bias perhaps represents yet another major ethical challenge in applications of AI. Most AI systems initially undergo training on historical datasets, and biased or non-representative datasets result in the possibility of biased models of AI. Bias in AI can take a range of forms: from hiring algorithms skewed to favor certain demographics to predictive policing systems that disproportionately affect marginalized communities.

Bias is an issue that is of not only legal significance but also one highly critical to ensuring AI-driven decisioning is fair and inclusive. If left unaddressed, bias directly erodes the credibility and value of AI systems, which may eventually result in unequal access to opportunities, goods, and services. It requires entrepreneurs to take a very proactive attitude toward detecting, mitigating, and correcting bias through sensitive curation of training data, performing fairness audits regularly, and diversification of development teams building AI. Ethical AI practices should focus on equality and inclusiveness, offering benefits through AI practices undivided among people and groups irrespective of their backgrounds and identity.

Accountability and Transparency Within AI Systems

The main ethical issue in artificial intelligence implementations pertains to a lack of transparency into the way AI systems work. Most AI models, especially those based on deep learning, are generally referred to as "black boxes," since their internal mechanisms have turned pretty complex. These systems can give out decisions and results that at times are beyond explanation even by the developers themselves, raising questions about issues of transparency and accountability.

This opacity comes with quite a few ethical challenges to businesspeople. People are very suspicious to trust AI systems, since either one cannot understand how the decisions were made, or the process is obscure. It is especially difficult in areas like healthcare, financial services, or legal services, as far as the consequences of AI-driven decisions may seriously affect people's lives. In these cases, transparency is more of a requirement than it is a moral obligation so that confidence and consistency with regulatory norms may be attained.

Explainability in AI, otherwise stated, is when entrepreneurs choose models or mechanisms of decision-making that can be understood. In other words, it may mean developing the AI system to give explanations for their outputs or provide a possibility for users to request human intervention or oversight in critical decision-making processes. By allowing transparency, entrepreneurs will further build trust with customers and stakeholders while continuing to comply with ethical and regulatory requirements.

Accountability for AI's Actions

Closely related to transparency, but often ignored, is the issue of accountability. As AI becomes increasingly independent and autonomous from direct human overview, decisions have to be made about who should bear responsibility in case something goes wrong. When an AI system creates harm-for example, a discriminatory hiring decision, denial of an application for a loan, or misdiagnosis of a patient-whom would one hold responsible: the developers, the business owners, or the AI itself?

There should, therefore, be clear lines of accountability for decisions made through AI in organizations by entrepreneurs. This calls for the design of systems that keep humans in the loop when the stakes are high and the creation of systems that can correct any adverse outcomes emanating from the performance of the AI system. Business applications will also be required to ensure conformance with the host of regulatory frameworks now being developed in response to needs for accountability from AI-in particular, the EU's General Data Protection Regulation requires that all automated decisions involving personal data should be explainable and subject to human review.

THE "BLACK BOX" PROBLEM

The black box problem involves a lack of explanation in how AI algorithms, particularly those using deep learning variants, come up with their decisions. While possibly returning highly accurate results, most of the time these algorithms do not present clear explanations of how they reach their conclusions. This lack of interpretability creates ethical risks, especially when AI is used in high-stakes environments like criminal justice, healthcare, or financial services.

For example, if an AI system denies an individual a loan or recommends one type of medical treatment, that person is entitled to an explanation of the rationale upon which that decision was founded. If the AI works like a black box, then it certainly creates feelings of frustration, confusion, and distrust among its users, especially when they do not feel that they have any recourse to question or understand why a particular result came about.

The challenge can be overcome by entrepreneurs through investing in XAI or, in other words, explainable AI: an AI system developed to give understandable and clear explanations for arriving at decisions. Explainable AI makes sure the developers and end-users have an insight into the behind-the-scenes decision-making, thus better transparency, accountability, and ethical responsibility on behalf of the developer and implementer of AI.

Ethical AI in Autonomous Decision-Making

With the sophistication in AI systems, they nowadays represent more and more autonomous decisions on transportation, finance, health, and customer service. While this increases efficiency and improves outcomes on the one hand, it also raises ethical concerns about the role of human judgment in the delegation of decision-making authority to machines.

For example, tests and deployments of autonomous vehicles are happening all over the world, raising many questions about liability in the case of an accident involving an AI-driven car. AI-powered algorithms of trading make decisions on their own in the financial domain, having considerable impacts on markets and individual investors. Entrepreneurs should consider, among other factors related to the autonomy of AI, the ethical implications and provide safeguards, monitoring systems, and mechanisms of human oversight that prevent negative consequences.

The Ethical Challenge of AI's Impact on Jobs

The other significant ethical issue related to the implementation of AI is that it may affect employment. With artificial intelligence gaining much importance and serving to automate more and more processes and activities, losing jobs due to automated machines has become one of the recurrent fears people have. While AI indeed guarantees huge productivity gains and cost savings, it may also lead to the discontinuance of a few jobs, considering those that are routine or involve much manual work.

Among others, entrepreneurs are going to have to consider the ethical impact of AI on job losses, which is highly probable to affect the manufacturing industry, customer support and service, and logistics. The businesses must seek opportunities for reskilling or upskilling their employees so that these can assume new functions related to managing, overseeing, or cooperating with the new AI-driven systems. By taking multi-dimensional approaches-building a staff of better-educated employees and transitioning dislocated employees to new positions-business owners can balance the innovative benefits of AI with their ethical obligation to their employees.

Ethical issues regarding AI implementation are complex and multi-faceted. Entrepreneurs will have to balance innovation with responsibility while deploying the technology. In fact, it takes much proactive effort for entrepreneurs to address ethical AI in data privacy, bias, transparency, accountability, and job displacement. Ethics sewn right into the strategies and systems of AI at the very initial stages can help businesses create AI-driven solutions that will enhance their competitive advantage, foster well-being for society, trust, and fairness.

BUILDING RESPONSIBLE AI PRACTICES

Building responsible AI practices requires modern entrepreneurial pressure for the driving force to balance innovation with standards of ethics. In simple terms, responsible AI practices are about mitigating the risks associated with deploying AI while fostering trust, transparency, and fairness. The entrepreneur, through making responsible AI practices a priority, can differentiate their ventures with life-positive technology that protects against harm. Key steps in building responsible AI practices that guarantee ethical use of AI within entrepreneurial ventures are discussed below.

Integration of Ethical AI Principles into Business Models

It all begins by embedding the right set of ethical AI principles at the very core of a business model-a set that enshrines values such as equity, transparency, and accountability. That means the entrepreneurs will not only have to take a call on using AI in their operations but also make a conscious effort to align their AI applications with moral and societal values. Embedding such principles within the business strategy can enable entrepreneurs to ensure that their AI systems are designed to be biased as little as possible, more inclusive, and operate in manners explainable to users and stakeholders.

First, the entrepreneur has to make a risk assessment that should consider the potential social and ethical consequence of AI on business processes. It may include the chances of AI's subtle reinforcement of bias, privacy invasions, or unequal access to services. The identified risks can be mitigated by designing the AI systems in a way that the decision-making is done quite fairly and all AI-driven, dependent processes are transparent and subjected to human oversight if need be.

Furthermore, embedding ethics of AI into business models involves continuous stakeholder engagement through customers, employees, regulators, and advocacy groups. Diverse views will also give entrepreneurs the tools needed to develop AI systems that factor in different stakeholders' needs and considerations in deploying AI in a responsible and ethical manner.

Devolution of Ethical Guidelines for Development and Deployment of AI

Full ethical guidelines on how AI will be developed and deployed within the organization are paramount in the responsible building of AI. Such guidelines would in a way form a route map toward ethics within AI, directing developers and employees on what the company stands for and expects in terms of ethics (Shahid, 2024; Felzmann et al., 2020).

Ethical guidelines should indicate a way forward on issues such as data collection and usage, algorithmic transparency, bias detection and mitigation, and consent from users. For example, guidelines can provide that any information used for training AI models needs to be clearly obtained from users and stored according to data privacy regulations. On the other hand, different recommendations about algorithmic transparency will be binding upon many models of AI to provide explanation for decisions taken, particularly in high-impact sectors like health and finance, where accountability forms a very integral part of the process.

These guidelines should also provide ways through which ethical AI audits can be performed, periodic reviews during which AI systems are checked for conformance with ethical guidelines. Audits may help ascertain biases, the fairness of AI outcomes, and specific areas where AI systems may fall short of the ethical undertakings of the company. By institutionalizing such guides, a concern for ethics will be inculcated into the very culture of the enterprise at each and every level of AI development and deployment (Klímová et al., 2023).

Setting up AI Ethics Committees and Oversight Structures

The best manner of implementing responsible AI is through the formation of an AI Ethics Committee or the appointment of an AI Ethics Officer. An oversight structure plays the role of internal bodies responsible for monitoring the ethical implications of the AI technologies used by the business. The ethics committee has to be representative of a great variety of stakeholders, including the developers of AI, legal experts, ethicists, and representatives of different departments within the organization.

The purpose of the AI Ethics Committee is to evaluate and follow up on AI projects in terms of their plausible risks and to confirm that such initiatives are within the guidelines of the company's ethics. This committee should be integrated into an early development phase that provides input regarding ethical issues with respect to data usage, model design, and deployment strategies. Ongoing reviews from the ethics committee will ensure that AI systems meet not only regulatory requirements but also societal values.

In addition to that, businesses should set up internal accountability structures so that it is clear who is responsible for addressing ethical concerns in an AI project. It could perhaps be through the appointment of a chief AI ethics officer to lead the ethical execution of AI so that all initiatives in AI undergo a review to check on potential ethical issues; thus, clear lines of accountability will ensure that ethical considerations are realized at every point in the operations of entrepreneurs' AI.

Ensuring Transparency and Accountability in AI Systems

The very foundation of responsible AI practices is being transparent in how AI systems work and how decisions are made. Apart from its intrinsic value in building trust with users, transparency has greater implications for businesses to remain accountable for the output provided by their AI systems continuously. In the absence of transparency, AI systems risk being "black boxes" where the very developers of those systems do not understand how certain decisions are reached.

XAI models, therefore, would be a way through which entrepreneurs can boost transparency. Explainable AI is all about those AI systems that, after arriving at certain decisions or producing outputs, should be able to give plausible explanations in understandable human language. For example, loan approval using an AI network has to give explanations to applicants with regards to the approval or disapproval of the loan with particular specifications. This fairness in transparency calls for more equitable treatment of the user and leaves room for appeal upon dissatisfaction (Ossa, 2024).

In addition to the requirements of transparency, making accountable AI systems is also a must. Businesses have to set up processes through which users can contest AI decisions or simply ask for human reconsideration of any decision that significantly influences their life. For instance, in the health sector, AI diagnostic systems should not operate in a vacuum; they have to work alongside human doctors who could validate recommendations by AI and add more context or judgment. This will instil more trust and accountability through human oversight and explanations or interventions sought by users in AI processes. Finally, entrepreneurs can train employees on responsible ways of using AI.

Training Employees on Responsible AI Practices

Building responsible AI practices is not the sole responsibility of AI developers or management, but it is a commitment by the company to maintain ethical standards. Companies would do well to invest in responsible AI practices training for their employees. This kind of training makes them understand the ethical implications that may arise from AI, recognize potential risks, and contribute to building AI systems with core values of fairness, transparency, and accountability.

While developers may require very specialized training on algorithmic fairness and detection of bias, marketing teams would need training on how to clearly and honestly communicate AI-driven product features. This training will ensure that every category of employee is fully knowledgeable to easily identify and handle likely ethical issues arising.

Second, entrepreneurs should encourage an ethical innovative corporate culture; employees should be given the right and outlet to express concerns over the ethics of AI projects. Mechanisms for whistleblowing could be established in which workers can report problems anonymously regarding ethical issues. This can be achieved either by establishing different mechanisms for reporting ethical issues anonymously or by organizing open discussions related to AI ethics in the workplace. A culture of ethical responsibility promoted by a business can ensure that responsible AI practices are followed at every level in the organization.

Collaborating with External Experts and Regulatory Bodies

Ethical AI cannot be developed in isolation. Similarly, entrepreneurs must also engage proactively with independent experts, including ethicists, academic researchers, and interest groups, to get manifold perspectives on all issues related to the ethical consequences of AI. Interaction with third-party stakeholders helps businesses keep abreast of the latest information on hot trends in AI ethics, newly arising risks, and best practices in implementing responsible AI.

Second, entrepreneurs should be discussing with the regulatory body to make sure that the development is in line with national and international AI regulations. Though these regulations are still in the development process, renowned frames exist such as the EU's General Data Protection Regulation and the proposed Artificial Intelligence Act. This can also be done through keeping updated on recent regulatory developments and working closely with policy makers, whereby businesses will be well prepared for the new legal requirements and ensure that their AI systems are ethically appropriate.

Monitoring and Auditing AI Systems

Finally, the last keystone to responsible AI practices involves continuous monitoring and auditing of the AI systems. AI technologies are evolutionary in nature; they change over time as new data is fed into them, changing the way AI models behave. Regular audits will help in ascertaining whether AI systems remain in compliance with ethical guidelines and are free from bias and aligned with business objectives.

AI audits have to be performed regarding the performance, equity, and transparency of the system over time. These may include tests on algorithmic bias, data security vulnerability testing, and the capability for explainable output of the system. Auditing will enable the entrepreneur to discover problems that may arise early, so an appropriate corrective action could be taken before the issue causes significant harm (Jobin & Ienca, 2019).

Second, post-deployment monitoring needs to be performed to ensure AI systems are performing ethically even after deployment. It may comprise users' feedback, analyzing real-world outcomes, and making necessary edits to the AI models. The entrepreneur has to be ever-vigilant and proactive in managing AI systems to avoid negative unintended consequences.

Building responsible AI requires developing ethical guidelines for the creation and deployment of AI: transparency and accountability require that continuous monitoring of AI be done by entrepreneurs in such a way that ethical AI is emphasized to build trust, fairness, and social responsibility. Responsible AI practices can thus help companies realize the full potential of AI innovation to tackle a fairer and more sustainable future.

REGULATORY AND LEGAL CONSIDERATIONS

Ongoing evolution in AI technology itself, coupled with pervasive use of it, has made regulatory and legal considerations really frontline in responsible use. Grasping and managing through these regulatory frameworks and myriad legal requirements will go a long way in support for entrepreneurs in effectively managing risk and compliance while leveraging the innovation arising from AI. A few critical regulatory and legal issues relevant to AI implementation are briefly discussed in the following section.

Data Protection and Privacy Laws

Overview of Data Protection Regulations: Data protection and privacy laws are basic to regulation in the collection, storage, and usage of personal data by AI systems. Key regulations include the General Data Protection Regulation (GDPR) of the European Union and the California Consumer Privacy Act (CCPA) of the United States, which impose strict standards on the processing and handling of personal data. These regulations aim at the protection of the privacy rights of individuals and ensuring that personal data is used responsibly (Hoseini, 2023).

Data Protection Requirements: An organization shall ensure it obtains explicit consent when collecting personal data on him; retain the data securely, and provide him with the right to access, correct, and erase his personal data. Such requirements should be addressed at design in the AI system in the first place by embedding data protection principles (Mühling, 2023).

Algorithmic Accountability and Transparency

Algorithmic transparency creates understanding and access in the AI system's decision-making processes to the users. In this respect, the new landmark AI Act by the European Union, among other regulations, puts great emphasis on the dire need for transparency of AI systems, particularly for high-risk applications, which includes clear information on algorithms' workings, what data is considered, and why decisions are made.

Mechanisms of Accountability: There is a need for mechanisms through which it would be possible to track and address issues relating to the algorithmic decisions. This calls for comprehensive documentation in the process of developing AI, audit trails, and mechanisms that users can use to report concerns. Many of the regulatory frameworks require organizations to explain how they handle and resolve issues relating to AI decisions.

Ethical AI Guidelines and Standards

Ethics Guidelines: The sets of guidelines and standards focusing on ethics from various organizations and institutions have recently come to develop the overall concerns about fairness, bias, and discrimination in AI. These guidelines aim at promoting responsible development and use through providing a framework that guides ethical decision-making and accountability.

Standards: Entrepreneurs ought to keep up to date with newly emerging guidelines and standards in the field and then integrate these practices into their AI activities. This would mean the alignment of AI development practices with the industrial standards and participation in the development of ethical framework evolution. It helps in creating trust and commitment towards responsible AI practice.

IP and AI Innovations

Intellectual Property Considerations: Most AI technologies involve the creation of original algorithms, models, and software. Such innovations fall under intellectual property protection. Founders need to understand some basic intellectual property issues about patenting inventions in AI, protecting proprietary algorithms, and how to handle IP rights pertinent to the creation of AI-generated content.

Legal Protections and Challenges: An understanding of the nuances within various IP laws vis--vis protecting AI innovations involves dealing with challenges, such as issues of patent eligibility for inventions relating to AI, or issues of management in collaborative projects. Therefore, due to the legal difficulty, it is recommended that entrepreneurs take professional advice on the protection of their AI innovations and further follow through any disputes over its IP. The next issue is that of

Liability and Risk Management

Liability Issues: AI systems can introduce new liability concerns, especially in particular cases when they cause harm or adverse outcomes. Determining liability in cases where AI systems malfunction or produce unintended consequences can be very complex. Regulatory frameworks and legal precedents are evolving to address these issues and clarify responsibility.

Risk Management Strategies: For mitigating liability risks, the organization may adopt risk management strategies, such as an extensive testing and validation process of AI systems, specified terms of use, and adequate insurance coverage. Furthermore, appropriate incident response planning and potential effective actions to limit the damage may also minimize legal exposure.

Regulatory Compliance and Future Trends

Regulatory Compliance: Staying compliant with regulations probably is one big continuous process whereby an organization would have to stay updated with changes in the law and regulations relating to AI. This would also include monitoring new legislative developments, adapting to the evolution of regulatory requirements, and ensuring that AI practices are up to date with the applicable rule of law.

Anticipating the future trend: with emerging challenges and opportunities brought about by advancements in AI technology, its regulatory framework will also constantly evolve. Entrepreneurs should look ahead into the future of AI regulation by preparing for possible changes through engaging with policymakers, active participation in industry forums besides adapting practices to meet the evolving standards that arise (Hermann, 2021).

Posing regulatory and legal considerations is a significant method of implementation for AI responsibly. The entrepreneurs should take responsibility in data protection and privacy laws, algorithmic accountability and transparency, adherence to ethical guidelines, intellectual property issues, and liability and risk management. This will in turn enable the organization to make effective use of AI with sustained compliance and trust: understanding the current and future trends within the regulatory environment (Bakri, 2024).

THE ROLE OF STAKEHOLDERS IN ETHICAL AI

Ethical AI cannot be implemented without the active engagement and collaboration of various stakeholders. Each group has a very important role in ensuring that the AI technologies are responsibly advanced and deployed. This section discusses the stakeholders involved in Ethical AI and their respective roles toward responsible AI practices.

1. Developers and Data Scientists

Designing Responsible AI Systems: Developers and data scientists are at the very forefront of creating systems in AI. They have prime responsibility for embedding ethics into the design and development process; this would include avoiding potential biases in algorithms, making certain that data is private, and embedding transparency features. Developers can minimize risks and improve fairness and reliability by embedding principles from the start (Prikshat et al., 2022).

Continuous learning and adaptation: Considering the evolution in AI technology, it is incumbent on developers and data scientists to remain current with developing ethical guidelines and best practices. Continuous learning in this respect would help them adapt approaches for finding solutions to emerging challenges and further maintaining conformance with ethical standards.

2. Organizations and Business Leaders

The identification and implementation of ethical frameworks are very important, and here organizations and their business leaders also have a great role to play. This involves comprehensive policy development and guidelines on the development and deployment of AI. Business leaders must ensure that such frameworks reflect the organization's values and address key ethical concerns, such as fairness, transparency, and accountability.

Promoting a Culture of Ethics: Business leaders also have the responsibility to create a culture of ethics within their organizations. This consists of promoting ethical behavior, training in ethical AI practices, and encouraging employees to emphasize responsible AI use. A robust ethical culture ensures that all stakeholders are committed to maintaining high standards in the development and deployment of AI (Tang et al., 2023).

3. Regulators and Policymakers

Setting and Enforcement of Regulations: The regulators and policymakers have an important role regarding the shaping of legal and regulatory environments for AI. They would thus develop and implement regulations that guide data protection, algorithmic transparency, and other AI ethics aspects. Such regulation can effectively help the development and use of AI systems in a manner that protects individual rights and fosters well-being in society.

Address emerging challenges: Policymakers need to be informed of the developments in AI technology and even attempt to predict what challenges that may hold for regulations. It would prepare them in advance through the creation of regulations which tackle the emerging issues; adaptation to which changes occur in AI. Such a one will certainly seek involvement of stakeholders and experts to help design balanced and effective regulations.

4. Ethics and Compliance Experts

Ethical Practice Advice: Ethics and compliance consultants do advise on the institutionalization of ethical practices in AI. They help organizations navigate through tricky ethical issues, ethical audits, and the development of strategies addressing ethical dilemmas. Their expertise is invaluable in ensuring that AI systems align with ethical standards and regulatory requirements.

Best Practice Promotion: They even participate in the promotion of best practices related to ethical AI. Sharing experience and knowledge contribute to wide-ranging standard creation and guidelines within the industry. They assist organizations in implementing responsible AI practices that build trust among stakeholders.

5. Consumers and End Users

Feedback and Insights: Consumers and users are the very critical stakeholders in the ecosystem of ethical AI. Their feedback and experiences might be a source of valuable insight into how AI systems actually affect individuals and society. Sharing user experiences helps in deducing potential issues and areas for improvement in AI systems.

Advocacy for rights and transparency: Consumers have to play their role in the advocacy of their rights and demanding transparency in AI systems. They are in a position to influence organizations and policymakers by raising their voices on data privacy, algorithm fairness, and other ethical issues. Engaged and well-informed users help build a more accountable and responsible AI ecosystem.

6. Academic and Research Institutions

Performing ethical research: Many academic and research institutions contribute to the discourse of ethical AI through research and analysis. It does basic research on AI technology, development frameworks of AI ethics, and assessment of the impacts of AI systems on society. Their research helps inform best practices and regulatory approaches.

Education and Training: Besides their contribution to the education and training of future AI professionals, these institutions integrate ethical issues into curricula in order to prepare students for the ethical dilemmas created by AI so that they can go out into the world and assist in the development of responsible AI technologies.

7. Civil Society and Advocacy Groups

Civil society and its representational groups help to advocate for ethical standards and, where necessary, take organizations to task on account of AI practices. They address concerns on data privacy, algorithmic fairness, and transparency. In this way, it makes certain that the development and application of AI technologies are in concert with the values of society and protection of the rights of the individual.

Monitoring and Accountability: These groups also monitor the development of AI and raise awareness about potential ethical concerns. By interacting with policymakers, organizations, and the public, they help build a more responsible and transparent environment for AI.

Conclusion The commitment to ethical AI is wide-ranging and shared by all stakeholders. Designers and data scientists develop responsible AI systems, organizations and business leaders put in place ethical frameworks, regulators and policymakers craft and enforce regulations, and ethics experts advise best practices. Consumers, academic institutions, and civil society also play important roles in building and advocating for ethical AI practices. All of these stakeholders, by working together, will help develop and deploy the technology in innovative yet responsible ways.

FUTURE DIRECTIONS IN ETHICAL AI

As AI continues to evolve and find applications in additional facets of human life, the future of ethics in AI will be determined through emerging trends, changing technologies, and changing debates about how AI ought to be done responsibly. This section identifies the key forward-moving directions of ethical AI, focusing on technological advances, regulatory developments, and shifting roles of stakeholders.

1. Advancements in Explainable AI

Enhancing Explainability: With systems becoming increasingly complex and integral parts of critical decision-making processes, the demand for XAI will only increase. Future efforts will be channeled to ensuring explainability within AI models, making it easier for users to understand how a decision is reached with ease, while the AI system itself is transparent and accountable in its functioning.

New Techniques and Approaches: Research into new techniques and approaches will be further advanced in explainability. This will involve the development of methods for explaining complex models, such as deep learning networks, and create tools that provide clear and actionable insights into AI decision-making processes. This enhanced explainability will be of immense help in building trust and will also pave the way for the increased adoption of AI technologies.

2. Evolving Regulatory Frameworks

Global Harmonization: With AI technology crossing borders, the call for global harmonization of regulations would grow louder. Future developments may include attempts at developing international standards and agreements that consider ethical considerations in AI and consistency across different jurisdictions. This will help in cross-border collaborations and addressing global challenges associated with AI.

Adaptive Regulations: The regulatory framework will need to keep pace with the rapid speed at which these AI innovations are being developed. Future regulations are likely to embed flexible and adaptive approaches that permit continuous updating and adjusting in response to new technological developments and emerging ethical issues. Policymakers will have to strive for a delicate balance between innovation and imperatives for oversight and protection.

3. Enhanced Data Privacy and Security Measures

Privacy-enhancing technologies are the future of data privacy and security. Future development and implementation will be characterized by innovative privacy-enhancing technologies, especially the techniques of federated learning, differential privacy, and secure multi-party computation.

Stricter Data Protection Laws: These have arisen in regard to data privacy and security concerns. The scope may continue to increase in regard to the protection of data, meaning there could be further restrictions in the future on methods for processing data, increased transparency of data collection and usage, and additional rights accorded to individuals with regard to their personal information.

4. Ethics of AI in Emerging Technologies

Ethics of AI-enabled Technologies: With most emergent areas like autonomous systems, biotechnology, and smart cities introducing AI technologies, it also denotes that new ethical issues will emerge. It would require that in the future, research and discussions will have to be geared toward the implication of AI Ethics in those areas, including issues on autonomy, safety, and societal impact.

Cross-D disciplinary Approaches: The answer to the ethical challenges thrown up by emerging technologies cross-disciplinary approaches involving collaboration by technologists, ethicists, policy makers, and other stakeholders. The ultimate goal of this collaborative effort will be to make sure that ethical considerations form part of the development and deployment process of AI-enabled technologies.

5. Strengthening Public Engagement and Education

AI Literacy: Future directions in ethical AI will move in the direction of promoting AI literacy among the general public. This is achieved through building knowledge around the working of AI technologies and their capabilities and implications, so that persons can be better informed and make decisions or engage in discussions on AI ethics.

Governance with Public Participation in AI: Greater public involvement in decision-making regarding AI governance will be critical to appropriately place emerging technologies to reflect current values and priorities of interest. Potential ways forward could include providing pathways for public feedback on the development of AI policy and facilitating public deliberation on ethical issues related to AI, including opening up AI decision-making to scrutiny and more transparency.

6. Equity and Inclusion

Mitigation of bias and inequality: the work in ethical AI in the future will rest on the detection and mitigation of bias in AI systems, a feature of the methodology, making technologies inclusive, equitable as would be fostered within AI development teams.

Service to Underserved Communities Equity: There will be an increasing emphasis on ensuring that AI technologies serve all communities, including underserved and marginalized groups. Future efforts may well include targeted work to reduce gaps in access to AI technologies and distribute the benefits of AI equitably across diverse populations.

7. Collaboration and Industry Standards

Another key future direction is that of creating industry-wide standards for ethical AI. This shall be a function of active interaction among leading industrialists, academic institutions, and even regulatory bodies in setting up frameworks that can ensure responsible AI development and deployment are consistent and done responsibly across the AI landscape.

Alliances and Partnerships: In going forward, partnerships and alliances amongst stakeholders will be really very crucial towards moving forward with ethical AI practices. Such initiatives can share knowledge, promote best practices, and address common challenges in AI ethics for better development of a more responsible and ethical AI ecosystem.

The ethical AI of the future will be crafted upon three pillars: explainability, regulatory frameworks, and data privacy. New ethical issues and concerns will continually emerge as the AI technology is developed. Solutions to these challenges will depend on the collaboration of all stakeholders. The ways in which AI technologies are being developed and used will be improved, considering ethics principles and societal values, equity, and inclusion, besides industry standards.

CONCLUSION

The place of ethical practices in AI development is neither a regulatory nor a technical necessity but an ontological imperative in the assurance that AI technologies will serve the interest of society with considerations for basic values. Where AI continually evolves and shapes dimensions of our life, commitment to ethics in AI practices will define its impact on innovation, equity, and transparency. It is something at which all stakeholders-developers, business leaders, regulators, and consumers-need to be in it together to overcome the ethical challenges thrown up by AI. An emerging responsibility culture within an organization, strict guidelines on ethics, coupled with constant updates on emerging trends and regulations, can help us manage the complexity of the technology underlying AI and put it to work for meaningful societal change. The future of AI will heavily depend on our joint work of harmonizing between innovation and ethics for the design and deployment of AI systems, so that fairness and transparency are maintained along with general goals for humanity.

REFERENCES

Aggarwal, V., Maslen, C., Abel, R., Bhattacharya, P., Bromiley, P., Clark, E., ... & Poole, K. (2021). Opportunistic diagnosis of osteoporosis, fragile bone strength and vertebral fractures from routine ct scans; a review of approved technology systems and pathways to implementation. *Therapeutic Advances in Musculoskeletal Disease*, 13, 1759720X2110240. DOI: 10.1177/1759720X211024029

Bakri, B., Zm, A. A., Defitri, S. Y., & Mu'min, H. (2024). The effect of ai technology, innovation readiness, and digital entrepreneurship on competitive advantage in start up in jakarta. *West Science Interdisciplinary Studies*, 2(04), 841–850. DOI: 10.58812/wsis.v2i04.807

Bryndin, E. (2019). Practical development of creative life-saving artificial intelligence. *Communications*, 7(2), 31. DOI: 10.11648/j.com.20190702.11

Elvas, L., & Ferreira, J. (2021). Intelligent transportation systems for electric vehicles. *Energies*, 14(17), 5550. DOI: 10.3390/en14175550

Felzmann, H., Fosch-Villaronga, E., Lutz, C., & Tamò-Larrieux, A. (2020). Towards transparency by design for artificial intelligence. *Science and Engineering Ethics*, 26(6), 3333–3361. DOI: 10.1007/s11948-020-00276-4 PMID: 33196975

Giuggioli, G., & Pellegrini, M. (2022). Artificial intelligence as an enabler for entrepreneurs: A systematic literature review and an agenda for future research. *International Journal of Entrepreneurial Behaviour & Research*, 29(4), 816–837. DOI: 10.1108/IJEBR-05-2021-0426

Hermann, E. (2021). Artificial intelligence and mass personalization of communication content—An ethical and literacy perspective. *New Media & Society*, 24(5), 1258–1277. DOI: 10.1177/14614448211022702

Holmes, W., Iniesto, F., Anastopoulou, S., & Boticario, J. (2023). Stakeholder perspectives on the ethics of ai in distance-based higher education. *International Review of Research in Open and Distance Learning*, 24(2), 96–117. DOI: 10.19173/irrodl.v24i2.6089

Hoseini, F. (2023). Ai ethics: a call for global standards in technology development. aitechbesosci, 1(4), 1-3. DOI: 10.61838/kman.aitech.1.4.1

Jobin, A., Ienca, M., & Vayena, E. (2019). The global landscape of ai ethics guidelines. *Nature Machine Intelligence*, 1(9), 389–399. DOI: 10.1038/s42256-019-0088-2

Klímová, B., Pikhart, M., & Kacetl, J. (2023). Ethical issues of the use of ai-driven mobile apps for education. *Frontiers in Public Health*, 10, 1118116. Advance online publication. DOI: 10.3389/fpubh.2022.1118116 PMID: 36711343

Kolanu, N., Silverstone, E., Ho, B., Pham, H., Hansen, A., Pauley, E., Quirk, A. R., Sweeney, S. C., Center, J. R., & Pocock, N. (2020). Clinical utility of computer-aided diagnosis of vertebral fractures from computed tomography images. *Journal of Bone and Mineral Research : the Official Journal of the American Society for Bone and Mineral Research*, 35(12), 2307–2312. DOI: 10.1002/jbmr.4146 PMID: 32749735

Mühling, Ş. (2023). Utilizing artificial intelligence (ai) for the identification and management of marine protected areas (mpas): A review. *Journal of Geoscience and Environment Protection*, 11(09), 118–132. DOI: 10.4236/gep.2023.119008

Ossa, L. (2024). Integrating ethics in ai development: A qualitative study. *BMC Medical Ethics*, 25(1), 10. Advance online publication. DOI: 10.1186/s12910-023-01000-0 PMID: 38262986

Prikshat, V., Patel, P., Varma, A., & Ishizaka, A. (2022). A multi-stakeholder ethical framework for ai-augmented hrm. *International Journal of Manpower*, 43(1), 226–250. DOI: 10.1108/IJM-03-2021-0118

Radhakrishnan, R. (2024). Cultural impacts of artificial intelligence on sustainable entrepreneurship development., 201-230. DOI: 10.4018/979-8-3693-2432-5.ch010

Rojas, A., & Tuomi, A. (2022). Reimagining the sustainable social development of ai for the service sector: The role of startups. *Journal of Ethics in Entrepreneurship and Technology*, 2(1), 39–54. DOI: 10.1108/JEET-03-2022-0005

Salam, M. (2024). Social and environmental responsibility in ai-driven entrepreneurship., 173-193. DOI: 10.4018/979-8-3693-1842-3.ch012

Shahid, N. (2024). Ethical imperatives and frameworks for responsible ai adoption in digital entrepreneurship., 228-250. DOI: 10.4018/979-8-3693-1842-3.ch015

Tang, L., Li, J., & Fantus, S. (2023). Medical artificial intelligence ethics: A systematic review of empirical studies. *Digital Health*, 9, 20552076231186064. Advance online publication. DOI: 10.1177/20552076231186064 PMID: 37434728

Undheim, K., Erikson, T., & Timmermans, B. (2022). True uncertainty and ethical ai: Regulatory sandboxes as a policy tool for moral imagination. *AI and Ethics*, 3(3), 997–1002. DOI: 10.1007/s43681-022-00240-x

Winecoff, A. (2022). Artificial concepts of artificial intelligence: institutional compliance and resistance in ai startups. /arxiv.2203.01157DOI: 10.1145/3514094.3534138

Chapter 8
Artificial Intelligence as a Catalyst for Innovation in Islamic Entrepreneurship:
Balancing Ethics and Efficiency

Early Ridho Kismawadi
https://orcid.org/0000-0002-9420-5212
IAIN Langsa, Indonesia

Mohammad Irfan
https://orcid.org/0000-0002-4956-1170
Christ University, Bangalore, India

ABSTRACT

The study explores the intersection of AI and Islamic entrepreneurship, focusing on how AI can be effectively leveraged to improve business operations and innovation while adhering to Islamic ethical standards. Through a comprehensive analysis, the study identifies practical guidelines for Muslim entrepreneurs to adopt AI technology without sacrificing their commitment to Sharia-compliant practices. The study also provides actionable recommendations for businesses and policymakers to design and implement AI systems that align with Islamic values, ensuring transparency, fairness, and social responsibility in AI-driven initiatives. The findings have significant implications for the Islamic economic sector, providing a model for integrating cutting-edge technology with traditional values to achieve sustainable and socially responsible business practices.

DOI: 10.4018/979-8-3693-1495-1.ch008

INTRODUCTION

Artificial Intelligence (AI) advancement has been at the peak and changed numerous phases so quickly that all sectors have already begun this journey, including Entrepreneurship (Abbas & Bulut, 2024; Duong & Nguyen, 2024; Zhang & Wu, 2024). Nowhere is this truer than in the realm of business, and entrepreneurs are befitting from almost unparalleled opportunity to leverage AI for improving process efficiency or bringing innovation. But when it comes to participating in Islamic entrepreneurship, AI has been met with a certain level of derision; coping Sharia principles on ethical means of doing business and social responsibility related themes can be challenging. With the rise of Islamic economy, it is crucial to discover how AI can be used for profits in business while aligning its operations with a set of values that defines both Islamic finance and entrepreneurship.

It is oriented by the values of Islamic law (Sharia), and encourages business ventures to operate in a way that does not violate Sharia rules on commerce. The potential of AI when clashing with Islamic business process is very extensive. On one side, it can optimize trade mechanism on a quite high scale and it even initiates creative ideas to haft bring the new innovation from this technology but also by considering technological development through ethical domain as well Maintaining the right balance is necessary if AI-driven initiatives are to help business growth in a sustainable way while upholding pure Sharia compliance.

The study explores the corridor of AI and Islamic entrepreneurship, highlighting how AI could be utilized for good business operation with innovation following pure teachings of Islam. This article aims to take a closer look at the opportunities and challenges involved in adopting AI technologies within Islamic entrepreneurship in order to illustrate how technology may be used for sustainable growth, while preserving the ethical considerations on which the underpinning principles of an Islamic economic system rely. Therefore, the outcomes of this study could help in providing guidelines that may actually allow for developing behaviour-strategy AI techniques to not only further business interest but would also underpin Islamic entrepreneurship ethics as well and its sustainability norms which can pave a way towards more sustainable socially responsible businesses.

Researchers hope that this investigation will be of great practical importance to the players in the industry, especially for entrepreneurs and companies operating within Islamic economics. It is writing down some guidelines architected from the perspective of Muslim Entrepreneur in how to use AI in their business operations without violating Sharia principle. Simply put, this research is how one might identify the ways to use AI with efficiency, innovation and growth in businesses that adhere to Islamic ethics.

These are the recommendations companies can implement in designing and operating their AI technology based on Islamic values according to this research. For instance, with respect to the transparency and fairness that are important elements in Islamic entrepreneurship, AI can be employed within data management and automated decision-making as well as customer interaction. It also provides grounded alternatives for companies to manage the ethical dilemmas that surface from combining these more advanced technologies, as well as it concretizes how AI could be applied in a way without causing any problems with Sharia.

The other practical value of this paper is that the policymakers and regulators may be able to derive some insights from our results in formulating policies or regulations favouring AI adoption level within Islamic business sector. In that sense, this work is not only enabling AI at scale directly within industry but also ensuring the use of it in an ethical manner as a means to sustainable growth and well-being. The study therefore provides a much-needed roadmap for the operationalising of AI technology into Islamic business and ensures that rather than obstructing ethical economic logic, this technology is used as an enabler to strengthen established normative values subtending Muslim entrepreneurship.

This study provides an important contribution to enrich the literature of AI integration in Islamic entrepreneurship that remains relatively new and under researched domain. This research can therefore serve as a useful benchmark on how AI might be used in an Islamic economics perspective within business domains for practitioners, academics and policy makers working towards development of the industry. This investigation argues that the principal contribution is a new conceptual framework into which Islamic entrepreneurship can combine its AI technology with ethical, and operational basis. It will guide Muslim entrepreneurs to adopt advanced technologies in their business without compromising the ethics of Sharia, which is one pillar of Islamic Business. The research is a roadmap for companies who want to use AI in their operations and comply with the Shariah requirements, with good practices that application of AI fulfils justice, transparency and sustainability as mandated by Islam.

This research adds to our theoretical explanation of Islamic entrepreneurship by introducing and examining the interplay between AI as well as Sharia-driven entrepreneurship, for which further future theorization may emerge from these studies. The research also has significant policy implications as it provides guidance to policymakers in Muslim-majority countries on how they might stimulate the uptake of AI among Islamic business sectors and ensure that when this technology is employed, its use is done so responsibly through alignment with Sharia. This is getting more and more important in the face of new technology legislations. This is why this research holds relevance as well: to ensure that technological innovation does not merely feed economic growth but it also complements social good and environmental sustainability. With the world becoming more globalised and digital each day, we sure do need people that are able to blend ethics together with technology this research is definitely crucial in guiding us along those paths. In sum, this research not only contributes empirically to broader understanding of the applicability of AI in Islamic entrepreneurship but also provides a blueprint for how global business can adopt technology ethically and sustainably.

The Impact of AI Ethics on Business Sustainability

In the Islamic perspective, ethical AI adoption really matters in ensuring sustainability of businesses (Panta & Popescu, 2023; Trabucco & De Giovanni, 2021; Vrontis et al., 2023). The same will be true for any Islamic applications, which should take their starting point from the core values of justice, transparency and social responsibility that are central to Islam. The 1st principle of fairness says that AI systems must be built so they are free from bias and do not cause harm in other words, everyone should receive full and equal opportunity to lead a healthy life with no discrimination (in processes like hiring as well as business decisions) In so doing, businesses can preserve social cohesion and steer clear of conflictual situations that could harm their reputations or even disrupt operations. Transparency in the use of AI. This is another important factor by which stakeholders trust any business using AI. Transparency is a part of the principles of openness and honesty in Islam. As such companies need to emphasize the explainability of how an AI and its respective data was used, along with any decisions that the system made. This would prevent the doubts and suspicions that could be detrimental to business sustainability, as it breaks the relationship between company and society.

Social responsibility: This is also an important part of Islamic business ethics where it demands company to account for the social and ecological influence that its activities involve (Hassan et al., 2019; Ismaeel & Blaim, 2012; Khurshid et al., 2014). AI used humanely the problem, if some technology can mitigate the most negative consequences of its worst applications such as optimizing resource usage and reducing waste. Companies who prove devotion to social responsibility fulfil their ethical duty but also represent in the eyes of customers, a key factor driving loyalty and sustainability. Applying AI according to Islamic Ethics is not just for the sake of sustainable business growth but rather ensuring that your businesses are giving beneficial contribution to society and environment. By building ethical processes that shape technology, this reveals a way that ethics and technology need not be at odds but can work together to create an inclusive approach towards business in the future.

AI ethics in a company is building up from the ground, so that you can be better positioned to avoid future challenges. Closing Thoughts In a world more and more influenced by technology, companies that incorporate AI in an ethical manner will have tremendous competitive edge. Partly from the effectiveness of AI and innovation it brings to the table, but also partly from its strong ethical/societal side; 2. Enterprises can also remain more loyal to their stakeholders' customers, staff, partners and the community in general through commitment to certain ethical principles prescribed by Islam. By fostering trust with both the transparency and fairness, businesses will already be one step ahead by creating repeat customers who want to have a reliant relationship with the business within society. Doing so is vital in establishing a stable business ecosystem that enables growth to be sustained.

The obvious fact that the company is engaged in social responsibility, not only has a positive effect on branding but also operational continuity. By leveraging AI to optimize how resources are allocated and individual operations are conducted, companies can reduce overall operational costs while meeting increasingly stringent regulatory requirements around environmental impact. As a bonus, this brings added value to the company in pursuing investment and cooperation with parties that value their environmental/social commitments. We must not forget that in Islamic norms, business is for religion and the universe otherwise it will simply disappear. Thus, the use of AI in accordance with Islamic ethics not only serves to sustain businesses in their traditional sense for the long term but also becomes more congruent and supportive to fulfil "doing good" on a large scale. Therefore, the ethical adoption of AI by businesses will not only prosper in the long run but also become an agent of change that ultimately brings benefits to everyone.

AI as a Driver of Product and Service Innovation in Islamic Entrepreneurship

Most of the recent innovations in Islamic entrepreneurship, at least from a business perspective could be attributed to artificial intelligence (AI) (Dwivedi et al., 2021; Huang & Rust, 2018). As the global market is getting more and more competitive, developing innovative products and services which also comply with Islamic principles become crucial requirements. In Islamic entrepreneurship, whose bases are grounded in those principles (justice, honesty and responsibility towards society), AI is an exceptional tool for finding niches where business opportunities compliant to these ethics can be identified. Through AI technology analyses of consumer data, market trends and cultural preferences businesses can implement more appealing products & services which not only meet the demands from Muslim consumers but that are also in line with Islamic values. AI can be used to identify market opportunities in the development of new halal products. In today's market of halal products are related not only to the food and beverages but also cosmetics, medicines or other customer goods that like in this case have a respectful way with their traditions. As the population of Muslims increases around world, halal products are becoming more valuable as well. For businesses to stay ahead in this market, they will have to innovate and launch new products catering for the evolving tastes of Muslim consumers. AI can also be used to mine data from numerous areas, including consumer likings, market trends and changes in regulations among others that might lead it towards the discovery of a new product which is likely to attain achievement in this competitive world. EG, AI can crunch sales and consumer feedback numbers to pin-point your best-selling products let you know what consumers are looking for from those products. This information can, however, be used by businesses to create halal products which comply with sharia whilst catering for a more modern-day Muslim consumers.

The technology could be leveraged to create AI-powered Islamic services that are better aligned with the needs of Muslim customers. These include Islamic banking, education, healthcare and travel services based on sharia principles. For example, in Islamic banking AI can be implemented to create new financial products that comply with the principles of equity and transparency on which Islamic banking is based. It can analyse consumer data to understand more about what consumers want and need, which in turn could feed into the process of designing financial products that are not only Shariah-compliant but also be tailored specifically for different segments they cater towards. In the case of banks, AI can provide a helping hand in designing investment products that not achieve more competitive profits or yield as opposed to conventional banking products but are also sharia-compliant by steering clear from riba and gharar practices.

For one, AI could be utilized in the education space to create Islamic and Muslim-friendly educational services that meet local needs. Such as, AI can develop online learning platforms focusing on content compliant with Islamic principles and crafted for the Muslim learners countrywide etc. It can also lend its support in ensuring that customised curricula are developed and delivered to Muslim learners by analysing data records of learner preferences as well global academic trends. Education service providers can use AI to deliver a learning experience that is more personalized and with higher efficacy, making it possible for Muslim learners to achieve their maximum potential while still living up the values of Islam.

AI could also provide insights to better understand the cultural sensitivities of Muslim consumers from around the world. The Western press likes to portray the Muslim population as monolithic, but we see that is clearly not true. For businesses to thrive, they must know that Islamic entrepreneurship seeks out and appreciates these differences between cultures; it also does the kind of products which will be best suited for consumers depending on their cultural preferences. AI can be employed to scour data from multitude of sources including social media, consumer surveys and sales figures for detecting cultural trends that matter for Muslim consumer tastes. Such as AI can analyse Islamic fashion trends in each Muslim country and give advice to lingerie companies about collections should be sold based on the demand of each market therefore. Through AI to comprehend and cater for these cultural variations, businesses will have the potential produce services and products which are more meaningful & enchanting towards Muslim consumers globally.

AI can help with improving the efficiency of sharia-complaint operations as well. One example is utilizing AI to automate the process of halal certification, which can be a time-consuming and resource-intensive endeavour. Companies can also use AI to analyse documents as well production processes which would help them achieve product haleness at a faster pace. This ensures the software is error-free and reliable, which not only helps in saving time Ans money but also accelerates speed to business. Of course, AI can also be used to handle halal supply chains and make sure that the production process from start to end using sharia principles. Through managing this supply chain with AI, businesses can limit potential sharia breaches and build confidence in their products to the consumers.

But as important it is for its benefits in creating a new image-based Islamic entrepreneurship venture with the use of AI should also be cautious not to lose sight of what Islam and moral values hath represent. On the other hand, AI should not be responsible for allowing more businesses to exploit consumers or unknowingly producing products and services that contradicts sharia. AI as a tool for enabling fairness, transparency and social responsibility in businesses rather than the other way around. For instance, AI could be used in making sure that halal products developed are truly sharia compliant and do not contain non-halal predicates. AI can also help make the Islamic services offered are inclusive and not Favor specific groups.

As such, Muslim Startups are advised to collaborate with the Islamic Scholars and subject matter experts while developing as well implementing AI into their businesses. This way, entrepreneurs can also make sure that AI is being used according sharia principles and help to reach Islamic morality and ethical objectives through an involvement of clerics in the process. Consequently, employers will also have to make sure that AI usage complies with consumer privacy and rights considerations as well as the requirements not to deploy such technologies in an unethical or unauthorized manner. Through a cautious and responsible approach to the use of AI, Muslim entrepreneurs are well-equipped to harness this technology in ways that not only create new products or services but also align with Islamic values.

AI can become a main driver of innovation in Islamic entrepreneurship. To tap new markets in halal products and Islamic services, businesses can use AI to process massive amounts of consumer data as well market trends and cultural preferences. Nevertheless, these benefits would be best maximized if Muslim entrepreneurs apply

AI in ways that maintains the ethics of fairness, transparency and social responsibility. Properly harnessed, AI can aid businesses to make goods and services that not only attend the requirements of Muslim consumers but also align with Islamic moral prides. A stable, viable business is the end game; for one that not only makes financial profit but also has beneficial positive effects on society and environment.

AI in Optimizing Risk Management in Islamic Entrepreneurship

The business realm has long since needed AI, with risk management not excluded from this. Risk management is the biggest challenge in Islamic entrepreneurship as according to sharia principles, speculation must be fully avoided and adhere fairness, transparency with warning on social responsibility (E R Kismawadi, Irfan, M., Al Muddatstsir, U. D., & Abdulkarim, 2023; Ridho Kismawadi et al., 2023). So, by analysing risk in real-time and making more accurate predictions AI plays a key role to develop Islamic entrepreneurship but soliciting most possible business decisions always within the sharia guidelines.

The first is better risk identification using AI. In the business world, which is convoluted and subject to rapid fluctuations in contemporaneous reality things can very quickly bring a rise of risk by sources such as markets dynamics movement under corridor shift price political uncertainty operating risks; AI can simultaneously scrape and analyse data from multiple places, which ultimately allows companies to track a myriad of risks in less time either not having collected certain information without AI or at best making good guesses. For instance, you could use AI solutions to track real-time market data and look for patterns that might signal risks such as abnormal price movements or shifts in consumer behaviour. For example, AI can monitor data from sophisticated algorithms to ensure all company systems are in good shape and alert management when there is an anomaly that could risk the ability for a system to function properly. This is significant especially in Islamic entrepreneurship, as sharia compliance necessitates a strict-risk management protocol to rule out unsolicited speculation.

It can also proactively manage risk a role that AI will increasingly step into. When risks are spotted, the trick is to mitigate those so that effect on business can be reduced. One of its uses is for simulating possible risk scenarios through AI and identifying their effects on the business. Utilizing historical data and predictive models, AI can predict some of the potential outcomes so that management has a good chance to prepare effective mitigations. In Islamic banking, for instance, AI can help to reduce credit risk by using patterns of previous data on loans from many customers and provide more accurate prediction on that. This will permit banks, to some extent at least, better credit quality and lower the risk of default from their borrowers which certainly becomes a necessity for maintaining financial stability as well as complying with sharia principles.

In the context of Islamic entrepreneurship, AI used in risk management based on sharia principles or ethics. It must utilize AI in a transparent and fair way, taking into consideration the social impact of decisions made. For instance, AI algorithms used in credit scoring should not involve biases that could pick some group and leave others. This is because within Islam, justice has a high value and discrimination or injustice should not arise. Moreover, AI should also be utilised for corporate social responsibility – ensuring that environmental and social risks are taken into account when making decisions.

AI is useful for more than compliance with Sharia Requirements which differ even within Moslem countries. Sharia-based businesses are subject to other laws and regulations covering the practices of businesses; specifically, those which deal in interest (riba) bearing debts or products that have sharia prohibitions. AI can track the observance of these laws in a timely manner, send alerts about possible breaches and keep your enterprise compliant. As an example, we can apply AI on monitoring production processes in halal food industry to make sure that every single stage of the whole process meets a requirement from competent authority for these kinds of good (which is so-called as halal standards). As a result, the company does not face any reputational risks or other kinds of legal sanctions that may be imposed in case they do not comply with sharia restrictions.

AI can also improve the risk management policies within companies. AI helps enterprises to take a lot of data coming from different sources, and enables businesses through which they can track emerging risk trends, update their policies with changing market conditions. This flexibility ensures sharia-compliance but offers a form of dynamism to adapt and provide with the right solution, whether it be for existing issues or unexpected problems. For instance, AI may help in scanning the economics and other regulation changes happening across countries while updating company-wise risk policy to ensure it is conforming all laws. So, AI both reduces the risk that is managed by a company and helps it to keep up with its competitive edge when being compared globally.

Benefits aside, there are risks in using AI for risk management as well and one should be very wary of this. In instances where very real ethical and moral decisions have to be made, AI cannot and should not substitute for human judgment. In the context of Islamic entrepreneurship, where sharia is always at the forefronts AI should be a means to help in ethical and responsible decision-making frameworks. Let's say that in the risk assessment process, AI can be used to present relevant information and analysis but it will still require a decision by sharia principle competent management.

Much like any other field, AI has the capability to elevate risk management in Islamic entrepreneurship. AI can also help companies to better identify and manage risks by providing real-time data analysis, more accurate forecast predictions, complex process automation ensuring that all business decisions are made compliant with sharia principles. Nevertheless, to harness these benefits it is crucial that the deployment of AI contributes in an ethical transparent and responsible way. If done right, AI can help in a significant way to support the upcoming sustainable and growth of Islamic entrepreneurship on this digital era.

The Use of AI in Research and Development (R&D) for Islamic Entrepreneurship Innovation

The use of artificial intelligence (AI) in various sectors has been presented as significant for the development of research and development (R&D), including Islamic entrepreneurship (Kulkarni et al., 2024; Lyndgaard et al., 2024; Meyer et al., 2024; Tian et al., 2024). AI in this context enables efficient analysis of information; at the same time, it serves to reveal areas where innovation can be carried out in accordance with Islamic law. The potential of AI scale to optimize the use of Big Data in R&D, help companies with the development of products and services in line with Islamic values further, improve operational efficiency as well as bring in new technologies that support the growth path that shapes Islamic entrepreneurship is enormous. The first is that AI is able to analyse Big Data, making companies able to uncover current market trends and also distinguish consumer preferences and specific desires in the halal sector. In Islamic entrepreneurship, the products and services produced must be of good quality, meet halal requirements and other principles in accordance with sharia law, aka in Islam. Artificial intelligence and algorithms are used to determine emerging patterns or gaps within Muslim communities by exploring consumer data from publicly available sources such as social media, product reviews, or sales statistics. With this information, companies can effectively direct their R&D resources to develop more new products and services that are aligned with Islamic values; For example, halal food that tastes better or financial instruments that are in accordance with sharia that are cost-effective.

With an intelligent R&D process, AI can improve the quality of halal products. Using some in food and beverages, such as automated for the production process while ensuring that each stage produced successfully meets halal criteria. AI can detect product quality-related issues caused by contamination and other non-halal conditions by analysing production process data. This will allow companies to change their recipes along the way, ending up with a final product that is of better quality and God willing, meets the expectations of Muslim consumers. In addition, it is possible to apply AI in the development of new technologies that can help halal certification mechanisms as automated control systems based on recognized standards to ensure compliance with strict regulations along all stages of the production chain.

AI will give companies opportunities to find inefficiencies within their own processes, whether it be in production or distribution and even resource management. For instance, operational data mining reveals patterns (and anomalies) that might signal waste or inefficiency. This information can be used to create more effective and efficient production solutions, for example in automation of time-consuming processes or waste reduction during manufacturing. Islamic operational efficiency can also be viewed from a social perspective where companies are required to minimize resource and energy waste both in production processes and how they interact with the environment among others, considering Islam concepts of wise resources usage.

Meanwhile, AI could also be a force for technological innovation that helps create ecosystems supportive of Islamic entrepreneurship. Especially in sharia-related industries, without technological innovation companies and entrepreneurs will no longer be relevant to the global market. The use of AI in innovating new technologies that are in accordance with sharia can be considered to provide companies a competitive advantage. This includes the possibility for AI solutions also be applied to create more complex (and hence ethical) financial technologies such as digital payment platforms which are compatible with Islamic ban on riba and gharar. With aid of AI, businesses are able to construct algorithms which ensure every transaction is conducted transparently and fairly in accordance with sharia principles. Such technological advancements not only help these companies to be competitive, but they also build trustworthiness and authenticity amongst the Muslim consumers.

Nonetheless, the integration of AI in R&D for Islamic entrepreneurship should come with caution to truly consider all plausible moral and ethical outcome from any innovation. According to Islamic law, no custom can be a true tradition if it does not comply with the principles of sharia (law), social justice and transparency. Hence, companies need to equip their R&D process with collaboration between corporates and Islamic scholars/experts that not only let innovations meet the criteria of technical viability and commercial feasibility but also fit well in fundamental standards found in Islam. For example, companies must ensure that in the development of new products: their raw materials are halal; won't be contaminated by non-halal substance on processing stage at plant level and final product not to contain any elements prohibited under Islamic law. This perspective helps to ensure that AI becomes a powerful tool for the implementation of sharia-led innovation, and presents an innovative system free from kinks in conducting business.

Furthermore, AI could refine new segments for Sharia-compliant businesses to be developed. Detecting underserved markets with big potential for growth is one of the problems in R&D. For instance, AI can be used by companies in analyses of global market data to spot segments that have specific unserved needs not addressed and thus identified; such as Halal products or Islamic financial services outside Muslim countries. It is useful for companies to be more targeted in their R&D, provide products and services directives that are sharia compliant through business opportunities using Sharia-compliant as a value-added expansion of market segmentation. One use case is the analysis of demographic and sociable data in non-Muslim countries provided a good% for halal related product demand using AI, then that can be the initial of many innovative products meeting Islamic values.

But for R&D of Islamic entrepreneurship, AI still have some challenges and risks. One of the biggest obstacles is keeping AI analysis fair and accurate in avoiding unintended consequences due to data bias. Consequently, inaccurate or prejudiced data results in wrong conclusions and unethical decisions. Therefore, companies must take some responsibility for their R&D data being obtained ethically and managed properly. Also, the social consequence of these innovations too needs to be considered by companies as how it can affect work and well-being employees in an era where machines are replacing manpower. Social responsibility is part of Islamic values, and every innovation should be assessed by its impact on the society and environment.

The potential to harness AI in R&D provides a massive opening for breakthroughs within Islamic entrepreneurship. Through it, AI can also provide insights for companies to detect areas with potential breakthroughs, enhance the quality of halal products as well as operational efficiency and develop cutting edge technologies in line with sharia principles. However, as you cannot utilize these benefits unless it is allied with Islamic values and acts of goodness for the sake of businesses that are humane based essentially truth. In the digital era, Islamic entrepreneurship can develop and survive by utilizing AI provided it is correctly utilized.

CONCLUSION

AI innovation for research and development (R&D) of Islamic entrepreneurs can be an opportunity to accelerate sustainable business also align with sharia principles. Market trends, consume preferences and specific demands within the halal industry can all be quickly highlighted with AI's ability to analyse large amounts of data (Big Data) efficient. Through analysis like this, companies can target their R&D efforts towards creating new products and services that are in line with Islamic values such as increased halal product quality of life optimization efficiency improvements to operations or the creation of brand-new technologies that will support an entrepreneurial spirit based on localizing offerings. But if aide has several benefits, so companies must be held in their ethical and moral use of Islamic principles. This includes sourcing and safeguarding data that is used in the R&D process, as well as reflecting on social implications of the innovations. Within Islam, all forms of innovation are to be assessed for whether they align with sharia principles such as justice, accountability and social welfare. Furthermore, AI can assist corporations to discover new halal-compatible markets and improve business opportunities for expansion as well. With AI, organizations can scan data from the global market to see if some market segment with particular demand is overlooked by someone like halal goods or Islamic services in non-Muslim countries. The implementation of AI in R&D can serve as a powerful component to back the development and modernisation for Islamic entrepreneurship. With the correct interpretation, and according to sharia principles AI has less of a threat in making better companies competitive on the global scale than it can help generate sustainable businesses with equality emphasis.

Artificial intelligence also enables fast analysis of data which can help identify market trends and consumer preferences within the halal industry to create items that are more innovative, relevant to consumers. Similarly, AI enhances operational efficiencies and fosters innovation to underpin not just continued business viability but systems that are also compliant with the ethical considerations set by Islamic doctrines. This participation is assisting in Islamic business eccentricity to survive globally and also sharia compliant heavily as an outcome. Furthermore, the practice of AI in R&D applied to Islamic entrepreneurship will need extensive consequences as well due compliance that are following sharia. Optimistically, corporate must follow is the social and ethical impact of each innovation; implement strategies for working closely with Muslim scholars or experts in upholding Islamic values. Moreover, they are also compelling the policymakers to frame relevant regulations which facilitate AI adoption in halal with making sure that this democratic technology is used ethically and responsibly. If used wisely, AI can be another great enabler for sustainable growth within Islamic entrepreneurship.

REFERENCES

Abbas, M. H., & Bulut, M. (2024). Navigating the landscape of sustainable entrepreneurship research: A systematic literature review. *Discover Sustainability*, 5(1), 171. Advance online publication. DOI: 10.1007/s43621-024-00293-4

Duong, C. D., & Nguyen, T. H. (2024). How ChatGPT adoption stimulates digital entrepreneurship: A stimulus-organism-response perspective. *International Journal of Management Education*, 22(3), 101019. Advance online publication. DOI: 10.1016/j.ijme.2024.101019

Dwivedi, Y. K., Hughes, L., Ismagilova, E., Aarts, G., Coombs, C., Crick, T., Duan, Y., Dwivedi, R., Edwards, J., Eirug, A., Galanos, V., Ilavarasan, P. V., Janssen, M., Jones, P., Kar, A. K., Kizgin, H., Kronemann, B., Lal, B., Lucini, B., & Williams, M. D. (2021). Artificial Intelligence (AI): Multidisciplinary perspectives on emerging challenges, opportunities, and agenda for research, practice and policy. *International Journal of Information Management*, 57, 101994. Advance online publication. DOI: 10.1016/j.ijinfomgt.2019.08.002

Hassan, M. K., Rashid, M., Wei, A. S. T., Adedokun, B. O., & Ramachandran, J. (2019). Islamic business scorecard and the screening of Islamic businesses in a cross-country setting. *Thunderbird International Business Review*, 61(5), 807–819. DOI: 10.1002/tie.22038

Huang, M.-H., & Rust, R. T. (2018). Artificial Intelligence in Service. *Journal of Service Research*, 21(2), 155–172. DOI: 10.1177/1094670517752459

Ismaeel, M., & Blaim, K. (2012). Toward applied Islamic business ethics: Responsible halal business. *Journal of Management Development*, 31(10), 1090–1100. DOI: 10.1108/02621711211281889

Khurshid, M. A., Al-Aali, A., Soliman, A. A., & Amin, S. M. (2014). Developing an Islamic corporate social responsibility model (ICSR). *Competitiveness Review*, 24(4), 258–274. DOI: 10.1108/CR-01-2013-0004

Kismawadi, E. R., Irfan, M., Al Muddatstsir, U. D., & Abdulkarim, F. M. (2023). Fintech innovations: Risk mitigation strategies in Islamic finance. In *Fintech Applications in Islamic Finance* (pp. 35–58). AI, Machine Learning, and Blockchain Techniques., DOI: 10.4018/979-8-3693-1038-0.ch003

Kulkarni, A. V., Joseph, S., & Patil, K. P. (2024). Artificial intelligence technology readiness for social sustainability and business ethics: Evidence from MSMEs in developing nations. *International Journal of Information Management Data Insights*, 4(2), 100250. Advance online publication. DOI: 10.1016/j.jjimei.2024.100250

Lyndgaard, S. F., Storey, R., & Kanfer, R. (2024). Technological support for lifelong learning: The application of a multilevel, person-centric framework. *Journal of Vocational Behavior*, 153, 104027. Advance online publication. DOI: 10.1016/j.jvb.2024.104027

Meyer, L. M., Stead, S., Salge, T. O., & Antons, D. (2024). Artificial intelligence in acute care: A systematic review, conceptual synthesis, and research agenda. *Technological Forecasting and Social Change*, 206, 123568. Advance online publication. DOI: 10.1016/j.techfore.2024.123568

Panta, N., & Popescu, N.-E. (2023). Charting the Course of AI in Business Sustainability: A Bibliometric Analysis. *Studies in Business and Economics*, 18(3), 214–229. DOI: 10.2478/sbe-2023-0055

Ridho Kismawadi, E., Irfan, M., & Shah, S. M. A. R. (2023). Revolutionizing islamic finance: Artificial intelligence's role in the future of industry. In *The Impact of AI Innovation on Financial Sectors in the Era of Industry 5.0* (pp. 184–207). DOI: 10.4018/979-8-3693-0082-4.ch011

Tian, L., Li, X., Lee, C.-W., & Spulbăr, C. (2024). Investigating the asymmetric impact of artificial intelligence on renewable energy under climate policy uncertainty. *Energy Economics*, 137, 107809. Advance online publication. DOI: 10.1016/j.eneco.2024.107809

Trabucco, M., & De Giovanni, P. (2021). Achieving resilience and business sustainability during COVID-19: The role of lean supply chain practices and digitalization. *Sustainability (Basel)*, 13(22), 12369. Advance online publication. DOI: 10.3390/su132212369

Vrontis, D., Chaudhuri, R., & Chatterjee, S. (2023). Role of ChatGPT and Skilled Workers for Business Sustainability: Leadership Motivation as the Moderator. *Sustainability (Basel)*, 15(16), 12196. Advance online publication. DOI: 10.3390/su151612196

Zhang, N., & Wu, C. (2024). Application of deep learning in career planning and entrepreneurship of college students. *Journal of Computational Methods in Sciences and Engineering*, 24(4–5), 2927–2942. DOI: 10.3233/JCM-247531

Chapter 9
Entrepreneurial Success and Decision–Making Power With the Support of Assistive Technology

S. Srinivasan
 https://orcid.org/0009-0002-0179-9849
Department of Humanities and Social Sciences, Graphic Era University (Deemed), India

R. Vallipriya
Department of Physical Science, Institute of Education, India

ABSTRACT

The study mainly concentrates on entrepreneurial success and decision-making power and processes in a developing country like India. The study used qualitative and quantitative methods, adopting semi-structured interviews conducted with entrepreneurs in Dehradun City, Uttarakhand, India. The findings of the study were analyzed using SPSS version 23. The study focused on the following aspects: socio-economic characteristics of the entrepreneurs, problems faced by entrepreneurs at various levels such as family, financial, gender disparities, and education, as well as legal challenges encountered by the entrepreneurs. The significance of the study lies in how entrepreneurs, with the support of Artificial Intelligence, cope with problem-solving, risk identification, and decision-making processes. The study emphasizes that AI can play a vital role in improving both the entrepreneurs' lives and their businesses. This study can contribute to enhancing the future perspectives of AI and entrepreneurship-related aspects in research.

DOI: 10.4018/979-8-3693-1495-1.ch009

Copyright © 2025, IGI Global. Copying or distributing in print or electronic forms without written permission of IGI Global is prohibited.

INTRODUCTION

The entrepreneurial process involves identifying market opportunities and developing a business in a viable way to increase its success. The significance of the study lies in the entrepreneur's focus on feasibility, business planning, execution, and growth, which require a blend of innovation and strategic planning. Support for the entrepreneurial process can improve business market opportunities, develop viable business concepts, plan and execute business strategies, and manage growth. There is significant support involved in entrepreneurship, which contributes to shaping the mindset among entrepreneurs. It is incredibly rewarding for entrepreneurs. Entrepreneurs can start their businesses in the competitive world. According to the Global Entrepreneurship Monitor (GEM), entrepreneurs need to invest money, time, and resources. The GEM can help leverage strong data, which can influence the creation of an entrepreneurial culture to eradicate corruption. Successful entrepreneurs must follow entrepreneurial skills to improve creativity, leadership, and risk-taking. It is also important to understand better market strategies to provide a business model for the study.

AI can support entrepreneurial success by facilitating innovation and automating regular and routine tasks, enabling entrepreneurs to focus on problem-solving and strategic thinking (Garbuio & Lin, 2021; Nambisan et al., 2019). AI-powered robots can perform tasks with high accuracy and speed, increasing productivity and efficiency in industries. It can lead to overall manufacturing improvements; reduce costs, and lower inflation in the industry. The study emphasizes that AI can boost the entrepreneurial process and help individuals become successful entrepreneurs. AI can implement innovation in both theory and practice within the entrepreneurial process and can also provide protective support for AI technology, driving both the push and pull in the AI market. Further steps in the innovation funnel, as well as AI's role as a contributor to new product development, are explored. Finally, we discuss future directions for research in these fields.

The study highlights that AI can enhance entrepreneurial success by improving decision-making power. Entrepreneurship is important to the modern economy, and there are challenges for entrepreneurs in decision-making. The study highlights these challenges for entrepreneurs.

AI can play a vital role in improving decision-making capabilities. The proposed study mainly focuses on the theoretical framework for entrepreneurship with the help of AI technologies like machine learning and predictive analytics.

AI AND ENTREPRENEURIAL SUCCESS

Technology can improve entrepreneurs' business domains. The existing study provides a comprehensive analysis of the effect of AI systems on entrepreneurs' decision-making, through their mediation of customer preferences and business benchmarks. The study highlighted the key importance of entrepreneurial decision-making, which is enriched in an environment with an AI system. The system can implement customer preferences and industry benchmarks for employee involvement. The findings of the study provide AI tools for better decision-making in entrepreneurs' businesses, offering endless options and multiple ways to use AI systems. AI in the business sector is more useful for the decision-making process and addresses various social issues related to the impact machines have on humans and society. This study can make new technology more useful for businesses and enhance entrepreneurship (Amoako et al., 2021).

DECISION-MAKING IN ENTREPRENEURSHIP AND ARTIFICIAL INTELLIGENCE

The decision-making process for entrepreneurs involves identifying business plans to effectively solve issues and challenges related to entrepreneurial opportunities. The entrepreneurial process involves facing challenges and making judgments during the decision-making process to achieve organizational goals and plans. The term uses the decision-making process to identify plans and solve specific challenges and opportunities. It is the process of managing opportunities and challenges for the entrepreneur's long-term goals (Hellriegel et al., 2005; Stoner et al., 1995). The decision-making process identifies the best solution for effective business innovation and strategically plans for entrepreneurs through Assistive Technology (Hellriegel et al., 2005). Decision-making for entrepreneurs is the process of improving the business. Entrepreneurial decision-making is vital for the better process for employed and business entrepreneurs to exploit new business opportunities (Davidsson & Klofsten, 2003).

The process can identify the challenges, collect data, and create options to select the course of action. Additionally, the decision-making process refers to defining and selecting options based on the standards and preferences of the leader (Harris, 2009).Examine the study to process the discovery and exploit business opportunities to create market opportunities, acquire resources, refine business ideas, utilize technology, and recruit key employees, etc. (Davidsson and Klofsten, 2003). The study emphasizes that the decision-making process is a critical way to achieve long-lasting success and performance for the enterprise (Reuber and Fischer, 1997).

Entrepreneurs can explore with the support of AI and utilize it to gain information, knowledge, and experience.

Entrepreneurs use novel opportunities to create value for society. It can often involve creating new products, services, and technologies (Levine, 2019; Acs & Audretsch, 2005). It can improve jobs and increase living standards (Astebro & Tag, 2017; Carter, 2011).

The study clearly indicates that improving societal values and increasing the entrepreneurs' decision-making process addresses sustainability issues for both consumers and firms in a circular economy, which can be considered by AI. The effect of AI can enhance the decision-making process for entrepreneurs, offering one of many options to strategize how it is useful for market and business strategy, and to utilize opportunities in firms and society. The literature clearly mentions identifying opportunities in the decision-making process to explore entrepreneurial activity (Fairlie & Fossen, 2018; Shane, 2003; Shane & Venkatraman, 2000).

Entrepreneurs can influence opportunities to discover and exploit them, which can improve knowledge-based performance (Fairlie & Fossen, 2018). However, opportunities to improve society must be conducted in the light of societal and human dignity. The entrepreneurial decision-making process can be extensive and vary depending on various situations (Levine, 2019). Entrepreneurs deal with their business in a commercial way to explore opportunities. Entrepreneurs regularly make decisions concerning the worth of opportunities, pursuing available solutions to explore how they influence their knowledge (Fairlie & Fossen, 2018). Technology can play an important role in addressing entrepreneurs' knowledge of AI; it can facilitate credible interpretation and external data to enhance institutional memory.

ENTREPRENEURIAL DECISION-MAKING PROCESS FOR CUSTOMER PREFERENCE

Customer preferences are considered in the entrepreneurial decision-making process. It can support customers in improving entrepreneurs' decision-making and enhance customer excitement (Venkatraman et al., 2012). Customer preferences are used to construct business strategies that focus on customer relationships to improve decision-making for competitive advantage (Baiyere et al., 2020). Entrepreneurs identify customer preferences to tailor the products and services offered by their industry and business. To increase the global inventory for small businesses, entrepreneurs need proper services and goods, which can improve customer satisfaction and their experience (Venkatraman et al., 2012). The study plays a vital role in improving vibrant economies, providing jobs, and enhancing lives. Entrepreneurship contributes to the development of economic growth (Levasseur et al., 2019).

To explore the research study on how experiences influence the development of positive and negative attitudes towards a product and establish trends in consumer choices (Cullen & Kingston, 2009). This study highlights the trends and essentials for entrepreneurs' decision-making with the support of an Artificial Intelligence (AI) system for effective utilization.

ENTREPRENEURIAL DECISION MAKING PROCESS IN INDUSTRY

The entrepreneurial decision-making process in industry aims to provide the best products and services to enhance business performance (Harrington & Harrington, 1995; Dahlgaard et al., 1998). The focus of the study is on how better performance can be applied by entrepreneurs in the industry (Bogan & English, 1994; Raybourn & Cores, 2001). The study influences knowledge related to business information to improve and increase the quality of the decision-making process. The industry can refer to various markets among competitors to recognize best practices (Harrington & Harrington, 1995). The study clearly indicates the entrepreneurial decision-making process. Entrepreneurs make decisions to analyze situations and meet developmental standards. The study realistically examines the entrepreneurs' decision-making process and assesses practical success (Dahlgaard et al., 1998). The study mainly emphasizes the advancement of continuous learning for both experience and entrepreneurs. The study proceeds with the information and suggestions proposed. Business strategy in the industry focuses on decision-making in entrepreneurship and the crucial leadership qualities required. The significance of the study is to provide various practices for improving performance across different industries and to benchmark organizational processes. The best practice in the company process is defined within the peer group for comparison (Harrington & Harrington, 1995). This can improve the decision-making process by creating new strategies and developing specific best practices, which typically boost entrepreneurs' performance. It can highlight the industry benchmark and set high expectations to increase the entrepreneur's decision-making power.

EMPLOYEE INVOLVEMENT IN ENTREPRENEURSHIP THROUGH ARTIFICIAL INTELLIGENCE

Employee involvement in an organization where all employees are valued. The study mainly emphasizes engaging every employee to help them attain their goals. All the employees request their management to increase their salaries and provide bonuses. Employees and management should cherish each other's involvement to contribute to the organization's success (Aliyu, 2019). Employees can be involved in various activities within the organization to actively participate in events, improve their performance, and empower themselves to attain higher individual goals. The study mainly focuses on entrepreneurs and employee processes in decision-making within the industry to promote active participation and empower both individual and firm performance. The decision-making process is used to solve problems and improve the work process. The function of involvement in various industries in employee working conditions can ensure improvements in the decision-making process, impacting firms' quality and competitiveness. Employees can make strong decisions by participating in volunteer activities and taking responsibility for organizational goals (Sofijanova & Zabijakin-Chatleska, 2013).

The study addresses how employees engage with the organization and improve the workforce, contributing to better decision-making processes. The leader can encourage open communication to stabilize the industrial relationship with employees. Employees are involved in increasing and contributing to policies and documents that support the primary goals of employing their internal ideas, skills, and strategies to improve the thinking and decision-making processes. Employees can be involved in various decision-making processes to achieve excellence in organizational growth. Employees can improve cognitive and emotional support to achieve organizational goals and objectives. It can create a better environment for employees and influence decisions and actions that impact their roles (Aliyu, 2019). To examine the effect of employers and their efforts to participate in managing industry workers to enhance organizational efficacy (Macey & Schneider, 2008).

The study highlights the success of employee participation in entrepreneurial business strategy planning for improving organizational citizenship behavior (Harber et al., 1991). The study indicates the boost in employee commitment to their work. The employees can understand the importance of the relationship between employees and employers. It can empower the organization's decision-making (Bendix, 2010). The entrepreneurs' relationship with employees and their potential to engage in the problem-solving and decision-making process. The study can support the organization and its business objectives and goals in terms of turning over the business plan (Mullins & Christy, 2005). The study addressing employee interest and their involvement, and engaging participation, has increased (Frost, 2000), resulting in more active participation in organizational decision-making by employees. Employees adopt the method for assessing factors and their accountability. Technological systems support employee involvement and make it easier to complete tasks (Aliyu, 2019). To explore the existing literature on decision-making power with AI support to enhance and improve models for the entrepreneurial process. The significance of the study is to create employee participation centered on goods for a logical approach to market strategy planning (Vargo & Lusch, 2004).

AI TOOLS HELP ENTREPRENEURS GENERATE IDEAS AND SUCCEED

The Relationship Between Ai and Entrepreneurship

AI tools, since the 1950s, have been used in theoretical and machine learning models. The study can implement that the advancements of Industry 4.0 must provide theoretical models (French et al., 2021). The revolution in AI represents a tremendous change in advanced technology worldwide, with various applications spreading human intelligence (Oztemel & Gursev, 2018). The AI revolution in the digital era changes Industry 4.0 technological improvement. Industries are improving smart factories by connecting manufacturing systems to enhance human intervention and advance technological growth (Lasi et al., 2014). The study can emphasize that AI technology can control the entire system to improve business activities and human intervention for automated machines. Quality control for the outcome involves performing maintenance activities (Meziane et al., 2014; Murray, 2003).

AI can be used for augmented reality (AR) in digital systems to enhance human-computer interaction by blending real and virtual 3D objects to advance technology in real time (Azuma et al., 2001). AI is more useful for improving the accuracy and clarity of 3D image processing to handle robustness and correlate tasks (Sahu et al., 2020). The entrepreneurs use digital technology and AI to manage digital signatures, maintain ledgers, track staff details, and handle salaries, which leads to trusted and credible outcomes (Dinhand & Thai, 2018). The technological change for entrepreneurs in creating new ventures involves developing the process (Elia et al., 2020). AI can increase entrepreneurs' development and use design scales for the entrepreneurial step-by-step process (Chalmers et al., 2021). The radical improvement in AI can increase entrepreneurs' ability to create new and better opportunities (Obschonka & Audretsch, 2020). Even though AI techniques can improve entrepreneurs' decision-making power and lead to stronger, higher-quality, and more innovative decisions in their own business, they also enhance the effectiveness of business strategy performance (Kraus et al., 2020). AI drives the development of entrepreneurs' business models by using AI-based support. AI is crucial for creating entrepreneurial opportunities in the history of revolutionaries (Iansiti & Lakhani, 2020).

BACKGROUND OF THE STUDY

The background of the study on entrepreneurial success and the decision-making process, with the support of AI, clearly mentions that entrepreneurs use and utilize decision-making technology to identify resources through assistive technology in their businesses. The number of entrepreneurs is increasing every day, which is a positive aspect of economic development for the nation as well as for individuals. It creates job opportunities and fosters business innovation for entrepreneurial ventures. The modern era includes individuals from various backgrounds engaging in entrepreneurial ventures to boost economic growth and empower entrepreneurs (Abosede & Onakoya, 2013). An entrepreneur's success is linked to financial aspects, education, experience, and network. The study places more emphasis on technology, which has emerged as a critical aspect for entrepreneurs, reshaping their business styles and strategies in advanced ways.

Decision-making power is essential to entrepreneurial success. his study can navigate the various dynamics of the environment and entrepreneurs' strategic decisions to quickly adapt to changing market conditions. Effective decision-making power is one of the leadership qualities that enhances cognitive abilities. The study can support the advancement of the decision-making process in a data-driven approach to predict models that enhance entrepreneurs' decision-making power. Assistive technology emphasizes entrepreneurs' capabilities, enhancing their individual efforts and ability to improve through the use of AI. Technology can support broader business opportunities for entrepreneurs. Assistive technology includes decision support systems that improve efficiency and reduce cognitive load for entrepreneurs, allowing them to focus on strategic growth (Usman et al., 2024).

Entrepreneurs can enhance efficiency by using AI and access more opportunities. The AI aid tool simplifies the decision-making process regarding financial aspects and market trend analysis, helping entrepreneurs to identify and rectify barriers and support their efforts. Assistive technology can enhance the decision-making process by innovating new ideas for market strategy to improve business outcomes (Ferri, 2015).

The background mentions the research gap in how entrepreneurs utilize technology to improve their decision-making and achieve business success. To explore how technology can transform the entrepreneurial development process and strengthen economic improvement with limited access and traditional sources. The study investigates how assistive technology can enhance entrepreneurs' decision-making processes and overall success, especially in the context of traditional business improvement.

RESEARCH GAP, RESEARCH QUESTIONS AND RESEARCH OBJECTIVES

Hence, this chapter is an attempt to reduce the ambiguity of previous literature and it considers the following research questions:

RQ1. How can AI tools support idea generation and help entrepreneurs succeed in their business?

RQ2. How can AI support the business development plan?

RQ3. How can AI identify potential investors?

RQ4. How can AI identify the caliber of employees?

RQ5. What roles does AI play in improving Six Sigma for successful entrepreneurs?

RQ6. What strategies are adopted for success in improving the business?

RQ7. What are the problems at the initial stage for startup entrepreneurs, and what challenges do they face after starting the business? How do they successfully overcome these challenges?

RQ8. What are the familial, financial, and educational barriers faced by entrepreneurs?

RQ9. What are the legal barriers faced by entrepreneurs?

Major Objective of the Study

To identify the socio-economic conditions of entrepreneurs.

To assess the challenges faced at the initial stage and after starting the business.

To understand the strategies and methods adopted to innovate the business by the entrepreneurs.

To identify the decision-making processes during business promotion for the entrepreneurs.

The impact of AI tools on entrepreneurs' business activities.

Proposed Research Methodology

The proposed research study aims to conduct data collection systematically. The study will use mixed methods and a self-prepared questionnaire, including questions derived from previous model question papers. The study plans to conduct a snowball sample with 46 respondents in Dehradun city, Uttarakhand, India. It will focus on analyzing the demographic aspects of the entrepreneurs. The study will obtain informed consent from the respondents and ensure that the data remains confidential, with no information shared without the respondents' permission. The study plans to use SPSS software for descriptive statistics and cross-tabulation analysis. Factor analysis will be employed after the data has been collected.

LITERATURE REVIEW

Ai Helps Businesses Find Investors

Business: Entrepreneurs develop new strategic plans to enhance business processes, forecast sales, and generate more revenue in line with market trends. The streamlined process reduces costs and increases efficiency for entrepreneurs' businesses. To provide better customer service and assistance, enhancing customers' experiences. To advertise content for market optimization. To work efficiently on logistics and inventory for new entrepreneurs, identifying risk management strategies and potential risks for opportunities. To analyze market competitors and develop a strategic plan. Entrepreneurs create innovative strategic plans and generate new ideas. To use AI-powered tools. To use AI-powered tools to detect and prevent threats to entrepreneurs' businesses (Tekic & Fuller, 2023).

Investors: AI is used in their business to analyze market trends and increase company performance. AI can improve new entrepreneurs' strategic planning, help identify potential investor risks, and track stock prices in current market movements. AI is more useful for business evaluation and entrepreneurs' asset allocation. It provides real-time portfolio tracking for entrepreneurs and investors. It increases the effectiveness of AI-powered tools (Chishti, 2020).

AI-powered tools for the business and investors: The tools useful for investors include Natural Language Processing (NLP), Machine Learning (ML), Deep Learning models, Business Intelligence, Predictive Analysis, chatbots, blockchain and cryptocurrency analysis tools, sentiment analysis, and data visualization tools (Zwingmann, 2022).

Benefits of AI tools in the Business investors: AI tools are more useful for business investors to increase efficiency, improve decision-making power, and enhance accuracy. They help reduce costs, increase competitiveness, improve risk handling and management, enhance customer experience, provide better services, and boost revenue for faster business growth. Additionally, they offer strategic insights for entrepreneurs to improve growth and make informed decisions in their businesses (McGrath & MacMillan, 2000).

AI IDENTIFY THE CALIBER OF EMPLOYEES

AI can be used to identify employee involvement in their jobs, assess their dedication and interest, and evaluate their capabilities. To analyze employee skills, conduct technical problem-solving tests, and evaluate employee performance (Gravina et al., 2021). Data can be used to analyze productivity and project outcomes, leading to better quality work performance and identifying employee involvement. The study can address employees' future potential and high integrity in their job involvement (Anitha, 2014).

It is useful for analyzing employee communication, fast usage of the internet, and email chat activity. It provides better insights to address leadership qualities, teamwork, interpersonal skills, and active involvement in multi-level work. Employee feedback and interaction reflect their attitude and engagement. Employees play a vital role in 360-degree feedback, which involves both subordinates and supervisors, providing a comprehensive view of employee capabilities (Eisalou, 2014). The employee tracking system nowadays is more useful as AI can detect performance in a digital system and improve skill development over time. AI can appraise employee skills, experiences, and career improvement in projects, ensuring optimal utilization of their abilities. AI can implement transparency and respect for privacy while utilizing human judgment, which is the best approach for evaluating employee caliber (Pereira et al., 2023).

AI PLAYS IN IMPROVING SIX SIGMA FOR SUCCESSFUL ENTREPRENEURS

The study plays a vital role in improving AI by enhancing the sigma of successful entrepreneurs in their business. Six Sigma is useful for defining, measuring, analyzing, improving, and controlling processes. The study addresses how entrepreneurs can apply Six Sigma in their business to enhance their success. The first Sigma clearly indicates that entrepreneurs should define their situation, goals, and agenda for future business plans, including those for employees, employers, and management. They have clear objectives, milestones, vision, and mission for their business, and they improve entrepreneurs' skills and advancement with the support of assistive technology. The measures of the entrepreneur's Sigma level aim to increase the quality of production and use the number of given items and actions. The Sigma level indicates a lower rate of defects. The measure of Sigma can lead to business success by reducing defects and improving processes for capability, cost savings, and customer satisfaction. Adhering to timelines can also enhance employee engagement and help entrepreneurs achieve their business goals. Analyzing Sigma can improve through AI support by assessing data. If the stage is low, they need to work more; if it is high, they can maintain stability in their business. Analyze the data on employee performance and the strategic improvement of entrepreneurs' businesses. Improve and control processes for the entrepreneurs.

Figure 1. Six sigma

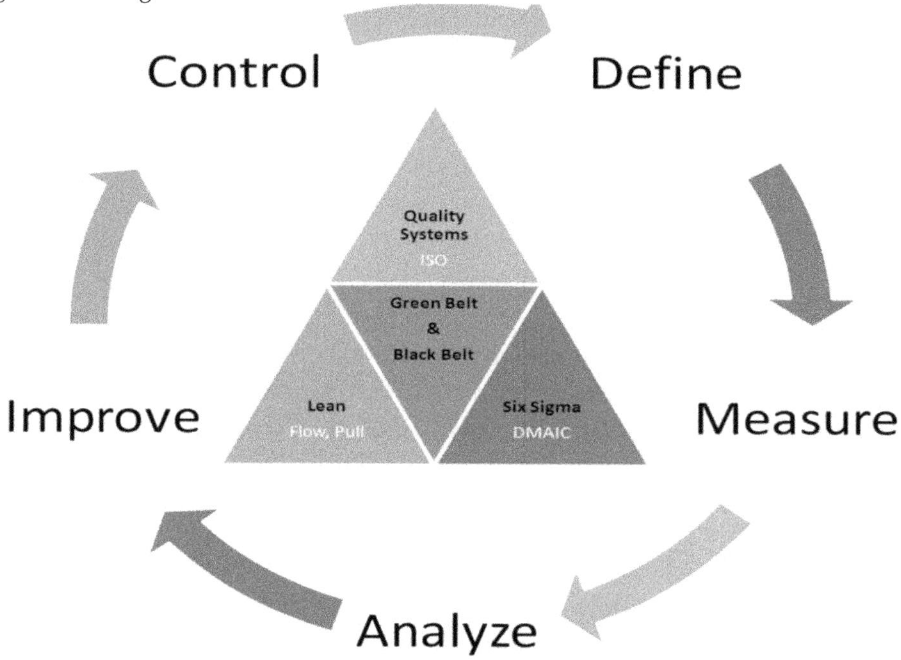

MANAGING THE ENTREPRENEURIAL CHALLENGES AND OVERCOMING THE ISSUES:

AI can address entrepreneurial strategies to identify prevalent problems and provide solutions to increase efficiency. Entrepreneurs face significant challenges that AI can address. Entrepreneurs encounter both biases and unbiased situations in their business decision-making, especially in hiring, marketing, and interacting with customers (Nouri & AhmadiKafeshani, 2020). The study can address issues with the help of assistive technology to ensure compliance with ethical guidelines. AI can address job displacement and societal challenges and help retain employees. Entrepreneurs face challenges in risk management in their business, especially at the initial stage. They may start their business with low capital and be unable to manage the situation effectively (Kanchana et al., 2013). Entrepreneurs without adequate manpower suffer from difficulties in identifying raw materials and selling their products, which makes it very challenging to face these problems. Network and association involvement is very low, making it difficult to handle customers, build rapport, and identify new stakeholders. Entrepreneurs face challenges from their own people in their business. Advertising business activities and products to the market, as well as maintaining finance and accounting, is very difficult to manage (Farquhar & Meidan, 2017). AI supports and drives massive changes in trends. It can utilize various gadgets and apps to address challenges, particularly using laptops and computers to manage stock. Additionally, platforms like WhatsApp, Twitter, Instagram, and Facebook are useful for easy communication, advertising products, and strengthening business networks. The study mainly emphasizes that Facebook is useful for easy communication and advertising products for business and networking. It highlights the responsibility of entrepreneurs to increase their contribution toward improving sustainable and equitable growth through AI in their business ventures (Gill et al., 2022).

FAMILIAL, FINANCIAL, AND EDUCATIONAL BARRIERS FACED BY ENTREPRENEURS

The study mainly discussed the entrepreneurs face their family level, financial level and educational leveled faced barriers related studies. According to the author the finding out the study to discussed that family business and their faced many barriers and obstacles clearly mentioned. The study highlighted lack of access information desiminated by their business support. The crucial family support in the family business and distribution work in their family members. The study can reveal that family business lower propensity for the collateral for transactions. The family level business it can overlap their own familial resources for the satisfied the requirement of support and their program services. The study can proceed for the novel approach it can develop the family entrepreneurial activity it is comparison between family and non-family firms to perceived their barriers (Domańska & Zajkowski, 2022).

Familial Barriers Faced by Entrepreneurs

The entrepreneurs faced familial issues in their business journey, particularly within the socio-economic context of the challenges.

Lack of Family Support: Due to business stress, the entrepreneurs need emotional support from their family. On the family side, a lack of encouragement can lead to low self-esteem, decreased enthusiasm at times, and a sense of isolation. The family cannot provide financial support to initiate their business, making it a struggle to start their ventures.

Family Commitment:

Women entrepreneurs have certain cultural and household responsibilities, while on the other hand, they are also responsible for their professional roles. They are playing a dual role in both their family and business life. That is the reason they face many physical and mental challenges, making it difficult for them to concentrate on their business life. Male entrepreneurs face certain problems related to increased risk-taking, especially in financial aspects. They often invest more money in their business, which can sometimes lead to negative outcomes, causing business losses. As a result, they worry about the future and may struggle to run their business smoothly.

Family Conflicts: The study discusses important aspects of family conflicts, focusing on different ideas and directions for their business in relation to entrepreneurial activities that are worth the effort. The conflict arises from their business when the entrepreneur's vision clashes with their family's expectations. The joint family system can be prevalent in increasing the multiple roles of entrepreneurs, leading to more conflicts in the decision-making process.

Time constraints for their Family Commitments: Entrepreneurs struggle to balance their life, business, and family commitments. It is especially challenging for those who face issues in their family and with dependent members. The lack of understanding among family members about the dedication required in entrepreneurship leads to frustration for entrepreneurs who juggle family and business responsibilities.

Economic Dependence for the Entrepreneurs:

Generally, entrepreneurs from low-income families face more barriers in their business and economic dependence on their family due to heavy pressure to contribute to the household. They may encounter more expenses in their business, and running their lives poses risks for the entrepreneurs. The entrepreneur's income may increase with more business, but decision-making can also increase fear and financial instability in the business.

These are the barriers for entrepreneurs; even though they overcome them and sustain their business life, it has a positive impact on their personal well-being. The strategist can facilitate more communication and establish clear boundaries between family and their business. Seeking mentorship can help mitigate their challenges.

FINANCIAL BARRIERS FACED BY ENTREPRENEURS

The entrepreneurs face several financial issues before starting the business, and after starting their business, they encounter many problems in addressing these financial issues. This study highlights how various obstacles affect entrepreneurs in their industry, business strategy, and personal background. The study can increase awareness of the common financial support and barriers faced by entrepreneurs.

Initial funding options: There are many entrepreneurs who struggle with their initial funding to start their business. There is financial support available, but it is often hesitant to lend to startups due to high risk, and they are falling behind in accessing resources.

Rate of Interest High: Entrepreneurs face problems getting loans, and even after obtaining them, it is difficult to pay the high interest rates, which pose a high risk for borrowers. This increases the financial pressure on the business. Entrepreneurs face high risks and financial pressure in their business. Many loans have very short repayment periods, making it difficult for entrepreneurs to run a new business and take the time needed to become profitable

Collateral Requirements: The entrepreneurs do not have assets. New entrepreneurs, particularly those in marginalized or vulnerable sections, need to provide collateral to banks and financial institutions. The financial risk can improve entrepreneurs' willpower and make them more confident. After achieving success, entrepreneurs can buy new assets, such as property, which helps secure their personal and financial stability.

Cash Flow Management: Small businesses may experience delayed payments from their clients and customers, leading to cash flow problems. Everyday expenses, including salaries and rent, have increased, while revenue generation is very slow, making it overwhelming for businesses.

Lack of Financial Literacy: Entrepreneurs with poor financial planning and limited financial literacy often lead to the mismanagement of funds, poor budgeting, and improper investment in their business. Entrepreneurs struggle with the financial aspects of completing their business plans.

Government Regulations and Taxes: Entrepreneurs face challenges in handling tax regulations, which lead to financial burdens and increase costs. The government somewhat lags behind in providing financial support, but while some schemes are available, many entrepreneurs face problems accessing them.

EDUCATIONAL BARRIERS FACED BY ENTREPRENEURS

Overcoming educational barriers can improve entrepreneurs' ability to start and sustain their business. These are barriers due to a lack of education, limiting access to entrepreneurial training. The study discusses how education supports management, financing, and marketing, yet entrepreneurs face problems because of educational barriers.

Lack of Formal Education: Entrepreneurs have limited knowledge in their field and lack education and financial resources for strategic decision-making. Without proper education, they are unable to handle financial planning and strategic decision-making. Entrepreneurs still struggle without formal education; they are unable to proceed with the business plan, understand tax laws, and comply with labor regulations, which can lead to costly mistakes.

Inadequate Entrepreneurial Education and Training: Most entrepreneurs in rural and underdeveloped areas need to conduct programs such as mass entrepreneurs' meetings and experience-sharing workshops and seminars, along with hands-on training. It can be more useful to address real-world business and entrepreneurs' challenges.

Limited Financial Literacy: Due to a lack of education, entrepreneurs are unable to maintain proper financial literacy and poor budgeting, pricing, and accounting skills, making it difficult for them to manage cash flow, increase profit, and control expenses effectively. Without educational knowledge, they lose opportunities, and entrepreneurs may struggle to create compelling business proposals to attract investors.

Educational support for the Technology: Entrepreneurs without sufficient technical education may struggle to adapt to technological changes and use digital tools for marketing, e-commerce, and operations management. Entrepreneurs still lack technological knowledge, which makes it difficult to innovate and scale their business using modern tools, like AI or online services.

RESULT & DISCUSSION

Table 1. Basic details of the respondents

Basic details of the Respondents			
Demographic Details	**Options**	**No of Respondents**	**Percentage**
Gender	Male	34	73.9
	Female	12	26.1
	Total	46	100
Education	Below 12th	17	37
	Diploma	15	32.6
	Under Graduate	7	15.2
	Post Graduate	7	15.2
	Total	46	100
Marital Status	Married	35	76.1
	Unmarried	11	23.9
	Total	46	100
Type of Family	Nuclear	30	65.2
	Joint	11	23.9
	Extent Family	5	10.9
	Total	46	100
Size of Family	Less than 3	10	21.7
	4-5	30	65.2
	More than 5	6	13.0
	Total	46	100.0
Previous Work Experience	Yes	30	65.2
	No	16	34.8
	Total	46	100
Previous work experience related in your current Business	Yes	13	28.3
	No	33	71.7
	Total	46	100

The entrepreneurs involved in their businesses consist of 73.9% males and 26.1% females. This reflects that the majority of the respondents are men, suggesting a gender imbalance in this study. The education level of the respondents shows that 37% have education below the 12th standard, while 32.6% of the entrepreneurs have a diploma. 15.2% of the respondents have UG and PG degrees. This reflects that the majority of the entrepreneurs have a lower educational background. It is suggested that the entrepreneurs' education level is very low in higher education. The marital statuses of the entrepreneurs are as follows: 76.1% of the respondents are married, while the remaining 23.9% are unmarried. This shows that most entrepreneurs pursue business after settling their family commitments. Family structure of the entrepreneurs: 65.2% belong to nuclear families, 23.9% to joint families, and 10.9% to extended families.

It is noted that nuclear families dominate, but these entrepreneurs also live in traditional and extended family structures. Previous work experience and employment status of the respondents: 65.2% of the entrepreneurs are employed, while 34.8% do not have prior experience. It indicates that most of the entrepreneurs have some prior experience in their own business. The entrepreneur's previous business involvement: 28% of the respondents were involved in their business previously, while 71% were not. It indicates that the majority of them do not own or manage their business. It is shown that the majority of the respondents are middle-aged. This reflects that the education level of the entrepreneurs is below 12th standard and that they hold a diploma. Many of the respondents are married and come from a nuclear family background. A small portion of the respondents was previously engaged in their business activities. The businesses were started in the age group between 26 and 45.

Figure 2. Age distribution of the respondents

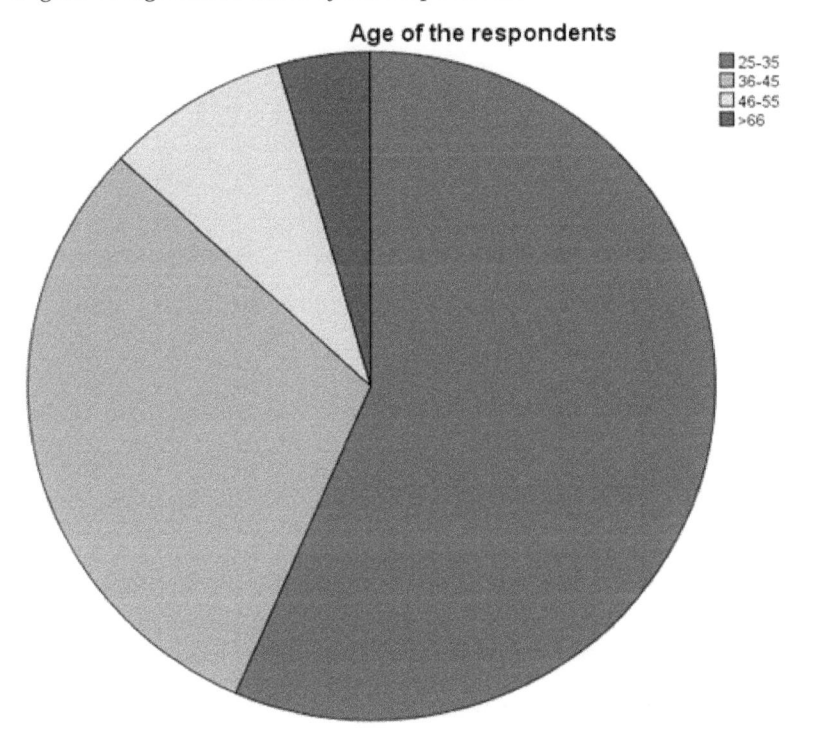

Age of the respondents

- 25-35
- 36-45
- 46-55
- >66

The figure clearly explains the age group of the respondents in their business during the time they were involved in their own business. In the age distribution of the respondents, the age group of 25-35 years has the majority, with 56.4% of them involved in their own business in the young adult group. The age group between 36-45 years comprises 30.4% of the entrepreneurs, making it the second largest group. In the 45-55 years age group, 8.7% of the respondents are included, and among those above 66 years, after retirement from the government and various organizations, 4.3% of the entrepreneurs started their own business in the older adult category.

Figure 3. Entrepreneurs age started in their business

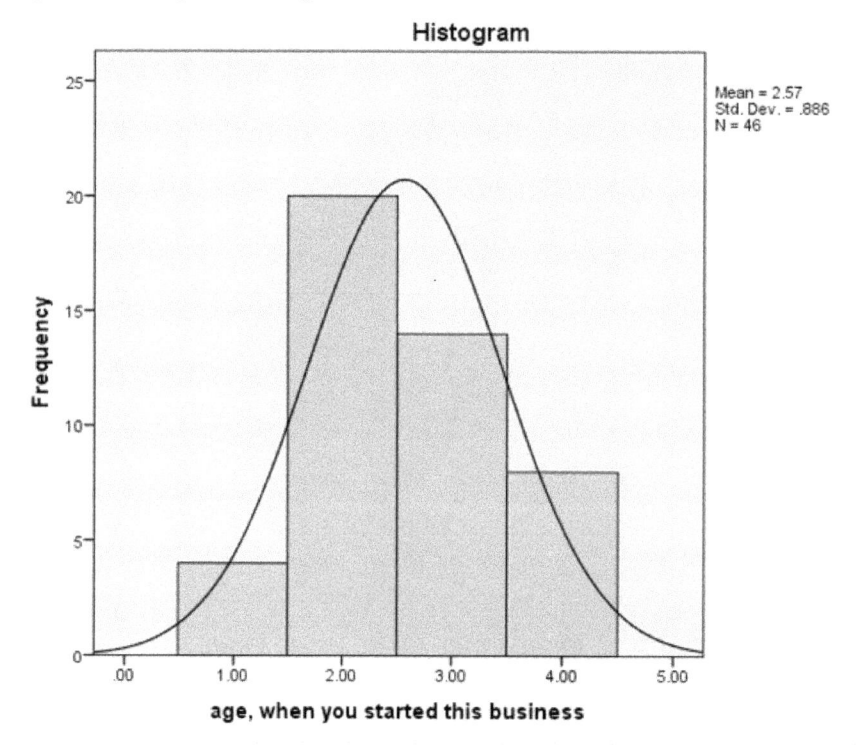

Histogram

[Histogram showing frequency distribution of age when started business. Mean = 2.57, Std. Dev. = .886, N = 46. X-axis: age, when you started this business (.00 to 5.00). Y-axis: Frequency (0 to 25).]

Figure 3 indicates that the majority of entrepreneurs start their business in the age range of 26 to 35, comprising 43.5% of the respondents. The age when they started their business: 30.4% of the respondents are in the 36 to 45 years group, 8.7% are under 25, and 17.4% are in the over 45 age group. It is clearly mentioned that the prime and protective age group to start a business is between 26 and 45 years of age.

Figure 4. Entrepreneur's years of running their business

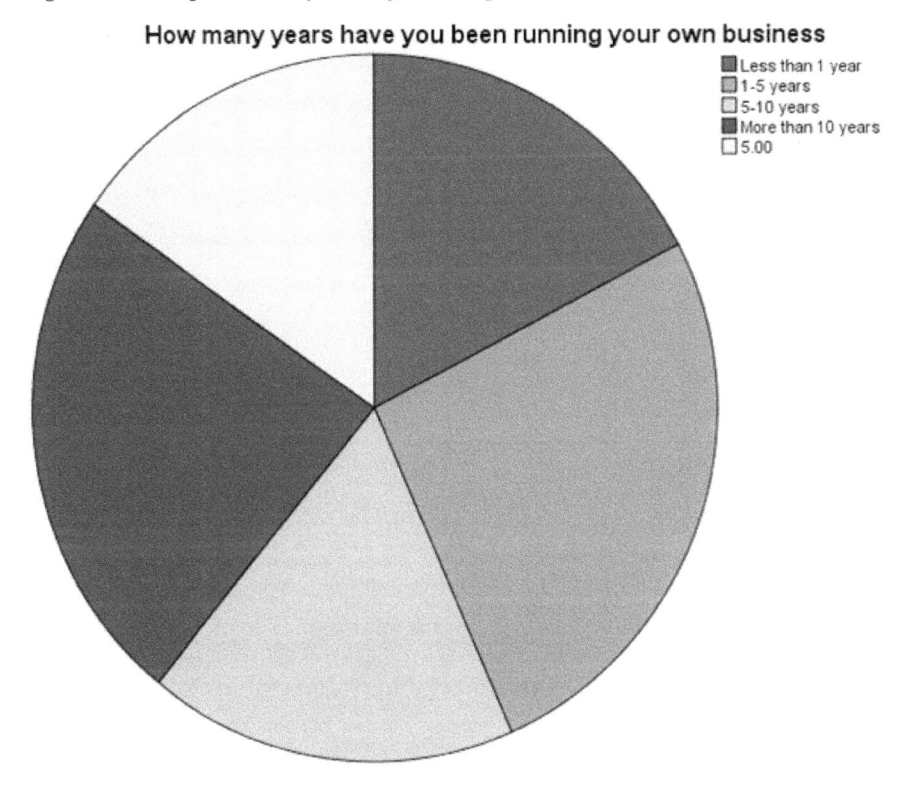

How many years have you been running your own business

- Less than 1 year
- 1-5 years
- 5-10 years
- More than 10 years
- 5.00

Figure 4 talks about business experience: the majority of the respondents, 26.1%, have one to five years of experience. More than 10 years of experience is reported by 23.9% of the respondents, indicating a high level of experience to handle risk conditions when they face problems. Additionally, 17.4% of the entrepreneurs have less than one year of experience, while 17.4% have 5 to 10 years of experience.

Table 2. Entrepreneurs business

Entrepreneurs Business Details			
Particulars	**Options**	**Frequency**	**%**
Entrepreneurs Business Sector	Trade	14	30.4
	Production	10	21.7
	Services	20	43.5
	Hand-craft	2	4.3
	Total	46	100

continued on following page

Table 2. Continued

Entrepreneurs Business Details			
Particulars	**Options**	**Frequency**	**%**
Number of employees in the enterprise	Less than 3	37	80.4
	>5	7	15.2
	>10	2	4.3
	Total	46	100
Legal ownership status of the Enterprises	Sole ownership	30	65.2
	Partnership	9	19.6
	Pvt ltd	5	10.9
	Cooperative	2	4.3
	Total	46	100
Prefer to start your own business	Family tradition	4	8.7
	Small investment is required	14	30.4
	To be self-employed	18	39.1
	No other alternative for income	6	13
	Brings high income	4	8.7
	Total	46	100
How initiated and started the business	Myself alone	24	52.2
	With the family	15	32.6
	With a friend/partner	7	15.2
	Total	46	100
Skill acquire for running your enterprise	Through formal training	19	41.3
	From past experience	15	32.6
	From family	12	26.1
	Total	46	100
Family Background in Business	Yes	29	63
	No	17	37
	Total	46	100
Revenue Growth	Yes	26	56.5
	No	20	43.5
	Total	46	100
Use of Online Apps for Orders	Whats app vido call	12	26.1
	Whats app	24	52.2
	Telegram	6	13
	Instagram	4	8.7
	Total	46	100

Entrepreneurs Business Details: the majority of the respondents, 43.5%, are in the service sector, engaging in service-oriented business activities. Thirty percent of the respondents are in trade, 21.7% are in production-based businesses, and 4.3% are in handcraft-related businesses. Regarding the number of workers in their businesses, the majority of the respondents are solo; nearly 80.4% have fewer than three members. This indicates that family members and related people support their businesses. Additionally, 15.2% of the respondents have 6 to 10 members working, and 4.3% have more than 11 to 15 members working in production and private limited businesses. The majority of the respondents have sole ownership of their businesses, indicating that entrepreneurs run their businesses independently. 19.6% of the respondents are in collaboration with partnerships, 10.9% are in private limited companies, and a small proportion of 4.3% are in cooperatives. It reflects that the majority of the respondents prefer individual and independent entrepreneurship.

The reason for starting their own business is to be self-employed: 39.1% of the entrepreneurs want to become entrepreneurs working independently. The small investment is a requirement for 30.4% of the entrepreneurs, and 13% of the respondents are engaged in side businesses or additional part-time work due to a lack of alternative income. Additionally, 8.7% of the respondents are motivated by family tradition to achieve higher income. This indicates a motivation to work in their own business for growth and economic development. 52.2% of the entrepreneurs initiated their business themselves, while 32.6% of the respondents received support from family members. Additionally, 15.2% started their business with friends and partnerships to generate income. 41.3% of the respondents are involved in formal training activities to enhance their product services, while 32.6% of the entrepreneurs have past experience in their business. Additionally, 26.1% of the respondents were suggested by family to start their own business, as they already have experience from family members who can easily guide them in developing business skills.

The entrepreneurs already have a family background in their business. The majority of the respondents, 63%, have family members who were entrepreneurs and have ownership in their businesses. This reflects that these entrepreneurs play a significant role in their business. 37% of the entrepreneurs do not have a family background in their business; they are operating independently and developing their business activities. The revenue growth for the respondents shows that 56.5% of them achieve significant income from their own business, which is a positive aspect of entrepreneurship. However, 43.5% of the respondents do not have proper revenue growth because they lack a mentor to guide them in improving their business. Technology plays a vital role in improving their business. Customer orders are placed through WhatsApp by 52.2% of the respondents, while 26.1% said they receive orders through video calls. Additionally, 13% use Telegram and Facebook Messenger, and 8.7% use Instagram to order their products through AI technology.

Table 3. Training program

Entrepreneurs Skill Training Program			
Particulars	Options	No of respondents	%
Formal Training Before Start-up	Yes	15	32.6
	No	31	67.4
	Total	46	100
Formal Training After Start-up	Yes	10	21.7
	No	36	78.3
	Total	46	100
Participation in Government-Supported Entrepreneurship Programs	Yes	9	19.6
	No	37	80.4
	Total	46	100
Satisfaction with Government Support for Women Entrepreneurs	Very satisfied	6	13
	Somewhat satisfied	18	39.1
	Not satisfied	22	47.8
	Total	46	100

The entrepreneurs' skill improvement and decision-making processes are supported through various training programs and government support services. Before starting their business, 36.6% of the people attended various training programs, while 67.4% did not attend any program before starting their business ventures. After starting their business, 27% of the respondents participated in formal training activities, while 78.3% did not attend any training program for their business. Nineteen percent of the people attended various government training programs, while 80.4% did not attend any program. The respondents cited a lack of awareness as the reason for not participating in the training programs. Additionally, 13% of the respondents were satisfied with the government training program, 39.1% were somewhat satisfied, and 47.8% were not satisfied, expressing the opinion that the program was conducted with only some formalities. The data clearly indicates that there is a lack of formal training programs before and after starting up their businesses, as well as a low rate of participation in government programs, which do not reach all entrepreneurs. There was low participation in the government-conducted programs involving the entrepreneurs. Almost half of the entrepreneurs are unsatisfied with the government program; it needs to conduct a strong policy to develop the entrepreneurs' skills training program.

Table 4. Challenges faced by entrepreneurs

Challenges Faced by Entrepreneurs			
Particulars	Options	No of Respondents	%
Gender-Based Discrimination in the Business World	Yes	20	43.5
	No	26	56.5
	Total	46	100
Challenges as a Woman Entrepreneur	Yes	17	37
	No	29	63
	Total	46	100
Challenges as a Woman	Limited access to networks	13	28.3
	Gender bias	6	13
	Lack of mentorship	17	37
	Difficulty accessing funding	10	21.8
	Total	46	100
Support Services Needed	Business training programs	8	17.4
	Access to funding options	22	47.8
	networking opportunities	9	19.6
	Mentorship programs	7	15.2
	Total	46	100
Facing Additional Business Challenges	Yes	32	69.6
	No	14	30.4
	Total	46	100

Table 4 mentions that gender-based discrimination affects 43.5% of the entrepreneurs, who have faced and experienced gender-based issues in their business, while 56.5% of the respondents have not encountered any challenges. This clearly indicates that nearly half of the women and men entrepreneurs face some kind of discrimination in their business. Thirty-seven percent of the respondents said that a lack of mentorship means there is no proper guidance to improve their business journey, and 28% of the entrepreneurs reported no network support to enhance business opportunities for women entrepreneurs. Twenty-one point eight percent of the entrepreneurs find it difficult to access funds for their own business. Thirteen percent of the people reported gender bias in their workplace, which is mostly common among entrepreneurs.

Forty-seven point eight percent of the women entrepreneurs are unable to secure the funding sources they need for support services in financial aspects, and 19.6% wish to join networking opportunities. This reflects their desire to join and enhance their business activities from a broader perspective. Seventeen point four percent of them need to participate in business training programs for further development in their business, while 15.2% of the people mentioned that mentorship activities are needed to reinforce their ability to face challenges in their business activities. Sixty-nine point six percent of the entrepreneurs face additional challenges in their business, including gender discrimination, while 30.4% did not report any issues or challenges. The data provide a comprehensive understanding of how women entrepreneurs deal with various problems that hinder their ability to face challenges, overcome issues, and succeed in their business.

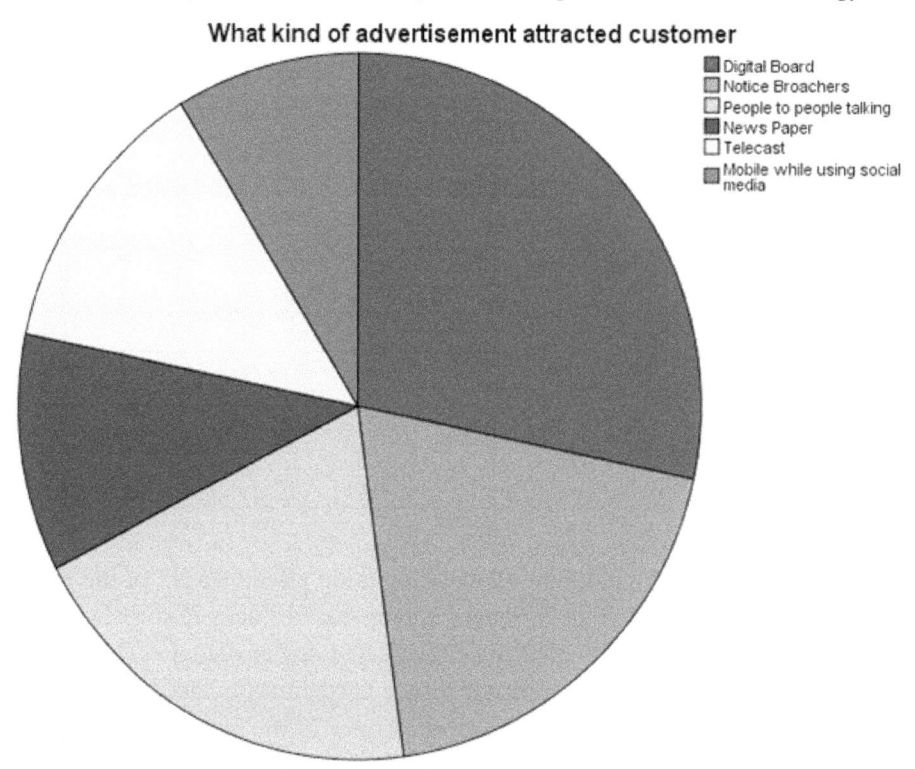

Figure 5. Kind of advertisement use for the entrepreneurs business strategy

What kind of advertisement attracted customer

- Digital Board
- Notice Broachers
- People to people talking
- News Paper
- Telecast
- Mobile while using social media

The entrepreneurs' business strategy to improve advertisement includes various aspects such as digital boards, notice brochures, individual talks to advertise their products, newspaper advertisements, TV broadcasts, and the use of mobile and mobile app platforms. Twenty-eight point three percent of the respondents use digital boards to increase the advertisement of their business, as these are predominant communication tools that provide more visibility to attract customers. Nineteen point six percent of the respondents use relationships and neighbors to promote their products, employing a business strategy that provides free samples and demonstrations to attract customers. Thirteen percent of the respondents advertise on local channels to promote their business and improve their business strategy. Ten point nine percent of the respondents use local newspapers to promote their business through media outlets and increase the number of customers. Eight point seven percent of the respondents use mobile devices to increase customer engagement through social media marketing, allowing them to contact and communicate easily.

Table 5. Entrepreneurs AI usage in their business

Entrepreneurs AI usage in their Business			
Particulars	**Options**	**Frequency**	**%**
Online shopping app like to prefer for customer	Myntra	24	52.2
	Flipkart	12	26.1
	Amazon	7	15.2
	Others	3	6.5
	Total	**46**	**100**
AI gadgets do you like to prefer	Laptop	13	35.1
	Mobile	11	29.7
	Smart watch	8	21.6
	Head phones	5	13.5
	Total	**37**	**100**
Business transaction method customer Prefer	UPI scanner	15	32.6
	UPI id through mobile number	15	32.6
	Master app	12	26.1
	Use bank app	4	8.7
	Total	**46**	**100**
Entrepreneurs business take customer feedback through use which AI tool	Whats app number	12	26.1
	Their own app customer service	16	34.8
	People-people contact	14	30.4
	Others	4	8.7
	Total	**46**	**100**

Entrepreneurs' AI Usage in Their Business Promotion and Communication Methods:

Regarding online platforms for selling products, the majority of entrepreneurs, 52.2%, use Myntra to sell their products through AI digital platforms. Among the respondents, 26.1% are using Flipkart. Fifteen point two percent of the respondents are using Amazon for e-commerce platforms. Six point five percent of them indicate that a small group of entrepreneurs is exploring different platforms. The entrepreneurs use various devices in their business. The majority of the respondents use these devices to easily access financial services and sell products, maintaining all the particular details on their laptops. Twenty-nine point seven percent of entrepreneurs use mobile devices for their own business. Twenty-one point six percent of them use smartwatches and various wearable devices for their business.

Thirteen point five percent of the respondents use technological devices such as headphones to enhance communication, which plays a role in their preferences. AI technology is used for business payment methods. Thirty-two point six percent of the respondents use UPI scanners and UPI IDs, while another 32.6% use online mode transactions. Additionally, 26.1% use MasterCard apps, and the remaining 8.7% use bank apps. The majority prefer UPI payments, which dominate due to their user-friendly nature. In customer service, thirty-four point eight percent of them have their own customer service apps that use advanced technology for customer engagement. Thirty point four percent of the respondents directly approach customers to advertise and inform them about product materials, while twenty-six point one percent use WhatsApp to collect products and facilitate easier communication. Eight point seven percent of them prefer specific customer service platforms.

CONCLUSION

The conclusion of the study addresses the impact of AI on successful entrepreneurship. It outlines how the findings align with the vision of the research paper. The study focused on how Artificial Intelligence (AI) plays an important role in enhancing entrepreneurial success and decision-making power. The significance of the study lies in providing strategic plans and innovations in the entrepreneurial process to improve business growth. It examines how entrepreneurs identify market strategies, manage risks, and optimize resource allocation. AI is highlighted as an important aspect in enhancing business innovation and strategies to promote better business environments.

POLICY IMPLICATIONS

Future research should focus on emerging trends in AI for entrepreneurship, particularly on developing new AI technologies that could further enhance entrepreneurs' success.

AI can play a vital role in improving entrepreneurs' decision-making power effectively. AI can enhance economic growth and support entrepreneurs in critical situations. Additionally, AI consistently provides innovations that improve business activities. Entrepreneurs can receive adequate education and support in AI, which will help them enhance their knowledge and skills to implement effective business strategies.

The government takes necessary action to improve AI tools to enhance entrepreneurs' usage, empower their communities, and increase high-level competitiveness within groups of people. AI can play a critical role in improving financial aspects, such as grants, tax details, and subsidies specific to AI technologies, to support startups and small businesses. AI adoption supports the reduction of financial barriers in entrepreneurs' business processes, improving both business and economic growth. AI technology can enhance business transparency, accountability, fairness, accuracy, and reliability in the entrepreneurs' business operations. Large data can be managed through AI technology, ensuring high quality while safeguarding the privacy and security of business plans. This technology can also significantly reduce manpower needs, leading to cost efficiency.

LIMITATION OF THE STUDY

The limitation of the study is that it was conducted among entrepreneurs in Dehradun city, Uttarakhand. The study focuses on regional aspects, including the geographical area and the diverse socio-economic, cultural, and technological backgrounds of the entrepreneurs. Additionally, the limitation of the study is that it focused on both male and female entrepreneurs.

OUTCOME OF THE STUDY

The outcome of the study is to identify entrepreneurs' socio-economic status and understand how they face challenges before and after the entrepreneurial process. AI can play and support for the business people. There are different strategy can lead to success for entrepreneurs. AI entrepreneurship can provide significant outcomes for decision-making power.

There are different types of strategies to support and improve their business livelihoods. The outcome of the study in various aspects improves AI detection changes, monitoring track for development, forecasting to project in the future to assessing the interpreted data. The strategies can be adopted for the power of buyers and bargaining power of suppliers, to manage the relevant substitutions. The study can be more useful to entrepreneurs to become successful business strategies like new ventures, industry support and ecological aspects increase the economic conditions of entrepreneurs—the technology to improve the politics of entrepreneurship. AI can improve the strategic plan like resource management and market adaptability. The entrepreneurial ecosystem can improve the increasing the sustainability of the business. AI can improve the entrepreneur's economic growth increase job opportunities and motivate and improve the innovation of their business. It can lead to a more diverse resilient economic condition with AI-driven entrepreneurship role to improve the successful entrepreneurs.

REFERENCES

Abosede, A. J., & Onakoya, A. B. (2013). Entrepreneurship, economic development and inclusive growth. *International Journal of Social Sciences and Entrepreneurship*, 1(3), 375–387. http://jesocin.com/index.php/jesocin/article/view/7

Acs, Z. J., & Audretsch, D. B. (2005). *Entrepreneurship, Innovation, and Technological Change* (Vol. 2105). Now Publishers Inc.

Aliyu, A. U. L. (2019). Effect of employee participation in decision making in an organization performance. *International Journal of the Economics of Business*, 3(2), 255–259.

Amoako, G., Omari, P., Kumi, D. K., Agbemabiase, G. C., & Asamoah, G. (2021). Conceptual framework—artificial intelligence and better entrepreneurial decision-making: The influence of customer preference, industry benchmark, and employee involvement in an emerging market. *Journal of Risk and Financial Management*, 14(12), 604. DOI: 10.3390/jrfm14120604

Anitha, J. (2014). Determinants of employee engagement and their impact on employee performance. *International Journal of Productivity and Performance Management*, 63(3), 308–323. DOI: 10.1108/IJPPM-01-2013-0008

Åstebro, T., & Tåg, J. (2017). Gross, net, and new job creation by entrepreneurs. *Journal of Business Venturing Insights*, 8, 64–70. DOI: 10.1016/j.jbvi.2017.06.001

Azuma, R., Baillot, Y., Behringer, R., Feiner, S., Julier, S., & MacIntyre, B. (2001). Recent advances in augmented reality. *IEEE Computer Graphics and Applications*, 21(6), 34–47. DOI: 10.1109/38.963459

Baiyere, A., Salmela, H., & Tapanainen, T. (2020). Digital transformation and the new logics of business process management. *European Journal of Information Systems*, 29(3), 238–259. DOI: 10.1080/0960085X.2020.1718007

Bendix, S. (2010). *industrial relations in South Africa*. Juta and Company Ltd.

Bogan, C. E., & English, M. J. (1994). Benchmarking for best practices: Winning through innovative adaptation. *(No Title)*. https://cir.nii.ac.jp/crid/1130000797322626048

Carter, S. (2011). The rewards of entrepreneurship: Exploring the incomes, wealth, and economic well–being of entrepreneurial households. *Entrepreneurship Theory and Practice*, 35(1), 39–55. DOI: 10.1111/j.1540-6520.2010.00422.x

Chalmers, D., MacKenzie, N. G., & Carter, S. (2021). Artificial intelligence and entrepreneurship: Implications for venture creation in the fourth industrial revolution. *Entrepreneurship Theory and Practice*, 45(5), 1028–1053. DOI: 10.1177/1042258720934581

Chishti, S. (2020). *The AI book: the artificial intelligence handbook for investors, entrepreneurs and fintech visionaries*. John Wiley & Sons. https://www.google.co.in/books/edition/The_AI_Book/oE3YDwAAQBAJ?hl=en&gbpv=0

Cullen, F., & Kingston, H. (2009). Analysis of rural and urban consumer behavior toward new food products using a food-related lifestyle instrument. *Journal of Foodservice Business Research*, 12(1), 18–41. DOI: 10.1080/15378020802671842

Dahlgaard, J. J., Kanji, G. K., & Kristensen, K. (2008). *Fundamentals of total quality management*. Routledge. doi; DOI: 10.4324/9780203930021

Davidsson, P., & Klofsten, M. (2003). The business platform: Developing an instrument to gauge and to assist the development of young firms. *Journal of Small Business Management*, 41(1), 1–26. DOI: 10.1111/1540-627X.00064

Dinh, T. N., & Thai, M. T. (2018). AI and blockchain: A disruptive integration. *Computer*, 51(9), 48–53. DOI: 10.1109/MC.2018.3620971

Domańska, A., & Zajkowski, R. (2022). Barriers to gaining support: A prospect of entrepreneurial activity of family and non-family firms in Poland. *Equilibrium. Quarterly Journal of Economics and Economic Policy*, 17(1), 191–224. https://www.ceeol.com/search/article-detail?id=1069305. DOI: 10.24136/eq.2022.008

Eisalou, M. R. (2014). *Human Resource 360-Degree Feedback*. LAP LAMBERT Academic Publishing. https://mc-caddogap.com/wp-content/uploads/Human-Resource-360-Degree-Feedback-by-Muhammad-Rouhi-Eisalou-1.pdf

Elia, G., Margherita, A., & Passiante, G. (2020). Digital entrepreneurship ecosystem: How digital technologies and collective intelligence are reshaping the entrepreneurial process. *Technological Forecasting and Social Change*, 150, 119791. DOI: 10.1016/j.techfore.2019.119791

Fairlie, R. W., & Fossen, F. M. (2018). Opportunity versus necessity entrepreneurship: Two components of business creation. DOI: 10.2139/ssrn.3140340

Farquhar, J., & Meidan, A. (2017). *Marketing financial services*. Bloomsbury Publishing. https://www.google.co.in/books/edition/Marketing_Financial_Services/lyBIEAAAQBAJ?hl=en&gbpv=0

Ferri, D. (2015). Does accessible technology need an 'entrepreneurial state'? The creation of an EU market of universally designed and assistive technology through state aid. *International Review of Law Computers & Technology*, 29(2-3), 137–161. DOI: 10.1080/13600869.2015.1055660

French, A. M., Shim, J. P., Risius, M., & Jain, H. (2019). The 4th industrial revolution powered by the integration of 5G, AI, and blockchain. https://aisel.aisnet.org/amcis2019/panel/panel/5/

Frost, A. C. (2000). Union involvement in workplace decision making: Implications for union democracy. *Journal of Labor Research*, 21(2), 265–286. https://www.proquest.com/openview/53064144eee6d0428a88224a5429b43e/1?pq-origsite=gscholar&cbl=48175. DOI: 10.1007/s12122-000-1047-7

Garbuio, M., & Lin, N. (2021). Innovative idea generation in problem finding: Abductive reasoning, cognitive impediments, and the promise of artificial intelligence. *Journal of Product Innovation Management*, 38(6), 701–725. DOI: 10.1111/jpim.12602

Gill, S. S., Xu, M., Ottaviani, C., Patros, P., Bahsoon, R., Shaghaghi, A., Golec, M., Stankovski, V., Wu, H., Abraham, A., Singh, M., Mehta, H., Ghosh, S. K., Baker, T., Parlikad, A. K., Lutfiyya, H., Kanhere, S. S., Sakellariou, R., Dustdar, S., & Uhlig, S. (2022). AI for next generation computing: Emerging trends and future directions. *Internet of Things : Engineering Cyber Physical Human Systems*, 19, 100514. DOI: 10.1016/j.iot.2022.100514

Giuggioli, G., & Pellegrini, M. M. (2023). Artificial intelligence as an enabler for entrepreneurs: A systematic literature review and an agenda for future research. *International Journal of Entrepreneurial Behaviour & Research*, 29(4), 816–837. DOI: 10.1108/IJEBR-05-2021-0426

Gravina, N., Nastasi, J., & Austin, J. (2021). Assessment of employee performance. *Journal of Organizational Behavior Management*, 41(2), 124–149. DOI: 10.1080/01608061.2020.1869136

Harber, D., Marriott, F., & Idrus, N. (1991). Employee participation in TQC: The effect of job levels on participation and job satisfaction. *International Journal of Quality & Reliability Management*, 8(5). Advance online publication. DOI: 10.1108/EUM0000000001638

Harrington, H. J., & Harrington, J. S. (1996). *High performance benchmarking: 20 steps to success*. McGraw-Hill.

Harris, R. 2009. Introduction to Decision Making. Available online: http://www.oppapers.com/subjects/robertharris-page1.html (accessed on 23 November 2021).

Hellriegel, D., Jackson, S. E., & Slocum, J. W. (2002). Management: A competency-based approach. *South-Western: Thomson Learning*.

Iansiti, M., & Lakhani, K. R. (2020). *Competing in the age of AI: Strategy and leadership when algorithms and networks run the world*. Harvard Business Press. https://www.google.co.in/books/edition/Competing_in_the_Age_of_AI/VH-JDwAAQBAJ?hl=en&gbpv=0

Kanchana, R. S., Divya, J. V., & Beegom, A. A. (2013). Challenges faced by new entrepreneurs. *International Journal of Current Research and Academic Review*, 1(3), 71–78. https://citeseerx.ist.psu.edu/document?repid=rep1&type=pdf&doi=a28a718c222b38298cf61f514efbe1d2688c329c

Kraus, M., Feuerriegel, S., & Oztekin, A. (2020). Deep learning in business analytics and operations research: Models, applications and managerial implications. *European Journal of Operational Research*, 281(3), 628–641. DOI: 10.1016/j.ejor.2019.09.018

Lasi, H., Fettke, P., Kemper, H. G., Feld, T., & Hoffmann, M. (2014). Industry 4.0. *Business & Information Systems Engineering*, 6(4), 239–242. DOI: 10.1007/s12599-014-0334-4

Levasseur, L., Tang, J., & Karami, M. (2019). Insomnia: An important antecedent impacting entrepreneurs' health. *Journal of Risk and Financial Management*, 12(1), 44. DOI: 10.3390/jrfm12010044

Levine, D. I. (2019). Automation as part of the solution. *Journal of Management Inquiry*, 28(3), 316–318. DOI: 10.1177/1056492619827375

Macey, W. H., & Schneider, B. (2008). The meaning of employee engagement. *Industrial and Organizational Psychology: Perspectives on Science and Practice*, 1(1), 3–30. DOI: 10.1111/j.1754-9434.2007.0002.x

McGrath, R. G., & MacMillan, I. C. (2000). *The entrepreneurial mindset: Strategies for continuously creating opportunity in an age of uncertainty* (Vol. 284). Harvard Business Press. https://www.google.co.in/books/edition/The_Entrepreneurial_Mindset/we7-hg9YGbgC?hl=en&gbpv=0

Meziane, F., Vadera, S., Kobbacy, K., & Proudlove, N. (2000). Intelligent systems in manufacturing: Current developments and future prospects. *Integrated Manufacturing Systems*, 11(4), 218–238. DOI: 10.1108/09576060010326221

Mullins, L. J. (2007). *Management and organisational behaviour*. Pearson education.

Murray, T. (2003). An Overview of Intelligent Tutoring System Authoring Tools: Updated analysis of the state of the art. *Authoring Tools for Advanced Technology Learning Environments: Toward Cost-Effective Adaptive, Interactive and Intelligent Educational Software*, 491-544. DOI: 10.1007/978-94-017-0819-7

Nambisan, S., Wright, M., & Feldman, M. (2019). The digital transformation of innovation and entrepreneurship: Progress, challenges and key themes. *Research Policy*, 48(8), 103773. DOI: 10.1016/j.respol.2019.03.018

Nouri, P., & AhmadiKafeshani, A. (2020). Do female and male entrepreneurs differ in their proneness to heuristics and biases? *Journal of Entrepreneurship in Emerging Economies*, 12(3), 357–375. DOI: 10.1108/JEEE-05-2019-0062

Obschonka, M., & Audretsch, D. B. (2020). Artificial intelligence and big data in entrepreneurship: A new era has begun. *Small Business Economics*, 55(3), 529–539. DOI: 10.1007/s11187-019-00202-4

Oztemel, E., & Gursev, S. (2020). Literature review of Industry 4.0 and related technologies. *Journal of Intelligent Manufacturing*, 31(1), 127–182. DOI: 10.1007/s10845-018-1433-8

Pereira, V., Hadjielias, E., Christofi, M., & Vrontis, D. (2023). A systematic literature review on the impact of artificial intelligence on workplace outcomes: A multi-process perspective. *Human Resource Management Review*, 33(1), 100857. DOI: 10.1016/j.hrmr.2021.100857

Raybourn, C., & Coers, M. (2001). *Benchmarking: a guide for your journey to best-practice processes*. Accent Press Ltd.

Reuber, A. R., & Fischer, E. (1997). The influence of the management team's international experience on the internationalization behaviors of SMEs. *Journal of International Business Studies*, 28(4), 807–825. DOI: 10.1057/palgrave.jibs.8490120

Sahu, C. K., Young, C., & Rai, R. (2021). Artificial intelligence (AI) in augmented reality (AR)-assisted manufacturing applications: A review. *International Journal of Production Research*, 59(16), 4903–4959. DOI: 10.1080/00207543.2020.1859636

Shane, S., & Venkataraman, S. (2000). The Promise of Entrepreneurship As a Field of Research. *Academy of Management Review*, 25(1), 217–226. Advance online publication. DOI: 10.5465/amr.2000.2791611

Shane, S. A. (2003). *A general theory of entrepreneurship: The individual-opportunity nexus*. Edward Elgar Publishing. https://www.google.co.in/books/edition/A_General_Theory_of_Entrepreneurship/0FxO_Wsh30kC?hl=en&gbpv=1&dq=Shane,+Scott+Andrew.+2003.+A+General+Theory+of+Entrepreneurship:+The+Individual-Opportunity+Nexus.+Northampton:+Edward+Elgar+Publishing.&pg=PR9&printsec=frontcover

Sofijanova, E., & Zabijakin-Chatleska, V. (2013). Employee involvement and organizational performance: Evidence from the manufacturing sector in Republic of Macedonia. https://eprints.ugd.edu.mk/8225/1/Trakia%20Journal%20of%20Sciences%28moj%20tekst%29.pdf

Stoner, J. A. F., Freeman, R. E., & Gilbert, D. R. (1995). *Management* (Cliffs, E., Ed.; 6th ed.). Prentice Hall.

Tekic, Z., & Füller, J. (2023). Managing innovation in the era of AI. *Technology in Society*, 73, 102254. DOI: 10.1016/j.techsoc.2023.102254

Usman, F. O., Eyo-Udo, N. L., Etukudoh, E. A., Odonkor, B., Ibeh, C. V., & Adegbola, A. (2024). A critical review of ai-driven strategies for entrepreneurial success. *International Journal of Management & Entrepreneurship Research*, 6(1), 200–215. DOI: 10.51594/ijmer.v6i1.748

Vargo, S. L., & Lusch, R. F. (2004). Evolving to a new dominant logic for marketing. *Journal of Marketing*, 68(1), 1–17. DOI: 10.1509/jmkg.68.1.1.24036

Venkatraman, V., Clithero, J. A., Fitzsimons, G. J., & Huettel, S. A. (2012). New scanner data for brand marketers: How neuroscience can help better understand differences in brand preferences. *Journal of Consumer Psychology*, 22(1), 143–153. DOI: 10.1016/j.jcps.2011.11.008

Zwingmann, T. (2022). *Ai-powered business intelligence*. " O'Reilly Media, Inc.". https://www.google.co.in/books/edition/AI_Powered_Business_Intelligence/54h0EAAAQBAJ?hl=en&gbpv=0

Chapter 10
AI-Driven Decision-Making in Startups:
Enhancing Strategic Choices Through Predictive Analytics

Mohit Yadav
https://orcid.org/0000-0002-9341-2527
O.P. Jindal Global University, India

Ajay Chandel
https://orcid.org/0000-0002-4585-6406
Lovely Professional University, India

Majdi Quttainah
https://orcid.org/0000-0002-6280-1060
Kuwait University, Kuwait

ABSTRACT

This chapter explores the transformative impact of AI-driven decision-making on startups, highlighting how predictive analytics enhances strategic choices and drives growth. It examines the evolution of AI in startup ecosystems, from ideation to scaling, and delves into specific tools and techniques for leveraging predictive analytics. The chapter also addresses the challenges and limitations associated with AI, including data quality, integration issues, and ethical considerations. Future trends such as AI-driven personalization, autonomous systems, and explainable AI are discussed, emphasizing their potential to reshape decision-making processes. The integration of AI with emerging technologies and the importance of balancing technological and human insights are also explored. This comprehensive analysis provides startups with actionable insights on harnessing AI for competitive advan-

DOI: 10.4018/979-8-3693-1495-1.ch010

tage and sustainable success.

INTRODUCTION

The pace at which the world of startups is moving demands an informed and well-plotted decision. With markets becoming increasingly complex, and the volume of data overwhelming, the conventional ways of making decisions are seriously insufficient to avail the required agility and accuracy for startups to thrive. This is where Artificial Intelligence, specifically predictive analytics, becomes such an important factor. AI-driven tools will, therefore, allow startups to tap into data's power for improved prediction of trends, identification of opportunities, and mitigation against risks-thus enhancing their strategic choices. Predictive analytics is a segment of AI that, with the use of machine learning algorithms coupled with statistical models applied to historical data, comes up with forecasts of future occurrences with uncanny accuracy (Giuggioli et al., 2024). Of course, the difference between failure and success may be an ability to predict changes in the market, customers, or operational problems. This chapter goes on to explore the transformative power of AI-driven decision-making in startups with regard to ways that predictive analytics may help entrepreneurs make smarter, faster, and strategic choices toward venture growth and innovation. To this end, recent evolution in the world of startup ecosystems is discussed in depth in the succeeding sections (Abuzaid & Alsbou, 2024).

Artificial Intelligence has been no different in the evolution of startup ecosystems, transforming how emerging companies solve problems, innovate, or even make decisions. Conventionally, decision-making processes in startups are intuitive, based on limited data, and reliant on manual analyses. As the volume of data available to businesses grew exponentially, so did their needs for more sophisticated tools to process and analyze the information effectively. Today, AI is no longer the domain of a handful of very large companies possessing lots of resources; advanced analytics has been democratized, and even the smallest company can apply AI in ways that were previously unimaginable (Afshan et al., 2021).

Early-day startups in AI adoption had used AI for automating routine tasks and improving operational efficiencies. But as AI advanced technically, its applications grew by leaps and bounds. Machine learning algorithms, natural language processing, and computer vision have now become essential parts of the strategies for many startups, helping them to innovate even more speedily and respond in a much timelier manner to market demands. AI-driven decision-making has turned into one of the most crucial differentiators in the realm of the startup ecosystem, whereby firms gain deeper insights into customers' behaviour, optimizing value chains and personalizing products or services on a large scale (Anane-Simon & Atiku, 2024).

This paradigm shift is causing probably the most fundamental shift in the operation of startups from traditional decision-making to AI-driven decision-making. While conventional methods are generally confined to rearview mirror analysis and subjective human judgment, AI makes it possible to have predictive and prescriptive insights drive the decisions of a startup, even anticipating future trends by making data-driven decisions in real time (Csaszar et al., 2024). This evolution has been particularly powerful in verticals such as fintech, healthtech, and e-commerce, where startups have to navigate strict regulatory ecosystems, rapid changes in consumer preference, and high levels of competition.

AI has not only built strategic capabilities for startups; rather, it has also triggered innovative initiatives in the AI industry per se. Many of the currently emerging startups are now at the very frontier of state-of-the-art AI technology development, developing solutions that push the boundaries of what can be achieved with data and machine learning. With AI still evolving, its place in the startup ecosystem will most likely continue to be felt by creating innovative paths and opportunities for growth and competitive advantage. This new breed of AI in startups would serve to show just how fundamental a place technology holds in shaping the future of entrepreneurship, as companies increasingly seek AI to transform data into insights and strategic advantage (Farayola et al., 2023).

Predictive Analytics: Tools and Techniques

Predictive analytics lies at the center of AI-driven decision-making and thus, avails several tools and techniques to startups that can help them predict trends likely to take place in the future, optimize their operations, and make informed strategic decisions. This section examines a few of the key tools and techniques that form the backbone of predictive analytics, with an explanation of their relevance and application in the startup ecosystem (Giuggioli et al., 2024).

1. Overview of Predictive Analytics Tools

Predictive analytics involves the application of statistical algorithms together with machine learning techniques in order to identify patterns in historic data and predict future outcomes. A set of tools has become indispensable in this domain, each offering unique capabilities that cater to different aspects of predictive analysis: (Gnilsen & Necula, 2023).

Data Mining Software: Applications such as RapidMiner, KNIME, and IBM SPSS Modeler can be used to extract meaningful patterns and correlations from big data. Such platforms support the goals of any startup through the analysis of large volumes of data for the discrimination of trends that could not have been easily observed (Heilig & Scheer, 2023).

Machine Learning Platforms: TensorFlow, PyTorch, Scikit-learn, among other machine learning platforms, help startups in the building, training, and deployment of predictive models. These are essential in building proprietary algorithms that will predict customer behavior, market trends, among other key metrics of interest (Jia & Stan, 2021).

Big Data Analytics Tools: Apache Hadoop, Spark, and Hive are examples of big data tools applied by startups within the contexts of data volume management and processing in efficient ways. These are important tools for a startup dealing with huge volumes of data, thus allowing real-time data analysis and thereby faster generation of actionable insights.

Predictive Modeling Tool: This is where advanced analytics SAS, Alteryx, and H2O.ai provide the comprehensive platform for predictive modeling. Such tools will enable a startup to get into serious statistical testing, machine learning, and data visualization in order to develop comprehensive models with unparalleled accuracy (Martins, 2024).

2. Machine Learning Algorithms and Their Applications

The core of predictive analytics includes a set of machine learning algorithms that can enable a startup to develop models capable of making predictions, assisted by historical data. There are numerous such algorithms, each having its own respect complexity and application; however, some of the most common ones in use by startups include: (Rana, 2022).

Regression Analysis: Linear and logistic regression are some of the important methods from predictive analytics (Orhan, 2023). Of these, linear regression could be contemplated when the outcome is continuous-for example, a sales forecast-whereas logistic regression is used for binary outcomes, such as predicting customer churn (Săniu ă & Filip, 2021).

Decision Trees and Random Forests: The decision trees are interpretable models, simple, and very useful for the tasks of classification and regression. An ensemble of decision trees, which is called a random forest, permits improvement in accuracy and robustness thanks to averages over several trees. This helps the startups predict customer segmentation, product recommendations, and a lot more.

Neural Networks: The famous neural network, deep learning models, is really very powerful regarding the management of complex and high-dimensional data. All the applications related to image recognition, natural language processing, and time series forecasting are brilliant in these models. Startups can predict the results of patients, fraud, and automate customer service right from healthtech to fintech (Suurmaa, 2024).

Clustering Algorithms: These are algorithms that perform the role of clustering similar data points together, such as K-means and hierarchical clustering. This proves beneficial in market segmentation, finding customer personas, and uncovering hidden patterns in large sets of data (Tunio, 2020).

Time Series Analysis: Time series analysis techniques like ARIMA and Prophet are specifically designed for the task of forecasting data indexed in time, such as sales data, stock prices, or website traffic. Startups use these to predict trends and seasonality that would inform decisions on inventory management, marketing campaigns, and financial planning (Tunio et al., 2021).

3. Sources and Types of Data Relevant for Predictive Analytics in Startups

Predictive analytics certainly rely on the quality and type of information that the models were subjected to and trained with. Because of this fact, startups typically rely on various sources of data to create a broad predictive model:

Internal Data: These could be data on sales records, customer interactions, website analytics, and other operations metrics that may be created within the startup. Generally, internal data sources are usually most accessible and more often than not, provide very rich feedback about performance and customer behavior in a firm (Yadav et al., 2024).

External Data: External data incorporates market research, social media trends, economic indicators, and data provided by third-party providers. Integrating external data will provide the ability for startups to understand the big picture of the market environment and all the external factors that influence their business.

Unstructured Data: Due to the ever-growing usages in predictive analytics, the amount of unstructured data comprising text, images, and videos keeps increasing. This would make it possible for techniques such as NLP and image recognition methods to enable startups to extract meaningful insights from social media posts, customer reviews, and other unstructured data sources (Afshan et al., 2021).

Streaming Data: Thanks to the rise in IoT devices and a new generation of real-time analytics, start-ups would use streaming data for immediate predictions with immediate decisions. Sensor data, live transaction data, and social media feeds are examples of streaming data sources critical for end-to-end startups who must have urgency in acting on rapidly changing conditions (Anane-Simon & Atiku, 2024).

4. Implementation Techniques in Predictive Analytics (Csaszar et al., 2024).

Alongside the right tools, predictive analytics requires a strategic approach in model development and deployment. Typical steps that startups go through in building predictive analytics include: Data Preprocessing: Before the actual creation of predictive models, a startup should clean and pre-process data to ensure quality (Orhan, 2023). This includes handling missing values, normalizing data, and encoding categorical variables. Data preprocessing is one of the main steps in the building of predictive models, which might greatly affect accuracy (Farayola et al., 2023).

Feature Engineering: Feature engineering selects and transforms the variables that would be used in the predictive model. Majorly, this step is important to perform in order to give higher performance to the model because well-engineered features may lead to better predictions. Some of the techniques are feature selection, dimensionality reduction, and interaction terms (Giuggioli et al., 2024).

Model Training and Validation: Generally, a startup divides its data into training and testing in order to build and validate predictive models. Techniques for cross-validation-k-fold validation among them-are normally applied to ensure that the model generalizes well to unseen data. The process is useful for tuning model hyperparameters and enhancing predictive accuracy (Gnilsen & Necula, 2023).

Model Deployment: The model, after training and validation, needs to be deployed to production. Startups leverage tools like Docker, Kubernetes, and cloud platforms-public ones like AWS or Google Cloud-to deploy models at scale with real-time predictions and integrate seamlessly into other systems (Heilig & Scheer, 2023).

Continuous Monitoring and Optimization: Predictive models must be continuously monitored to ensure their accuracy and relevance over time. A startup should regularly update its models with fresh data, retrain them if necessary, and check the performance metrics for any indications of model drift or degradation.

Case Studies and Applications

The case studies that follow will knit together various successful stories about startups that gain advantage using predictive analytics tools and techniques. Maybe how predictive analytics helped some startup to make a forecast of precise demand from customers, optimize its marketing campaigns, or develop better products (Jia & Stan, 2021). Such real-world examples are just pragmatic ways in which a startup might apply predictive analytics to generate growth and innovation.

In a nutshell, predictive analytics equips startups with a powerful set of tools and methodologies that transform raw data into actionable insights. By judiciously selecting the appropriate tools and applying leading-edge machine learning algorithms, strategic implementations of predictive models will drive startups toward much better decision-making capabilities, enabling them to predict changes in the market, optimize operations, and achieve a competitive advantage in respective industries (Martins, 2024).

AI EMPOWER STRATEGIC DECISION MAKING

AI amplifies the potential of strategic decision-making, ushering startups into a new paradigm where complex business environments can be navigated with unprecedented precision and speed. The next section will dwell upon how AI, through predictive analytics, transforms strategic decision-making, thereby equipping the startup with the means to make wiser, quicker, and more substantiated decisions with respect to growth and innovation (Orhan, 2023).

1. The Role of AI-Driven Insights in Business Strategy

AI-driven insight is the bedrock of modern business strategy and provides a huge competitive advantage to any start-up that embraces it. On the one hand, traditional decision-making rests a lot on human intuition and historical trends; whereas on the other hand, AI gives a start-up the capability to analyze huge volumes of data in real time and get patterns which may not have been perceivable before (Rana, 2022). The power of such insights for any startup, to gauge what might be in store for the future, provides valuable foresight into changes in customer preference, market dynamics, or operational challenges-enabling a proactive rather than reactive decision (Săniu ă & Filip, 2021).

For example, AI can help startups seek out emerging market opportunities by processing social media trends, customer feedback, and industry reports. By running the data through machine learning algorithms, startups can predict what products or services will thrive in the market and thus prioritize investments and optimally allocate resources. Similarly, AI helps in pricing strategy optimization through the competitor price, customer purchasing behavior, and prevailing market conditions analysis so that startups remain competitive but maintain profitability at the same time (Shaikh et al., 2022).

2. Case Studies of Successful AI-Driven Decisions in Startups

Real-life cases will provide evidence of the transformative power AI-driven decision-making can unleash in a startup. Consider a startup e-commerce company that deploys AI to observe customer browsing and buying behaviors so personalized marketing campaigns can be provided to help improve customer conversion rates and customer loyalty. Equipped with AI-powered recommendation engines, the startup offers tailored product recommendations, thereby registering higher average order values and repeat purchases (Tunio, 2020).

It could be applied, for example, in fintech to calculate credit risks through data analysis that emanates from non-traditional sources, including social media activities and transaction history. A startup will henceforth offer credit access to the underserved, minimizing the possibility of defaults. Another remarkable application of AI in FinTech firms is within the fraud detection area in real time (Tunio et al., 2021).

Another good example might be a healthtech startup that applies AI to predict the outcomes for patients using electronic health records and genetic data. Afterwards, the company can develop targeted interventions through the identification of high-risk patients, therefore enhancing patient care while reducing healthcare costs. These case studies illustrate how AI-powered decision-making empowers strategic choices to drive concrete business outcomes to meet growth and success (Usman et al., 2024).

3. Balancing Human Intuition with AI Recommendations

While AI offers huge benefits in strategic decision-making, the key for startups is all about finding a balance between AI-driven insights and human intuition. AI does amazingly well with huge datasets in pattern identification and predictions from past trends, but it sometimes falls short of qualitative factors such as organizational culture, ethical considerations, or market sentiment that often are crucial in making decisions (Yadav et al., 2024).

Startups can strike a balance in this regard by going hybrid, where AI will provide recommendations based on data analysis and then human decision-makers are supposed to evaluate them. For instance, a startup may make use of AI in generating forecasts related to product demand, while final decisions about production levels would be based on factors affecting brand reputation, customer relationships, and long strategic goals. This approach helps ensure that AI is used to complement human judgment, and thereby enhance the quality of decisions, rather than replace it, so the outcome can indeed be holistic and informed (Abuzaid & Alsbou, 2024).

The second reason incorporating humans into decision-making is important is to nullify certain limitations that AI operates within-for instance, biases in the dataset or model. Human oversight, on the other hand, is in a position to identify these biases and correct them to ensure that the decisions made have no hint of discrimination but are ethical and well within the boundaries set by the ethos and values of the startup. Also, by incorporating employees into a startup's AI-driven decision-making, an innovative culture and continuous learning will be developed in which teams can try new ideas and approaches (Afshan et al., 2021).

4. Integrating AI into the Strategic Planning Process

The startups will have to embed AI tools and techniques in all aspects of decision-making, starting from data collection and its analysis down to the formulation and execution of strategy, in order to fully exploit the benefits of AI in strategic decision-making. With that, the case will always be that AI-driven insights inform strategic decisions (Csaszar et al., 2024).

One is to have a centralized AI strategy team with full responsibility for the rollout of AI technologies across the organization. The department, which closely works with other departments like marketing, operations, and finance, identifies where AI can add value. In an effort to align all AI initiatives with the overall strategic goals of the startup, the team ensures AI-driven insights contribute toward the attainment of key business objectives (Farayola et al., 2023).

Another vital component of integrating AI into the strategic planning of an organization touches on infrastructure development. To this end, startups should invest in systems for data management, cloud computing resources, and AI development platforms that will support the deployment and scaling of AI models. Second, a startup needs to bring about a data-driven culture that enables employees to be harbored towards the habit of using data and AI tools in daily decision-making (Giuggioli et al., 2024).

5. Challenges to Overcome in AI-Driven Strategic Decision-Making

Though AI offers huge advantages in strategic decision-making, a start-up should also be able to converge the challenges related to the implementation of AI. One is the data quality and availability. The AI models have to be fed with voluminous data of high quality for generating business-critical predictions. It solely depends on the start-up whether relevant data sources are available or not, and this data is clean, accurate, and up-to-date. It is also important that a startup understand data privacy and keep to legally binding practices in collecting and using data (Heilig & Scheer, 2023).

Another major challenge: the bias or inaccuracy of AI models. This may happen due to several reasons, be it badly representative general population training datasets or models not correctly validated. Testing and validation checks should, therefore, be strong for any startup to ensure the AI models are reliable and unbiased. In addition, the performance of AI models developed should be continuously monitored in production, with adjustments done as necessary to maintain accuracy and fairness.

Finally, startups have to address the human and organizational dimensions of AI's adoption: training employees to make use of AI tools, building a culture where AI experts and business leaders work out solutions together, and communicating well what AI does within the organization. If done properly, these items can help maximize the full power of AI-driven decision-making in attaining strategic objectives (Jia & Stan, 2021).

6. Impact of AI on Culture and Leadership of a Startup

Artificial intelligence used in strategic decision-making has a profound impact on altering startup culture and leadership. This AI-driven insight has helped the leadership make more intuitive and data-driven decisions, probably affecting their credibility and effectiveness as a leader. It is only the open leaders who will move forward with ease into realms of uncertainty for opportunity identification and driving innovation within organizations (Orhan, 2023).

AI also has the power to shape how the teams interact with one another and make decisions in a startup team. The access to current data and predictive insights provided by AI brings much-needed transparency and inclusiveness into decision-making. Teams can tap into this AI-powered functionality to test hypotheses, consider probable outcomes, and map their approach against the overall objectives of the startup. That would mean more cohesive and motivated teams, as employees are more involved in decision-making (Rana, 2022).

By contrast, the adoption of AI means that startup leaders have to develop new skills and competencies. Leaders must comprehend the basics of AI and predictive analytics in order to lead effectively or ensure strategic decisions are made within their teams. It is arguably possible to do this with a focused investment in AI literacy, data-driven decision-making, and leadership development programs in any setting. Moreover, leaders will need to contemplate the ethics of AI and accept responsibility for assuring that the use of AI serves the values of the start-up and society as a whole (Săniu ă & Filip, 2021).

7. Future Directions in AI-Supported Strategic Decision Making

As AI continues to evolve, its involvement in strategic decision-making is bound to further increase. Variants of XAI and autonomous decision-making systems will go on to enhance explainability and interpretability of AI models, further easing the ability for startups to trust and act upon AI-driven insights. Advancements in NLP and AI-driven analytics platforms will enable startups to analyze unstructured data more effectively, uncovering new insights and opportunities (Suurmaa, 2024).

In the future, AI-driven decision-making may also be further integrated into other emerging technologies, such as blockchain and IoT. For example, startups might apply AI to real-time data coming from IoT devices in order to achieve supply chain optimization, equipment performance monitoring, and enhanced customer experiences. Blockchain technology may further bolster the security and transparency of AI-driven decisions, and thus provide a more robust basis for strategic planning to startups (Tunio, 2020).

Eventually, in any case, how well the startups adapt to the changing landscape and innovate within it will shape the future of AI-driven strategic decision-making. Only then can a startup position itself favorably to thrive best in an ever-competitive and data-driven world by embracing AI and showing inquisitiveness toward new ways of integrating it into their strategic processes (Tunio et al., 2021).

In all, AI-driven decision-making presents a tremendous opportunity for startups to leap forward in their strategy-making process for long-term success. A startup can draw maximum value from AI toward the fruition of a competitive and sustainable advantage in its industry by leveraging predictive analytics, balancing AI insights with human intuition, and overcoming the challenges presented by AI adoption (Usman et al., 2024).

AI in Different Startup Phases

Artificial Intelligence can transform a startup from the very initial stages of its inception to scaling and beyond. At each development stage in a startup, there is a set of specific challenges and opportunities; AI might be highly instrumental for startups to negotiate these phases more efficiently. The section details how AI might be used in various phases of a startup while outlining specific benefits and applications that will help a business thrive during each respective phase (Yablonsky, 2020).

1. Ideation and Conceptualization Phase

It includes the ideation or conceptualization at the initial stage of a start-up, whereby different ideas are brainstormed and created by the founders, which might disrupt the market. AI could be a strong tool in this phase for the validation of ideas and identification of market opportunities (Yadav et al., 2024).

AI-driven market research tools can analyze vast amounts of data from social media, industry reports, and patterns of consumer behavior to identify gaps in the market and emerging trends. Founders will, therefore, be able to develop their idea further and assure its relevance to a current market need. For instance, AI-powered sentiment analysis may avail to the founder an understanding of what the general public thinks about certain topics, products, or services; thus, providing valuable insights toward shaping the value proposition of the startup (Abuzaid & Alsbou, 2024).

AI will also support competitive analysis by scanning and analyzing competitor activities, product launches, and market positioning. This helps the startup differentiate from an existing player and works out a USP that the target audience understands and accepts (Afshan et al., 2021).

2. Early-Stage Development

After validation, the next logical step for any startup will be to actually build the product or service. During this development phase, AI can ensure that design, prototyping, and testing phases are orchestrated and hastened toward the market (Anane-Simon & Atiku, 2024).

AI-driven design software can automatically create better prototypes for startups with a product development focus. A tool could create different design iterations from a set of parameters, and a startup will test and iterate on their products more effectively. AI will be able to simulate hundreds of scenarios and give valuable predictions of what the product will do under live conditions. This reduces the chances of costly errors and reworks (Csaszar et al., 2024).

This next level of application helps AI-powered coding assistants in software development develop the efficiency and accuracy of the code. The facility can propose code snippets, identify bugs, and even generate code from natural language descriptions so that developers can use scarce resources on higher levels of problem-solving. Besides that, AI-driven testing will also help get the issues identified and fixed on automated grounds to render the product robust and ready for launch (Farayola et al., 2023).

3. Market Entry and Growth Phase

During the market entry and growth phase of a startup, AI can really drive a competitive edge in customer acquisition, marketing, and sales strategies. Indeed, at this stage, the focus is to build the customer base, revenue generation, and scaling of operations.

AI-powered marketing tools help in discovering the best customer acquisition strategy through the analysis of customer data and identification of the most apt channel, messages, and tactics to reach target audiences. For example, AI-powered customer segmentation tools divide customers into behavioral, preference, and demographic variables that allow startups to create focused marketing campaigns that resonate with certain segments. This can lead to better conversion rates in such marketing campaigns and improve customer loyalty (Gnilsen & Necula, 2023).

This could also be seen in predictive lead scoring, where AI stipulates the most promising leads based on historical data and behavioral signals. Concentrating on these leads will increase the chances of closing deals and securing maximum revenue. AI-driven chatbots and virtual assistants can also be forwarded to interact with customers, answer their queries, and guide them through the purchase to make the customer experience seamless and effective (Heilig & Scheer, 2023).

AI-powered pricing optimization tools can make this easy by helping startups set competitive prices which also maximize profitability while remaining attractive to customers. These tools analyze market conditions, competitor pricing, and customer willingness to pay price to help the startup make an informed, data-driven pricing call aligned with growth objectives.

4. Scaling and Expansion Phase

During this scale-up phase, operations are expanded; new markets are attained, which means so many more complexities. AI can be a strong facilitator for startups in scaling up efficiently with operational excellence.

AI-driven supply chain management will go a long way in enabling them to optimize inventory levels, streamline logistics, and predict demand so that startups can effectively meet customer demand without overextending resources (Jia & Stan, 2021). This would analyze data flowing from various sources such as sales trends, weather patterns, and supplier performance to enable them to make very accurate predictions for optimizing the supply chain operations. This is very important to those with physical products, given that efficient supply chain management might imply great profitability and customer satisfaction (Martins, 2024).

Market entry analysis Artificial Intelligence-IFT tools for startups entering new markets can value the viability of different markets according to a host of consumer behaviors, economic conditions, and regulatory environments. This can help indicate where the most potential for success lies in the marketplace and will enable the startup to tailor their strategies appropriately (Orhan, 2023).

AI can also enable talent management and organizational scaling through automation of recruitment processes and identification of the skills and competencies that are required for further growth. AI-driven HR tools screen resumes, conduct preliminary interviews, and even predict the performance of employees to help startups build high-performing teams very fast and efficiently (Rana, 2022).

5. Maturity and Optimization Phase

Every time a startup advances towards maturity, attention shifts to the optimization of operation, maximizing profitability, and retaining their competitive edge. In that sense, AI in this phase can be utilized to fine tune its business processes and make better decisions (Săniu ă & Filip, 2021).

AI-powered analytics can track key performance indicators in real time and also arm the startup with actionable insights on how to sustain operational efficiency. For example, AI makes analysis of customers' feedback and operations possible that can help in pointing out areas where production costs should be minimized, product quality enhanced, or customer service improved. Essentially, optimization of operation is the key to profitability and the ultimate guarantee of long-term growth for any startup (Shaikh et al., 2022).

More importantly, AI can help bridge a role in innovating new opportunities for product development, market expansion, or business model evolution. For example, AI-powered trend analysis tools can predict changes in consumer tastes and preferences, enabling startups to be a step ahead of the curve by introducing new products or services that meet emerging needs. Such proactive innovation will help startups survive and remain relevant in an ever-changing marketplace (Suurmaa, 2024).

6. AI in Pivoting and Reinvention

Where relevant, the market may shift, or internal or competitive pressures may set in that will force the firm to pivot or reinvent. AI comes in handy in such crucial transitions and helps the startups figure out what is the most feasible strategy for pivoting and execute it successfully (Tunio, 2020).

AI-powered scenario analysis tools can model the possible outcomes of any one of several pivot strategies so that startups understand the risks versus rewards for each available option before choosing. For example, a startup might use AI to determine how entering a new market, introducing a new product line, or altering its business model could work for it. By analyzing information on their pivot decisions derived from diverse data sources, AI will help startups understand the true impact of their decisions (Tunio et al., 2021).

Besides, AI can support the implementation of pivot strategies through process automation, optimization of resource distribution, and performance monitoring. In times of remarkable change within the startup world, AI can help turn forces of change into much-needed agility and flexibility in adapting quickly and effectively to new circumstances (Usman et al., 2024).

7. Exit Strategies and AI's Role

Precisely at the juncture when the startup gets ready to contemplate its exit, whether through merger, acquisition, or IPO, AI can be quite helpful in preparing for and executing the exit strategy. AI-powered valuation tools make use of complicated algorithms to arrive at an estimate of the market value of the startup in view of the financial performance of the company, prevailing market conditions, and industry trends (Yablonsky, 2020). The insight drawn out of this analysis would be of immense help to the founders and investors in deciding about the opportune moment and terms of exit.

AI can also facilitate due diligence processes by automating the analysis of financial statements, contracts, and other important documents for complete clarity and accuracy in understanding the value proposition, risks, and opportunities for potential buyers or investors. In addition, AI negotiation tools leverage market trends and comparable deals to drive startups toward negotiating favorable terms for their exit (Yadav et al., 2024).

In sum, AI is variously implicated in multilayers of a startup's phases while equipping it with various tools and insights to surmount each stage of growth. By effectively making use of AI, a startup will be able to make better decisions, streamline operations, and thus sustain growth for long-term success in a competitive market.

CHALLENGES AND LIMITATIONS

1. Data Quality and Availability

One of the key challenges to the application of AI for decision-making in startups is data quality and availability. The proper functionality of AI algorithms requires volumes of good-quality data, which, however, is difficult to ensure, considering that a lot of startups have poor resources in terms of data (Abuzaid & Alsbou, 2024). It is difficult for a startup in its formative years to collect enough historical data on which to train the AI models properly; hence, the output cannot be always accurate and reliable. Moreover, the data could be incomplete, biased, or inconsistencies might pop up, which again leads to less-than-perfect insights and decisions. Setting up strong data intake and management practices will help overcome these challenges, but it's expensive and may require specialized expertise that small teams often lack (Afshan et al., 2021).

2. Integration with Existing Systems

One of the major challenges with AI tools is their integration into the already established business processes of a startup. Most startups have lean infrastructures and many times rely on a patchwork of software solutions that may or may not easily support advanced AI capabilities. Integration might be complex in nature, where technical expertise is definitely required to make the AI systems integrate smoothly with their existing tools, databases, and workflows. In other cases, the adoption of AI requires them to do a complete overhaul of the legacy systems, which can become far too costly and disruptive. Start-ups must keenly evaluate their current technology stack and strategize on the integration challenges that might interrupt their normal working (Anane-Simon & Atiku, 2024).

3. Cost and Resource Constraints

Implementation of AI solutions is expensive, especially for a startup that has small budgets. The expenses associated with acquiring the technologies, skilled people to run the AI technologies, and maintenance costs stand in the way of most of the startups (Csaszar et al., 2024). The cost at the same time keeps on increasing because of continuous investment in data storage, processing power, and software updates. Resource constraints also make it difficult for startups to invest in the level of sophistication that larger companies with deeper pockets can achieve. This will, of course, place the startups at a competitive disadvantage, particularly when competing against AI-driven businesses with more considerable resources.

4. Ethical and Legal Considerations

The use of AI in decision-making brings a host of ethical and legal considerations that startups are going to have to grapple with. AI systems can continue reflecting biases found in the data upon which they have been trained and, in this respect, may arrive at decisions that are either unfair or discriminatory. Startups will have to be specially sentinel in the area of bias to avoid reputational harm and potentially serious legal consequences. Thirdly, the use of AI in profiling customers, hiring, pricing, etc., may raise some privacy issues, especially in jurisdictions with tight data protection laws. Some of these regulations are very intricate and expensive to adhere to; thus, a startup should establish clear ethical guidelines and lawful frameworks that will guide its use of AI (Farayola et al., 2023).

5. Interpretability and Trust

Another limitation with AI-driven decision-making has to do with the "black box" nature of many AI models, especially deep learning algorithms. These models can be immensely complex and hard to interpret, hence making it hard for startup leaders to tell through what means decisions are being made (Giuggioli et al., 2024). This might provide a barrier to transparency and, in turn, mistrust in AI-driven insights, especially when the decisions have bigger business implications. So, the trade-off for a startup becomes how to balance the need for sophisticated models with a need for interpretability, perhaps using simpler models that will give more transparency in cases where key decisions are made.

6. Scalability and Flexibility

Whereas AI may bring a lot of value to decision-making, scaling the AI solutions as the startup grows may be a challenge. While AI models work great for small-scale operations, as the business scales greater, so does the need for constant adaptation and retraining (Gnilsen & Necula, 2023). Most startups also have to change direction or pivot based on market feedback, and an inflexible AI system may not adapt well to new business strategies or operational changes. Yet building flexible AI solutions that could scale with the business takes foresight, investment in infrastructure, and sustained technical support.

7. Talent Acquisition and Retention

The scarcity of AI talent is well-chronicled across industries, and startups are particularly vulnerable given their resources. This will be the major challenge a startup has to face because most of the time it has to compete with other big and respected companies which offer high salaries, greater resources, and job security. Even when some startups can bring in a prospective AI expert on board, sometimes retaining them is not that easy, especially in a competitive job market. Startups may have to consider other options, such as academic partnerships, utilizing AI-as-a-service offerings, or reskilling their employees to get around this shortage in skills (Heilig & Scheer, 2023).

8. Dependence on Technology and Risk of Over-Reliance

While AI offers a distinct advantage in decision-making, there exists a risk that startups might heavily overutilize AI systems, slipping into a position where human intuition and experience may well become second best. It reduces critical thinking and the ability to respond to challenges that are unpredictable, out of the scope of AI models. Besides, AI systems are not infallible, with many of them sure to make mistakes in completely new situations they have never been trained on (Jia & Stan, 2021). A delicate balance defines how much startups can use AI to accentuate their strengths while keeping the human factor at the heart of decision-making.

While AI-driven decision-making opens a world of opportunities for startups, equally importantly, many challenges and shortcomings are tagged along with the implementation of this technology. Overcoming these challenges proactively, whether related to data, integration, cost, ethics, interpretability, scalability, talent, or reliance, will let startups tap the complete potential of this technology while avoiding imminent risks and ensuring sustainability (Martins, 2024).

FUTURE TRENDS IN AI-DRIVEN DECISION MAKING

1. AI-driven personalization

Perhaps one of the most exciting future trends in AI-driven decision-making is the increased focus on personalization. As AI technologies continue to develop and advance, this will enable more sophisticated algorithms to be utilized by startups in delivering highly personalized experiences for customers. Everything from omnichannel marketing messages and product recommendations to UI and customer service interactions will be tailored for personalization (Orhan, 2023). By being able to analyze vast pools of data with AI, startups can go deep into the preferences of behaviors and needs of people and, thus, build more relevant and engaging experiences for customers. In the future, AI systems will evolve, which would perform much better in predicting the need of consumers in real time and meet them, leading to better levels of customer satisfaction and loyalty.

2. Autonomous Decision-Making Systems

Next would be the development of autonomous decision-making systems. It doesn't just help make decisions but creates its very own on its own. Therefore, startups are increasingly reaching out to this trend for industries such as finance, logistics, and healthcare industries. These could be autonomous systems analyzing real-time data, assessing related risks, and making decisions on their own with very little involvement of human force. This again, results in higher speed and efficiency. With more reliable and sophisticated AI models, human oversight might finally be reduced in areas where AI increasingly assumes responsibility for routine and even strategic decisions (Rana, 2022).

3. Explainable AI-XAI

As AI increases its integration into everyday decision-making, there will be an increased emphasis on explainable AI-aka XAI. Much concern has been long raised by the "black box" nature of many AI models, especially in high-stake decisions where understanding the rationale behind a decision is important. In the future, XAI approaches will be increasingly taken up by startups to provide so much more transparency and interpretability in AI-driven decisions (Săniu ă & Filip, 2021). These systems would be designed in such a way that they could provide clear explanations for their outputs, thus enabling users to understand how and why a particular decision was arrived at. This will be particularly true in regulated industries where accountability and complete transparency cannot be compromised.

4. AI-Boosted Human-AI Collaboration

In the time to come, AI-driven decision-making would be less about replacing human decision-makers and more about enhancing collaboration between humans and AI. AI would be looked at as a tool that enhances human capabilities, offering insights and recommendations to enable better, faster, and more informed decisions. Startups will increasingly move towards hybrid models wherein AI and human expertise come together to make decisions, with AI doing data-driven analysis and humans providing contextual insights and ethical understanding. This will help make sure that decisions not only stand on data but also value alignment of the startup culture and long-term goals (Shaikh et al., 2022).

5. Integration of AI with Emerging Technologies

Meanwhile, the integration of emerging technologies such as blockchain, IoT, and 5G with AI will also be the shaping factors in the future of AI-driven decision-making. For instance, AI combined with blockchain would ensure a higher level of transparency and security in decision-making processes, particularly in domains involving supply chain management and finance. Meanwhile, AI-powered IoT devices will facilitate the ability of startups to access real-time data from various sources to make more accurate and timely decisions. Further, the rollout of 5G networks will further accelerate this pace as such networks will have the speed and connectivity required to support complex and data-intensive AI applications in real time (Suurmaa, 2024).

6. Ethical AI and Governance

With AI-driven decision-making becoming mainstream, there will be far greater emphasis on ethical AI and governance. This means that startups will have to come up with strong structures concerning the use of AI responsibly by their products or systems, and to make certain that decisions arrived at by these systems are non-discriminatory, transparent, and well aligned with society's values. It also means issues around bias, privacy, and accountability would need to be taken up. In this respect, it will be common to expect from new startups entering the world of business that they will periodically audit their AI, apply methods of bias mitigation, and be transparent with stakeholders regarding decision-making (Tunio, 2020).

7. AI-Driven Competitive Intelligence

With the help of AI, startups will enable themselves to competitively gain insight by closely monitoring competition, market trends, and imminent threats using advanced data analytics. For instance, AI can filter through the deserts of data created by news articles, social media, financial reports, and even patents to identify patterns and insights that may be too subtle for the human eye (Tunio et al., 2021). This allows the startups to see changes in the market before they happen, find new opportunities, and make strategic decisions that keep them ahead of the game. In the future, AI is going to be a very critical tool for startups operating in such dynamic markets, where the ability to access information and agility are critical determinants of success.

8. Continuous Learning and Adaptive AI

Finally, the future of AI-driven decision-making is one that is also going to be typified by continuous learning and adaptation. The AI will be self-enhancing and keep learning continuously from new data and feedback so as to improve its decision-making capabilities. AI models that quickly adapt to changes in the marketplace, customer preference, or even internal operations will benefit the startups. The capability for continuous learning will make AI systems more resilient and effective over time, thus enabling startups to better navigate uncertainty and maintain competitiveness within fast-evolving settings (Usman et al., 2024).

In all, personalization, autonomy, transparency, and collaboration are some of the features that will characterize the future in AI-powered decision-making in startups (Yablonsky, 2020). Accordingly, startups that embrace these trends will be well-positioned to leverage AI as a strategic asset that drives innovation and growth while navigating the complex challenges of an ever-evolving business landscape.

CONCLUSION

AI-driven decision-making, therefore, represents one of the most transformative forces in such a setting, as it opened new avenues to realize strategic decisions and triggered growth for a startup. While startups sail through the complexities in their respective markets, the integration of AI technologies could therefore allow them to tap into vast volumes of data to develop actionable insights, which could optimize operations and trigger innovation. Whether it is ideation, scaling, or expansion, AI provides the tools which can significantly boost the ways toward efficiency, accuracy, and competitiveness (Yadav et al., 2024).

While huge opportunities exist with AI, several challenges and limitations, on the other hand, need to be duly considered by any startup. Data quality, integration, affordability, ethics, and acquisition of talent are some of the critical variables that might affect how well a solution can be delivered or implemented. Moreover, because technology is evolving continuously, the specific demands it puts on human societies will evolve over time, thus forcing continuous adaptation and watchfulness to keep AI systems in concert with the goals and ethical standards of a startup (Abuzaid & Alsbou, 2024).

Going ahead, the path for AI-driven decision-making is even more astounding. Some of the coming trends in AI-driven decision-making, such as AI-powered personalization, autonomous decision-making systems, and explainable AI, will reshape how startups go about making crucial decisions. Development in integrated AI with upcoming technologies, a move toward ethical AI, and continuous learning systems adds to the capability of AI in driving success in startups (Afshan et al., 2021).

This art of using AI in decision-making would, more than often, find its balance between technological sophistication and insight that is intrinsically human. Startups that can play these dynamics would emerge not only better in their capabilities to make decisions but also position themselves for continued success in an ever-growing competitive data-driven world. Embracing the potential of AI while overcoming its challenges, startups can secure this resource that will drive innovation, optimize operations, and achieve their long-term objectives (Anane-Simon & Atiku, 2024).

REFERENCES

Abuzaid, A. N., & Alsbou, M. K. K. (2024, April). AI and Entrepreneurship: Enablers, Obstacles, and Startups' Role in Shaping the Future Economy. In *2024 International Conference on Knowledge Engineering and Communication Systems (ICKECS)* (Vol. 1, pp. 1-6). IEEE. DOI: 10.1109/ICKECS61492.2024.10616645

Afshan, G., Shahid, S., & Tunio, M. N. (2021). Learning experiences of women entrepreneurs amidst COVID-19. *International Journal of Gender and Entrepreneurship*, 13(2), 162–186. DOI: 10.1108/IJGE-09-2020-0153

Anane-Simon, R., & Atiku, S. O. (2024). Artificial Intelligence and Automation for the Future of Startups. In *Ecosystem Dynamics and Strategies for Startups Scalability* (pp. 133–153). IGI Global.

Csaszar, F. A., Ketkar, H., & Kim, H. (2024). Artificial Intelligence and Strategic Decision-Making: Evidence from Entrepreneurs and Investors. *arXiv preprint arXiv:2408.08811*. DOI: 10.2139/ssrn.4913363

Farayola, O. A., Abdul, A. A., Irabor, B. O., & Okeleke, E. C.Oluwatoyin Ajoke FarayolaAdekunle Abiola AbdulBlessing Otohan IraborEvelyn Chinedu Okeleke. (2023). Innovative business models driven by ai technologies: A review. *Computer Science & IT Research Journal*, 4(2), 85–110. DOI: 10.51594/csitrj.v4i2.608

Giuggioli, G., Pellegrini, M. M., & Giannone, G. (2024). Artificial intelligence as an enabler for entrepreneurial finance: A practical guide to AI-driven video pitch evaluation for entrepreneurs and investors. *Management Decision*. Advance online publication. DOI: 10.1108/MD-10-2023-1926

Gnilsen, M., & Necula, M. (2023). GDPR Compliance Strategies for AI-Driven Diagnostic Startups: How can AI-driven Diagnostic Startups in the Breast Cancer Screening Domain Leverage their Business Strategies and Compliance Strategies to gain a Competitive Advantage?.

Heilig, T., & Scheer, I. (2023). *Decision Intelligence: Transform Your Team and Organization with AI-Driven Decision-Making*. John Wiley & Sons.

Jia, P., & Stan, C. (2021). Artificial intelligence factory, data risk, and VCs' mediation: The case of ByteDance, an AI-powered startup. *Journal of Risk and Financial Management*, 14(5), 203. DOI: 10.3390/jrfm14050203

Kamyar, A. G. Artificial Intelligence Startups in Italy: Their role in Decision-Making.

Martins, M. M. R. (2024). Startup Guide to AI: Integrating Technology for Business Success. *Valley International Journal Digital Library*, 1264-1274.

Orhan, Ö. B. (2023). The Role of AI (Artificial Intelligence) in Cloud Service Provider Selection for Startups.

Rana, M. B. (2022). OF AI-DRIVEN HEALTHCARE STARTUPS.

Săniu ă, A., & Filip, S. O. (2021). Artificial Intelligence: An overview of European and Romanian startups landscape and the factors that determine their Success. *Strategica. Shaping the Future of Business and Economy*, 872-884.

Shaikh, E., Tunio, M. N., Khoso, W. M., Brahmi, M., & Rasool, S. (2022). The COVID-19 pandemic overlaps entrepreneurial activities and triggered new challenges: a review Study. Managing Human Resources in SMEs and Start-ups: International Challenges and Solutions, 155-182.

Suurmaa, P. (2024). The data-driven decision-making in start-ups.

Tunio, M. N. (2020). Role of ICT in promoting entrepreneurial ecosystems in Pakistan. [JBE]. *Journal of Business Ecosystems*, 1(2), 1–21. DOI: 10.4018/JBE.2020070101

Tunio, M. N., Chaudhry, I. S., Shaikh, S., Jariko, M. A., & Brahmi, M. (2021). Determinants of the sustainable entrepreneurial engagement of youth in developing country—An empirical evidence from Pakistan. *Sustainability (Basel)*, 13(14), 7764. DOI: 10.3390/su13147764

Usman, F. O., Eyo-Udo, N. L., Etukudoh, E. A., Odonkor, B., Ibeh, C. V., & Adegbola, A. (2024). A critical review of ai-driven strategies for entrepreneurial success. *International Journal of Management & Entrepreneurship Research*, 6(1), 200–215. DOI: 10.51594/ijmer.v6i1.748

Yablonsky, S. A. (2020). AI-driven digital platform innovation. *Technology Innovation Management Review*, 10(10), 4–15. DOI: 10.22215/timreview/1392

Yadav, P. V., Kollimath, U. S., Giramkar, S. A., Pisal, D. T., Badave, S. S., Dhole, V., & Phule, P. N. (2024, August). Exploring the nexus between AI in Technical Recruitment and Start-ups' Success. In *2024 4th International Conference on Emerging Smart Technologies and Applications (eSmarTA)* (pp. 1-7). IEEE.

Chapter 11
AI-Powered Talent Development:
Nurturing Skills and Leadership in Entrepreneurial Teams

Deepak Kumar Sahoo
 https://orcid.org/0009-0004-5703-8701
Biju Patnaik University of Technology, Rourkela, India

Thi Mai Le
 https://orcid.org/0000-0001-9720-308X
Vietnam National University, Hanoi, Vietnam

Anish Kumar
 https://orcid.org/0000-0002-8047-4227
O.P. Jindal Global University, India

Ajay Chandel
 https://orcid.org/0000-0002-4585-6406
Lovely Professional University, India

ABSTRACT

AI in entrepreneurship is one of the latest methods of talent development that transforms the conventional ways of skill enhancement, leadership, and team dynamics. In this chapter, the transformative power of AI will be discussed to identify, develop, and manage talent-what recent advances in AI technologies, including deep learning and natural language processing, have integrated with developing tools like AR, VR, and blockchain. It looks at trends such as personalized learning, AI-driven leadership development, and improving diversity and inclusion. The chapter also discusses a number of challenges and ethical issues that include algorithmic bias, data privacy,

DOI: 10.4018/979-8-3693-1495-1.ch011

and the balance between AI and human judgment. Understanding these trends and taking ethical concerns seriously can help organizations effectively deploy AI to build strong, diverse, and high-performing teams that drive innovation and success.

INTRODUCTION

AI and the Evolution of Talent Development Artificial Intelligence is driving new ways in which the conceptualization of talent development has been done, especially for fast-moving entrepreneurial settings. Traditionally, the process of talent development has been highly dependent on human-driven assessments, mentorship, and structured learning programs. Whereas in the past, organizations were limited to developing one-size-fits-all talent development processes, AI now allows companies to tap into vast datasets to create talent development processes that are personal, dynamic, and effective (Bashynska et al., 2023). In their stead, AI holds the keys to analyzing real-time performance, learning preferences, and potential for an individually tailored approach to building skills and developing leaders. This switch in focus is particularly paramount for entrepreneurial teams, which survive on agility, innovation, and leadership to fuel their growth.

AI-driven systems can provide deep insight into the strengths individuals possess, as well as where they need improvement. Talent development, in effect, becomes an ongoing adaptive process. Moreover, AI will let companies make sure that future skill requirements and leadership gaps can be predicted while developing employees not only for the needs of today but also for the challenges of tomorrow. This will indeed be a sea change in developing talents, as AI moves beyond traditional frameworks into fostering entrepreneurial teams and custom pathways for personal and professional growth. While doing so, AI fosters an environment where the talent can thrive, hence ensuring that the leaders are developed faster, and teams are empowered to meet the evolved demands of modern business (Chen et al., 2021).

AI Tools for Identification of Talent

Artificial intelligence greatly helped this process by providing tools that can evaluate candidates more efficiently and objectively than traditional methods. AI-driven tools are changing the way organizations source, evaluate, and select talent in entrepreneurial settings where getting the right talent fast is tantamount to innovating and just survival. These utilities deploy the power of machine learning algorithms, natural language processing, and data analytics to sift through volumes of candidate data and identify people who possess the required skills, experience, and leadership potential. AI identification of talent offers a number of benefits (Fountaine et al., 2019). For one, AI takes out human bias in hiring. In most traditional hiring, unconscious biases lead to missed opportunities for diverse talents. AI-powered platforms can check the qualification, past performance, and behavioral pattern of a candidate without getting biased due to his or her personal attributes, such as gender, race, or age. This makes their talent-seeking process much more inclusive in nature; hence, promoting diversity within their entrepreneurial teams for a wide range of perspectives becomes an essential ingredient for innovation (Ghafar, 2020).

AI-powered tools can predict future performance based on various data points gathered from resumes, social media profiles, previous work experience, and other sources. These tools can judge soft skills-which often cannot be judged through standard interviews or assessments-such as the problem-solving ability, creativity, and leadership potential. For instance, AI-driven psychometric assessments and behavioral analysis tools can spot candidates with high emotional intelligence-a critical trait for leadership in entrepreneurial ventures.

Furthermore, AI can help match candidates with certain roles through predictive analytics. This means that beyond identifying talent with the right skill set, AI tools can assess how well an individual would fit into a particular team or into the organizational culture (Goldstein & Gafni, 2019). Using data regarding past successes of employees within similar roles, AI systems can predict whether or not a candidate is likely to thrive in the entrepreneurial environment and reduce turnover to ensure long-term success.

Apart from improving the hiring process, AI-powered talent identification tools make the process of searching for internal talent easier. Indeed, several organizations are currently using AI in the identification of high-potential employees in their workforce. These AI systems go through data about employee performance, training records, and even communication patterns that underline those individuals who may be ready for leadership positions or other critical future roles. This identification within ensures that the venture can develop and retain talent from within, engendering loyalty and decreasing hiring costs (Khan, 2024).

More generally, AI-powered talent identification tools create a competitive advantage for entrepreneurial teams by much more rapidly identifying the optimal candidates to meet their highly particularized needs. Equipped with data-driven insights, reduced bias, and predictions about future performance, AI will enable more accuracy, equity, and alignment in identifying top talent within fast-moving entrepreneurial ventures.

Personalized Learning and Skill Development

Artificial Intelligence-driven personalized learning and skill development are changing the very way in which entrepreneurial teams pick up new competencies and grow into their roles. Professional development in the past has been one-size-fits-all, offering standardized training that doesn't consider learning styles, career goals, or expertise levels. AI has modified this by making more personalized, dynamic learning, elastically tuned to the particular needs of each team member. In as much as rapid growth and continuous skill acquisition are concerned, AI-driven personalized learning platforms provide a critical competitive advantage to the entrepreneurial team (Kolarov, 2023). The heart of AI-powered personalized learning is the capability for data analysis in large volumes, resting on individual learning patterns, preferences, and performance. It does so continuously, using machine learning algorithms to modify content, pace, and method of delivery. This provides employees at no point with standardized training but instead personal mentorship that builds upon one's strong points and fills in the gaps in knowledge and/or ability. For example, AI platforms can recommend learning modules, courses, or even practical experiences an end user should engage with, based on user's previous progress and performance. This focused approach ensures an effective acquisition of skills, especially in an entrepreneurial environment that is time-sensitive.

Artificially intelligent platforms enable learners themselves to check their progress and make improvements through real-time feedback. In the process, it creates this continuous feedback loop that not only accelerates learning but also makes it much more engaging since employees can see their development in real time and understand how their new skills apply to current roles or future career paths. For entrepreneurial teams, that means employees can quickly acquire the skills needed to address immediate business challenges while preparing for longer-term growth and leadership opportunities (Meacham, 2020).

Besides that, AI in personalized learning covers the development of soft skills, emotional intelligence, communication, and leadership, which goes further than hard skills and technical training. These skills are much more difficult to teach through traditional methods but are among the most important elements that make a person an entrepreneurial success. AI-powered platforms can simulate real-world scenarios, giving learners a chance to practice decision-making, collaboration, and conflict resolution in a safe environment. They could develop, through AI-powered personalized soft-skill development, leadership capabilities they would need to thrive in such an entrepreneurial environment. Arguably perhaps among the most convincing features of AI for personalized learning is scalability. Traditional training requires a great deal of resources since months or years may elapse just for designing and delivering curated training material to hundreds of employees (Nechytailo, 2023).

On the other hand, AI systems can scale personalized learning experiences across large and geographically dispersed teams, ensuring high-quality training begets no compromise irrespective of the location. This scalability is very important to keep the workforce cohesive and skilled for entrepreneurs leading remote or global teams.

AI-powered personalized learning platforms can also predict the skills employees will need to have in the future to meet the demands of industry trends and organizational objectives. Based on data analysis regarding market changes, new technologies, and changes in customer needs, AI can advise on early learning pathways to prepare employees for challenges in store for them. Such a forward-looking approach toward developing new skills is of prime importance in entrepreneurial teams that thrive on innovation and the ability of continuous adaptation (Nwosu, 2023).

AI-driven personalized learning and skill development provide personalized, efficient, and future-oriented professional development. For entrepreneurial teams, it is a game-changer to enable them to facilitate such a tailored learning experience aligned with the needs of the individuals and organizations. By applying AI to adaptive learning pathways, real-time feedback, and developing hard and soft skills, organizations will be able to create a highly competent and agile workforce that drives innovation and leadership within a constantly changing business environment (Prakash et al., 2021).

AI-Powered Leadership Development

AI-powered leadership development is revolutionizing how entrepreneurial teams develop tomorrow's leaders with new approaches to identifying, developing, and amplifying leadership competencies. The traditional development programs for leadership usually relied on manual processes like mentoring, self-assessment, and structured training programs, which were time-consuming and can be less adaptive to individual needs. Still, with Artificial Intelligence, the forthcoming scenarios enable organizations, especially fast-paced entrepreneurial ventures, to leverage data-driven insights in accelerating leadership development, tuned to particular strengths, weaknesses, and growth potential of each member in the team (Rashed Khan, 2024).

Among the key benefits of AI-driven leadership development is the ability to continuously assess and fine-tune how one views leadership potential through advanced analytics. The AI systems analyze everything from performance metrics to behavioral patterns with the intent of ascertaining which employees will have what it takes to lead. This is a far more objective and complete process compared to traditional assessment that enables organizations to identify their emerging leaders early in their careers. Thus, AI systems focus on data points such as emotional intelligence, effective decision making, and adaptability that are not easily quantifiable, enabling the entrepreneurial teams to ensure the promotion of people who would lead effectively within dynamic, high-pressure environments (Rizal et al., 2022).

In addition, leadership development programs powered by AI come with customized learning styles and growth requirements. These platforms can provide personalized training schemes using machine learning algorithms, focused on the particular skills a future leader should develop. If, for example, a budding leader is a brilliant technical resource, he may need to develop his communication or conflict resolution skills; thus, AI will make out a program with a bias toward those areas. This makes sure that leadership development is personalized, but also attuned to the demands of an entrepreneurial business environment where leaders must be versatile and capable of managing a variety of challenges.

Besides personalized training, most AI-driven leadership development platforms have real-time feedback and coaching. For example, AI systems can simulate real-life leadership scenarios, such as crisis management, strategic decision-making, or team motivation, in which an individual can afford to practice and fine-tune his or her skills with minimum risk. The entrepreneurial team is especially well-placed to utilize simulations of this nature because the leaders may face a greater degree of uncertainty and be called upon to render informed decisions without much deliberation (Saari et al., 2021). The fact that each of these simulations automatically provides feedback is a great way for potential leaders to learn from their mistakes and change their approaches, thereby catalysing the development process in their favor.

AI can also go a long way in helping leadership coaching through data-driven insights that might escape the conventional radar of a human coach. For example, AI platforms are able to watch communication patterns, meeting behavior, and even email interactions to give feedback on effective leadership. It is in this continuous objective feedback loop that leaders gain acute self-awareness-an attribute very crucial for any leader. In entrepreneurial teams where self-awareness and the ability to adapt remain key in negotiating fast-changing environments, AI-driven coaching can become a game-changer in developing strong, resilient leadership (Sundarapandiyan Natarajan et al., 2024).

Moreover, AI helps the entrepreneurial venture create an inclusive leadership development program by mitigating unconscious biases that may affect talent identification and promotion. Human judgment is inherently biased and often passes over underrepresented candidates through classic leadership pipelines. AI systems, however, make their choices strictly based on empirical data in the form of performance metrics and leadership traits, which are blind to variables like gender, ethnicity, and background. Fairness and representation means that there continues to be an inflow of creativity and innovation into an entrepreneurial environment.

A second powerful use of AI in the leadership development process is the potential of AI itself to predict, for an organization, what that basic level of future leadership will look and feel like. AI tools can track market trends, industry shifts, and organizational growth trajectories to predict just what skills and competencies leaders will need in the future. By doing so, entrepreneurial teams can start developing their leaders with the skills and competencies needed to deal with impending challenges ahead, which will ensure business sustainability for the future. This is specifically valuable in an entrepreneurial world where businesses have to constantly remodel and redefine themselves just to stay afloat (Thangaraja et al., 2024).

AI-driven leadership development is outstandingly more efficient, personalized, and inclusive in developing future leaders for the entrepreneurial teams. Advanced data analytics and real-time coaching, with predictive insights through AI, segregate leadership potential from the beginning, shape development programs according to individual needs, and prepare them for challenges unique to the entrepreneurial environment. With AI as a strong enabler, the ventures can develop agile, adaptive, and diverse leaders who would become ready for leading their way of innovating and guide their organizations toward continued success (Ye et al., 2021).

AI Empowering Team Performance

The role of AI in team dynamism is increasingly becoming an important aspect, especially within entrepreneurial settings, where collaboration, innovation, and effective communication are still key drivers of success. In these fast-moving settings, teams must become agile and cohesive in adapting to the rapidly changing market conditions and evolving business strategies. AI offers powerful tools for improvement in the way teams interact, communicate, and collaborate with each other in order to optimize the overall performance of the team and strong backbone of entrepreneurial ventures.

It comes first through better communication. AI-powered tools of communication can analyze how the members of a team are interacting with one another and provide much-needed insight into the patterns, bottlenecks, and areas where clarity in communications is needed. These tools can indicate whether certain team members dominate discussions or whether some voices simply are not being heard, which is a critical ingredient for a balanced and inclusive team environment. AI points out areas for improvement by analyzing such things as the use of language, the frequency of communications, and responsiveness; therefore, AI gives each team member an opportunity to meaningfully participate in the discussion. This aspect has particular relevance in entrepreneurial environments since groundbreaking ideas may pop up regardless of rank or seniority (Zichu, 2019).

Among other things, AI analyzes patterns of communications that make collaboration easier. AI can also facilitate better collaboration by smoothing workflow coordination and project management. AI-driven platforms can distribute the work by considering strengths and skills of individual team members in concert with their availability to make sure the right people are doing the right work at the right time (Bashynska et al., 2023). In automating this, AI reduces bottlenecks by helping with task assignment and prioritization. Thirdly, AI tools can monitor project development in real-time to make sure delays or problems are seen well in advance before things get bigger. With this, teams can be really proactive in resolving challenges to ensure better efficiency and collaboration in general. AI has also been helping ensure perfect team cohesion. For instance, AI-powered tools can analyze and give recommendations on team constitution by studying personality traits and working styles of individual team members among other motivations. AI can use predictive analytics to propose how to select teams that will work well together, guaranteeing complementary skills and minimal conflicts. Entrepreneurial teams consist of people with different backgrounds and expertise in general, so every insight of this kind is valuable in enabling the team to do its job better, foster creativity, and drive innovation (Chen et al., 2021).

It can also mediate conflicts within teams by analyzing the behavior of team members and suggesting solutions to enhance harmony in the teams. AI tools identify tension or friction in communication-from e-mail or chat platforms to meeting transcripts-and suggest ways to resolve these issues. Such suggestions may include mediation strategies or team role switches, as successfully used in previous conflict resolutions. It helps to maintain a positive and productive team atmosphere, essential for any entrepreneurial venture, and nips conflicts in the bud (Fountaine et al., 2019).

Other than conflict resolution, another critical area in team dynamics where AI is improving is through real-time feedback and performance management. AI-powered platforms have the ability to track the performance of each individual and teams over time and convey information regarding their strengths and weaknesses. These could provide automated, data-driven feedback to team members about how their contributions align with the goals of the team, where they may need to make improvements, and so on. A continuous feedback loop supports a culture of transparency and accountability by letting team members adjust their performance to meet certain clear, objective measures of success (Ghafar, 2020). This would vastly improve the effectiveness and morale of the team through constant, real-time feedback, which is especially helpful in an entrepreneurial environment characterized by rapid iteration and learning from failures.

AI also supports diversity and inclusion among teams, highly essential in thinking innovatively and solving problems. An AI system can indicate an imbalance in representation using demographic, communication, and team dynamic data. It will, in turn, help the entrepreneurial team ensure that diverse voices have been represented and integrated into decision-making within various teams. AI-powered tools will go further: to suggest what to do in order to enhance inclusiveness, such as rotating leadership during meetings or giving extra support to team members in underrepresented groups (Goldstein & Gafni, 2019).

Finally, AI makes collaboration among remote and global teams easier-nearly a norm within the entrepreneurial ecosystem today. Through automation of workflows, synchronization of schedules, and facilitation of error-free communication across locations, AI tools can transcend barriers brought about by time zones and geographic scattering of members. Application of AI in virtual collaboration makes every team cohesive and productive irrespective of the physical distances. This is quite important for start-ups or entrepreneurial ventures since often they depend on the remote workforce to scale up faster with minimum operational costs • (Khan, 2024).

AI is changing how entrepreneurial teams communicate, collaborate, and perform. AI helps teams work both wiser and harmoniously through analysis of communications, advising on team composition for optimizations, conflict resolution, and feedback in real time. AI brings diversity by supporting the fostering of inclusiveness and supporting teams working remotely. Putting it all together, AI-driven tools will make entrepreneurial teams agile, innovative, and resilient in order for them to be able to compete successfully over the long term in today's competitive business environment.

Artificial Intelligence for Diversity and Inclusion in Talent Development

Artificial Intelligence is increasingly playing a critical role in fostering diversity and inclusion within talent development, especially in entrepreneurial ventures where multiple diverse viewpoints and inclusive practices are paramount for innovation and growth. Traditionally, talent development has involved biased decision-making with regards to recruitment, training, and leadership development and, more often than not, excluded those that are already from underrepresented groups. AI might now offer objective data-driven insights to help reduce bias in an effort to create a more level playing field for developing talent. This is crucial in an entrepreneurial space because diverse teams are most likely to invent creative solutions and help further success (Kolarov, 2023).

One of the most important benefits of using AI in D&I within talent development is its ability to reduce bias in recruiting and hiring. Most traditional hiring tends to depend on human judgment, which might unconsciously favor some candidates over others based on considerations that have nothing to do with the latter's ability to perform-a woman or a man, black or white, or which school she or he graduated from. AI-powered recruitment tools, however, will judge a candidate on skills, experience, and potential without any identifiers to set off bias. These systems use algorithms to sift through resumes, hold initial interviews, and rank applicants based on their qualifications rather than prejudices. This objectivity ensures a wider outlook in general for any position, especially in underrepresented groups, thereby making more candidates available to select talent within entrepreneurial teams.

Beyond the sphere of recruitment, AI has also helped in finding and developing the leadership potential in highly diversified ways. Most organizations have problems with regard to the promotion of diverse employees to senior leadership positions, either due to biases that may be entrenched or lack of visibility regarding the potential of such candidates as leaders. AI-powered tools address the issue through performance metrics analysis, peer feedback analysis, and communication pattern analysis-enabling them to spot high-potential talent for leadership positions from underrepresented groups that conventional processes of talent identification probably missed (Meacham, 2020). That's where AI's greatest contribution lies: providing a data-oriented perspective on potential leaders, ensuring people from all walks of life get an equal opportunity to rise, hence more diversified leadership pipelines.

AI also supports diversity in training and development by offering personalized learning pathways that are relevant to the individual needs of diverse employees. For example, AI-driven learning platforms suggest tailored training modules that help employees from underrepresented backgrounds bridge particular gaps or prepare for leadership positions. These would also make adjustments in the learning experience to individual preference, learning style, and accessibility needs to make the training programs all-inclusive for employees with different learning abilities. AI helps tailor talent development programs to suit the needs of diverse employees, thus leveling the playing field for more equitable opportunities to grow professionally (Nechytailo, 2023).

Additionally, AI-powered analytics could provide organizations with insights about their general D&I initiatives and, therefore, allow them to monitor the progress of the same, and explore areas where such progress is weak. For instance, AI might analyze employee demography, promotion, and retention data in trying to underline disparities that may be prevalent between different groups. These insights will help the entrepreneurial team take concrete steps toward addressing diversity gaps in talent development and preparing for a more inclusive workplace. Moreover, AI's tracking and measurement of various diversity-related metrics help ensure that the talent development initiatives further inclusions, rather than surface-level diversity alone (Nwosu, 2023).

AI supports reducing biases beyond internal processes into external stakeholder engagement. AI can support job postings and company branding in the finding and mitigation of biases for entrepreneurial ventures looking to create teams that are diverse. Language analysis tools scan job descriptions to find gendered or exclusive language and suggest more inclusive alternatives to make the language inviting to candidates in recruitment. This is especially crucial for startups desiring to attract a diverse pool of candidates since wording in job posts can make a huge difference in who applies to them (Prakash et al., 2021).

Secondly, AI-powered platforms assure that mentorship and networking opportunities can make talent development programs inclusive for their underrepresented employees. For instance, AI algorithms can match employees from minority groups with mentors or coaches to guide and support their career development. In that way, AI helps to establish a strong network of support systems so crucial for diverse talent in entrepreneurial ventures where access to mentorship may make all the difference in one's career path. The kind of mentorship provided through such programs enables inclusion and empowers underrepresented groups for successful leadership.

Among the many issues that organizations face in the name of diversity, retaining the same is one important area, and AI can play a very key role in it. AI-powered retention analytics tools help make predictions about probable quiters by taking data inputs like engagement level, performance, and feedback. Perhaps these AI-powered tools can also extend to offer customized retention strategies for underrepresented groups-say, accesses to more support resources or professional development opportunities-so that more diversified employees feel valued and likely to stay. In entrepreneurial settings, where the holding onto of talent is so core to growth, such insight becomes pivotal in building and sustaining diverse work teams (Rashed Khan, 2024).

Finally, AI enables the creation of a more inclusive organizational culture with increased transparency and accountability. For instance, AI-powered tools are able to analyze workplace communication, such as emails, transcripts of conversations from meetings, or results of employee surveys, for any signs or signals of exclusionary behaviors or unconscious biases. Such insights enable organizations to act in time by offering training or policy change before things begin to deteriorate further. By fostering a more inclusive culture, AI ensures that all employees from different backgrounds feel invited and supported, something very important to innovative and collaborative entrepreneurship (Rizal et al., 2022).

Artificial intelligence is great support in the direction of diversity and inclusion within talent development, particularly in an entrepreneurial ecosystem where that could be a key motivator toward innovation. From reducing bias in recruitment and leadership development to providing personalized learning pathways and mentorship opportunities, AI opens a playing field wherein talent can bloom with so much greater equity. Driven by AI insights gained therein, entrepreneurial teams might launch into diverse and inclusive teams, competencies that better meet contemporary business challenges and support long-term success (Saari et al., 2021).

AI in Talent Retention and Succession Planning

AI is slowly but surely becoming an indispensable tool in talent retention and succession planning, especially within entrepreneurial settings that rely on speed, agility, and innovation-ingredients that mean the right talent in the right jobs. Traditional talent retention and succession planning heavily rely on manual assessment and subjective judgment, often characterized by missed opportunities to retain high-potential employees and then make smooth transitions in leadership. This is where AI brings in more precision, with its vast data analytics for predictive insights, to hold on to critical talent and plan future leadership requirements for an entrepreneurial venture (Sundarapandiyan Natarajan et al., 2024). Probably one of the most powerful means by which AI strengthens talent retention is through predictive analytics. AI tools may analyze employee data, such as performance metrics, level of engagement, feedback, career development, and more, looking for patterns that might indicate an employee is likely to quit. Such predictive models will indicate an early warning sign-for example, the level of engagement suddenly shows a decline, productivity is decreased, or dissatisfaction with career development opportunities. If such patterns are spotted in the early stage, entrepreneurial teams can proactively intervene, address issues, and try to find ways to retain key employees. For example, AI-driven insights might recommend offering employees who are in flight risk additional development opportunities, mentorship, and flexible work arrangements. The data-driven approach makes sure retention efforts are not only targeted but, at the same time, aim at ensuring that turnover is low and high-value talents important for entrepreneurial ventures' growth are preserved (Thangaraja et al., 2024).

More than predicting turnover, AI can drill down into the causes of employee satisfaction and retention, uncovering rich insight into what keeps employees happy and motivated. From surveys and general feedback to patterns in workplace communication, AI opens the box on company culture, work-life balance, career development, and leadership-issues at the center of driving retention. Such insights enable entrepreneurial ventures to shape tailored retention programs that meet the particular needs of their workforce (Ye et al., 2021). This is reflected in the way an AI could identify how employees in a certain department are looking for added leadership opportunities, where the organization could accommodate leadership training programs or paths to internal promotions in order to retain those workers on account of amplified engagement and motivation. This type of precise approach has become crucial during fast-paced entrepreneurial environments in which high turnover could disrupt growth.

AI can also help in retention by managing personalized career development through the alignment of employee aspirations with organizational goals. The AI platform, through machine learning algorithms, may analyze an employee's current skillset, interests, and career path and make recommendations for training or development that will make them a more valuable asset to the organization as they progress through the latter. This personal touch in employee development satisfies not only the employee but also helps the entrepreneurial team grow internal talent toward future leadership positions. Workers are likely to stay longer with the companies if they see a growth path ahead and only at scale will AI be able to provide personalized career planning. By making employee development in line with business needs, the entrepreneurial venture is able to ensure that it retains and develops talent capable of driving long-term organizational success (Zichu, 2019).

Regarding succession planning, AI provides powerful tools that are needed to assure smooth leadership transitions and future-proof the leadership pipeline. Traditional succession planning mechanisms rely on subjective evaluations about leadership potential that might very easily pass over high-potential employees or provide inadequate leadership during transitional periods. On the other hand, AI-driven succession planning tools use data to objectively determine a person's leadership potential based on his or her past performance, leadership behaviors, or team dynamics. Based on a synthesis of these data points, AI can also point to employees who can assume responsibility as leaders but are likely to shine in those roles based on demonstrated competencies and behaviors (Bashynska et al., 2023).

AI can also develop a detailed succession plan by charting future leadership requirements in terms of growth trajectory and market trends. For example, AI systems can predict what leadership positions would become highly critical in the future as the organization expands, diversifies, or enters new markets. These insights help the entrepreneurial venture to identify and develop well in advance those employees who can fill these positions so that when required, they are ready to take up the mantle (Chen et al., 2021). In a high-growth startup or an entrepreneurial venture where leadership changes happen in quick succession, AI-driven succession planning prevents leadership voids that may disrupt the continuity of the business.

AI-powered succession planning tools also support organizations to avoid dependence on a single person for succession to leadership positions by identifying more than one high-potential employee for each of the critical roles. In this respect, if any of the key leaders leaves the entrepreneurial venture without prior notice, it will not leave the latter in a vulnerable position. A well-prepared potential successor will mean smooth management of transitions and reduce potential operational disruptions (Fountaine et al., 2019). AI's ability to objectively evaluate a wide range of employees for leadership potential also tends to promote a more diverse leadership pipeline, whereby people of different backgrounds and perspectives are considered for leadership positions.

AI-driven succession planning also lets one monitor and make adjustments continuously. In traditional succession planning, when a plan is set, it may remain static for years, even as the business evolves. In turn, AI gives way to dynamic succession planning through constant analysis of employee performance, organizational needs, and market trends. These analyses will be in real time, setting up the business to adjust the succession plans accordingly and at any time so that at any moment, the right persons come up to assume leadership roles. This dynamic approach would perhaps be even more useful for entrepreneurial teams where flexibility and adaptability are essential (Ghafar, 2020).

In this case, AI also facilitates knowledge transfer between leaders at times of transition and makes sure that any critical knowledge and competencies have been transmitted to the next leaders. The use of AI-driven technologies allows for the documentation of the outgoing leaders' knowledge, skill, and decision-making processes and affords a chance for creating a knowledge repository on which successors can draw valuable leadership knowledge. Indeed, as it will be discussed below, that way an entrepreneurial venture will manage to evade such loss of indispensable institutional knowledge during transitions because of the new leaders' learning process from experience and insight that new leaders have (Goldstein & Gafni, 2019).

AI is revolutionizing the way talent retention and succession planning operate through data-driven, customized, and forward-looking approaches to fit the unique needs of entrepreneurial ventures. Predictive analytics powered by AI help organizations identify at-risk employees and allow for effective retention strategies that can prevent employee churn and ensure stability. Meanwhile, AI-driven succession planning ensures that the future leadership need is responded to through the identification and development of high-potential employees who will make the leadership pipeline diverse and dynamic. The use of AI helps entrepreneurial teams take action on talent at the right time and way in advance, ensuring the right people driving growth and innovation for long-term success (Khan, 2024).

Challenges and Ethical Considerations

With AI increasingly integrated into talent development, it is going to bring enormous opportunities and serious challenges, most especially within entrepreneurial settings where agility and innovation continue to lie at the heart. Since AI may reshape the process of identifying, developing, and leading talent, critical ethical issues will need consideration. Such issues that ought to be focused on must relate directly to fairness, transparency, and accountability for the same. These include everything from algorithmic bias and data privacy to over-reliance on AI at the expense of human judgment. These are critical issues for entrepreneurial ventures seeking both effective teams and the maintenance of trust and integrity within their respective organizations (Kolarov, 2023).

1. Algorithmic Bias and Fairness

One of the hottest ethical debates around AI in talent development revolves around the possibility of algorithmic bias. While AI is often asserted to be completely neutral, its very backbone is in the data from which it was created. If this training data, then encompasses biases along lines of gender, race, age, or socio-economic backgrounds, an AI could become complicit in-and possibly even exacerbate-such biases (Meacham, 2020). For example, AI-driven recruitment tools could favor candidates with profiles similar to those of candidates who have proved successful in the past, provided they use historical data to make decisions. This could make underrepresented groups even more marginalized. This would be counterproductive to efforts of ensuring diversity and inclusion in teams, which are highly supportive factors in driving innovation.

To mitigate this risk, it is of essence that organizations audit and closely monitor the data used to train AI algorithms. For example, entrepreneurs and teams of HR have to ensure that AI systems feed on diverse and representative data so that it captures the broad range of skills, backgrounds, and experiences that can help in the success of a team. Second, regular checks on AI results would be required to ensure that the systems do not perpetuate biases and discriminatory practices. Accountability structures should be clearly defined, with clarity concerning the use of AI in talent development and responsibility for any unintended biases arising (Nechytailo, 2023).

2. Data Privacy and Security

The use of AI in talent development will mean the collection and analysis of abundant data about each individual touching on performance reviews, patterns of behavior, styles of communication, and engagement metrics, among many other parameters. Although this information is essential to be fed into an AI system to make appropriate predictions and recommendations, it does raise significant concerns regarding data privacy and security. Employees may feel uneasy in knowing that every interaction they have is tracked and analyzed by AI; therefore, it could create a feeling of potential distrust or resistance to the AI-powered tools (Nwosu, 2023). Moreover, sensitive information about employees could be released through improper channels or accessed by other employees who are not authorized to access it. These might lead to leakage of privacy, which would hurt an organization's reputation and violate the requirements of law.

Data protection has thus become an essential aspect of entrepreneurship; hence, there is a need for the proper data security measures and actual conduction in its regulation, such as the General Data Protection Regulation in Europe and the California Consumer Privacy Act in the United States. This includes anonymization of data where possible, security of data storage and transmission, and clear control by the employee over the use of personal data. An organization should be transparent regarding what data will be collected, how that data is used, and who will have access to it. Ensuring AI systems comply with the ethical use of data standards will be paramount in maintaining employee trust and avoiding possible legal liabilities (Prakash et al., 2021).

3. Transparency and Explainability

One of the major challenges in using AI for talent development deals with the lack of transparency and explainability in AI-driven decision-making processes. Most AI algorithms are "black boxes," by which it is meant that their recommendations or predictions cannot be easily comprehended or explained. In many cases, this could be a problem since critical decisions on hiring, promotion, or succession planning would need sound reasoning. They can be suspicious or apprehensive about the result decided by AI without any idea of how or why it was arrived at. It leads to mistrust in an entrepreneurial ecosystem where everything runs based on open communication and trust among individuals (Rashed Khan, 2024).

The organizational AI systems should therefore be able to explain the rationale behind the decisions arrived at with the help of AI to the managers as well as employees in clear terms. It turns into a problem of AI explainability when AI recommendations become intuitively applicable for high-stakes decisions, for instance, selecting the future leaders or plan who gets training and development opportunities. Entrepreneurs need to work with AI vendors to select systems with features of transparency that help users understand what factors have influenced certain outcomes. Thus, AI decisions need supplementation with human judgment to make critical talent development decisions based on a blend of AI insights and human expertise (Rizal et al., 2022).

4. Over-Reliance on AI and the Loss of Human Intuition

While AI is well-placed to offer powerful insights and efficiencies in talent development, there is a very real danger of over-reliance on AI at the expense of human intuition and judgment. Above all, entrepreneurial teams sail smoothly on imagination, adaptability, and human relationships-all attributes that an AI system cannot completely replicate. In return for AI's extreme dependence in making talent-related decisions, organizations may let go of the most important nuances of human behavior, personality, and potential for building successful teams (Saari et al., 2021). For example, where AI can predict such things as technical skills and qualifications, it cannot necessarily capture softer characteristics necessary to attain desired leadership development, such as empathy, resilience, and emotional intelligence, within entrepreneurial environments.

If companies want to avoid this mistake, they must consider AI as a tool to enhance human decision-making instead of completely replacing it. AI may give insights that might be quintessential to decisions, but it should also be interpreted in tandem with intuition and knowledge from the human mind. Entrepreneurial leaders must use AI in a way to complement their intuition about team dynamics, individual potential, and organizational culture to make sure decisions are fully rounded and reflective of that human element so essential to innovation and leadership (Sundarapandiyan Natarajan et al., 2024).

5. Ethical Use of AI in Employee Monitoring

In addition, most AI talent development enhancement tools offer employee behavior monitoring, such as email tracking, communication pattern analysis, and productivity metrics. While these provide useful data to help improve team dynamics and find the best employees, they also raise ethical concerns about employee surveillance. Again, excessive monitoring may create a culture of mistrust in which the employees feel under constant observation and judgment, resulting in stress, burnout, or disengagement. This is particularly concerning in entrepreneurial ventures, where cultivating a creative culture and employee autonomy is critical to success (Thangaraja et al., 2024).

Organizations have to find a balance between the benefits of AI, intended for insight gathering, and employee privacy, respect for employee autonomy. Communication is the operative word: it should be explained to employees exactly what data is monitored and why, and employees should be able to say something about how to deploy AI tools to assess them. But while doing so, clear boundaries need to be prescribed to not make AI tools intrusive or overwhelming. Similarly, organizations must make their working environment supportive, making employees empowered rather than tracked down (Zichu, 2019).

6. The Risk of Job Displacement and Workforce Anxiety

With AI automating all aspects of talent development, from recruitment, learning, and succession planning, many have valid concerns that AI will displace the human resources and management functions, translating into job losses or highly changed job responsibilities. This can make employees anxious feelings of losing one's job or value because of AI. When the roles and responsibilities can already be fluid in entrepreneurial teams, this might exacerbate these anxieties of employees as against management (Bashynska et al., 2023). It is because of this that organizations should focus on upskilling their people, therefore, and on integrating AI in ways which supplement rather than replace human capital. Organizations can, however, foster a much more positive outlook toward AI by underlining how AI can contribute to employees doing their jobs more efficiently through things like reducing administrative tasks, personalized development, or data-driven insights. The entrepreneurial leaders should also focus on transparent communication about how the workforce will be affected by the AI as such and reassure those around them that AI is but an enhancement tool, not meant for eliminating human contributions.

AI will most definitely revolutionize talent development in entrepreneurial settings, while it is riddled with a host of complex ethical considerations. It would include issues like algorithmic bias, data privacy, and striking a balance between transparency and organizational needs from the AI-driven insight. Basic principles that should be integral in the approach to integrating AI into processes in organizations are fairness, accountability, and human values. If applied in a considerate and responsible way, AI can unlock an augmented path of talent development for entrepreneurial ventures while preserving employee welfare and trust (Chen et al., 2021).

Future Trends in AI-Powered Talent Development

Soon, artificial intelligence will continue to grow and improve; thus, this is directly going to affect the future of talent development it powers. In order to stay ahead of such emerging trends, entrepreneurial ventures have to use AI in a way that it guarantees complete results added with efficiency for sustaining competitive advantage (Fountaine et al., 2019). Considering AI-powered talent development, a number of key trends will shape the future and promise transformation in the way identification, nurturing, and managing talent are done in organizations. These three trends include the advancements being made in AI technologies themselves; the integration of AI with other emerging technologies, such as blockchain, the Cloud, and the Internet of Things; and the evolution in approaches taken to talent management. Here's a closer look at these future trends:

1. Improvement in AI Technologies

AI technologies are fast improving, from machine learning algorithms and NLP to predictive analytics; they have a sharp rise. These improvements will make AI far more capable at talent development, where systems will be able to perform much more precisely, efficiently, and adaptively.

- **Deep Learning and Neural Networks:** Continuous development with deep learning and neural network models will constantly empower AI in the future. Such models can process complex data patterns with high accuracy, enabling AI tools to provide better predictions about employee performance, spotting potential leaders, or recommending personalized development plans. In other words, the more advanced the model, the more accurate the insights into talent development (Ghafar, 2020).
- **Natural Language Processing:** The new dimensions of NLP will equip AI with the capacity to understand and analyze human communication in its written and spoken forms. That way, AI can comprehend what employees are saying through their feedback, analyze sentiments, and make much more subtle recommendations regarding their development. Enhanced NLP improvements also house better prospects for interactive and conversational AI-driven coaching and mentorship (Goldstein & Gafni, 2019).
- **Real-Time Analytics and Adaptability:** With the future AI in talent development, real time analytics may well be possible to enable an organization to monitor employee performance and engagement on a dynamic basis. The AI systems can adapt quickly to changing circumstances; timely insights and recommendations that align with evolving business needs and employee aspirations.

2. Integration with Emerging Technologies

And it is here that integration with other emerging technologies is moving apace, creating powerful synergies which can further enhance the talent development processes.

- **AR and VR**: AI integrated with AR and VR technologies is bound to bring about a sea change in training and development. AI-powered AR and VR platforms can create an immersive learning environment that simulates real-life environments where employees practice and develop the skills sans risk. This will really facilitate more engaging and effective training experiences, especially for complex or hands-on skills (Khan, 2024).
- **Verification of Skill by Blockchain:** Verification with the help of Blockchain technologies is considered one of the standard verification tools in proving

employee skills and credentials. AI systems can make use of Blockchain in tracking and recording-with full security-the development of skills, certifications, and achievements of employees to provide a transparently tamper-proof record of the qualifications of an employee. This will instil a higher degree of confidence and accuracy in the talent development process (Kolarov, 2023).
- **Internet of Things (IoT)**: AI connected to the IoT devices would mean that organizations will be able to gather information from the wearables to smart office equipment and everything else in between. Such information may offer insights related to employee wellness, productivity, and engagement that enable personalized and timely talent development strategies (Meacham, 2020).

3. Personalized Learning and Development

AI-driven talent development will be about personalization, wherein the model for AI systems will build up more and more toward meeting the specific needs of each employee.

- **Adaptive Learning Platforms:** Artificial Intelligence-powered adaptive learning platforms will provide a tailored learning experience by adjusting the content and delivery methodology according to the learning style, progress, and performance of the employees. Such platforms will continuously observe every individual learner's behavior and use AI in adapting in such a way that training is relevant, effective, and engaging for all (Nechytailo, 2023).
- **Career Pathing and Development:** AI will be very instrumental in career pathing for workers with personalized recommendations on developing their skills, a job that one will undertake, and career growth. AI systems will analyze data about individual career goals, performance data, and trends in the industry to develop customized development plans that meet both employee aspirations and organizational needs.
- **Real-time Feedback and Coaching:** The future AI will provide real-time feedback and coaching to enhance continuous performance and skills improvement among employees. AI-driven tools will analyze interactions, work output, and behavior, extract valuable insights, and give actionable guidance to continuously tune and enhance performance (Nwosu, 2023).

4. Enhanced Diversity and Inclusion

AI will continue propelling developments in D&I with enabling tools and insights that will make the workplace more equitable.

- **Bias Detection and Mitigation:** AI systems in the future will have more enhanced capacities for detecting and mitigating biases in talent development processes. These will be through sophisticated algorithms that help identify any potential biases in recruitment, performance evaluation, and promotion decisions to have a more inclusive and diverse workforce.
- **Inclusive Talent Strategies**: AI will underpin and develop diverse talent strategies on the basis of data around workforce composition, representation, and engagement. Organizations will use this to inform and build evidence-based D&I initiatives, giving them alignment of talent development policy with greater inclusion objectives (Prakash et al., 2021).
- **Accessibility Enhancements:** AI will improve the accessibility of those employees who might have a disability with the help of adaptive technologies and personalized support. AI-driven tools will offer solutions for inclusive recruitment, real-time translation, and speech-to-text capabilities-all ensuring equal access to development opportunities. The next might be customized learning experiences (Rashed Khan, 2024).

5. Ethical AI Practices and Governance

AI ethics and governance are likely to be organizational focuses of the future as AI becomes embedded in the talent development life cycle.

- **Ethical Frameworks and Guidelines:** The future will entail detailed ethical frameworks and guidelines on AI uses for talent development. Organisations will have to make policies and practices that deal with issues like algorithmic bias, data privacy, and transparency in their process; hence, AI deployment will be fair and accountable (Saari et al., 2021).
- **AI Governance and Oversight:** Organizations will go on to develop mechanisms for the governance of AI that will include oversight committees, ethics review boards, and frequent audits to make certain that AI systems are deployed responsibly. These are mechanisms that facilitate accountability and help organizations address any ethical concerns arising from their use of AI for talent development (Rizal et al., 2022).
- **Explainability and Transparency:** Organizations in the future will give more emphasis to transparency and explainability as far as AI systems are concerned. Organizations should, first of all, be able to understand AI-driven decisions internally and be in a position to explain them to employees for trust and confidence in the technology.

6. Human-AI Collaboration

The AI of the future in talent development will be all about collaboration between humans and AI, where both will work together for the best possible outcome.

- **Enhanced Human Decision-Making:** AI will enhance, but not replace, human judgment. It furnishes data-driven insights and recommendations to enhance decision-making. Freeing human managers and leaders from an exclusive reliance on data analysis and routine by leveraging AI will provide much more available time for the strategic and interpersonal areas of people development (Sundarapandiyan Natarajan et al., 2024).
- **AI Collaboration Tools:** Collaboration tools using AI will be developed in the future that can effectively collaborate with human users through appropriate and user-friendly interfaces or interaction features. In this respect, they will be supportive of real-time communication, feedback, and decision-making to make the process of development of talent even more holistic and collaborative.
- **Empower the Talent Development Professional:** AI will empower talent development professionals by equipping them with more advanced tools and insights to advance the work. Automation of administrative tasks and AI-driven recommendations will free HR and talent development professionals to devote their time to strategic work and culture-building in the organization (Thangaraja et al., 2024).

The future of AI-powered talent development is characterized by exciting development and evolutionary trends that will really revolutionize identification, nurturing, and managing talents in organizations. From the mere development in AI technologies with integrations, to emerging tools, personalized learning, and extending more diverse efforts, these are the trends that shape the next generations of talent development practices. Ahead of these trends and addressing ethical considerations, the entrepreneurial ventures will, in that way, have the momentum to tap into AI's potential to build strong, diverse, high-performing teams that drive innovation and success (Ye et al., 2021).

CONCLUSION

Talent development is a new transformation opportunity that entrepreneurial ventures can present through the incorporation of AI. It promises to revolutionize how organizations identify, nurture, and manage their talent. It is interesting to see AI technologies evolve continuously and offer unparalleled power for data analysis, anticipation of trends, and customization of development strategies. From complex algorithms enabling predictive analytics to integrating AI into emerging technologies like AR, VR, and blockchain, the future of talent development will be much more exciting and responsive. These advances will ultimately enable organizations to offer personalized learning, improve leadership development, and create inclusions, bottom-line talent management approaches.

On the flip side, opening talent development to AI also means being aware of several ethical hurdles and pitfalls. Algorithmic bias, data privacy, and transparency are pressing concerns, as is over-reliance on AI itself. Organizations must establish robust ethical frameworks and ensure that business is conducted transparently. They also have to strike a balance between AI insights and human judgment. Proactive confronting of these challenges helps the organizations realize all the potential of AI applications while maintaining the trust and integrity of the talent development process.

Moving forward, AI will continue to create value in the future of talent development- it enables and enhances human insight, not replaces it. It is this synergy between AI and human experience that will make informed judgments, instill a culture of continuous learning, and assure innovation in teams-entrepreneurial or otherwise. As organizations find their way around this dynamic landscape, they must be agile, ethical, and forward-looking, leveraging AI to build a workforce empowered, skilled, and diverse. This will not only make them better at developing talent but also set them up for continued growth and success in a very competitive marketplace.

REFERENCES

Bashynska, I., Prokopenko, O., & Sala, D. (2023). Managing human capital with AI: Synergy of talent and technology. *Zeszyty Naukowe Wyższej Szkoły Finansów i Prawa w Bielsku-Białej*, 27(3), 39–45.

Chen, S., Wang, W., & Lu, C. (2021). Exploring the development of entrepreneurial identity in a learning-by-doing entrepreneurial project environment. *Education + Training*, 63(5), 679–700. DOI: 10.1108/ET-07-2020-0195

Fountaine, T., McCarthy, B., & Saleh, T. (2019). Building the AI-powered organization. *Harvard Business Review*, 97(4), 62–73.

Ghafar, A. (2020). Convergence between 21st century skills and entrepreneurship education in higher education institutes. *International Journal of Higher Education*, 9(1), 218. DOI: 10.5430/ijhe.v9n1p218

Goldstein, A., & Gafni, R. (2019). Learning entrepreneurship through virtual multicultural teamwork. *Issues in Informing Science and Information Technology*, 16, 277–305. DOI: 10.28945/4332

Khan, M. R. (2024). Application of artificial intelligence for talent management: Challenges and opportunities. In *Intelligent Human Systems Integration (IHSI 2024): Integrating People and Intelligent Systems* (Vol. 119, pp. 119).

Kolarov, K., & Hadjitchoneva, J. (2023). Opportunities and limitations of digital educational tools in shaping entrepreneurial mindset and competences. *Digital Age in Semiotics & Communication*, 6, 32–56. DOI: 10.33919/dasc.23.6.3

Meacham, M. (2020). *AI in talent development: Capitalize on the AI revolution to transform the way you work, learn, and live*. Association for Talent Development.

Nechytailo, A. (2023). Using AI-powered tools for improving talent acquisition processes.

Nwosu, L., Enwereji, P. C., Enebe, N. B., & Segotso, T. (2023). Determining the roles of school management teams in fostering entrepreneurship among learners. *International Journal of Learning Teaching and Educational Research*, 22(9), 478–500. DOI: 10.26803/ijlter.22.9.26

Prakash, K. B., Reddy, A. A. S., & Yasaswi, R. K. K. (2021). AI-powered HCM: The analytics and augmentations. In *Beyond human resources: Research paths towards a new understanding of workforce management within organizations* (pp. 155).

Rashed Khan, M. (2024). Application of artificial intelligence for talent management: Challenges and opportunities.

Rizal, M., Novrizal, N., Irawan, D., & Patricia, M. C. (2022, December). Human potential in the AI era: Strategies for cultivating exceptional talent. In *The International Conference on Education, Social Sciences and Technology (ICESST)* (Vol. 1, No. 2, pp. 260-268).

Saari, A., Rasul, M., Yasin, R., Rauf, R., Ashari, Z., & Pranita, D. (2021). Skills sets for workforce in the 4th industrial revolution: Expectation from authorities and industrial players. *Journal of Technical Education and Training*, 13(2). Advance online publication. DOI: 10.30880/jtet.2021.13.02.001

Sundarapandiyan Natarajan, D. K. S., Subbaiah, B., Dhinakaran, D. P., Kumar, J. R., & Rajalakshmi, M. (2024). AI-powered strategies for talent management optimization. *Journal of Informatics Education and Research*, 4(2).

Thangaraja, T., Maharudrappa, M., Bakkiyaraj, M., Johari, L., & Muthuvel, S. (2024). AI-powered HR technology implementation for business growth in industrial 5.0. In *Multidisciplinary applications of extended reality for human experience* (pp. 171–200). IGI Global.

Ye, S., Xiao, Y., Yang, B., & Zhang, D. (2021). The impact mechanism of entrepreneurial team expertise heterogeneity on entrepreneurial decision. *Frontiers in Psychology*, 12, 732857. Advance online publication. DOI: 10.3389/fpsyg.2021.732857 PMID: 34671301

Zichu, Y. (2019). Can group intelligence help entrepreneurs find better opportunities? *Frontiers in Psychology*, 10, 1141. Advance online publication. DOI: 10.3389/fpsyg.2019.01141 PMID: 31156522

Chapter 12
AI and Social Media Analytics:
Leveraging Real-Time Data for Entrepreneurial Growth

Shashank Mittal
O.P. Jindal Global University, India

Ajay Chandel
https://orcid.org/0000-0002-4585-6406
Lovely Professional University, India

Phuong Mai Nguyen
https://orcid.org/0000-0002-2704-9707
Vietnam National University, Hanoi, Vietnam

ABSTRACT

This chapter explores the transformative impact of AI and social media analytics on entrepreneurial growth. It delves into how these technologies enable businesses to harness real-time data for personalized marketing, customer engagement, and market research. The discussion highlights key trends such as advanced personalization, AI-driven content creation, and predictive analytics, alongside the integration of AI with augmented and virtual reality. Challenges, including data privacy concerns, integration issues, and the complexity of AI models, are also addressed. The chapter concludes with insights into future innovations and their potential to drive sustainable growth. Entrepreneurs are encouraged to leverage these tools effectively while navigating the associated challenges to remain competitive in the digital age.

DOI: 10.4018/979-8-3693-1495-1.ch012

INTRODUCTION

The digital revolution has reshaped the entrepreneurial landscape, and at the fulcrum of this change lies social media, which is increasingly becoming an important tool for driving business growth and customer engagement. In this light, Artificial Intelligence embedded in social media analytics is expected to unlock new ways in which entrepreneurs would mine the mountains of data generated on the platform. The ability to parse and make meaningful insights from social media information in real time is increasingly becoming a decisive factor for businesses desiring to stay competitive in today's fast-paced and information-driven market. This chapter examines the pivotal role played by AI in improving social media analytics, focusing on how real-time data can be leveraged in fuelling entrepreneurial growth and innovation (Biswas, 2023).

Today, the entrepreneur is not only obliged to be reactive in the sea of change characterizing markets; he or she has to be proactive in order to anticipate which changes in trends and consumer behavior are next. Social media platforms like Facebook, Twitter, Instagram, and LinkedIn generate a huge amount of data every second. Such data involves user interactions, sentiments, preferences, and trends-a rich source of insights, should one interpret it properly and promise immense competitive advantage. But this volume and velocity make the data hard to process and analyze using conventional methods. This is where AI comes into play, providing those tools and techniques that allow the processing of real-time social media data to make sense out of it (Jaiswal, 2024).

AI-driven analytics of social media arms the entrepreneur with the power to make informed decisions in the blink of an eye. Hence, through the power of machine learning algorithms combined with NLP, AI can filter through gigantic datasets to come up with patterns and trends that no human would have been able to observe in real time. In fact, such knowledge could enlighten many areas of a company, from the development and marketing strategy of a product down to customer service and customer engagement (Khatua et al., 2021). For instance, opinion analysis tools run measures of general opinion regarding a product launch and may suggest certain on-the-spot modifications to strategy, while AI will track emerging trends that help entrepreneurs stay one step ahead of their competition in taking advantage of fresh opportunities. Also, AI improves the accuracy and efficiency of social media marketing. AI makes businesses more efficient in reaching the target audience by enabling them to make personalized content recommendations, run effective target advertising, and conduct predictive analytics to ensure a maximum return on investment. The analyses of data in real time allow dynamic changes to take place in marketing campaigns, ensuring relevance and impact. This level of agility is important in today's market, where consumer preferences can change in a snap and often makes the difference between success and failure (Lejeune et al., 2022).

Notwithstanding the immense opportunity that integration of AI in social media analytics presents, its integration does not come devoid of challenges. Data privacy concerns, algorithmic biases, and ethical ways to deploy AI are some of the critical issues entrepreneurs need to handle with care. Yet, the overall benefits of leveraging AI-driven social media analytics for entrepreneurial growth far outweigh the challenges. Since AI technology is continuously evolving, the part played in social media analytics is hence very likely to be core to the success of entrepreneurship, providing new ways and means of driving growth inside an increasingly competitive digital marketplace (Leung, 2023).

Different ways will be clearly outlined in this chapter concerning how applications of AI can be used in social media analytics to ensure growth in entrepreneurial development. A discussion on the types of data on social media, difficulties in extracting it from its raw form, and its analysis, as well as relevant ethics, will be presented. We will demonstrate, through case studies and practical examples, how AI-driven social media analytics can provide what the entrepreneur needs to be successful in such a fast-paced market (Lewis & Moorkens, 2020).

Understanding AI Technologies in Social Media Analytics

Artificial intelligence technologies have lately turned into an integral part of modern social media analytics-their meaningful part-playing in processing and making sense of such extensive amounts of data flowing from multiple sources. Artificial Intelligence-powered machine learning, NLP, and deep learning are at the forefront of making this transformation possible (Masih, 2023). Machine learning algorithms detect pattern and predict patterns using data, thereby empowering businesses to understand user behavior and preference for trends. NLP enables AI to understand human language and subsequently analyze text, sentiment, and conversations across social media platforms. Deep learning, as a subset of machine learning, extends this capability even further whereby an AI system can process complex big data like images and videos with unrivaled accuracy.

These technologies work together to provide valuable insight into social media activities, ranging from brand mentions and sentiment analysis to trending topics. AI, therefore, saves the entrepreneurs valuable time and resources by automating the job of analysis so that they can focus on strategic decisions. Of particular importance is the ability to analyze data in real time, as this allows companies to quickly respond to changes in consumer sentiment or competitor activity and to changes in market dynamics (Millagala, 2023).

Enhancing Data Collection and Interpretation

Perhaps the strongest point of AI in social media analytics is how it can help improve data collection and interpretation. The volume and type of information produced on social media are hard for traditional data analysis methods to keep up with. AI accomplishes this through automated data collection, where no piece of information is too small to slip through unnoticed. This includes not only direct mentions of a brand or product but also the more covert cues, such as changed consumer sentiment or the diffusion of emerging trends (Mohamed, 2024).

AI-driven tools can crawl data from multiple social media platforms and provide a unified view of the brand presence online. Such a holistic approach lets enterprises see the big picture and understand how different channels of social media influence and interact with one another. Also, the interpretation of data through AI goes beyond mere numerals to contextualize information: it identifies the underlying emotions, attitudes, and intentions behind such social media posts. Such insight is priceless for entrepreneurs in tailoring strategies that will meet the needs of their audience (Noranee & Othman, 2023).

AI-Driven Social Media Analytics Tools

The market has been Flooded with AI-powered social media analytics tools; each offers a variety of features and functionality. Tools like Hootsuite Insights, Sprout Social, and Brandwatch all use AI for real-time analytics, sentiment analysis, and predictive insights. The basis of these platforms is to use various machine learning algorithms that track brand mentions and sentiment, then convert into actionable insights from the data collected. For example, AI can pick up not just what is being said but also the tone and context of the conversations that exist around a brand in order to accurately judge public opinion (Ophir et al., 2020).

Another domain in which AI really dominates is predictive analytics. Looking at historic data and the latest trend, AI can make predictions on how likely a certain marketing campaign will be to succeed or how probable customer churn will occur. That foresight helps entrepreneurs make data-driven decisions that could save them from making a costly mistake. Automation features also come with many AI tools, allowing businesses to schedule posts, respond to customers' inquiries, and manage campaigns (Panda et al., 2019).

Real-World Applications and Case Studies

The real-world applications of AI in social media analytics span across a wide and variant spectrum-from small to large, benefits abound for business concerns in every respect. Major brands like Coca-Cola and Nike have, over the course of these recent times, had the right application of AI in developing their social media strategies. For instance, Coca-Cola uses AI in scanning social conversations on the platforms in real-time, thereby helping the company to fine-tune its marketing strategies based on consumer feedback (Somani et al., 2023). Nike does this with AI-driven sentiment analysis to understand the customer's emotion for the new launch, allowing it to tweak its messaging and campaigns accordingly. These case studies demonstrate very practical advantages of integrating AI into social media analytics. With deeper insights and more accurate predictions, AI helps companies stay ahead of the curve so as to adapt to changing market conditions and consumer preferences sooner and efficiently (Singh et al., 2023).

Basically, AI has completely revolutionized insights into social media analytics for entrepreneurs by granting them unparalleled capabilities to collect, analyze, and interpret data. This provides insight into consumer behavior, market trends, and brand sentiments, which is possible with AI technologies like machine learning, NLP, and deep learning. Agreed, if acted upon in real time, such insights will go a long way in competitive advantage and growth of a company in the digital marketplace (Sufi, 2023). In fact, AI will continue to evolve with each passing day, no doubt playing an increasingly crucial role in the social media analytics that underpin successful entrepreneurial ventures (Yiğitcanlar et al., 2020).

THE IMPORTANCE OF REAL-TIME DATA IN ENTREPRENEURSHIP

Today's digital economy moves at a fast pace, and the ability to access and make full use of real-time data is now key for any entrepreneur. Most analytical methods adopt historical data, and the business intelligence that comes from these sources usually arrives well after the fact. In contrast, real time data lets the entrepreneur make decisions based upon current, up-to-the-minute information (Varsha et al., 2021). This immediacy is important in dynamic markets where changes in consumer preferences, competitive circumstances, and other external factors are likely to happen very fast. Equipped with real-time data in the process of decision-making, entrepreneurs can respond much more effectively to emerging trends, optimize their strategies on the fly, and seize the day when opportunities present themselves.

Real-time data is particularly invaluable for social media analytics because it represents immediate consumer reaction and behavior. Social networks showcase flows of user-generated content through postings, comments, likes, shares, and many others, which often carry consumer sentiment and market trends. However, this can only be interpreted in context and with a deep understanding of consumer preference by real-time analysis of the data so that the entrepreneurs have a fairly clear idea about what is working amongst target audiences and help reformulate their strategies. It is all about the ability to adapt at a greater speed than what others are used to, and this gives an edge over competitors in the fast pace of entrepreneurship (Ziakis, 2023).

How Real-Time Insights Drive Strategic Decisions

Real-time insights play a very key role in making strategic decisions on each and every front-be it product development, marketing, customer service, or supply chain management. For instance, product development receives real-time feedback from social media, which helps the entrepreneur to identify those features or aspects of a product that the consumer loves or dislikes. This allows iterative improvements and faster innovation cycles whereby the product fits very closely with the needs and expectations of the consumers. As with marketing, in real time, the entrepreneur is able to get a view of his campaign's results as they unfold for opportunities to make messaging tweaks, targeting adjustments, or shifts in resources for maximum impact.

Customer Service Real-time data becomes indispensable in monitoring and responding promptly to customer inquiries or complaints when such situations occur. Social media sites have become a key channel for customer interaction, and firms that respond in a timely way to customer issues are more likely to engender loyalty and positive perception of the brand. Furthermore, real-time data can facilitate supply chain management by providing insight into demand fluctuations, allowing businesses to adjust inventory levels and logistics in real time to meet consumer demand without overstocking or understocking (Pigni et al., 2016).

Case Studies: Real-Time Data in Action

Several firms have already demonstrated how strong a driver real-time data can be for entrepreneurial decisions. For example, global fashion retailer Zara uses real-time in-store and social media data to decide which products to manufacture and keep in stock at any one time. Given that it has ongoing access to current sales data and consumer responses, it is fairly straightforward for Zara to identify which items are hot at the moment and cut back on those that are not. Such agility can put Zara ahead in fashion with reduced wastes, hence the reason for the success in fast fashion (Seyi-Lande et al., 2024).

Another example is Netflix, which puts real-time data into action for personalized content recommendations to its users. By analyzing the user's viewing habits and preferences in real time, Netflix is able to suggest those shows and movies more likely to keep users engaged, further enhancing user satisfaction and retention. Real-time personalization has been one of the major elements in Netflix's strategy to hold the top position in the highly competitive streaming market (Pigni et al., 2016).

REAL-TIME DECISION-MAKING AND COMPETITIVE ADVANTAGE

Those entrepreneurs who successfully make use of real-time data gain a real competitive advantage. The possibility to make data-driven decisions in real time enables business entities to become even more agile, responsive, and active. Real-time data is the last nail in the coffin when there are highly competitive environments where slowing down on decisions can yield missed opportunities. In this way, an entrepreneur may continuously process and analyze the real-time data to stay one step ahead of the competition and anticipate a market shift in order to adjust their strategies to meet the evolving needs of their customers (Shahid & Sheikh, 2021).

Moreover, risks can be at a minimum with the use of real-time data. With real-time analytics, entrepreneurs can make an early corrective action through warnings that may be set up for them in cases of adverse customer feedback or a dramatic drop in demand. Such an early move protects the business from further loss and helps in enhancing its reputation due to responsiveness to customer concerns.

Real-time data, therefore, acts as a potent catalyst for entrepreneurial decisions, wherein one receives immediate insight on strategic actions throughout the spectrum of a business. Offering real-time data in a market that's changing dynamically, therefore, enhances the ability to make informed decisions regarding competitiveness, innovation, and growth. Success in today's digital economy calls for the ability to respond promptly to market dynamics, customer feedback, and any emerging trends. It is real-time data that avails the tools necessary for such agility. The role of real-time data in entrepreneurship will only reify with emerging technology, hence becoming an indispensable asset for any future business leader (Cao et al., 2019).

The Vast Reservoir of Social Media Data

Social media sites have turned up as explicit sources of data, and no other earlier media have ever provided such effortless access to information related to consumer behavior, preference, and trend. Every interaction-liking, sharing, commenting, posting-data gets generated that could be analyzed for insight generation. This data varies in nature: starting from textual content, multimedia postings, user engagement metrics, and network connections, anything can be built upon. All this, as a bundle of information, is like a goldmine to the entrepreneurs for understanding their target audience, finding the gap in the market, and creating ways that would click with consumers. The volume of data generated over these social media sites is something astonishing (Gundersen, 2018). Billions of users host social media platforms like Facebook, Twitter, Instagram, and LinkedIn, generating and interacting with the content continuously. This innate flow of information provides a real-time snapshot of global conversations, opinions, and trends that can be fetched from social media- an invaluable source for any business wanting to stay ahead of the curve. The true value of this data, however, lies in the fact that it can be analysed and interpreted effectively enough to turn raw pieces of information into actionable insights to drive business growth.

Types of Data Available on Social Media Platforms

Social media platforms host various sources through which data can be extracted for its eventual application to business intelligence. Demographic, behavioral, and sentiment data are the most frequent forms. Demographic data can show age, gender, location, and other personal attributes, hence enabling businesses to make distinctions in their audience and tailor marketing strategies accordingly. Behavioral data monitors the actions of users on social media, including likes, shares, comments, and clicks, which demonstrate trends in consumer behavior and preference. Sentiment data is arguably the most subtle because it seeks to examine the mood and attitude that underpin social media content. Applying NLP techniques, AI can evaluate the content as positive, negative, or neutral; hence, providing business insights into the perception of the public about their brand or products. Other critical data, trend data, represents the currently hot topics, hashtags, and themes on social media and the opportunities for businesses to position their messaging with what is hot (Barham, 2017).

Challenges in Data Extraction and Quality Management

While social media does contain a treasure of data, it does have its own particular problems with regards to how it can be extracted and managed. One of the major complications regarding social media data is its huge and unstructured nature. Unlike traditional datasets, social media data can be somewhat messy because it contains numerous pieces of text and images, among other forms of multimedia that require advanced tools to process and analyze. Its unstructured nature makes this data hard to standardize and categorize; therefore, useful insights are rarely derived from it. Another major issue is the quality of the data in itself (Janssen et al., 2017). It has a lot of noise that might come in with irrelevant or redundant information mixed in with important insights. The dynamic nature of social media data contributes greatly toward making the data outdated pretty fast. These could be overcome only when the companies start deploying highly advanced AI-driven tools for filtering, cleaning, and organizing data. Such tools have been of immense help to businesses in presenting accurate, relevant, timely data for analysis, hence making sure that any insights derived are reliable.

Ethics in Social Media Data Use

Increased use of social media data brings into light some important ethical issues businesses need to be very careful about. There are many issues in this context, yet all relate to the privacy of the data provided. Social media collates immense personal information in their databases from their subscribers, and companies have to keep laws regarding the protection of personal data strictly, as is done in the case of GDPR in Europe. This would, in turn, incorporate informed consent by users before the collection and analysis of data, the secure storage of such data, and the responsible usage of that data (Tien, 2017).

The other ethical issue is the potential for algorithmic bias in AI-powered social media analytics; biases in algorithms result in biased insights that would perpetuate stereotypes or exclude certain groups from consideration. This includes, among others, business ethics in AI, such as regular auditing for bias in algorithms and complete transparency in data collection and use. Demonstrating these ethical concerns helps businesses build trust with their audience by proving a commitment to responsible data use.

Social media is a goldmine of data that is extensive, dynamic, and even boundless, with information on consumer behavior, market trends, and public sentiment unmatched by any other source for businesses. While proper extraction of this data can surely help entrepreneurs find new avenues of growth, innovation, and consumer interface, challenges in data extraction, quality management, and ethical consideration have to be taken care of with utmost attention. Yet, with technology still evolving, social media analytics' role in business strategy will continue to climb upwards. Meaning, as a business owner, one needs to be better-equipped with skills and tools to navigate this ever-complicating landscape (Janssen et al., 2017).

LEVERAGING SOCIAL MEDIA ANALYTICS FOR MARKET RESEARCH

It has evolved into an integral part of market research, wherein an enterprise taps into copious streams of real-time data as well as consumer behavior, preferences, and emerging trends. This methodology differs from various conventional techniques for market research studies, which are often dependent on questionnaires, focus groups, and past data. The technique offers a bottom-up, vibrant perspective of the market. This changing trend from conventional to digital analytics is the big paradigm shift in how businesses get to approach market research and make informed, timely decisions.

Consumer Preference Identification and Trend Analysis

Probably one of the most important advantages of using social media analytics in market research is that it gives the company a way to acquire consumer preferences and trends at an emergent stage. Social media sites burst with conversations, reviews, and user updates about their interests and opinions on just about anything. Businesses, by processing this information, can thus detect emerging trends early and thereby timely adjust strategies and offerings as appropriate (Păvăloaia et al., 2019).

It shows companies, for instance, the level of customer interest in some products, services, or industries based on trending hashtags, keywords, or topics. Immediate knowledge from this area will, therefore, give a business the competitive edge of offering new products or services that are trending in consumer interest. Social media analytics can also uncover changing consumer sentiments, helping the business see how their brand or products are perceived in the marketplace.

Competitor Analysis and Benchmarking

Social media analytics also has a major role in competitor analysis and benchmarking. Through observation of social media activities of competitors, businesses can gain valuable insight into the strategies adopted, strengths, and weaknesses of competitors. This analysis will also allow companies to benchmark their performance against industry peers and understand areas where they are capable of competing positively and/or improving.

Precisely, through social media analytics, the engagement metrics of the competitors may be located through tracking likes, shares, and comments received from their posts and will also know what kind of content works well with audiences. Data such as that helps a company refine its own social media strategy to ensure its content is more engaging and aligns closely with consumer preferences (Zhang et al., 2022). Furthermore, sentiment analysis has the added advantage of showing companies how their brand perception stacks up against their competitors and may pinpoint areas where companies would want to improve regarding their public image or consumer satisfaction.

Improve Customer Segmentation and Targeting

Customer segmentation and targeting are some of the most important activities in marketing, with social media analytics housing some of the most powerful tools for refinement. Through social media data, a firm can develop much more precise customer segments based on demographics, behaviors, and interests. This granular level of segmentation allows for personalized marketing strategies that can upscale engagement and conversion rates.

Social media platforms also provide rich demographic information such as age, sex, geography, and language (Ziakis, 2023). Interest and behavioral data on users are also available. When combined with engagement metrics, business users can determine which groups within a target audience may be most responsive to a specific marketing message. This focused approach also helps increase marketing campaigns' effectiveness to allow for the correct use of marketing budgets by focusing resources on customer segments that show the most promise.

Measuring Campaign Effectiveness and ROI

Among the most conspicuous advantages brought about by using social media analytics in market research includes the aspect of having to measure how well a marketing campaign has been going on in real time. Most of the traditional approaches toward measuring the success of a campaign require either backdated data or even incomplete data. This makes the proper assessment of the correct impact of marketing quite impossible to get. This is in contrast to the fact that with social media analytics, immediate feedback is given regarding how a campaign is doing and, therefore, allows businesses to make changes based on data in real time (Yiğitcanlar et al., 2020).

Additionally, other metrics-cum-measures, such as engagement rate, click-through rate, and conversion rate, give valuable insight into the efficiency of specific campaigns or marketing messages. It is these which will, in turn, provide an indication to the firms regarding which strategy works best and which one requires re-evaluation. Moreover, social media analytics helps a company to measure the return on investment of campaigns much more accurately and, thus, to have a fine view of what value has been created due to the marketing activities.

Gaining Insights into Customer Feedback and Sentiment

Social media is an extremely powerful tool to collate customer feedback and sentiment. Customers share their experiences about products and services across various social media platforms; hence, their appreciation, criticism, or suggestions for improvement. The analysis of such feedback, with the help of social media analytics, enables businesses to get an insight into knowing customer satisfaction and realize where they need to shape their offerings (Varsha et al., 2021).

Sentiment analysis is the core of social media analytics and helps a business to measure the tone of customer feedback, whether it be positive, negative, or neutral. It will help one to work toward quick resolutions of their grievances to allow product improvement and relationship building with customers. Therefore, a business always has an keen eye on the feedback through continuous social media monitoring and is normally proactive in their customer service to stay ahead of the issues.

Hence, social media analytics for market research opens up a sea of opportunities to learn more about consumer behavior and preferences, emerging trends, consumer sentiment, competitor analysis, and optimization of marketing strategy. Every business can harness the power of this data to reach informed decisions, match offerings with market demand, and drive entrepreneurial growth (Sufi, 2023).

Social Media Analytics for Understanding Customer Engagement

Customer engagement is the key to creating long-lasting relationships with one's customers, and social media may turn out to be a unique platform to build their interest. Through analytics, business organizations get deep insight into how customers interact with their brand online. This would mean monitoring the likes, shares, comments, and direct messages-albeit important indicators of how an audience is engaging with the brand's content. Knowing this interaction will, in turn, enable any business to build up their strategies in such a way that the needs and preferences of its audience are best met, hence more meaningful and sustained engagement (Sufi, 2023).

Through the analysis of engagement metrics, businesses identify what kind of content their audience is most engaged in-be it informative, in-depth blog posts, fun videos, or polls. Knowing what fuels engagement will allow brands to create content that captures attention and spurs further interaction. Besides timing, social media analytics can also let a business know when the best times are to post for better reach and engagement, allowing businesses to touch their audience at the right moments consistently (Somani et al., 2023).

Personalization: A Key to Deepening Customer Relationships

Personalization is the surest way to enhance customer engagement. The analytics from social media show a business what a particular customer wants, does, and likes. Equipped with such intelligence, brands can create and deliver personalized content, offers, and experiences relevant to each particular customer, thus making them feel related.

This could be anything from personalized social media ads, based on a user's patterns of interaction in the past, to even personalized messages and offers via direct messages. For instance, a brand can use social media analytics to identify which customers more often interact with posts related to a specific category of product and target them with personalized promotions or content of the said category. This level of personalization not only increases engagement but also builds a more personal attachment of the customer to the brand (Singh et al., 2023).

Moreover, analytics on social media may allow the business to segment its audience into groups that differ in demographics, behaviors, and preference. In that respect, branding will be able to deliver content and campaigns that are more targeted, meaning the right messages are portrayed to each customer based on their individual interests. Due to this, customers will most likely interact with the brand, share positive experiences, and start showing loyalty (Perakakis et al., 2019).

ENHANCING CUSTOMER ENGAGEMENT AND BRAND LOYALTY

Brand loyalty is the eventual outcome of customer engagement strategy, and social media analytics plays a vital role in building up and measuring brand loyalty. Repetition will make loyal customers repeat their purchases, advocate on behalf of the brand, and provide positive word-of-mouth marketing. Businesses, in creating this loyalty, strive to connect with their customers in a consistent manner so that the value proposition from the brand matches customer expectations.

Social media analytics can also identify customer sentiment over time, providing them with clear insight into a brand. By tracking sentiment, companies are able to identify areas in which they excel and areas where they may need to improve. For example, if there was a dip in positive sentiment for that brand after a product launch, they could study the causes and take remedial action before problems begin to affect customer loyalty (Panda et al., 2019).

Social media analytics can also enable an enterprise to quantify the effectiveness of loyalty programs and campaigns. Through tracking engagement and conversion metrics attributed to loyalty programs, companies can understand what works well with their customers and make data-driven changes to optimize those programs. For instance, if a certain loyalty campaign delivers high levels of social media engagement but a low volume of conversions, the brand could perhaps try adjusting the offer or messaging to more align with customer expectations (Ophir et al., 2020).

Building Loyalty with User-Generated Content

One of the ways to increase customer engagement and loyalty toward a brand is through user-generated content. Creating and sharing content on a brand, be it in photo, video, or testimonial form, instantly makes the consumer part of that brand's story. This can help foster a sense of community among customers, no doubt, but more importantly, perhaps, the authenticity of the message increases with UGC.

Social media analytics can also help in identification and amplification of UGC by observing mentions, hashtags, and other indicators related to customer-generated content. The business can give kudos to customers by showcasing and sharing UGC across official brand channels, which strengthens the relationship even more. The effect becomes a greater number of social engagements that drive other customers to create and share content on their own, further fueling the interaction-loyalty continuous cycle (Noranee & Othman, 2023).

In addition, UGC provides insight into how customers perceive and utilize the product in their daily lives. This kind of information will be useful during the fine-tuning of marketing strategies, product development, and enhancing customer service to ensure brand loyalty.

Through social media, customers are telling companies what they want, and it is a trend that will only continue to grow considering the rise of the online population. Social media will enable the development of personalized experiences, sentiment measurement, and user-generated content that allow businesses to be closely connected with their customers (Mohamed, 2024). These will not only enhance engagement but also build loyalty to appreciate the brand for many successful years ahead. The competitive advantage will remain with the ability to leverage analytics to better drive user interaction and loyalty as these platforms continue to evolve.

CHALLENGES AND LIMITATIONS

Whereas the potential of AI and analytics is huge in driving entrepreneurial growth, there are many challenges and limitations that need to be overcome with a view to maximizing these technologies. In such a way, entrepreneurs and businesses will be able to make full sense of how to implement AI-driven strategies.

Data Privacy and Ethical Concerns

The issue of privacy of data and ethics is considered one of the major challenges associated with analytics on social media. The collection and analysis of reams of personal information raise concerns about the uses that are made of that information, how it is stored, and with whom it is shared. In this respect, as consumers become more aware of their digital footprint, so too does their demand for transparency regarding the use of their personal information and more control over that information (Millagala, 2023). This heightened sensitivity in recent times has also brought about sterner regulation, such as the General Data Protection Regulation in Europe, which drastically tightens the reins of rules on businesses regarding data collection and use.

This means that entrepreneurs must navigate a maze of privacy laws and ethical issues. Non-compliance with these results in significant fines, apart from the loss of reputation for any company involved. Furthermore, even while adhering to the letter of the law, businesses have to take into account the ethical dimensions of their data handling. The challenge is to balance the need to use data as a means of growth against the responsibility for consumer privacy and ethical conduct.

Data Quality and Integration Problems

Data quality and integration are major areas where the potential benefits of AI and social media analytics rest. Poor data quality includes inaccuracies, inconsistencies, and incompleteness, which mislead insights and inept strategies. For instance, if the data gathered from social networking sites is incomplete or outdated, the AI models developed on this would tend to give biased results, leading to poor decision-making (Masih, 2023).

The other challenge is how to integrate the data coming from diverse social media platforms. Each platform has its unique data structures, formats, and APIs, and putting it all together in a holistic way and analyzing the data is really difficult.

This is where entrepreneurs are to ensure that the data they use isn't just high-quality but also well-integrated across a number of channels to give a comprehensive view of their audience and the market.

The Complexity of AI Models

AI models are usually very complicated and difficult to decipher, especially those employed in social media analytics. Such models can handle a lot of data and provide insight into patterns that no human could find, yet they often act as "black boxes" that prevent users from discerning how the system came up with this or that conclusion or prediction. The lack of transparency could amount to a situation where AI-generated insights are not trusted, and there is a lack of confidence in using these tools on which to base critical business decisions (Lewis & Moorkens, 2020).

However, the element of complexity is a big limiting factor for entrepreneurs. Without an exact understanding of how AI models work, it's difficult to validate their results and confidently apply the gained knowledge to business strategy. This challenge, therefore, puts forward the need not only to have advanced AI tools at one's command but also the necessary expertise to interpret and validate their output.

Rapidly Evolving Social Media Landscape

The social media landscape is ever-changing; new platforms crop up, along with new features and trends in user behavior. The fast-moving surroundings are quite challenging for businesses that try to be on top of the trends and use social media analytics intelligently. AI models and analytical tools would constantly need updating regarding this, lest they fall behind (Leung, 2023).

Change in social media often is an extremely resource-consuming affair on the part of entrepreneurs, as continuous monitoring, adaptation, and at times even overhauling of existing strategies are often required. The test then lies in how agile and responsive one can be towards changes while keeping the core elements of AI and analytics involved fresh and effective.

High Costs and Resource Requirement

Most of the time, implementations of AI and social media analytics tools require considerable investment-not just in buying the technology, but also in continuous costs required to maintain data, train models, and pay for the required talent. This may be costly for a startup or small business; therefore, it is impossible for these businesses to adopt and apply AI in its entirety.

Moreover, effective AI-powered social media analytics requires a strong technological infrastructure to be in place, entailing processing power and storage of big volumes of data in a secure manner. It is here that this challenge can easily be overlooked, with the entrepreneurs having to balance resource investments against the funding of leading technology on limited budgets (Lejeune et al., 2022).

Overreliance on AI and Data

There is, however, a very great risk with AI and analytics on social media that these technologies could start being relied upon too much. Businesses could start to lean far too heavily on the data-driven insights derived and not take into consideration other important aspects like human intuition, creativity, and the wider context within which decisions are made. AI models are never perfect and can easily miss nuances that human judgment might perceive (Khatua et al., 2021).

But the balancing act for an entrepreneur remains in order to make decisions based on data-driven insights, yet dominated by human judgment. AI is a tool and not a substitute for critical thinking or strategic insight-the hallmark of the successful entrepreneurship spirit.

While the benefits of AI and analytics in regard to social media toward entrepreneurship growth cannot be denied, there are challenges and limitations to these technologies, too. There are indeed obstacles to overcome, from data privacy concerns and integration issues to the potential complexity of AI models and the ever-changing landscape within social media (Jaiswal, 2024). Fully comprehending and meeting these challenges will in turn enable these businesses to harness the power of artificial intelligence and analytics concerning social media with better ease in an effort toward growth and continued success in today's digital world.

FUTURE TRENDS AND INNOVATIONS

As AI and analytics further advance into the realms of social media, there are some future trends and innovations that promise to shape the future of how these technologies are applied by entrepreneurs in driving growth. These developments ensure increased capability of AI tools, deeper insights, and new ways for better audience engagement.

Advanced Personalization with AI

The most important trends in AI and social media analytics include going hyper-personal. As AI algorithms continue with their ever-evolving cycle of improvement, they are going to be far better prepared to analyze a large quantum of data to create highly personalized experiences for the users (Ziakis, 2023). This results from the improvements in machine learning, natural language processing, and predictive analytics that enable businesses to understand customer preference, behavior, and need with high accuracy at an individual level.

For entrepreneurs, that means the ability to curate marketing campaigns, content, and product recommendations based on users' explicit preferences-higher engagement rates and stronger brand loyalty. In addition, personalization in the future probably is going to go down to even more granular segmentation, where AI identifies micro-moments and contexts within which customers are most responsive to a certain message or offer (Yiğitcanlar et al., 2020).

Integration of AI with Augmented Reality (AR) and Virtual Reality (VR)

Other trends that are going to continue changing the face of social media analytics include the fusion of AI with augmented and virtual reality. As AR and VR reach mainstream status, they offer new ways for businesses to engage customers and source valuable data from them. AI can amplify such experiences by analyzing user interactions in real time and drawing insights into how customers interact with virtual environments and content (Varsha et al., 2021).

For example, it might track in a virtual retail store which products a customer interacts with, how long they stay on a certain item, and even their emotional responses. This can then be used to optimize the virtual shopping experience and make personalized recommendations. AI in combination with augmented and virtual reality will open completely new dimensions in market research, customer engagement, and product development (Sufi, 2023).

Growth of Predictive Analytics for Social Media

Predictive analytics will play a very important role in the context of analytics on social media. Through the analysis of past data and noticeable trends, AI is able to predict future trends, customer behaviors, and market shifts. This capability will be even more important as businesses try to outpace the competition in a rapidly changing digital landscape.

Predictive analytics for entrepreneurs will facilitate proactive decisions on how to anticipate the needs of their customers, develop better marketing strategies, and explore new opportunities before these become mainstream. This trend will also stretch into social listening tools, where AI can predict potential brand crises or viral trends that enable businesses to respond with swiftness and effectiveness (Somani et al., 2023).

AI-Driven Content Creation and Curation

Another emerging trend in the field is leveraging AI to create and curate content. As AI has already begun to assist in content creation, from social media posts and blogs down to video content, advanced tools for creating AI-driven content will hit the market. Such tools will not only create the content but will also optimize it for particular audiences, platforms, and contexts.

This means that, for entrepreneurs, there is the ability to scale the production of content without sacrificing quality; AI churns out personalized content at a fraction of the time and cost it would take with a human team. Additionally, AI can curate content from across the web, giving businesses a ready supply of relevant and engaging material to share with their audience (Singh et al., 2023).

Enhanced Social Media Monitoring and Sentiment Analysis

As social media continues to be a key channel for customer feedback and brand perception, the AI technology driving sentiment analysis will only evolve. In the future, more innovations in this trend will be centered on improving the accuracy and depth of sentiment analysis rather than just capturing the emotions and opinions of customers.

This will be enhanced sentiment analysis that shall avail to entrepreneurs real-time actionable insight into how their brand is perceived and make proper decisions about the development of the product, customer service, or crisis management. The capability to detect subtle shifts in sentiment will also help businesses identify potential issues before they escalate, allowing for more effective reputation management (Perakakis et al., 2019).

Ethical AI and Transparency in Social Media Analytics

With AI being more embedded within the process of analytics on social media, the focus shall be on ethical AI practices and transparency. Ethical use of AI-by both consumers and regulators-is a fast-emerging topic in three broad areas: data privacy, bias, and transparency of AI-driven decisions.

In return, companies will be mandated to introduce more transparent AI practices into their operations: ensuring that their algorithms work equitably without bias, and are explainable in nature. This trend will further inspire innovation in AI tools that take ethics into consideration, such as privacy-preserving analytics and those that enable users to understand how their data is being used (Panda et al., 2019).

Customer Service Powered by AI in Real Time

AI will be the main influencer in shaping the future of customer service on social media. Though already being utilized, chatbots and virtual assistants are assigned to handle customer inquiries; future innovations in these technologies will render them even smarter in understanding every query- no matter how complex-and responding to each personally in real time.

AI-powered customer support can enable entrepreneurs to offer hour support to customers round the clock, therefore, enabling customer satisfaction and loyalty to be enhanced. As these support tools become smarter, so can they cope with issues that are complex in nature. Due to this, they require lesser interference of humans intervening in the resolution of issues and, therefore, reduce operational costs (Ophir et al., 2020).

They are amazing prospects that are embedded in the future of AI and social media analytics for an entrepreneur. More powerful tools have continuously been leading to more ways for businesses to drive growth and innovation through personalization, predictive analytics, AR, and VR integration, and even AI-driven content creation. Yet, these possibilities come with challenges, especially concerning ethical issues, transparency, and quality of data. In fact, being abreast of the trends and turning towards new innovations are some of the ways entrepreneurs can stay ahead in the digital economy, maintaining growth through AI and analytics on social media (Noranee & Othman, 2023).

CONCLUSION

The level of integration between AI and social media analytics is changing the entrepreneurial landscape, offering unbridled growth opportunities, innovation, and customer engagement. By delivering the power of live data, entrepreneurs make wiser decisions, offer personalized marketing, and forge better relationships with their audiences. While these technologies are continuously evolving, there is a growing need to negotiate other issues around responsible AI, information privacy, and increasing congestion experienced in information management. From the new level of predictive analytics and integrations of AR and VR to AI-driven content creation, it really does get even brighter. Invariably, with these innovations, the possibilities are endless for an entrepreneur who will take up the very pathway to sustained success in an increasingly competitive digital world.

REFERENCES

Barham, H. (2017, July). Achieving competitive advantage through big data: A literature review. In *2017 Portland International Conference on Management of Engineering and Technology (PICMET)* (pp. 1-7). IEEE. DOI: 10.23919/PICMET.2017.8125459

Biswas, S. (2023). The function of chat GPT in social media: According to chat GPT. Available at *SSRN* 4405389. DOI: 10.2139/ssrn.4405389

Cao, G., Duan, Y., & Cadden, T. (2019). The link between information processing capability and competitive advantage mediated through decision-making effectiveness. *International Journal of Information Management*, 44, 121–131. DOI: 10.1016/j.ijinfomgt.2018.10.003

Gundersen, S. (2018). The rise of a new competitive intelligence: Need of real-time competitive intelligence and the impact on decision-making (Master's thesis, Universidade NOVA de Lisboa (Portugal)).

Jaiswal, A., Shah, A., Harjadi, C., Windgassen, E., & Washington, P. (2024). Ethics of the use of social media as training data for AI models used for digital phenotyping. *JMIR Formative Research*, 8, e59794. DOI: 10.2196/59794 PMID: 39018549

Janssen, M., Van Der Voort, H., & Wahyudi, A. (2017). Factors influencing big data decision-making quality. *Journal of Business Research*, 70, 338–345. DOI: 10.1016/j.jbusres.2016.08.007

Khatua, A., Khatua, A., Xu, C., & Wang, Z. (2021). Artificial intelligence, social media and supply chain management: The way forward. *Electronics (Basel)*, 10(19), 2348. DOI: 10.3390/electronics10192348

Lejeune, A., Robaglia, B., Walter, M., Berrouiguet, S., & Lemey, C. (2022). Use of social media data to diagnose and monitor psychotic disorders: Systematic review. *Journal of Medical Internet Research*, 24(9), e36986. DOI: 10.2196/36986 PMID: 36066938

Leung, R. (2023). Using AI–ML to augment the capabilities of social media for telehealth and remote patient monitoring. *Health Care*, 11(12), 1704. DOI: 10.3390/healthcare11121704 PMID: 37372822

Lewis, D., & Moorkens, J. (2020). A rights-based approach to trustworthy AI in social media. *Social Media + Society*, 6(3), 205630512095467. DOI: 10.1177/2056305120954672

Masih, D. (2023). Enhancing employee efficiency and performance in industry 5.0 organizations through artificial intelligence integration. *EEL*, 13(4), 300–315. DOI: 10.52783/eel.v13i4.589

Millagala, K. (2023). Navigating the confluence of artificial intelligence and social media marketing. *International Journal of Research Publications*, 133(1). Advance online publication. DOI: 10.47119/IJRP1001331920235473

Mohamed, E., Osman, M. E., & Mohamed, B. A. (2024). The impact of artificial intelligence on social media content. *Journal of Social Sciences (New York, N. Y.)*, 20(1), 12–16. DOI: 10.3844/jssp.2024.12.16

Noranee, S., & Othman, A. (2023). Understanding consumer sentiments: Exploring the role of artificial intelligence in marketing. *Jmm17 Jurnal Ilmu Ekonomi Dan Manajemen*, 10(1), 15-23. https://doi.org/DOI: 10.30996/jmm17.v10i1.8690

Ophir, Y., Tikochinski, R., Asterhan, C., Sisso, I., & Reichart, R. (2020). Deep neural networks detect suicide risk from textual Facebook posts. *Scientific Reports*, 10(1), 16685. Advance online publication. DOI: 10.1038/s41598-020-73917-0 PMID: 33028921

Panda, G., Upadhyay, A., & Khandelwal, K. (2019). Artificial intelligence: A strategic disruption in public relations. *Journal of Creative Communications*, 14(3), 196–213. DOI: 10.1177/0973258619866585

Păvăloaia, V. D., Teodor, E. M., Fotache, D., & Danileț, M. (2019). Opinion mining on social media data: Sentiment analysis of user preferences. *Sustainability (Basel)*, 11(16), 4459. DOI: 10.3390/su11164459

Perakakis, E., Mastorakis, G., & Kopanakis, I. (2019). Social media monitoring: An innovative intelligent approach. *Designs*, 3(2), 24. DOI: 10.3390/designs3020024

Pigni, F., Piccoli, G., & Watson, R. (2016). Digital data streams: Creating value from the real-time flow of big data. *California Management Review*, 58(3), 5–25. DOI: 10.1525/cmr.2016.58.3.5

Seyi-Lande, O. B., Johnson, E., Adeleke, G. S., Amajuoyi, C. P., & Simpson, B. D. (2024). Enhancing business intelligence in e-commerce: Utilizing advanced data integration for real-time insights. *International Journal of Management & Entrepreneurship Research*, 6(6), 1936–1953. DOI: 10.51594/ijmer.v6i6.1207

Shahid, N. U., & Sheikh, N. J. (2021). Impact of big data on innovation, competitive advantage, productivity, and decision making: Literature review. *Open Journal of Business and Management*, 9(02), 586–617. DOI: 10.4236/ojbm.2021.92032

Singh, P., Verma, A., Vij, S., & Thakur, J. (2023). Implications & impact of artificial intelligence in digital media: With special focus on social media marketing. *E3S Web of Conferences, 399*, 07006. https://doi.org/DOI: 10.1051/e3sconf/202339907006

Somani, S., Buchem, M., Sarraju, A., Hernandez-Boussard, T., & Rodríguez, F. (2023). Artificial intelligence–enabled analysis of statin-related topics and sentiments on social media. *JAMA Network Open*, 6(4), e239747. DOI: 10.1001/jamanetworkopen.2023.9747 PMID: 37093597

Sufi, F. (2023). A new social media analytics method for identifying factors contributing to COVID-19 discussion topics. *Information (Basel)*, 14(10), 545. DOI: 10.3390/info14100545

Tien, J. M. (2017). Internet of things, real-time decision making, and artificial intelligence. *Annals of Data Science*, 4(2), 149–178. DOI: 10.1007/s40745-017-0112-5

Varsha, P., Akter, S., Kumar, A., Gochhait, S., & Patagundi, B. (2021). The impact of artificial intelligence on branding. *Journal of Global Information Management*, 29(4), 221–246. DOI: 10.4018/JGIM.20210701.oa10

Yiğitcanlar, T., Kankanamge, N., Preston, A., Gill, P., Rezayee, M., Ostadnia, M., Xia, B., & Ioppolo, G. (2020). How can social media analytics assist authorities in pandemic-related policy decisions? Insights from Australian states and territories. *Health Information Science and Systems*, 8(1), 37. Advance online publication. DOI: 10.1007/s13755-020-00121-9 PMID: 33078073

Zhang, H., Zang, Z., Zhu, H., Uddin, M. I., & Amin, M. A. (2022). Big data-assisted social media analytics for business model for business decision making system competitive analysis. *Information Processing & Management*, 59(1), 102762. DOI: 10.1016/j.ipm.2021.102762

Ziakis, C., & Vlachopoulou, M. (2023). Artificial intelligence in digital marketing: Insights from a comprehensive review. *Information (Basel)*, 14(12), 664. DOI: 10.3390/info14120664

Compilation of References

Nechytailo, A. (2023). Using AI-powered tools for improving talent acquisition processes.

Rashed Khan, M. (2024). Application of artificial intelligence for talent management: Challenges and opportunities.

Rawashdeh, A. (2023). The consequences of artificial intelligence: An investigation into the impact of AI on job displacement in accounting. *Journal of Science and Technology Policy Management*. https://doi.org/DOI: 10.1108/JSTPM-02-2023-0031

Holzinger, A., Weippl, E., Tjoa, A. M., & Kieseberg, P. (2021, August). Digital transformation for sustainable development goals (SDGs)—A security, safety and privacy perspective on AI. In *International cross-domain conference for machine learning and knowledge extraction* (pp. 1-20). Cham: Springer International Publishing. DOI: 10.1007/978-3-030-66151-9_1

Khan, M. R. (2024). Application of artificial intelligence for talent management: Challenges and opportunities. In *Intelligent Human Systems Integration (IHSI 2024): Integrating People and Intelligent Systems* (Vol. 119, pp. 119).

Ligozat, A. L., Lefèvre, J., Bugeau, A., & Combaz, J. (2021). Unraveling the hidden environmental impacts of AI solutions for the environment. *arXiv preprint arXiv:2110.11822*.

Pfau, W., & Rimpp, P. (2021). AI-enhanced business models for digital entrepreneurship. In *Digital Entrepreneurship: Impact on Business and Society* (pp. 121-140). Springer International Publishing. DOI: 10.1007/978-3-030-53914-6_7

Prakash, K. B., Reddy, A. A. S., & Yasaswi, R. K. K. (2021). AI-powered HCM: The analytics and augmentations. In *Beyond human resources: Research paths towards a new understanding of workforce management within organizations* (pp. 155).

Aaker, D. A. (1991). *Managing Brand Equity: Capitalizing on the Value of a Brand Name*. Free Press.

Abbas, M. H., & Bulut, M. (2024). Navigating the landscape of sustainable entrepreneurship research: A systematic literature review. *Discover Sustainability*, 5(1), 171. Advance online publication. DOI: 10.1007/s43621-024-00293-4

Abosede, A. J., & Onakoya, A. B. (2013). Entrepreneurship, economic development and inclusive growth. *International Journal of Social Sciences and Entrepreneurship*, 1(3), 375–387. http://jesocin.com/index.php/jesocin/article/view/7

Abraham, S. (2021). The Future of Fashion is Here: Integration of AI in Marketing Practices of Leading Fashion Retail Businesses (Doctoral dissertation, Toronto Metropolitan University).

Abuzaid, A. N., & Alsbou, M. K. K. (2024, April). AI and Entrepreneurship: Enablers, Obstacles, and Startups' Role in Shaping the Future Economy. In *2024 International Conference on Knowledge Engineering and Communication Systems (ICKECS)* (Vol. 1, pp. 1-6). IEEE. DOI: 10.1109/ICKECS61492.2024.10616645

Acs, Z. J., & Audretsch, D. B. (2005). *Entrepreneurship, Innovation, and Technological Change* (Vol. 2105). Now Publishers Inc.

Afshan, G., Shahid, S., & Tunio, M. N. (2021). Learning experiences of women entrepreneurs amidst COVID-19. *International Journal of Gender and Entrepreneurship*, 13(2), 162–186. DOI: 10.1108/IJGE-09-2020-0153

Agarwal, R., & Mangal, S. (2020). Robotic process automation in business: Insights and implications. *Journal of Business Process Management*, 26(3), 245–262. DOI: 10.1108/JBPM-05-2019-0263

Aggarwal, V., Maslen, C., Abel, R., Bhattacharya, P., Bromiley, P., Clark, E., … & Poole, K. (2021). Opportunistic diagnosis of osteoporosis, fragile bone strength and vertebral fractures from routine ct scans; a review of approved technology systems and pathways to implementation. Therapeutic Advances in Musculoskeletal Disease, 13, 1759720X2110240. DOI: 10.1177/1759720X211024029

Agrawal, A., Gans, J., & Goldfarb, A. (2018). *Prediction Machines: The Simple Economics of Artificial Intelligence*. Harvard Business Review Press.

Ahlstrom, D. (2010). Innovation in small and medium-sized enterprises: A review of the literature. *International Journal of Management Reviews*, 12(4), 401–426. DOI: 10.1111/j.1468-2370.2009.00268.x

Akella, K., Venkatachalam, N., Gokul, K., Choi, K., & Tyakal, R. (2017). Gain customer insights using NLP techniques. *SAE International Journal of Materials and Manufacturing*, 10(3), 333–337. DOI: 10.4271/2017-01-0245

Aldunate, Á., Maldonado, S., Vairetti, C., & Armelini, G. (2022). Understanding customer satisfaction via deep learning and natural language processing. *Expert Systems with Applications*, 209, 118309. DOI: 10.1016/j.eswa.2022.118309

Aliyu, A. U. L. (2019). Effect of employee participation in decision making in an organization performance. *International Journal of the Economics of Business*, 3(2), 255–259.

Aljarboa, S. (2024). Factors influencing the adoption of artificial intelligence in e-commerce by small and medium-sized enterprises. *International Journal of Information Management Data Insights*, 4(2), 100285. DOI: 10.1016/j.jjimei.2024.100285

Alshareef, N., & Tunio, M. N. (2022). Role of leadership in adoption of blockchain technology in small and medium enterprises in Saudi Arabia. *Frontiers in Psychology*, 13, 911432. DOI: 10.3389/fpsyg.2022.911432 PMID: 35602740

Alves Gomes, M., & Meisen, T. (2023). A review on customer segmentation methods for personalized customer targeting in e-commerce use cases. *Information Systems and e-Business Management*, 21(3), 527–570. DOI: 10.1007/s10257-023-00640-4

Amoako, G., Omari, P., Kumi, D. K., Agbemabiase, G. C., & Asamoah, G. (2021). Conceptual framework—artificial intelligence and better entrepreneurial decision-making: The influence of customer preference, industry benchmark, and employee involvement in an emerging market. *Journal of Risk and Financial Management*, 14(12), 604. DOI: 10.3390/jrfm14120604

Anane-Simon, R., & Atiku, S. O. (2024). Artificial Intelligence and Automation for the Future of Startups. In *Ecosystem Dynamics and Strategies for Startups Scalability* (pp. 133–153). IGI Global.

Anastasia, O. (2023). Mediating effects of entrepreneurship education on personality dimensions and venture creation of Nigerian graduates: An empirical approach. *Journal of Economics Management & Business Administration*, 2(1), 15–28. DOI: 10.59075/jemba.v2i1.235

Anitha, J. (2014). Determinants of employee engagement and their impact on employee performance. *International Journal of Productivity and Performance Management*, 63(3), 308–323. DOI: 10.1108/IJPPM-01-2013-0008

An, J., Kwon, H., & Park, H. (2014). The impact of artificial intelligence on marketing strategies: An empirical study. *Journal of Business Research*, 67(7), 1401–1410. DOI: 10.1016/j.jbusres.2013.08.015

Åstebro, T., & Tåg, J. (2017). Gross, net, and new job creation by entrepreneurs. *Journal of Business Venturing Insights*, 8, 64–70. DOI: 10.1016/j.jbvi.2017.06.001

Azuma, R., Baillot, Y., Behringer, R., Feiner, S., Julier, S., & MacIntyre, B. (2001). Recent advances in augmented reality. *IEEE Computer Graphics and Applications*, 21(6), 34–47. DOI: 10.1109/38.963459

Baiyere, A., Salmela, H., & Tapanainen, T. (2020). Digital transformation and the new logics of business process management. *European Journal of Information Systems*, 29(3), 238–259. DOI: 10.1080/0960085X.2020.1718007

Bakri, B., Zm, A. A., Defitri, S. Y., & Mu'min, H. (2024). The effect of ai technology, innovation readiness, and digital entrepreneurship on competitive advantage in start up in jakarta. *West Science Interdisciplinary Studies*, 2(04), 841–850. DOI: 10.58812/wsis.v2i04.807

Balaji, K. "Blockchain Based Banking Transactions Enabled by Big Data," *2023 5th International Conference on Energy, Power and Environment: Towards Flexible Green Energy Technologies (ICEPE)*, Shillong, India, 2023, pp. 1-6, DOI: 10.1109/ICEPE57949.2023.10201613

Balaji, K. "Exploring the Drivers and Effects on Supply Chain Resilience and Performance in an Emerging Market Using Artificial Intelligence," *2023 3rd International Conference on Smart Generation Computing, Communication and Networking (SMART GENCON)*, Bangalore, India, 2023, pp. 1-6, DOI: 10.1109/SMARTGENCON60755.2023.10442071

Balaji, K. (2024). Charting the Path to Global Prosperity: Unveiling the Impact and Promise of Sustainable Development. In Ordóñez de Pablos, P., Anshari, M., & Almunawar, M. (Eds.), *Harnessing Green and Circular Skills for Digital Transformation* (pp. 1–22). IGI Global., DOI: 10.4018/979-8-3693-2865-1.ch001

Balaji, K. (2024). Harnessing AI for Financial Innovations: Pioneering the Future of Financial Services. In Jermsittiparsert, K., Phongkraphan, N., & Lekhavichit, N. (Eds.), *Modern Management Science Practices in the Age of AI* (pp. 91–122). IGI Global., DOI: 10.4018/979-8-3693-6720-9.ch004

Balaji, K. (2024). The Nexus of Smart Contracts and Digital Twins Transforming Green Finance With Automated Transactions in Investment Agreements: Leveraging Smart Contracts for Green Investment Agreements and Automated Transactions. In Jafar, S., Rodriguez, R., Kannan, H., Akhtar, S., & Plugmann, P. (Eds.), *Harnessing Blockchain-Digital Twin Fusion for Sustainable Investments* (pp. 287–315). IGI Global., DOI: 10.4018/979-8-3693-1878-2.ch012

Balaji, K. "Unlocking the Potential of BI-Enhancing Banking Transactions Through AI&ML Tools," *2023 International Conference on Applied Intelligence and Sustainable Computing (ICAISC)*, Dharwad, India, 2023, pp. 1-6, DOI: 10.1109/ICAISC58445.2023.10200018

Balaji, K., & Babu, M. K. (2017). A study on the affect of technology on unplanned purchase behaviour among the customers across selected corporate retail chains of Andhrapradesh, India. *International Journal of Economic Research*, 14(4), 277–288.

Balaji, K., & Babu, M. K. (2017). A study on the role of the external and internal factors on consumer impulse buying behaviour in selected retail outlets of Andhra Pradesh, India. *International Journal of Applied Business and Economic Research*, 15(4), 171–185.

Balaji, K., Karim, S., & Rao, P. S. "Unleashing the Power of Smart Chatbots: Transforming Banking with Artificial Intelligence," *2024 International Conference on Advances in Computing, Communication and Applied Informatics (ACCAI)*, Chennai, India, 2024, pp. 1-7, DOI: 10.1109/ACCAI61061.2024.10602456

Balaji, K., & Kishore Babu, M. (2016). A study on consumer shopping patterns in current retail scenario across selected retail stores in Andhra Pradesh, India. *International Journal of Economic Research*, 13(4), 1629–1640.

Barham, H. (2017, July). Achieving competitive advantage through big data: A literature review. In *2017 Portland International Conference on Management of Engineering and Technology (PICMET)* (pp. 1-7). IEEE. DOI: 10.23919/PICMET.2017.8125459

Bashynska, I., Prokopenko, O., & Sala, D. (2023). Managing human capital with AI: Synergy of talent and technology. *Zeszyty Naukowe Wyższej Szkoły Finansów i Prawa w Bielsku-Białej*, 27(3), 39–45.

Benanav, A. (2020). *Automation and the Future of Work*. Verso Books.

Benbya, H., Davenport, T. H., & Pachidi, S. (2020). Artificial intelligence in organizations: Current state and future opportunities. *MIS Quarterly Executive*, 19(4).

Bendix, S. (2010). *industrial relations in South Africa*. Juta and Company Ltd.

Bhuiyan, M. S. (2024). The role of AI-enhanced personalization in customer experiences. *Journal of Computer Science and Technology Studies*, 6(1), 162–169. DOI: 10.32996/jcsts.2024.6.1.17

Birkinshaw, J. (2004). A dynamic capabilities perspective on innovation. *Journal of Product Innovation Management*, 21(5), 319–336.

Biswas, A., & Wang, H. C. (2023). Autonomous vehicles enabled by the integration of IoT, edge intelligence, 5G, and blockchain. *Sensors (Basel)*, 23(4), 1963. DOI: 10.3390/s23041963 PMID: 36850560

Biswas, S. (2023). The function of chat GPT in social media: According to chat GPT. Available at *SSRN* 4405389. DOI: 10.2139/ssrn.4405389

Bogan, C. E., & English, M. J. (1994). Benchmarking for best practices: Winning through innovative adaptation. *(No Title)*. https://cir.nii.ac.jp/crid/1130000797322626048

Boldureanu, G., Ionescu, A., Bercu, A., Bedrule-Grigoruă, M., & Boldureanu, D. (2020). Entrepreneurship education through successful entrepreneurial models in higher education institutions. *Sustainability (Basel)*, 12(3), 1267. DOI: 10.3390/su12031267

Bossuwé, E. (2023). AI-DRIVEN BUSINESS MODELS AIMED AT PROMOTING A CIRCULAR ECONOMY (Doctoral dissertation, Ghent University).

Bouncken, R. B., & Kraus, S. (2022). Entrepreneurial ecosystems in an interconnected world: Emergence, governance and digitalization. *Review of Managerial Science*, 16(1), 1–14. DOI: 10.1007/s11846-021-00444-1

Bourechak, A., Zedadra, O., Kouahla, M. N., Guerrieri, A., Seridi, H., & Fortino, G. (2023). At the confluence of artificial intelligence and edge computing in iot-based applications: A review and new perspectives. *Sensors (Basel)*, 23(3), 1639. DOI: 10.3390/s23031639 PMID: 36772680

Brem, A., Giones, F., & Werle, M. (2021). The AI digital revolution in innovation: A conceptual framework of artificial intelligence technologies for the management of innovation. *IEEE Transactions on Engineering Management*, 70(2), 770–776. DOI: 10.1109/TEM.2021.3109983

Bryndin, E. (2019). Practical development of creative life-saving artificial intelligence. *Communications*, 7(2), 31. DOI: 10.11648/j.com.20190702.11

Brynjolfsson, E., & McElheran, K. (2016). The digitization of business: How IT has changed the nature of work. *Harvard Business Review*, 94(11), 85–92. https://hbr.org/2016/11/the-digitization-of-business

Bughin, J., Seong, J., Manyika, J., Chui, M., & Joshi, R. (2019). *Notes from the AI Frontier: Tackling Europe's Gap in Digital and AI*. McKinsey Global Institute.

Burns, P. (2016). *Entrepreneurship and Small Business*. Macmillan International Higher Education. DOI: 10.1007/978-1-137-43034-2

Burström, T., Parida, V., Lahti, T., & Wincent, J. (2021). AI-enabled business-model innovation and transformation in industrial ecosystems: A framework, model and outline for further research. *Journal of Business Research*, 127, 85–95. DOI: 10.1016/j.jbusres.2021.01.016

Bu, S., Jeong, U. A., & Koh, J. (2022). Robotic process automation: A new enabler for digital transformation and operational excellence. *Business Communication Research and Practice*, 5(1), 29–35. DOI: 10.22682/bcrp.2022.5.1.29

Cachon, G. P., & Terwiesch, C. (2009). Matching Supply with Demand: An Introduction to Operations Management. McGraw-Hill/Irwin.

Cambria, E., Poria, S., Gelbukh, A., & Hussain, A. (2017). Sentiment analysis: A review and comparative analysis. *Affective Computing and Intelligent Interaction*, 2(4), 301–320. DOI: 10.1007/s40063-017-0072-5

Candelon, F., & Reeves, M. (Eds.). (2022). *The Rise of AI-Powered Companies*. Walter de Gruyter GmbH & Co KG. DOI: 10.1515/9783110775112

Cantamessa, M., Gatteschi, V., Perboli, G., & Rosano, M. (2018). Startups' roads to failure. *Sustainability (Basel)*, 10(7), 2346. DOI: 10.3390/su10072346

Cao, G., Duan, Y., & Cadden, T. (2019). The link between information processing capability and competitive advantage mediated through decision-making effectiveness. *International Journal of Information Management*, 44, 121–131. DOI: 10.1016/j.ijinfomgt.2018.10.003

Carter, S. (2011). The rewards of entrepreneurship: Exploring the incomes, wealth, and economic well–being of entrepreneurial households. *Entrepreneurship Theory and Practice*, 35(1), 39–55. DOI: 10.1111/j.1540-6520.2010.00422.x

Chalmers, D., MacKenzie, N. G., & Carter, S. (2021). Artificial intelligence and entrepreneurship: Implications for venture creation in the fourth industrial revolution. *Entrepreneurship Theory and Practice*, 45(5), 1028–1053. DOI: 10.1177/1042258720934581

Chen, H., Chiang, R. H. L., & Storey, V. C. (2012). Business intelligence and analytics: From big data to big impact. *Management Information Systems Quarterly*, 36(4), 1165–1188. DOI: 10.2307/41703503

Chen, L., Zhang, X., & Wu, Z. (2014). Barriers to artificial intelligence adoption in small businesses: An empirical study. *International Journal of Information Management*, 34(4), 467–473. DOI: 10.1016/j.ijinfomgt.2014.02.005

Chen, S., Wang, W., & Lu, C. (2021). Exploring the development of entrepreneurial identity in a learning-by-doing entrepreneurial project environment. *Education + Training*, 63(5), 679–700. DOI: 10.1108/ET-07-2020-0195

Chen, Y., & Biswas, M. (2021). Turning crisis into opportunities: How a firm can enrich its business operations using artificial intelligence and big data during COVID-19. *Sustainability (Basel)*, 13(22), 12656. DOI: 10.3390/su132212656

Chen, Y., Zhang, X., & Xu, J. (2022). Comparative analysis of AI and traditional forecasting methods in supply chain management. *International Journal of Forecasting*, 38(4), 789–804. DOI: 10.1016/j.ijforecast.2021.12.008

Chesbrough, H. (2003). *Open Innovation: The New Imperative for Creating and Profiting from Technology*. Harvard Business Press.

Chishti, S. (2020). *The AI book: the artificial intelligence handbook for investors, entrepreneurs and fintech visionaries*. John Wiley & Sons. https://www.google.co.in/books/edition/The_AI_Book/oE3YDwAAQBAJ?hl=en&gbpv=0

Choi, J., Lee, H., & Kim, S. (2022). Machine learning algorithms for predictive analytics: A comprehensive review. *Journal of Data Science and Analytics*, 14(2), 117–135. DOI: 10.1007/s41060-021-00264-0

Choi, T. M., Wallace, S. W., & Wang, Y. (2018). Big data analytics in operations management. *European Journal of Operational Research*, 271(3), 558–569. DOI: 10.1016/j.ejor.2018.05.048

Chowdhury, R. H.Rakibul Hasan Chowdhury. (2024). AI-driven business analytics for operational efficiency. *World Journal of Advanced Engineering Technology and Sciences*, 12(2), 535–543. DOI: 10.30574/wjaets.2024.12.2.0329

Christensen, C. M. (1997). *The innovator's dilemma: When new technologies cause great firms to fail*. Harvard Business Review Press.

Christensen, C. M., & Raynor, M. E. (2003). *The Innovator's Solution: Creating and Sustaining Successful Growth*. Harvard Business Press.

Chung, D. (2023). Machine learning for predictive model in entrepreneurship research: Predicting entrepreneurial action. *Small Enterprise Research*, 30(1), 89–106. DOI: 10.1080/13215906.2022.2164606

Ćirković, A. (2020). Evaluation of four artificial intelligence–assisted self-diagnosis apps on three diagnoses: Two-year follow-up study. *Journal of Medical Internet Research*, 22(12), e18097. DOI: 10.2196/18097 PMID: 33275113

Cockburn, I. M., Henderson, R., & Stern, S. (2019). The impact of artificial intelligence on innovation. *Innovation Policy and the Economy*, 19(1), 41–58.

Csaszar, F. A., Ketkar, H., & Kim, H. (2024). Artificial Intelligence and Strategic Decision-Making: Evidence from Entrepreneurs and Investors. *arXiv preprint arXiv:2408.08811*. DOI: 10.2139/ssrn.4913363

Cullen, F., & Kingston, H. (2009). Analysis of rural and urban consumer behavior toward new food products using a food-related lifestyle instrument. *Journal of Foodservice Business Research*, 12(1), 18–41. DOI: 10.1080/15378020802671842

D'Aveni, R. A. (2010). Competitive pressures and innovation in small firms: Evidence from artificial intelligence applications. *Small Business Economics*, 34(3), 211–229. DOI: 10.1007/s11187-009-9205-1

Daft, R. L. (2017). *Organization Theory and Design*. Cengage Learning.

Dahlgaard, J. J., Kanji, G. K., & Kristensen, K. (2008). *Fundamentals of total quality management*. Routledge. doi: DOI: 10.4324/9780203930021

Dastin, J. (2022). How Amazon uses AI to optimize supply chain operations. Reuters. Retrieved from https://www.reuters.com/business/amazon-ai-supply-chain

Davenport, T. H. (2000). *Mission Critical: Realizing the Promise of Enterprise Systems*. Harvard Business Press.

Davenport, T. H., & Harris, J. G. (2007). *Competing on analytics: The new science of winning*. Harvard Business Review Press.

Davenport, T. H., & Ronanki, R. (2018). AI is the future of work: How artificial intelligence is transforming business operations. *Harvard Business Review*, 96(4), 108–116.

Davenport, T. H., & Ronanki, R. (2018). Artificial intelligence for the real world. *Harvard Business Review*, 96(1), 108–116. https://hbr.org/2018/01/artificial-intelligence-for-the-real-world

Davidsson, P., & Klofsten, M. (2003). The business platform: Developing an instrument to gauge and to assist the development of young firms. *Journal of Small Business Management*, 41(1), 1–26. DOI: 10.1111/1540-627X.00064

Davis, M., & Thompson, L. (2015). Preparing entrepreneurs for artificial intelligence: Education and training challenges. *Entrepreneurship Education*, 18(2), 113–130. DOI: 10.1016/j.ejbe.2014.08.002

Dean, J., & Ghemawat, S. (2004). MapReduce: Simplified data processing on large clusters. In *6th Symposium on Operating System Design and Implementation (OSDI'04)*, San Francisco, CA, USA.

Dew, R. (2018). *Customer experience innovation: How to get a lasting market edge*. Emerald Group Publishing. DOI: 10.1108/9781787547865

Dinh, T. N., & Thai, M. T. (2018). AI and blockchain: A disruptive integration. *Computer*, 51(9), 48–53. DOI: 10.1109/MC.2018.3620971

Dolnicar, S., Grün, B., Leisch, F., & Schmidt, K. (2020). Nature and Management of Airbnb Accommodation in Disruptive Times. *Current Issues in Tourism*, 23(13), 1602–1617.

Domańska, A., & Zajkowski, R. (2022). Barriers to gaining support: A prospect of entrepreneurial activity of family and non-family firms in Poland. *Equilibrium. Quarterly Journal of Economics and Economic Policy*, 17(1), 191–224. https://www.ceeol.com/search/article-detail?id=1069305. DOI: 10.24136/eq.2022.008

Duan, W., Gu, B., & Whinston, A. B. (2008). The dynamics of online word-of-mouth and product sales—An empirical investigation of the movie industry. *Journal of Retailing*, 84(2), 233–242. DOI: 10.1016/j.jretai.2008.04.005

Duhigg, C. (2012). *The Power of Habit: Why We Do What We Do in Life and Business*. Random House.

Duong, C. D., & Nguyen, T. H. (2024). How ChatGPT adoption stimulates digital entrepreneurship: A stimulus-organism-response perspective. *International Journal of Management Education*, 22(3), 101019. Advance online publication. DOI: 10.1016/j.ijme.2024.101019

Du, Y. R. (2023). Personalization, echo chambers, news literacy, and algorithmic literacy: A qualitative study of AI-powered news app users. *Journal of Broadcasting & Electronic Media*, 67(3), 246–273. DOI: 10.1080/08838151.2023.2182787

Dwivedi, Y. K., Hughes, L., Ismagilova, E., Aarts, G., & Baabdullah, A. M. (2021). Artificial Intelligence (AI): Multidisciplinary perspectives on emerging challenges, opportunities, and agenda for research, practice, and policy. *International Journal of Information Management*, 57, 102–126.

Dwivedi, Y. K., Hughes, L., Ismagilova, E., Aarts, G., Coombs, C., Crick, T., Duan, Y., Dwivedi, R., Edwards, J., Eirug, A., Galanos, V., Ilavarasan, P. V., Janssen, M., Jones, P., Kar, A. K., Kizgin, H., Kronemann, B., Lal, B., Lucini, B., & Williams, M. D. (2021). Artificial Intelligence (AI): Multidisciplinary perspectives on emerging challenges, opportunities, and agenda for research, practice and policy. *International Journal of Information Management*, 57, 101994. DOI: 10.1016/j.ijinfomgt.2019.08.002

Eisalou, M. R. (2014). *Human Resource 360-Degree Feedback*. LAP LAMBERT Academic Publishing. https://mc-caddogap.com/wp-content/uploads/Human-Resource-360-Degree-Feedback-by-Muhammad-Rouhi-Eisalou-1.pdf

Eisenmann, T. R. (2013). *HBS Case: Airbnb, Inc*. Harvard Business School Publishing.

Elia, G., Margherita, A., & Passiante, G. (2020). Digital entrepreneurship ecosystem: How digital technologies and collective intelligence are reshaping the entrepreneurial process. *Technological Forecasting and Social Change*, 150, 119791. DOI: 10.1016/j.techfore.2019.119791

Ellahham, S., Ellahham, N., & Simsekler, M. C. E. (2020). Application of artificial intelligence in the health care safety context: Opportunities and challenges. *American Journal of Medical Quality*, 35(4), 341–348. DOI: 10.1177/1062860619878515 PMID: 31581790

Elvas, L., & Ferreira, J. (2021). Intelligent transportation systems for electric vehicles. *Energies*, 14(17), 5550. DOI: 10.3390/en14175550

Engidaw, A. (2022). Small businesses and their challenges during COVID-19 pandemic in developing countries: In the case of Ethiopia. *Journal of Innovation and Entrepreneurship*, 11(1), 1. Advance online publication. DOI: 10.1186/s13731-021-00191-3 PMID: 35036286

Etzioni, A. (2014). The ethics of artificial intelligence: Balancing innovation and responsibility. *AI & Society*, 29(3), 225–233. DOI: 10.1007/s00146-013-0462-0

Evangelista, P. N. (2019). Artificial intelligence in fashion: how consumers and the fashion system are being impacted by AI-powered technologies.

Fairlie, R. W., & Fossen, F. M. (2018). Opportunity versus necessity entrepreneurship: Two components of business creation. DOI: 10.2139/ssrn.3140340

Fang, J. (2023). Research on the design of business models and transformation management of new entrepreneurial ventures driven by artificial intelligence. *BCP Business & Management*, 49, 36–41. DOI: 10.54691/bcpbm.v49i.5383

Farayola, O.Oluwatoyin Ajoke FarayolaAdekunle Abiola AbdulBlessing Otohan IraborEvelyn Chinedu Okeleke. (2023). Innovative business models driven by AI technologies: A review. *Computer Science & IT Research Journal*, 4(2), 85–110. DOI: 10.51594/csitrj.v4i2.608

Farquhar, J., & Meidan, A. (2017). *Marketing financial services*. Bloomsbury Publishing. https://www.google.co.in/books/edition/Marketing_Financial_Services/lyBIEAAAQBAJ?hl=en&gbpv=0

Felzmann, H., Fosch-Villaronga, E., Lutz, C., & Tamò-Larrieux, A. (2020). Towards transparency by design for artificial intelligence. *Science and Engineering Ethics*, 26(6), 3333–3361. DOI: 10.1007/s11948-020-00276-4 PMID: 33196975

Ferri, D. (2015). Does accessible technology need an 'entrepreneurial state'? The creation of an EU market of universally designed and assistive technology through state aid. *International Review of Law Computers & Technology*, 29(2-3), 137–161. DOI: 10.1080/13600869.2015.1055660

Fitriah, A. (2024). The relationship of entrepreneurship education and entrepreneurial motivation to entrepreneurial innovation through entrepreneurial mindset as an intervening variable in vocational school students in Mojokerto. *East Asian Journal of Multidisciplinary Research*, 2(12), 5021–5034. DOI: 10.55927/eajmr.v2i12.6870

Floridi, L., & Cowls, J. (2019). A unified framework of five principles for AI in society. *Harvard Data Science Review*, 1(1), 1–13.

Fountaine, T., McCarthy, B., & Saleh, T. (2019). Building the AI-powered organization. *Harvard Business Review*, 97(4), 62–73.

French, A. M., Shim, J. P., Risius, M., & Jain, H. (2019). The 4th industrial revolution powered by the integration of 5G, AI, and blockchain. https://aisel.aisnet.org/amcis2019/panel/panel/5/

Frost, A. C. (2000). Union involvement in workplace decision making: Implications for union democracy. *Journal of Labor Research*, 21(2), 265–286. https://www.proquest.com/openview/53064144eee6d0428a88224a5429b43e/1?pq-origsite=gscholar&cbl=48175. DOI: 10.1007/s12122-000-1047-7

Garbuio, M., & Lin, N. (2021). Innovative idea generation in problem finding: Abductive reasoning, cognitive impediments, and the promise of artificial intelligence. *Journal of Product Innovation Management*, 38(6), 701–725. DOI: 10.1111/jpim.12602

Garcia, A., & Adams, J. (2023). Data-driven decision making: Leveraging analytics and AI for strategic advantage. *Research Studies of Business*, 1(02), 77–85.

Ghafar, A. (2020). Convergence between 21st century skills and entrepreneurship education in higher education institutes. *International Journal of Higher Education*, 9(1), 218. DOI: 10.5430/ijhe.v9n1p218

Gharajedaghi, J. (1999). *Systems thinking: Managing chaos and complexity*. Butterworth-Heinemann.

Gill, S. S., Xu, M., Ottaviani, C., Patros, P., Bahsoon, R., Shaghaghi, A., Golec, M., Stankovski, V., Wu, H., Abraham, A., Singh, M., Mehta, H., Ghosh, S. K., Baker, T., Parlikad, A. K., Lutfiyya, H., Kanhere, S. S., Sakellariou, R., Dustdar, S., & Uhlig, S. (2022). AI for next generation computing: Emerging trends and future directions. *Internet of Things : Engineering Cyber Physical Human Systems*, 19, 100514. DOI: 10.1016/j.iot.2022.100514

Giuggioli, G., & Pellegrini, M. M. (2023). Artificial intelligence as an enabler for entrepreneurs: A systematic literature review and an agenda for future research. *International Journal of Entrepreneurial Behaviour & Research*, 29(4), 816–837. DOI: 10.1108/IJEBR-05-2021-0426

Giuggioli, G., Pellegrini, M. M., & Giannone, G. (2024). Artificial intelligence as an enabler for entrepreneurial finance: A practical guide to AI-driven video pitch evaluation for entrepreneurs and investors. *Management Decision*. Advance online publication. DOI: 10.1108/MD-10-2023-1926

Gnilsen, M., & Necula, M. (2023). GDPR Compliance Strategies for AI-Driven Diagnostic Startups: How can AI-driven Diagnostic Startups in the Breast Cancer Screening Domain Leverage their Business Strategies and Compliance Strategies to gain a Competitive Advantage?.

Goldstein, A., & Gafni, R. (2019). Learning entrepreneurship through virtual multicultural teamwork. *Issues in Informing Science and Information Technology*, 16, 277–305. DOI: 10.28945/4332

Goodfellow, I., Bengio, Y., & Courville, A. (2016). *Deep learning*. MIT Press.

Goswami, M. J. (2020). Leveraging AI for cost efficiency and optimized cloud resource management. *International Journal of New Media Studies: International Peer Reviewed Scholarly Indexed Journal*, 7(1), 21–27.

Gravina, N., Nastasi, J., & Austin, J. (2021). Assessment of employee performance. *Journal of Organizational Behavior Management*, 41(2), 124–149. DOI: 10.1080/01608061.2020.1869136

Gundersen, S. (2018). The rise of a new competitive intelligence: Need of real-time competitive intelligence and the impact on decision-making (Master's thesis, Universidade NOVA de Lisboa (Portugal)).

Guttentag, D. (2015). Airbnb: Disruptive innovation and the rise of an informal tourism accommodation sector. *Current Issues in Tourism*, 18(12), 1192–1217. DOI: 10.1080/13683500.2013.827159

Hagendorff, T. (2020). The Ethics of AI Ethics. *Minds and Machines*, 30(1), 99–120. DOI: 10.1007/s11023-020-09517-8

Hain, D. S., & Jurowetzki, R. (2020). The promises of machine learning and big data in entrepreneurship research. In *Handbook of Quantitative Research Methods in Entrepreneurship* (pp. 176–220). Edward Elgar Publishing. DOI: 10.4337/9781786430960.00014

Hamel, G. (2009). Moon shots for management. *Harvard Business Review*, 87(2), 91–98. PMID: 19266704

Harber, D., Marriott, F., & Idrus, N. (1991). Employee participation in TQC: The effect of job levels on participation and job satisfaction. *International Journal of Quality & Reliability Management*, 8(5). Advance online publication. DOI: 10.1108/EUM0000000001638

Harrington, H. J., & Harrington, J. S. (1996). *High performance benchmarking: 20 steps to success*. McGraw-Hill.

Harris, R. 2009. Introduction to Decision Making. Available online: http://www.oppapers.com/subjects/robertharris-page1.html (accessed on 23 November 2021).

Hassan, M. K., Rashid, M., Wei, A. S. T., Adedokun, B. O., & Ramachandran, J. (2019). Islamic business scorecard and the screening of Islamic businesses in a cross-country setting. *Thunderbird International Business Review*, 61(5), 807–819. DOI: 10.1002/tie.22038

Hedman, J., Sarker, S., & Veit, D. (2016). Digitization in business models and entrepreneurship. *Information Systems Journal*, 26(5), 419–420. DOI: 10.1111/isj.12119

Heilig, T., & Scheer, I. (2023). *Decision Intelligence: Transform Your Team and Organization with AI-Driven Decision-Making*. John Wiley & Sons.

Hellriegel, D., Jackson, S. E., & Slocum, J. W. (2002). Management: A competency-based approach. *South-Western: Thomson Learning*.

Henderson, R. M., & Clark, K. B. (1990). Architectural innovation: The reconfiguration of existing product technologies and the failure of established firms. *Administrative Science Quarterly*, 35(1), 9–30. DOI: 10.2307/2393549

Hermann, E. (2021). Artificial intelligence and mass personalization of communication content—An ethical and literacy perspective. *New Media & Society*, 24(5), 1258–1277. DOI: 10.1177/14614448211022702

Herrmann, H. (2023). What's next for responsible artificial intelligence: A way forward through responsible innovation. *Heliyon*, 9(3), e14379. Advance online publication. DOI: 10.1016/j.heliyon.2023.e14379 PMID: 36967876

He, Z., & Wang, J. (2014). The relationship between AI adoption and business performance: Evidence from digital entrepreneurship. *Journal of Business Research*, 67(11), 2286–2294. DOI: 10.1016/j.jbusres.2014.06.001

Hitt, L. M. (1997). Computing productivity: Firm-level evidence. *The Review of Economics and Statistics*, 79(3), 391–406. DOI: 10.1162/003465397558244

Holmes, W., Iniesto, F., Anastopoulou, S., & Boticario, J. (2023). Stakeholder perspectives on the ethics of ai in distance-based higher education. *International Review of Research in Open and Distance Learning*, 24(2), 96–117. DOI: 10.19173/irrodl.v24i2.6089

Ho, S. Y., & Bodoff, D. (2014). The effects of web personalization on user attitude and behavior. *Management Information Systems Quarterly*, 38(2), 497–510. DOI: 10.25300/MISQ/2014/38.2.08

Hoseini, F. (2023). Ai ethics: a call for global standards in technology development. aitechbesosci, 1(4), 1-3. DOI: 10.61838/kman.aitech.1.4.1

Huang, M. H., & Rust, R. T. (2021). Artificial intelligence in service. *Journal of Service Research*, 23(1), 1–17. DOI: 10.1177/1094670520959723

Huang, M.-H., & Rust, R. T. (2018). Artificial Intelligence in Service. *Journal of Service Research*, 21(2), 155–172. DOI: 10.1177/1094670517752459

Hwang, J., Kim, S., & Choi, K. (2023). Ethical considerations in the use of artificial intelligence in digital entrepreneurship. *Business Ethics Quarterly*, 33(1), 55–78. DOI: 10.1017/beq.2022.45

Iansiti, M., & Lakhani, K. R. (2020). *Competing in the age of AI: Strategy and leadership when algorithms and networks run the world*. Harvard Business Press. https://www.google.co.in/books/edition/Competing_in_the_Age_of_AI/VH-JDwAAQBAJ?hl=en&gbpv=0

Ikwue, U., Eyo-Udo, N. L., Onunka, O., Ekwezia, A. V., Nwankwo, E. E., & Daraojimba, C. (2023). Entrepreneurship: Scalability strategies in entrepreneurial ventures: A comprehensive literature review. *Agricultural Extension & Development Countries*, 1(2), 78–88. DOI: 10.26480/aedc.02.2023.78.88

Ismaeel, M., & Blaim, K. (2012). Toward applied Islamic business ethics: Responsible halal business. *Journal of Management Development*, 31(10), 1090–1100. DOI: 10.1108/02621711211281889

Jacobides, M. G., Brusoni, S., & Candelon, F. (2021). The evolutionary dynamics of the artificial intelligence ecosystem. *Strategy Science*, 6(4), 412–435. DOI: 10.1287/stsc.2021.0148

Jaiswal, A., Shah, A., Harjadi, C., Windgassen, E., & Washington, P. (2024). Ethics of the use of social media as training data for AI models used for digital phenotyping. *JMIR Formative Research*, 8, e59794. DOI: 10.2196/59794 PMID: 39018549

Janssen, M., Van Der Voort, H., & Wahyudi, A. (2017). Factors influencing big data decision-making quality. *Journal of Business Research*, 70, 338–345. DOI: 10.1016/j.jbusres.2016.08.007

Jarrahi, M. H. (2018). Artificial intelligence and the future of work: Human-AI symbiosis in organizational decision-making. *Business Horizons*, 61(4), 577–586.

Jarrahi, M. H., Kenyon, S., Brown, A., Donahue, C., & Wicher, C. (2023). Artificial intelligence: A strategy to harness its power through organizational learning. *The Journal of Business Strategy*, 44(3), 126–135. DOI: 10.1108/JBS-11-2021-0182

Jia, P., & Stan, C. (2021). Artificial intelligence factory, data risk, and VCs' mediation: The case of ByteDance, an AI-powered startup. *Journal of Risk and Financial Management*, 14(5), 203. DOI: 10.3390/jrfm14050203

Jia, Y., Wang, X., & Li, R. (2021). Predictive maintenance using machine learning: A case study in manufacturing. *International Journal of Production Economics*, 236, 108–123. DOI: 10.1016/j.ijpe.2021.108123

Jobin, A., Ienca, M., & Vayena, E. (2019). The global landscape of ai ethics guidelines. *Nature Machine Intelligence*, 1(9), 389–399. DOI: 10.1038/s42256-019-0088-2

Johnson, H., & Smith, L. (2023). Scaling business analytics with AI: A comparative study. *Journal of Business Analytics*, 12(1), 65–78. DOI: 10.1080/09720529.2023.2145145

Jordan, M. I., & Mitchell, T. M. (2015). Machine learning: Trends, perspectives, and prospects. *Science*, 349(6245), 255–260. DOI: 10.1126/science.aaa8415 PMID: 26185243

Judijanto, L., Asfahani, A., Bakri, A. A., Susanto, E., & Kulsum, U. (2022). AI-supported management through leveraging artificial intelligence for effective decision making. *Journal of Artificial Intelligence and Development*, 1(1), 59–68. DOI: 10.3390/ai.v1n1.5

K. Balaji, S. Karim, N. G. Naidu, T. Venkatesh, P. V. Ranjitha and S. ChandraSekhar, "Examining the Potential of Cryptocurrencies as An Asset Class-An Empirical Study," *2023 International Conference on Applied Intelligence and Sustainable Computing (ICAISC)*, Dharwad, India, 2023, pp. 1-6, .DOI: 10.1109/ICAISC58445.2023.10200309

Kalogiannidis, S., Kalfas, D., Papaevangelou, O., Giannarakis, G., & Chatzitheodoridis, F. (2024). The role of artificial intelligence technology in predictive risk assessment for business continuity: A case study of Greece. *Risks*, 12(2), 19. DOI: 10.3390/risks12020019

Kamyar, A. G. Artificial Intelligence Startups in Italy: Their role in Decision-Making.

Kanchana, R. S., Divya, J. V., & Beegom, A. A. (2013). Challenges faced by new entrepreneurs. *International Journal of Current Research and Academic Review*, 1(3), 71–78. https://citeseerx.ist.psu.edu/document?repid=rep1&type=pdf&doi=a28a718c222b38298cf61f514efbe1d2688c329c

Khang, A., Jadhav, B., & Dave, T. (2024). Enhancing Financial Services. Synergy of AI and Fintech in the Digital Gig Economy, 147.

Khatua, A., Khatua, A., Xu, C., & Wang, Z. (2021). Artificial intelligence, social media and supply chain management: The way forward. *Electronics (Basel)*, 10(19), 2348. DOI: 10.3390/electronics10192348

Khurshid, M. A., Al-Aali, A., Soliman, A. A., & Amin, S. M. (2014). Developing an Islamic corporate social responsibility model (ICSR). *Competitiveness Review*, 24(4), 258–274. DOI: 10.1108/CR-01-2013-0004

Kim, Y., & Chen, X. (2024). Building innovation ecosystems through AI collaboration: A study of digital entrepreneurship. *Journal of Innovation & Knowledge*, 9(1), 101–114. DOI: 10.1016/j.jik.2022.04.001

Kismawadi, E. R., Irfan, M., Al Muddatstsir, U. D., & Abdulkarim, F. M. (2023). Fintech innovations: Risk mitigation strategies in Islamic finance. In *Fintech Applications in Islamic Finance* (pp. 35–58). AI, Machine Learning, and Blockchain Techniques., DOI: 10.4018/979-8-3693-1038-0.ch003

Klímová, B., Pikhart, M., & Kacetl, J. (2023). Ethical issues of the use of ai-driven mobile apps for education. *Frontiers in Public Health*, 10, 1118116. Advance online publication. DOI: 10.3389/fpubh.2022.1118116 PMID: 36711343

Kline, S. J., & Rosenberg, N. (1986). An overview of innovation. In Landau, R., & Rosenberg, N. (Eds.), *The positive sum strategy: Harnessing technology for economic growth* (pp. 275–305). National Academy Press.

Klintong, N., Vadhanasindhu, P., & Thawesaengskulthai, N. (2012, February). Artificial intelligence and successful factors for selecting product innovation development. In *2012 Third International Conference on Intelligent Systems Modelling and Simulation* (pp. 397-402). IEEE. DOI: 10.1109/ISMS.2012.86

Kolanu, N., Silverstone, E., Ho, B., Pham, H., Hansen, A., Pauley, E., Quirk, A. R., Sweeney, S. C., Center, J. R., & Pocock, N. (2020). Clinical utility of computer-aided diagnosis of vertebral fractures from computed tomography images. *Journal of Bone and Mineral Research : the Official Journal of the American Society for Bone and Mineral Research*, 35(12), 2307–2312. DOI: 10.1002/jbmr.4146 PMID: 32749735

Kolarov, K., & Hadjitchoneva, J. (2023). Opportunities and limitations of digital educational tools in shaping entrepreneurial mindset and competences. *Digital Age in Semiotics & Communication*, 6, 32–56. DOI: 10.33919/dasc.23.6.3

Kraus, M., Feuerriegel, S., & Oztekin, A. (2020). Deep learning in business analytics and operations research: Models, applications and managerial implications. *European Journal of Operational Research*, 281(3), 628–641. DOI: 10.1016/j.ejor.2019.09.018

Kristian, A., Goh, T. S., Ramadan, A., Erica, A., & Sihotang, S. V. (2024). Application of AI in optimizing energy and resource management: Effectiveness of deep learning models. *International Transactions on Artificial Intelligence*, 2(2), 99–105. DOI: 10.33050/italic.v2i2.530

Kruger, S., & Steyn, A. A. (2021). A conceptual model of entrepreneurial competencies needed to utilise technologies of Industry 4.0. *International Journal of Entrepreneurship and Innovation*, 22(1), 56–67. DOI: 10.1177/1465750320927359

Kshetri, N. (2018). Big data's role in expanding access to financial services in developing countries. *Journal of Business Research*, 91, 60–71. DOI: 10.1016/j.jbusres.2018.06.023

Kulkarni, A. V., Joseph, S., & Patil, K. P. (2024). Artificial intelligence technology readiness for social sustainability and business ethics: Evidence from MSMEs in developing nations. *International Journal of Information Management Data Insights*, 4(2), 100250. Advance online publication. DOI: 10.1016/j.jjimei.2024.100250

Kuratko, D. F. (2005). The emergence of entrepreneurship education: Development, trends, and challenges. *Entrepreneurship Theory and Practice*, 29(5), 577–598. DOI: 10.1111/j.1540-6520.2005.00099.x

Lasi, H., Fettke, P., Kemper, H. G., Feld, T., & Hoffmann, M. (2014). Industry 4.0. *Business & Information Systems Engineering*, 6(4), 239–242. DOI: 10.1007/s12599-014-0334-4

Leavy, B. (2018). Airbnb's Approach to Data Science, with Surabhi Gupta. Retrieved from https://www.airbnb.com/resources/hosting-homes/a/airbnbs-approach-to-data-science-with-surabhi-gupta-164

Lee, K., & Lee, S. (2022). Optimizing logistics with AI: A case study of route planning and inventory management. *Logistics Research*, 15(2), 210–225. DOI: 10.1007/s12159-022-00222-x

Lejeune, A., Robaglia, B., Walter, M., Berrouiguet, S., & Lemey, C. (2022). Use of social media data to diagnose and monitor psychotic disorders: Systematic review. *Journal of Medical Internet Research*, 24(9), e36986. DOI: 10.2196/36986 PMID: 36066938

Leung, R. (2023). Using AI–ML to augment the capabilities of social media for telehealth and remote patient monitoring. *Health Care*, 11(12), 1704. DOI: 10.3390/healthcare11121704 PMID: 37372822

Levasseur, L., Tang, J., & Karami, M. (2019). Insomnia: An important antecedent impacting entrepreneurs' health. *Journal of Risk and Financial Management*, 12(1), 44. DOI: 10.3390/jrfm12010044

Levine, D. I. (2019). Automation as part of the solution. *Journal of Management Inquiry*, 28(3), 316–318. DOI: 10.1177/1056492619827375

Lewis, D., & Moorkens, J. (2020). A rights-based approach to trustworthy AI in social media. *Social Media + Society*, 6(3), 205630512095467. DOI: 10.1177/2056305120954672

Liao, S. H., Wu, C. H., & Hu, D. C. (2017). Exploring the effects of artificial intelligence on the operational efficiencies of startups. *International Journal of Production Economics*, 192, 115–126. DOI: 10.1016/j.ijpe.2017.06.011

Li, G., & Fung, R. Y. (2008). A predictive model for stock market behavior using multiple classifiers. *Decision Support Systems*, 45(4), 834–851.

Lockett, A., & Thompson, S. (1988). The role of technology in competitiveness: The impact of the technological revolution on competitive strategy. *Research Policy*, 17(2), 95–107. DOI: 10.1016/0048-7333(88)90031-1

Lopez, R., Martinez, P., & Santos, M. (2021). The hype of artificial intelligence in entrepreneurship: A critical review. *Journal of Business Venturing Insights*, 15, e00201. DOI: 10.1016/j.jbvi.2021.e00201

Luo, X., Tong, S., Fang, Z., & Qu, Z. (2021). Frontiers: Machines vs. humans: The impact of AI chatbot disclosure on customer purchases. *Marketing Science*, 40(5), 914–926.

Lyndgaard, S. F., Storey, R., & Kanfer, R. (2024). Technological support for lifelong learning: The application of a multilevel, person-centric framework. *Journal of Vocational Behavior*, 153, 104027. Advance online publication. DOI: 10.1016/j.jvb.2024.104027

M. A., Idris, A. A., & Odukoya, J. A. (. (2021). The impact of artificial intelligence on customer engagement in digital entrepreneurship. *Journal of Business Research*, 123, 412–423. DOI: 10.1016/j.jbusres.2020.09.033

Macey, W. H., & Schneider, B. (2008). The meaning of employee engagement. *Industrial and Organizational Psychology: Perspectives on Science and Practice*, 1(1), 3–30. DOI: 10.1111/j.1754-9434.2007.0002.x

Magalhaes Azevedo, D., & Kieffer, S. (2021). User reception of AI-enabled mHealth Apps: The case of Babylon health.

March, J. G. (1991). Exploration and exploitation in organizational learning. *Organization Science*, 2(1), 71–87. DOI: 10.1287/orsc.2.1.71

Markula, A. (2023). The use of artificial intelligence in dynamic pricing strategies. *Pricing Studies Review Journal*, 21(3), 34–56.

Marletto, G. (2019). Who will drive the transition to self-driving? A socio-technical analysis of the future impact of automated vehicles. *Technological Forecasting and Social Change*, 139, 221–234. DOI: 10.1016/j.techfore.2018.10.023

Martins, M. M. R. (2024). Startup Guide to AI: Integrating Technology for Business Success. *Valley International Journal Digital Library*, 1264-1274.

Masih, D. (2023). Enhancing employee efficiency and performance in industry 5.0 organizations through artificial intelligence integration. *EEL*, 13(4), 300–315. DOI: 10.52783/eel.v13i4.589

McAfee, A., & Brynjolfsson, E. (2017). *Machine, Platform, Crowd: Harnessing Our Digital Future*. W. W. Norton & Company.

McGrath, R. G., & MacMillan, I. C. (2000). *The entrepreneurial mindset: Strategies for continuously creating opportunity in an age of uncertainty* (Vol. 284). Harvard Business Press. https://www.google.co.in/books/edition/The_Entrepreneurial_Mindset/we7-hg9YGbgC?hl=en&gbpv=0

Meacham, M. (2020). *AI in talent development: Capitalize on the AI revolution to transform the way you work, learn, and live*. Association for Talent Development.

Meadows, D. (2015). *Thinking in Systems: A Primer*. Chelsea Green Publishing.

Mele, C., Spena, T. R., & Peschiera, S. (2018). Value creation and cognitive technologies: Opportunities and challenges. *Journal of Creating Value*, 4(2), 182–195. DOI: 10.1177/2394964318809152

Meyer, L. M., Stead, S., Salge, T. O., & Antons, D. (2024). Artificial intelligence in acute care: A systematic review, conceptual synthesis, and research agenda. *Technological Forecasting and Social Change*, 206, 123568. Advance online publication. DOI: 10.1016/j.techfore.2024.123568

Meziane, F., Vadera, S., Kobbacy, K., & Proudlove, N. (2000). Intelligent systems in manufacturing: Current developments and future prospects. *Integrated Manufacturing Systems*, 11(4), 218–238. DOI: 10.1108/09576060010326221

Millagala, K. (2023). Navigating the confluence of artificial intelligence and social media marketing. *International Journal of Research Publications*, 133(1). Advance online publication. DOI: 10.47119/IJRP1001331920235473

Mohamed, E., Osman, M. E., & Mohamed, B. A. (2024). The impact of artificial intelligence on social media content. *Journal of Social Sciences (New York, N. Y.)*, 20(1), 12–16. DOI: 10.3844/jssp.2024.12.16

Monica, R., & Soju, A. V. (2024). Artificial Intelligence and Service Marketing Innovation. In AI Innovation in Services Marketing (pp. 150-172). IGI Global.

Mourey, D. A., & Martin, I. M. (2017). Share a Coke: Brand personalization and the sharing economy. *Journal of Consumer Psychology*, 27(3), 397–405.

Mühling, Ş. (2023). Utilizing artificial intelligence (ai) for the identification and management of marine protected areas (mpas): A review. *Journal of Geoscience and Environment Protection*, 11(09), 118–132. DOI: 10.4236/gep.2023.119008

Mullins, L. J. (2007). *Management and organisational behaviour*. Pearson education.

Murray, T. (2003). An Overview of Intelligent Tutoring System Authoring Tools: Updated analysis of the state of the art. *Authoring Tools for Advanced Technology Learning Environments: Toward Cost-Effective Adaptive, Interactive and Intelligent Educational Software*, 491-544. DOI: 10.1007/978-94-017-0819-7

Muthukalyani, A. R. (2023). Unlocking Accurate Demand Forecasting in Retail Supply Chains with AI-driven Predictive Analytics. *Information Technology Management*, 14(2), 48–57.

Nambisan, S., Wright, M., & Feldman, M. (2019). The digital transformation of innovation and entrepreneurship: Progress, challenges and key themes. *Research Policy*, 48(8), 103773. DOI: 10.1016/j.respol.2019.03.018

Nedelcheva, I. (2020). DATA-DRIVEN CONTENT IN INTEGRATED DIGITAL MEDIA. In Communication Management: Theory and Practice in the 21st Century (pp. 254-263). Факултет по журналистика и масова комуникация, Софийски университет „Св. Кл. Охридски

Neff, J. (2007). Coca-Cola Gets Boost from Juice Brands. *Advertising Age*.

Nguyen, T., Tran, D., & Vu, H. (2021). Advantages of AI-driven analytics over traditional methods in operational efficiency. *Journal of Operations Management*, 39(6), 953–970. DOI: 10.1016/j.jom.2021.04.002

Noranee, S., & Othman, A. (2023). Understanding consumer sentiments: Exploring the role of artificial intelligence in marketing. *Jmm17 Jurnal Ilmu Ekonomi Dan Manajemen, 10*(1), 15-23. https://doi.org/DOI: 10.30996/jmm17.v10i1.8690

Nouri, P., & AhmadiKafeshani, A. (2020). Do female and male entrepreneurs differ in their proneness to heuristics and biases? *Journal of Entrepreneurship in Emerging Economies*, 12(3), 357–375. DOI: 10.1108/JEEE-05-2019-0062

Núñez, M. T. (2021). The Implementation Of AI. In *Marketing*. Universidad Pontificia de Comillas.

Nwosu, L., Enwereji, P. C., Enebe, N. B., & Segotso, T. (2023). Determining the roles of school management teams in fostering entrepreneurship among learners. *International Journal of Learning Teaching and Educational Research*, 22(9), 478–500. DOI: 10.26803/ijlter.22.9.26

O'Reilly, C. A.III, & Tushman, M. L. (2013). Organizational ambidexterity: Past, present, and future. *The Academy of Management Perspectives*, 27(4), 324–338. DOI: 10.5465/amp.2013.0025

O'Reilly, T. (2007). What Is Web 2.0: Design Patterns and Business Models for the Next Generation of Software. *Communications & Stratégies*, 65(1), 17–37.

Obschonka, M., & Audretsch, D. B. (2020). Artificial intelligence and big data in entrepreneurship: A new era has begun. *Small Business Economics*, 55(3), 529–539. DOI: 10.1007/s11187-019-00202-4

Ophir, Y., Tikochinski, R., Asterhan, C., Sisso, I., & Reichart, R. (2020). Deep neural networks detect suicide risk from textual Facebook posts. *Scientific Reports*, 10(1), 16685. Advance online publication. DOI: 10.1038/s41598-020-73917-0 PMID: 33028921

Orhan, Ö. B. (2023). The Role of AI (Artificial Intelligence) in Cloud Service Provider Selection for Startups.

Oskam, J., & Boswijk, A. (2016). Airbnb: The future of networked hospitality businesses. *Journal of Tourism Futures*, 2(1), 22–42. DOI: 10.1108/JTF-11-2015-0048

Ossa, L. (2024). Integrating ethics in ai development: A qualitative study. *BMC Medical Ethics*, 25(1), 10. Advance online publication. DOI: 10.1186/s12910-023-01000-0 PMID: 38262986

Oztemel, E., & Gursev, S. (2020). Literature review of Industry 4.0 and related technologies. *Journal of Intelligent Manufacturing*, 31(1), 127–182. DOI: 10.1007/s10845-018-1433-8

Page, L. (2017). What I learned at work this week: Google's social responsibility. Financial Times. Retrieved from https://www.ft.com/content/5dd0eb00-3b26-11e7-ac89-b01cc67cfeec

Panda, G., Upadhyay, A. K., & Khandelwal, K. (2019). Artificial intelligence: A strategic disruption in public relations. *Journal of Creative Communications*, 14(3), 196–213. DOI: 10.1177/0973258619866585

Panta, N., & Popescu, N.-E. (2023). Charting the Course of AI in Business Sustainability: A Bibliometric Analysis. *Studies in Business and Economics*, 18(3), 214–229. DOI: 10.2478/sbe-2023-0055

Park, G. (2019). The changing wind of data privacy law: A comparative study of the European Union's General Data Protection Regulation and the 2018 California Consumer Privacy Act. *UC Irvine L. Rev.*, 10, 1455.

Patricia, E. (2021). Value proposition design. https://doi.org/DOI: 10.31219/osf.io/kpd3b

Păvăloaia, V. D., Teodor, E. M., Fotache, D., & Danileț, M. (2019). Opinion mining on social media data: Sentiment analysis of user preferences. *Sustainability (Basel)*, 11(16), 4459. DOI: 10.3390/su11164459

Perakakis, E., Mastorakis, G., & Kopanakis, I. (2019). Social media monitoring: An innovative intelligent approach. *Designs*, 3(2), 24. DOI: 10.3390/designs3020024

Pereira, V., Hadjielias, E., Christofi, M., & Vrontis, D. (2023). A systematic literature review on the impact of artificial intelligence on workplace outcomes: A multi-process perspective. *Human Resource Management Review*, 33(1), 100857. DOI: 10.1016/j.hrmr.2021.100857

Pfau, W., & Rimpp, P. (2021). AI-enhanced business models for digital entrepreneurship. Digital Entrepreneurship: Impact on Business and Society, 121-140.

Pigni, F., Piccoli, G., & Watson, R. (2016). Digital data streams: Creating value from the real-time flow of big data. *California Management Review*, 58(3), 5–25. DOI: 10.1525/cmr.2016.58.3.5

Porter, M. E., & Millar, V. E. (1985). How information gives you competitive advantage. *Harvard Business Review*, 63(4), 149–160.

Prasetyo, P., Setyadharma, A., & Kistanti, N. (2021). The collaboration of social entrepreneurship and institutions for sustainable regional development security. *Open Journal of Business and Management*, 9(5), 2566–2590. DOI: 10.4236/ojbm.2021.95141

Prikshat, V., Patel, P., Varma, A., & Ishizaka, A. (2022). A multi-stakeholder ethical framework for ai-augmented hrm. *International Journal of Manpower*, 43(1), 226–250. DOI: 10.1108/IJM-03-2021-0118

Quelch, J. A. (2020). *Greater Good: How Good Marketing Makes for Better Democracy*. Harvard Business Press.

Radhakrishnan, R. (2024). Cultural impacts of artificial intelligence on sustainable entrepreneurship development., 201-230. DOI: 10.4018/979-8-3693-2432-5.ch010

Radinsky, K. (2012). Learning to predict from big data. *Proceedings of the ACM Web Science Conference*, Evanston, IL, USA.

Raihan, A. (2024). A review of the digitalization of the small and medium enterprises (SMEs) toward sustainability. *Global Sustainability Research*, 3(2), 1–16. DOI: 10.56556/gssr.v3i2.695

Ramírez, J. G. C. (2023). Incorporating Information Architecture (ia), Enterprise Engineering (ee) and Artificial Intelligence (ai) to Improve Business Plans for Small Businesses in the United States. *Journal of Knowledge Learning and Science Technology ISSN: 2959-6386 (online)*, 2(1), 115-127.

Rana, M. B. (2022). OF AI-DRIVEN HEALTHCARE STARTUPS.

Raybourn, C., & Coers, M. (2001). *Benchmarking: a guide for your journey to best-practice processes*. Accent Press Ltd.

Reuber, A. R., & Fischer, E. (1997). The influence of the management team's international experience on the internationalization behaviors of SMEs. *Journal of International Business Studies*, 28(4), 807–825. DOI: 10.1057/palgrave.jibs.8490120

Ridho Kismawadi, E., Irfan, M., & Shah, S. M. A. R. (2023). Revolutionizing islamic finance: Artificial intelligence's role in the future of industry. In *The Impact of AI Innovation on Financial Sectors in the Era of Industry 5.0* (pp. 184–207). DOI: 10.4018/979-8-3693-0082-4.ch011

Rizal, M., Novrizal, N., Irawan, D., & Patricia, M. C. (2022, December). Human potential in the AI era: Strategies for cultivating exceptional talent. In *The International Conference on Education, Social Sciences and Technology (ICESST)* (Vol. 1, No. 2, pp. 260-268).

Roberts, D. L., & Candi, M. (2024). Artificial intelligence and innovation management: Charting the evolving landscape. *Technovation*, 136, 103081. DOI: 10.1016/j.technovation.2024.103081

Rogers, E. M. (2003). *Diffusion of innovations* (5th ed.). Free Press.

Rojas, A., & Tuomi, A. (2022). Reimagining the sustainable social development of ai for the service sector: The role of startups. *Journal of Ethics in Entrepreneurship and Technology*, 2(1), 39–54. DOI: 10.1108/JEET-03-2022-0005

Rok, B., & Kulik, M. (2020). Circular start-up development: The case of positive impact entrepreneurship in Poland. *Corporate Governance (Bradford)*, 21(2), 339–358. DOI: 10.1108/CG-01-2020-0043

Rudall, Y. (2012). Business model generation. *Kybernetes*, 41(5/6), 823–824. DOI: 10.1108/03684921211261761

Ryan, M. (2020). The future of transportation: Ethical, legal, social and economic impacts of self-driving vehicles in the year 2025. *Science and Engineering Ethics*, 26(3), 1185–1208. DOI: 10.1007/s11948-019-00130-2 PMID: 31482471

Saari, A., Rasul, M., Yasin, R., Rauf, R., Ashari, Z., & Pranita, D. (2021). Skills sets for workforce in the 4th industrial revolution: Expectation from authorities and industrial players. *Journal of Technical Education and Training*, 13(2). Advance online publication. DOI: 10.30880/jtet.2021.13.02.001

Sahu, C. K., Young, C., & Rai, R. (2021). Artificial intelligence (AI) in augmented reality (AR)-assisted manufacturing applications: A review. *International Journal of Production Research*, 59(16), 4903–4959. DOI: 10.1080/00207543.2020.1859636

Salam, M. (2024). Social and environmental responsibility in ai-driven entrepreneurship., 173-193. DOI: 10.4018/979-8-3693-1842-3.ch012

Săniuă, A., & Filip, S. O. (2021). Artificial Intelligence: An overview of European and Romanian startups landscape and the factors that determine their Success. *Strategica. Shaping the Future of Business and Economy*, 872-884.

Schilling, M. A., & Phelps, C. (2007). Interfirm collaboration networks: The impact of large partners. *Management Science*, 53(3), 1030–1042. DOI: 10.1287/mnsc.1060.0687

Schmidt, E., & Rosenberg, J. (2014). *How Google Works*. Grand Central Publishing.

Seyi-Lande, O. B., Johnson, E., Adeleke, G. S., Amajuoyi, C. P., & Simpson, B. D. (2024). Enhancing business intelligence in e-commerce: Utilizing advanced data integration for real-time insights. *International Journal of Management & Entrepreneurship Research*, 6(6), 1936–1953. DOI: 10.51594/ijmer.v6i6.1207

Shahid, N. (2024). Ethical imperatives and frameworks for responsible ai adoption in digital entrepreneurship., 228-250. DOI: 10.4018/979-8-3693-1842-3.ch015

Shahid, N. U., & Sheikh, N. J. (2021). Impact of big data on innovation, competitive advantage, productivity, and decision making: Literature review. *Open Journal of Business and Management*, 9(02), 586–617. DOI: 10.4236/ojbm.2021.92032

Shaik, A. S., Alshibani, S. M., Jain, G., Gupta, B., & Mehrotra, A. (2024). Artificial intelligence (AI)-driven strategic business model innovations in small-and medium-sized enterprises. Insights on technological and strategic enablers for carbon neutral businesses. *Business Strategy and the Environment*, 33(4), 2731–2751. DOI: 10.1002/bse.3617

Shaikh, E., Tunio, M. N., Khoso, W. M., Brahmi, M., & Rasool, S. (2022). The COVID-19 pandemic overlaps entrepreneurial activities and triggered new challenges: a review Study. Managing Human Resources in SMEs and Start-ups: International Challenges and Solutions, 155-182.

Shane, S. A. (2003). *A general theory of entrepreneurship: The individual-opportunity nexus*. Edward Elgar Publishing. https://www.google.co.in/books/edition/A_General_Theory_of_Entrepreneurship/0FxO_Wsh30kC?hl=en&gbpv=1&dq=Shane,+Scott+Andrew.+2003.+A+General+Theory+of+Entrepreneurship:+The+Individual-Opportunity+Nexus.+Northampton:+Edward+Elgar+Publishing.&pg=PR9&printsec=frontcover

Shane, S., & Venkataraman, S. (2000). The Promise of Entrepreneurship As a Field of Research. *Academy of Management Review*, 25(1), 217–226. Advance online publication. DOI: 10.5465/amr.2000.2791611

Sharma, A. (2019, November). Entrepreneurship and role of AI. In *Proceedings of the 2019 2nd International Conference on Signal Processing and Machine Learning* (pp. 122-126). IEEE. DOI: 10.1145/3372806.3374910

Shepherd, D. A., & Majchrzak, A. (2022). Machines augmenting entrepreneurs: Opportunities (and threats) at the Nexus of artificial intelligence and entrepreneurship. *Journal of Business Venturing*, 37(4), 106227. DOI: 10.1016/j.jbusvent.2022.106227

Singh, P., Verma, A., Vij, S., & Thakur, J. (2023). Implications & impact of artificial intelligence in digital media: With special focus on social media marketing. *E3S Web of Conferences, 399*, 07006. https://doi.org/DOI: 10.1051/e3sconf/202339907006

Smith, T., Stiller, B., Guszcza, J., & Davenport, T. (2019). Analytics and AI-driven enterprises thrive in the Age of With. Deloitte Insights, 16.

Smith, R. (2018). *The Growth Hacker's Guide to the Galaxy: 100 Proven Growth Hacks for the Digital Marketer*. Routledge.

Sofijanova, E., & Zabijakin-Chatleska, V. (2013). Employee involvement and organizational performance: Evidence from the manufacturing sector in Republic of Macedonia. https://eprints.ugd.edu.mk/8225/1/Trakia%20Journal%20of%20Sciences%28moj%20tekst%29.pdf

Somani, S., Buchem, M., Sarraju, A., Hernandez-Boussard, T., & Rodríguez, F. (2023). Artificial intelligence–enabled analysis of statin-related topics and sentiments on social media. *JAMA Network Open*, 6(4), e239747. DOI: 10.1001/jamanetworkopen.2023.9747 PMID: 37093597

Stoner, J. A. F., Freeman, R. E., & Gilbert, D. R. (1995). *Management* (Cliffs, E., Ed.; 6th ed.). Prentice Hall.

Sudmann, A. (2019). *The democratization of artificial intelligence. Net politics in the era of learning algorithms*. Transcript.

Sudmann, A. (2019). The democratization of artificial intelligence: Net politics in the era of learning algorithms. *Transcript*, 45(2), 78–92. DOI: 10.14361/ai.v45n2.56

Sufi, F. (2023). A new social media analytics method for identifying factors contributing to COVID-19 discussion topics. *Information (Basel)*, 14(10), 545. DOI: 10.3390/info14100545

Sundarapandiyan Natarajan, D. K. S., Subbaiah, B., Dhinakaran, D. P., Kumar, J. R., & Rajalakshmi, M. (2024). AI-powered strategies for talent management optimization. *Journal of Informatics Education and Research*, 4(2).

Suurmaa, P. (2024). The data-driven decision-making in start-ups.

Tak, A., & Chahal, S. (2024). Sprint planning and AI/ML: How to balance iterations with data complexity. *Journal of Technology and Systems*, 6(2), 56–72. DOI: 10.47941/jts.1817

Tang, L., Li, J., & Fantus, S. (2023). Medical artificial intelligence ethics: A systematic review of empirical studies. *Digital Health*, 9, 20552076231186064. Advance online publication. DOI: 10.1177/20552076231186064 PMID: 37434728

Tekic, Z., & Füller, J. (2023). Managing innovation in the era of AI. *Technology in Society*, 73, 102254. DOI: 10.1016/j.techsoc.2023.102254

Thangaraja, T., Maharudrappa, M., Bakkiyaraj, M., Johari, L., & Muthuvel, S. (2024). AI-powered HR technology implementation for business growth in industrial 5.0. In *Multidisciplinary applications of extended reality for human experience* (pp. 171–200). IGI Global.

Tian, L., Li, X., Lee, C.-W., & Spulbăr, C. (2024). Investigating the asymmetric impact of artificial intelligence on renewable energy under climate policy uncertainty. *Energy Economics*, 137, 107809. Advance online publication. DOI: 10.1016/j.eneco.2024.107809

Tidd, J., & Bessant, J. (2018). *Managing innovation: Integrating technological, market and organizational change* (6th ed.). Wiley.

Tien, J. M. (2017). Internet of things, real-time decision making, and artificial intelligence. *Annals of Data Science*, 4(2), 149–178. DOI: 10.1007/s40745-017-0112-5

Trabucco, M., & De Giovanni, P. (2021). Achieving resilience and business sustainability during COVID-19: The role of lean supply chain practices and digitalization. *Sustainability (Basel)*, 13(22), 12369. Advance online publication. DOI: 10.3390/su132212369

Tucker, K. D., & Miller, V. D. (2013). Thinking about the future: Guidelines for strategic foresight. *Social Science Research*, 42(3), 617–628.

Tunio, M. N. (2020). Role of ICT in promoting entrepreneurial ecosystems in Pakistan. [JBE]. *Journal of Business Ecosystems*, 1(2), 1–21. DOI: 10.4018/JBE.2020070101

Tunio, M. N., Chaudhry, I. S., Shaikh, S., Jariko, M. A., & Brahmi, M. (2021). Determinants of the sustainable entrepreneurial engagement of youth in a developing country—An empirical evidence from Pakistan. *Sustainability (Basel)*, 13(14), 7764. DOI: 10.3390/su13147764

Tunio, M. N., Jariko, M. A., Børsen, T., Shaikh, S., Mushtaque, T., & Brahmi, M. (2021). How entrepreneurship sustains barriers in the entrepreneurial process—A lesson from a developing nation. *Sustainability (Basel)*, 13(20), 11419. DOI: 10.3390/su132011419

Tunio, M. N., Shaikh, E., Katper, N. K., & Brahmi, M. (2023). Nascent entrepreneurs and challenges in the digital market in developing countries. *International Journal of Public Sector Performance Management*, 12(1-2), 140–153. DOI: 10.1504/IJPSPM.2023.132244

Tushman, M. L., & Anderson, P. (1986). Technological discontinuities and organizational environments. *Administrative Science Quarterly*, 31(3), 439–465. DOI: 10.2307/2392832

Tussyadiah, I. P., & Pesonen, J. (2016). Impacts of peer-to-peer accommodation use on travel patterns. *Journal of Travel Research*, 55(8), 1022–1040. DOI: 10.1177/0047287515608505

Undheim, K., Erikson, T., & Timmermans, B. (2022). True uncertainty and ethical ai: Regulatory sandboxes as a policy tool for moral imagination. *AI and Ethics*, 3(3), 997–1002. DOI: 10.1007/s43681-022-00240-x

Upadhyay, N., Upadhyay, S., & Dwivedi, Y. K. (2022). Theorizing artificial intelligence acceptance and digital entrepreneurship model. *International Journal of Entrepreneurial Behaviour & Research*, 28(5), 1138–1166. DOI: 10.1108/IJEBR-01-2021-0052

Usman, F. O., Eyo-Udo, N. L., Etukudoh, E. A., Odonkor, B., Ibeh, C. V., & Adegbola, A. (2024). A critical review of AI-driven strategies for entrepreneurial success. *International Journal of Management & Entrepreneurship Research*, 6(1), 200–215. DOI: 10.51594/ijmer.v6i1.748

Vargo, S. L., & Lusch, R. F. (2004). Evolving to a new dominant logic for marketing. *Journal of Marketing*, 68(1), 1–17. DOI: 10.1509/jmkg.68.1.1.24036

Varsha, P., Akter, S., Kumar, A., Gochhait, S., & Patagundi, B. (2021). The impact of artificial intelligence on branding. *Journal of Global Information Management*, 29(4), 221–246. DOI: 10.4018/JGIM.20210701.oa10

Venkatraman, V., Clithero, J. A., Fitzsimons, G. J., & Huettel, S. A. (2012). New scanner data for brand marketers: How neuroscience can help better understand differences in brand preferences. *Journal of Consumer Psychology*, 22(1), 143–153. DOI: 10.1016/j.jcps.2011.11.008

Volkmann, C., Fichter, K., Klofsten, M., & Audretsch, D. (2019). Sustainable entrepreneurial ecosystems: An emerging field of research. *Small Business Economics*, 56(3), 1047–1055. DOI: 10.1007/s11187-019-00253-7

Vrontis, D., Chaudhuri, R., & Chatterjee, S. (2023). Role of ChatGPT and Skilled Workers for Business Sustainability: Leadership Motivation as the Moderator. *Sustainability (Basel)*, 15(16), 12196. Advance online publication. DOI: 10.3390/su151612196

Wang, D., Churchill, E., Maes, P., Fan, X., Shneiderman, B., Shi, Y., & Wang, Q. (2020, April). From human-human collaboration to human-AI collaboration: Designing AI systems that can work together with people. In *Extended abstracts of the 2020 CHI conference on human factors in computing systems* (pp. 1–6). ACM., DOI: 10.1145/3334480.3381069

Weber, S. (2010). *The Success of Open Source*. Harvard University Press.

Werther, W. B.Jr, & Chandler, D. (2011). *Strategic Corporate Social Responsibility: Stakeholders in a Global Environment*. SAGE Publications.

Winecoff, A. (2022). Artificial concepts of artificial intelligence: institutional compliance and resistance in ai startups. /arxiv.2203.01157DOI: 10.1145/3514094.3534138

Wu, C. J., Raghavendra, R., Gupta, U., Acun, B., Ardalani, N., Maeng, K., & Hazelwood, K. (2022). Sustainable AI: Environmental implications, challenges, and opportunities. *Proceedings of Machine Learning and Systems*, 4, 795–813. DOI: 10.48550/arXiv.2110.12044

Wu, Y., Chen, S., & Pan, C. (2019). Entrepreneurship in the internet age. *International Journal on Semantic Web and Information Systems*, 15(4), 21–30. DOI: 10.4018/IJSWIS.2019100102

Yablonsky, S. A. (2020). AI-driven digital platform innovation. *Technology Innovation Management Review*, 10(10), 4–15. DOI: 10.22215/timreview/1392

Yadav, P. V., Kollimath, U. S., Giramkar, S. A., Pisal, D. T., Badave, S. S., Dhole, V., & Phule, P. N. (2024, August). Exploring the nexus between AI in Technical Recruitment and Start-ups' Success. In *2024 4th International Conference on Emerging Smart Technologies and Applications (eSmarTA)* (pp. 1-7). IEEE.

Ye, S., Xiao, Y., Yang, B., & Zhang, D. (2021). The impact mechanism of entrepreneurial team expertise heterogeneity on entrepreneurial decision. *Frontiers in Psychology*, 12, 732857. Advance online publication. DOI: 10.3389/fpsyg.2021.732857 PMID: 34671301

Yiğitcanlar, T., Kankanamge, N., Preston, A., Gill, P., Rezayee, M., Ostadnia, M., Xia, B., & Ioppolo, G. (2020). How can social media analytics assist authorities in pandemic-related policy decisions? Insights from Australian states and territories. *Health Information Science and Systems*, 8(1), 37. Advance online publication. DOI: 10.1007/s13755-020-00121-9 PMID: 33078073

Yoffie, D. B., & Kim, R. C. (2011). *Coca-Cola: Residual income valuation*. Harvard Business School.

Zervas, G., Proserpio, D., & Byers, J. W. (2016). The rise of the sharing economy: Estimating the impact of Airbnb on the hotel industry. *JMR, Journal of Marketing Research*, 54(5), 687–705. DOI: 10.1509/jmr.15.0204

Zhang, H., Zang, Z., Zhu, H., Uddin, M. I., & Amin, M. A. (2022). Big data-assisted social media analytics for business model for business decision making system competitive analysis. *Information Processing & Management*, 59(1), 102762. DOI: 10.1016/j.ipm.2021.102762

Zhang, H., & Zhao, X. (2010). Innovation and entrepreneurship in the context of artificial intelligence: An integrative framework. *The Journal of Technology Transfer*, 35(3), 292–307. DOI: 10.1007/s10901-009-9147-6Afolabi

Zhang, N., & Wu, C. (2024). Application of deep learning in career planning and entrepreneurship of college students. *Journal of Computational Methods in Sciences and Engineering*, 24(4–5), 2927–2942. DOI: 10.3233/JCM-247531

Zhou, H., Li, Y., & Zhao, W. (2020). The impact of AI-powered chatbots on customer satisfaction: Evidence from the retail industry. *Journal of Retailing and Consumer Services*, 54, 102012. DOI: 10.1016/j.jretconser.2019.102012

Ziakis, C., & Vlachopoulou, M. (2023). Artificial intelligence in digital marketing: Insights from a comprehensive review. *Information (Basel)*, 14(12), 664. DOI: 10.3390/info14120664

Zichu, Y. (2019). Can group intelligence help entrepreneurs find better opportunities? *Frontiers in Psychology*, 10, 1141. Advance online publication. DOI: 10.3389/fpsyg.2019.01141 PMID: 31156522

Zwingmann, T. (2022). *Ai-powered business intelligence.* " O'Reilly Media, Inc.". https://www.google.co.in/books/edition/AI_Powered_Business_Intelligence/54h0EAAAQBAJ?hl=en&gbpv=0

About the Contributors

Muhammad Nawaz Tunio, an accomplished scholar in Business, Management, and Policy, brings much experience and expertise to the academic arena. With a Ph.D. in Entrepreneurship, Innovation, and Economic Development from Alpen Adria University, Klagenfurt, Austria, Dr. Tunio has established himself as a leading authority in his field. Currently serving as an Assistant Professor at the Department of Business Administration, University of Sufism and Modern Sciences, Bhitshah, Pakistan, he has also held positions at esteemed institutions such as Greenwich University and Mohammad Ali Jinnah University. Dr. Tunio's research interests include Entrepreneurship, Innovation, Economic Development, Youth Development, CSR, and Qualitative Methods. His scholarly contributions extend far beyond the confines of academia, with numerous research articles published in top-tier journals and prestigious book chapters with reputable publishers. With an impressive research profile boasting over 1000 citations, an H-Index of 18, and an i10-index of 31, Dr. Tunio's work has significantly impacted the academic community. His consultancy experience includes projects with organizations such as the National Rural Support Program and the Small and Medium Enterprises Development Authority, where he has provided invaluable expertise on issues related to small business restoration and brand management for women entrepreneurs. Dr. Tunio's dedication to academic excellence is further evidenced by his teaching and administrative roles at various universities, where he has mentored students, organized international conferences, and contributed to developing curricula in Business Administration and Management.

***

K. Balaji is an Assistant Professor in Business and Management, CHRIST University, Bengaluru. He did Ph.D. from KLU Business School, KL University, Vijayawada. He is having 12 years of teaching experience. He has to his credit 23 Research Articles published in reputed National and International Journals. He has participated and presented more than 12 papers in both National and International Seminars/Conferences and also attended more than 50 workshops/FDPS organized by various reputed organizations. He has also participated in more than 50 seminars / webinars organized by various reputed organizations. He has also attended in 6 Short Term Training programs.He has successfully conducted 3 webinars, one 5 day FDP and one International Conference on Reimaging marketing in New Normal. He is a ratified as Assistant Professor by both JNTUH, JNTU Anantapur and Sri Venkateswara University,Tirupati. His specialized areas include, Accounting and Financial management, Marketing Management, Retailing Management, Consumer Behavior studies, Entrepreneurship and Business Laws.

Ajay Chandel is working as an Associate Professor at Mittal School of Business, Lovely Professional University, Punjab. He has 14 years of teaching and research experience. He has published papers in SCOPUS, WOS, and UGC listed Journals in areas like Social Media Marketing, E-Commerce, and Consumer Behaviour. He has published cases on SMEs and Social Entrepreneurship in The Case Centre, UK. He also reviews The Case Journal, Emerald Group Publishing, and International Journal of Business and Globalisation, Inderscience. He has authored and developed MOOCs on Tourism and Hospitality Marketing under Epg-Pathshala- A gateway to all postgraduate courses (a UGC-MHRD project under its National Mission on Education Through ICT (NME-ICT).

|**Shivani Dhand** is an Associate Professor (14+ years of experience),a Certified SHRM (Society for Human Resource Management)faculty in the department of Mittal School of Business of Lovely Professional University.She is NLP(Neuro Linguistics Programming) Practioner She is also a member of the Indian Society for Training and Development (ISTD) and the Indian Society of Labour Economics. She is also a core committee member and Mentor of an NGO(Shalini Fellowship) Shivani Dhand has worked in an IT company as an HR. She has published 15 research papers in various journals which include Scopus-indexed, UGC care and peer-reviewed journals. She is a certified POSH trainer. She has worked with CPSC (Columbo Plan Staff College) Manila Philippines, and trained the faculty and Principals of various Institutions in Bhutan (2015). In 2016, She worked on one of the projects," Austria as an Innovation leader in EU in Austria and was awarded as best presentation and Excellent paper. Her research is situated in the field of Startups, HR Practices Human Resource Management, Entrepreneurship, and social entrepreneurship with a special focus on academic entrepreneurship.

Mohammad Irfan is presently working as an Associate Professor at School of Business and Management, Christ University, Bengaluru, Karnataka, India. Dr. Irfan has done his Ph.D. from the Central University of Haryana. He is MBA (Finance), M.Com (Account and Law), and MA (Economics). He has qualified UGC-JRF/SRF/NET in Management and Commerce. Dr. Irfan certified NSEs (NCFM) and BSEs certification. He has experience of more than sixteen years in the area of SAPM, Artificial Intelligence, Machine Learning, Blockchain, Cryptocurrency, Financial Engineering, Fintech, Green Finance, and Alternative Finance. He has to his credit more than 40+ Scopus Indexed articles, includes The Journal of Economic Cooperation and Development (Q2), International Journal of Business Excellence (IJBEX), International Journal of Economics and Management (IJEM), Montenegrin Journal of Economics (Q2), Cogent Business & Management (Taylor & Francis) (Q2), Indian Journal of Finance (IJF) and Journal of Islamic Monetary Economics and Finance (JIMF). His citations reached 319+ along with 11 H-index. Dr. Irfan has published 8 books in Springer, IGI Global Publication (Scopus indexed).

Preet Kanwal completed her Post-Doctoral Fellowship at the ESG, University of Quebec in Montreal, Canada, furthering research expertise in her field. During her Post Doctoral Fellowship, she worked on exploring demographic sensitivity and its impact on discrimination in HEIs while considering insights from Canada and India. Dr. Kanwal is an academician and researcher with over 20 years of experience in Human Resource Management. She holds a PhD in Human Resource Management from I.K. Gujral Punjab Technical University, Punjab, India, where she conducted an empirical study on the quality of work life in the textile industry of Punjab, India. She also has international experience teaching MBA students from Victoria University (Online), Australia, and Sunway University (Online), Malaysia. Dr. Kanwal's research interests revolve around the quality of work-life, work-life balance, industrial relations, labour laws, social security and labour welfare, organizational stress, and behaviour, particularly in the context of the textile industry. She has presented her research at numerous national and international conferences and published her work in Scopus-indexed and UGC-listed Journals. Additionally, she has authored several book chapters on related topics, underscoring her commitment to advancing knowledge in her field. Her contributions extend beyond teaching and research; she has been actively involved in organizing and leading training sessions, workshops, and conferences, both as a participant and as a session chair. Currently she is working on a funded project titled, "Empowering Women Artisans for Vision Viksit Bharat@2047: Financial Inclusion, Market Access, and Skill Development in Selected States of India".

Early Ridho Kismawadi, S.E.I, MA is a lecturer at the Department of Islamic Banking, Faculty of Islamic Economics and Business IAIN Langsa, Aceh, Indonesia, he has been a lecturer since 2013, he has completed a doctoral program in 2018 majoring in Sharia economics at the State Islamic University of North Sumatra. He was appointed head of the Islamic economics Law study program (2023) Islamic banking study program (2020) and Islamic financial management study program (2019) at Langsa State Islamic Institute (IAIN Langsa), Aceh, Indonesia. His research interests include financial economics, applied econometrics, Islamic economics, banking, and finance. He has published articles in national and international journals. In addition, he is also a reviewer of several reputable international journals such as Finance Research Letters, Financial Innovation, Cogent Business &; Management, Journal of Islamic Accounting and Business Research. He has also presented his papers at various local and international seminars. Dr. Early Ridho Kismawadi, S.E.I, MA, can be contacted at kismawadi@iainlangsa.ac.id.

Vineet Mehan received the B.Tech. degree from Kurukshetra University, M.E. degree from NITTTR Chandigarh and Ph.D. degree from NIT Jalandhar. He is currently a Professor with the Department of Artificial Intelligence and Machine Learning, NIET, NIMS University, Jaipur, India. He has published over 50 papers in peer-reviewed international journals and conferences. Her research interests include Machine Learning, AI, Bio-informatics and DIP.

Shashank Mittal has done his FPM in Organizational behavior and Human Resource from Indian Institute of Management Raipur. He holds B. Tech from I.E.T. Lucknow. His post FPM work experience includes almost five years of industry and academics exposures in multiple roles. Prior to joining FPM, he has over two years of industrial experience and three years of teaching experience in various organizations. He has published multiple papers in ABDC ranked and SSCI indexed journals of international repute such as Journal of Knowledge Management, Journal of Behavioral and Experimental Finance, International Journal of Conflict Management, Journal of Management and Organization and Current Psychology. His current research interest includes Social identity, Knowledge exchanges, Status, Proactive helping, Employer branding, Organizational justice, and Humanitarian relief management. He enjoys badminton and cycling during leisure time.

Sandeep Kumar Singh is a faculty in the area of Information Systems and Analytics at Jindal Global Business School, O.P. Jindal Global University, Sonipat. Prior to joining Jindal Global Business School, he worked as an Assistant Professor at JKLU Jaipur for two years. He has earned his Ph.D. in computational physics from Antwerpen University, Belgium. His PhD work focused on mathematical modeling and simulation of two-dimensional materials. Post to his PhD, he worked as a research scientist in Sweden for four years in energy storage systems, bioelectronics. He also did MTech in industrial mathematics and scientific computing from IIT Madras, Chennai. His current research interests are to apply complex mathematical modeling in the business and financial world.

Srinivasan Vasan has been working in the Department of Humanities and Social Sciences at Graphic Era (Deemed to be University) as an Assistant Professor. With a wealth of experience, Mr. Srinivasan has accumulated 14 years of extensive teaching and field-level expertise. Prior to his current role, he served in the Ministry of Health and Family Welfare, Government of India, and gained valuable experience. He also contributed as a Guest Faculty at the university level and served for nearly 2 years in the State Government Public Works Department as a Mobilization Training Specialist. In the past year, Mr. S. Srinivasan has enriched his experience by actively participating in a tuberculosis project funded by GFATM and USAID, providing a platform for further exploration of his research and practical field-based knowledge. His scholarly contributions include publishing 24 papers, with 18 more under peer review in various UGC-CARE, SCOPUS, and peer-reviewed journals.

Mohit Yadav is an Associate Professor in the area of Human Resource Management at Jindal Global Business School (JGBS). He has a rich blend of work experience from both Academics as well as Industry. Prof. Mohit holds a Ph.D. from Department of Management Studies, Indian Institute of Technology Roorkee (IIT Roorkee) and has completed Master of Human Resource and Organizational Development (MHROD) from prestigious Delhi School of Economics, University of Delhi. He also holds a B.Com (Hons.) degree from University of Delhi and UGC-JRF scholarship. He has published various research papers and book chapters with reputed publishers like Springer, Sage, Emerald, Elsevier, Inderscience etc. and presented research papers in national and International conferences both in India and abroad. He has many best paper awards on his credit too. He is reviewer of various international journals like Computers in Human Behavior, Policing etc. His areas of interest are Organizational Behavior, HRM, Recruitment and Selection, Organizational Citizenship Behavior, Quality of work life and role.

Index

A

AI 1, 2, 3, 4, 5, 6, 7, 8, 9, 10, 11, 12, 13, 14, 15, 16, 17, 18, 19, 21, 22, 23, 24, 25, 26, 27, 28, 29, 30, 31, 32, 33, 34, 35, 36, 37, 38, 39, 40, 41, 42, 43, 44, 45, 46, 47, 48, 49, 50, 51, 56, 57, 58, 59, 60, 61, 62, 63, 64, 65, 66, 67, 68, 71, 72, 73, 74, 75, 76, 77, 78, 79, 80, 81, 82, 83, 84, 85, 86, 87, 88, 89, 90, 91, 92, 93, 94, 95, 96, 97, 99, 100, 101, 102, 103, 104, 105, 106, 107, 108, 109, 110, 111, 112, 113, 114, 115, 116, 117, 118, 119, 120, 121, 122, 123, 125, 126, 127, 137, 138, 139, 140, 141, 142, 143, 144, 145, 146, 147, 148, 149, 150, 151, 152, 153, 154, 155, 156, 157, 158, 159, 160, 161, 162, 163, 165, 166, 167, 168, 169, 170, 171, 172, 173, 174, 175, 176, 177, 178, 179, 181, 182, 183, 184, 185, 186, 187, 188, 189, 190, 191, 192, 193, 196, 197, 204, 207, 208, 209, 210, 212, 213, 214, 215, 216, 217, 218, 219, 220, 223, 224, 225, 226, 227, 228, 229, 230, 231, 232, 233, 234, 235, 236, 237, 238, 239, 241, 242, 243, 244, 245, 246, 247, 248, 249, 250, 251, 252, 253, 254, 255, 256, 257, 258, 259, 260, 261, 262, 263, 264, 265, 267, 268, 269, 270, 271, 274, 275, 281, 282, 283, 284, 285, 286, 287, 288
AI-driven decision-making 7, 79, 217, 218, 219, 223, 224, 226, 227, 233, 234, 235, 236, 237, 238, 256
AI-driven Personalization 15, 99, 120, 123, 217, 234
AI Innovation 18, 34, 38, 137, 153, 176, 179
AI Integration 6, 7, 8, 27, 28, 43, 167
AI Transparency 71, 84, 85, 92
Algorithmic Transparency 2, 144, 150, 154, 157

Artificial Intelligence 1, 2, 3, 5, 8, 11, 14, 16, 17, 18, 19, 21, 22, 23, 24, 27, 28, 31, 32, 33, 34, 35, 36, 37, 38, 39, 43, 44, 45, 46, 47, 49, 50, 51, 56, 57, 58, 60, 66, 71, 72, 76, 80, 84, 88, 93, 94, 95, 96, 99, 100, 106, 116, 119, 122, 126, 137, 138, 145, 146, 148, 152, 162, 163, 165, 166, 169, 174, 177, 178, 179, 181, 183, 185, 208, 211, 212, 213, 215, 218, 226, 227, 229, 238, 239, 242, 244, 245, 249, 251, 258, 260, 264, 265, 268, 269, 283, 288, 289, 290
augmented reality 187, 211, 215, 284
Autonomous Supply Chains 99, 123
autonomous systems 160, 217, 234

B

Business Automation 23, 99, 119, 120, 123
Business Innovation 21, 22, 24, 27, 31, 32, 33, 35, 37, 42, 43, 47, 91, 183, 188, 209
Business Model Optimization 73, 76, 77, 78, 79, 80, 84, 87, 92

C

Case Studies 1, 2, 8, 9, 10, 11, 14, 21, 22, 29, 31, 35, 59, 130, 143, 222, 223, 224, 269, 271, 272

D

Data Privacy 2, 5, 7, 12, 14, 18, 22, 27, 36, 42, 59, 71, 84, 87, 91, 92, 113, 122, 138, 140, 145, 148, 150, 157, 158, 159, 161, 225, 241, 254, 255, 258, 261, 263, 267, 269, 281, 283, 286
data quality 111, 217, 225, 231, 237, 281
Decision Making 94, 95, 114, 121, 185, 211, 213, 214, 223, 226, 234, 245, 289, 290
Decision-Making 1, 2, 4, 5, 7, 8, 11, 13, 15, 21, 25, 27, 28, 32, 39, 40, 47, 49, 50, 51, 52, 53, 54, 57, 58, 59, 60, 61, 64, 66, 71, 72, 75, 76, 77, 79, 80, 84, 86, 88, 89, 90, 91, 92, 99, 101, 106,

108, 114, 115, 116, 118, 119, 120, 121, 122, 123, 133, 141, 146, 147, 148, 149, 154, 159, 160, 167, 173, 181, 182, 183, 184, 185, 186, 187, 188, 189, 190, 192, 194, 196, 204, 208, 209, 210, 211, 217, 218, 219, 222, 223, 224, 225, 226, 227, 231, 232, 233, 234, 235, 236, 237, 238, 239, 244, 246, 249, 254, 256, 257, 262, 271, 273, 281, 288

Deep Learning 15, 93, 95, 126, 146, 147, 159, 179, 190, 214, 220, 233, 241, 259, 269, 271

Digital Entrepreneurship 1, 2, 3, 4, 11, 12, 13, 14, 15, 17, 18, 19, 21, 24, 25, 26, 27, 28, 29, 31, 32, 33, 34, 35, 36, 37, 38, 39, 40, 41, 42, 43, 46, 47, 96, 162, 163, 178, 212

Diversity and Inclusion 241, 248, 249, 251, 255, 260

Dynamic Pricing 71, 80, 81, 84, 86, 96, 142

E

Emerging visionaries 49, 50, 51, 52, 53, 54, 55, 56, 60, 61, 62, 63, 64, 65, 66, 67

Entrepreneurial Process 17, 97, 182, 183, 186, 208, 209, 212

Entrepreneurial Strategies 192

Entrepreneurial Success 22, 24, 26, 62, 97, 109, 110, 181, 182, 183, 188, 208, 216, 239, 244

Entrepreneurial trajectories 49, 50, 51

Entrepreneurs 1, 2, 3, 4, 5, 6, 7, 8, 9, 10, 11, 12, 13, 14, 15, 17, 19, 21, 22, 24, 25, 26, 27, 28, 29, 30, 33, 34, 39, 40, 41, 42, 43, 45, 47, 48, 49, 50, 51, 52, 53, 54, 55, 56, 57, 58, 59, 60, 61, 62, 63, 64, 65, 66, 67, 71, 72, 73, 74, 75, 76, 77, 78, 80, 84, 87, 88, 91, 92, 93, 94, 97, 99, 100, 101, 102, 103, 104, 105, 106, 107, 108, 109, 110, 111, 112, 113, 114, 115, 116, 117, 118, 119, 122, 123, 126, 129, 130, 131, 132, 134, 138, 139, 140, 141, 142, 143, 144, 145, 146, 147, 148, 149, 150, 151, 152, 153, 154, 155, 162, 165, 166, 167, 171, 175, 176, 181, 182, 183, 184, 185, 186, 187, 188, 189, 190, 191, 192, 193, 194, 195, 196, 197, 198, 199, 200, 201, 203, 204, 205, 206, 207, 208, 209, 210, 211, 212, 213, 214, 215, 218, 238, 245, 255, 256, 265, 267, 268, 269, 270, 271, 272, 273, 274, 275, 281, 282, 283, 284, 285, 286, 287

Entrepreneurship 1, 2, 3, 4, 8, 9, 10, 11, 12, 13, 14, 15, 17, 18, 19, 21, 22, 24, 25, 26, 27, 28, 29, 31, 32, 33, 34, 35, 36, 37, 38, 39, 40, 41, 42, 43, 45, 46, 47, 49, 50, 51, 56, 57, 58, 59, 60, 61, 63, 66, 67, 68, 71, 72, 73, 75, 79, 93, 94, 95, 96, 97, 101, 102, 103, 114, 117, 118, 119, 124, 130, 131, 132, 137, 139, 141, 144, 162, 163, 165, 166, 167, 168, 169, 170, 171, 172, 173, 174, 175, 176, 177, 178, 179, 181, 182, 183, 184, 185, 187, 194, 197, 203, 204, 208, 209, 210, 211, 212, 215, 216, 219, 238, 239, 241, 251, 256, 264, 269, 271, 272, 273, 283, 289

Ethical AI 33, 36, 87, 91, 122, 137, 138, 139, 140, 141, 144, 146, 147, 148, 149, 150, 152, 153, 154, 156, 157, 158, 160, 161, 163, 168, 235, 236, 237, 261, 286

Ethical AI Practices 33, 122, 146, 156, 158, 161, 261, 286

Ethical Considerations 2, 8, 13, 14, 27, 40, 42, 46, 58, 60, 71, 84, 85, 87, 92, 99, 112, 122, 138, 139, 142, 144, 150, 159, 160, 166, 177, 217, 224, 254, 258, 262

Explainable AI 85, 87, 137, 147, 151, 158, 217, 234, 235, 237

F

Future Directions 41, 137, 158, 160, 182, 213, 226

Future Trends 1, 11, 12, 30, 48, 72, 73, 74, 77, 115, 118, 119, 121, 155, 217, 219, 234, 258, 283, 284

I

Industry leaders 49, 51, 55, 58
Innovation 1, 2, 4, 5, 7, 9, 10, 11, 13, 14, 15, 16, 17, 18, 19, 21, 22, 24, 25, 26, 27, 28, 29, 30, 31, 32, 33, 34, 35, 36, 37, 38, 39, 40, 41, 42, 43, 44, 45, 46, 47, 49, 50, 51, 52, 53, 54, 55, 56, 57, 58, 59, 60, 61, 62, 63, 64, 65, 66, 67, 68, 72, 73, 80, 82, 83, 84, 87, 88, 89, 90, 91, 92, 93, 94, 95, 100, 101, 102, 103, 105, 106, 107, 108, 109, 110, 119, 120, 123, 129, 130, 131, 132, 134, 135, 136, 137, 138, 139, 141, 142, 143, 144, 148, 149, 153, 159, 161, 162, 165, 166, 167, 169, 171, 174, 175, 176, 177, 179, 182, 183, 188, 209, 210, 211, 213, 215, 216, 218, 222, 223, 226, 230, 236, 237, 239, 242, 243, 245, 246, 247, 248, 249, 251, 252, 254, 255, 257, 262, 263, 268, 272, 273, 275, 286, 287, 289
integration challenges 232
Iterative Planning 71, 72, 73, 75, 76

L

Leadership Development 226, 241, 245, 246, 247, 249, 251, 257, 263

M

Machine Learning 2, 4, 6, 14, 22, 23, 30, 31, 32, 33, 34, 35, 36, 37, 38, 39, 41, 57, 59, 71, 72, 75, 76, 77, 78, 79, 80, 82, 85, 86, 87, 94, 95, 96, 97, 105, 115, 125, 126, 142, 178, 182, 187, 190, 218, 219, 220, 222, 223, 242, 244, 246, 252, 259, 268, 269, 270, 271, 284
Market Dynamics 53, 61, 131, 223, 269, 273
Models 1, 3, 4, 5, 8, 12, 13, 14, 16, 18, 22, 25, 27, 29, 31, 32, 33, 34, 41, 42, 54, 55, 56, 69, 71, 72, 73, 75, 76, 77, 78, 79, 80, 81, 84, 85, 86, 87, 88, 89, 90, 91, 93, 94, 95, 96, 111, 119, 129, 131, 132, 133, 134, 141, 142, 143, 144, 145, 146, 149, 150, 151, 152, 153, 154, 159, 172, 186, 187, 188, 190, 214, 218, 220, 221, 222, 225, 226, 231, 233, 234, 235, 236, 238, 252, 259, 267, 281, 282, 283, 288

N

Natural Language Processing 2, 6, 14, 22, 23, 29, 34, 35, 41, 71, 76, 77, 80, 93, 142, 190, 218, 220, 241, 242, 259, 284

O

Operational Efficiency 4, 7, 21, 26, 29, 32, 37, 59, 66, 78, 79, 82, 101, 102, 103, 105, 109, 110, 117, 125, 126, 130, 133, 134, 174, 175, 176, 230

P

Personalization 3, 10, 12, 15, 17, 26, 29, 35, 37, 47, 69, 78, 79, 80, 81, 88, 89, 91, 92, 93, 99, 116, 120, 123, 126, 142, 162, 217, 234, 236, 237, 260, 267, 273, 279, 284, 286
predictive analytics 2, 4, 6, 8, 14, 18, 29, 30, 34, 35, 48, 59, 72, 75, 76, 77, 84, 88, 105, 114, 115, 116, 118, 125, 142, 182, 217, 218, 219, 220, 221, 222, 223, 226, 227, 243, 248, 252, 254, 259, 263, 267, 268, 270, 284, 285, 286, 287

R

real-time data 12, 27, 29, 73, 75, 82, 88, 90, 108, 118, 121, 174, 220, 226, 234, 235, 267, 268, 271, 272, 273, 276
Responsible AI 27, 33, 34, 36, 91, 137, 144, 149, 150, 151, 152, 153, 154, 156, 157, 158, 161, 163, 287

S

social media analytics 267, 268, 269, 270, 271, 272, 275, 276, 277, 278, 279, 280, 281, 282, 283, 284, 286, 287, 290
Stakeholders 7, 13, 28, 29, 36, 42, 43, 54,

70, 72, 84, 89, 90, 91, 107, 113, 122, 137, 138, 139, 140, 146, 149, 150, 152, 156, 157, 158, 160, 161, 168, 169, 192, 236
Strategic Insights 190
Successful Business 43, 84, 210
Sustainable Business 28, 123, 168, 176

T

Talent Development 241, 242, 249, 250, 251, 254, 255, 256, 257, 258, 259, 260, 261, 262, 263, 264
Transformative impact 26, 35, 49, 50, 51, 55, 58, 59, 99, 217, 267

V

virtual reality 267, 284